World

For E

World at Risk

ULRICH BECK

Translated by Ciaran Cronin

polity

Polity Press
65 Bridge Street
Cambridge CB2 1UR, UK

Polity Press
350 Main Street
Malden, MA 02148, USA

The translation of this work was supported by a grant from the Goethe-Institut that is funded by the German Ministry of Foreign Affairs.

ISBN-13: 978-0-7456-4200-0
ISBN-13: 978-0-7456-4201-7(pb)

A catalogue record for this book is available from the British Library.

Typeset in 10 on 12 pt Stempel Garamond
by SNP Best-set Typesetter Ltd., Hong Kong
Printed and bound in Great Britain by MPG Books Ltd, Bodmin, Cornwall

The publisher has used its best endeavours to ensure that the URLs for external websites referred to in this book are correct and active at the time of going to press. However, the publisher has no responsibility for the websites and can make no guarantee that a site will remain live or that the content is or will remain appropriate.

Every effort has been made to trace all copyright holders, but if any have been inadvertently overlooked the publisher will be pleased to include any necessary credits in any subsequent reprint or edition.

For further information on Polity, visit our website: www.polity.co.uk

Contents

Acknowledgements   vii

1   Introduction: Staging Global Risk   1

2   Relations of Definition as Relations of Domination:
Who Decides What is and is Not a Risk?   24

3   The 'Cosmopolitan Moment' of World Risk Society or:
Enforced Enlightenment   47

4   Clash of Risk Cultures or: The Overlapping of the State of
Normalcy and the State of Exception   67

5   Global Public Sphere and Global Subpolitics or: How Real is
Catastrophic Climate Change?   81

6   The Provident State or: On the Antiquatedness of Linear
Pessimism Concerning Progress   109

7   Knowledge or Non-Knowing? Two Perspectives of
'Reflexive Modernization'   115

8   The Insurance Principle: Criticism and Counter-Criticism   129

9   Felt War, Felt Peace: Staging Violence   140

10   Global Inequality, Local Vulnerability: The Conflict
Dynamics of Environmental Hazards Must be Studied
within the Framework of Methodological
Cosmopolitanism   160

11   Critical Theory of World Risk Society   187

12 Dialectics of Modernity: How the Crises of Modernity
   Follow from the Triumphs of Modernity   212

Notes   235
References and Bibliography   243
Index   261

Acknowledgements

Risk Society was published in German in 1986. In 1999, *World Risk Society* appeared in English and was translated into more than ten languages, though not into German. The attempt to translate it into German in a lightly revised version proved to be untenable. Too much has occurred in the meantime, the learning curve in responding to global risks is simply too vast. Hence this new book.

There was no shortage of reasons for writing it. They reside, first, in the endless chain of events in which reality and the mass media are co-authoring ever new chapters of 'world risk society'. What seemed larger than life twenty years ago has proved to be the script that reality has been following: 'We are all trapped in the global danger zone' (*Tagesanzeiger*, Zurich, 2006). On the other hand, the trend towards a globalization of risks is also reflected in the reception of *Risk Society*. My analyses have by now been translated into more than thirty languages and have triggered heated debates across nations and specialist fields – in sociology and political science, in law and history, in philosophy, anthropology, ecology and engineering. Furthermore, studies on diverse topics in the most varied empirical contexts have contributed to articulating the contours, paradoxes and contradictions of (world) risk society. This worldwide discourse on *Risk Society* stimulated me to further reflection and to write *World at Risk*. I would like to mention here just the inspiring works of Joost van Loon (*Risk and Technological Culture: Towards a Sociology of Virulence*) and Piet Strydom (*Risk, Environment and Society: Ongoing Debates, Current Issues and Future Prospects*).

Earlier versions of one or more of the chapters presented here were commented upon by Jakob Arnoldi, Boris Holzer, Edgar Grande, Christoph Lau, Daniel Levy, Stefan May, Martin Muslow, Angelika Poferl and Natan Sznaider, to whom I am also sincerely grateful. The context for this book was provided by cooperation and discussion within the Collaborative Research Centre 'Reflexive Modernization', which enjoys the generous support of the German Research Foundation. Without Raimund Fellinger, friend and editor, this book would never have been written. I would also like to thank Almut Kleine and Waltraud Zoldos for their work in typing the manuscript.

On this occasion, Elisabeth Beck-Gernsheim encouraged me to tame my academicism and to indulge my pleasure in writing. Hence this book is addressed not to sociologists alone but to all of those who are keen to understand our age of man-made uncertainties.

1

Introduction: Staging Global Risk

The academic debate concerning climate change is over, but the political and moral responses have reached a new level. . . . Human beings, as researchers have established with a unanimity rare with such multi-faceted issues, bear the primary blame for global warming. . . . The real novelty, perhaps even the historic message of this report, is the conclusiveness with which all evasions and doubts concerning the human causation of climate change are dispelled.

Müller-Jung 2007 (referring to IPCC 2007)

The anticipation of catastrophe is changing the world

A suicide bomber attack in which terrorists with British passports planned to blow up several passenger aircraft en route from Heathrow to the United States with liquid explosives did *not* occur during the summer of 2006 under the spotlight of the global mass media because the British police, in cooperation with international colleagues, managed to intervene on time and arrest the suspected perpetrators. On 6 November, barely three months after the thwarted attack, a new EU-wide regulation came into force that imposes severe restrictions on the transport of liquids in aircraft cabins. The new security measures are the worldwide reaction to *anticipated* terrorist attacks which, as stated, did *not* occur in a certain place, i.e. London. They place restrictions on the freedom of millions of passengers for the foreseeable future. The passengers, in whose minds the terrorist threat has become lodged, accepted such restrictions on their liberties without demur.

The power of the powerless or: The risk to the reputation of banks

The pressure exerted by a small Westphalian environmental group is jeopardizing a multibillion dollar nuclear generation project in Bulgaria. Following protests by this internationally networked civic group opposed to nuclear power, Deutsche Bank and the HypoVereinsbank withdrew their financing of the Belene nuclear power station. The justification offered was the 'high reputation risk' that forced the banks on to the defensive. Allegedly this had nothing to do with the evaluation of the project, even from an environmental point of view. The measure was solely due to the protests of the group Urgewalt, Ausgestrahlt and its European partners. The anticipated nuclear threat which might be posed by the planned Bulgarian nuclear power plant in the future was publicly denounced by a small West German group active across Europe in protest actions picked up by the media – for example, outside the Deutsche Bank – with the result that the silent powerbrokers of global capitalism, the banks, gave in without a murmur.

Segregating risk embryos

The successes of human genetics and reproductive medicine mean that parents can now select embryos whose genetic profiles promise a reduced risk of illness. They are taking advantage of the opportunities provided by reproductive medicine to 'weed out' embryos with predispositions, for instance, for cancer – which will not break out in later life with certainty but only with a certain degree of probability – and to bring potentially healthy children into the world. All couples, whether they like it or not, will be confronted with this difficult decision sooner or later. They will have to assess whether their wish to prevent suffering, even though they cannot be certain that it will occur, justifies the conscious selection of an embryo and the 'rejection' of potential children who are bearers of a 'risk gene', however the latter is identified. This can lead simultaneously to a lowering of inhibitions. The growing interest in the early detection and elimination of the risk of cancer through 'genetic screening' is symptomatic of a growing tolerance for genetic selection. It is also contributing to the use of pre-implantation diagnosis to identify indicators that are less concerned with serious illnesses and ultimately even give effect to preferences and prejudices. And although there are in the meantime thousands of apparently healthy babies in the United States who underwent these interventions at the pre-embryonic stage, concerns over their unknown long-term effects cannot be simply brushed aside.

The inundation of London, New York and Tokyo

In November 2006, the British foreign minister Margaret Beckett stated that wars fought over limited resources – land, drinking water, oil – are as old as human history. Furthermore, she stated that climate change is threatening to reduce the availability of these resources in some of the most unstable regions of the world, with Africa and the Middle East being the most dramatically affected. If climate change represents a foreign policy issue in this sense, then the converse also holds, namely, foreign policy must become part of the solution to the problems thrown up by climate change. If global warming leads to increases the temperature of the earth by 4 to 5 degrees Celsius, London, New York and Tokyo could disappear into the sea. In order to prevent 'local' problems, such as the inundation of London, therefore, global initiatives, and ultimately a 'global deal', are required. To this end, it is not only necessary to spur the environmental offender number one, the United States, into action. We must also succeed in finding or inventing a compromise formula for global justice in a world in which both wealth and risks are radically unequally distributed. At any rate, this is becoming a tangible task and a concrete utopia to which every country should contribute simply because it is in its own most basic national interest.

Changing sides

A paradigm shift is taking place in climate policy. It is becoming apparent that the sovereignty of the market represents a fatal threat given the danger of catastrophic climate change. As a result, major sectors of the transnational economy have switched sides and are jostling for favourable starting positions in the competition over the markets for environmental technologies and renewable energy sources. But this also means that a new alliance between civic movements and the large corporations is emerging. In January 2007, American companies called on President George W. Bush to make an environmental conversion. The managers pleaded for an improved climate policy based on state regulation on a global scale.

In Europe and California, the state and environmental movements are forming an alliance against the motor industry. Because voluntary undertakings on the part of the firms have proven to be ineffective, EU Commissioner Stavros Dimas and Governor Arnold Schwarzenegger of California are resorting to compulsory measures, namely, sharp reductions in carbon dioxide emissions. This is painful for the motor industry, especially for the German. In both Germany and in California the neoliberal alliance between state and capital is open to challenge.

World ugliness contest

The 'existential concern' which is being awakened across the world by global risks has long since led to a risky game for survival, to a world 'ugliness contest' over the suppression of large-scale risks. The incalculable threats to which climate change is giving rise are supposed to be 'combated' with the incalculable threats associated with new nuclear power stations. Many decisions over major risks do not involve a choice between safe and risky alternatives, but one between different risky alternatives, and often a choice between alternatives whose risks concern qualitatively different dimensions which are scarcely commensurable. Current scientific and public discourses are rarely a match for such considerations. One source of temptation towards inadmissible simplifications is to represent the decision in question as one between safe and risky alternatives by playing down the imponderabilities of one's preferred proposal while simultaneously focusing on the hazardousness of the other risks.

1   Risk

Threat and insecurity have always been among the conditions of human existence; in a certain sense this was even more the case in the past than it is today. The threat to individuals and their families through illness and premature death and the threats to the community through famines and plagues were greater in the Middle Ages than today. From this kind of threat we must distinguish the *semantics of risk* associated since the beginning of the modern period with the increasing importance of decision, uncertainty and probability in the process of modernization. The semantics of risk refer to the present thematization of future threats that are often a product of the successes of civilization. It also makes possible new, post-utopian mobilizations of societies, for example, as we have seen, cosmopolitan initiatives against climate change and shifting alliances between civic movements, states and companies.

The two faces of risk – chance and danger – became an issue in the course of industrialization, starting with intercontinental merchant shipping. Risk represents the perceptual and cognitive schema in accordance with which a society mobilizes itself when it is confronted with the openness, uncertainties and obstructions of a self-created future and is no longer defined by religion, tradition or the superior power of nature but has even lost its faith in the redemptive powers of utopias.

As a gulf opened up between God and risk, the European novel entered into an association with risk. When risk appeared on the stage, God had to renounce his role as lord of the universe, with all the subversive consequences that this entailed. *The Art of the Novel* (Kundera 2003) revealed the many faces of risk in terms of its own logic and explored its existential dimension. In the figure of Don Quixote, human life, whose future no longer bows down before the power of the gods or before God's wisdom, has become a never-ending adventure. For, in God's absence, risk unfolds its fateful and terrible, inscrutable ambiguity. The world is not as it is; rather its existence and its future depend on *decisions*, decisions which play off positive and negative aspects against one another, which connect progress and decline and which, like all things human, are bearers of error, ignorance, hubris, the promise of control and, ultimately, even the seed of possible self-destruction.

Don Quixote, one of the first modern European novels, was completed with the appearance of the second part in 1616. The reaction of the sciences to the unforeseen was swift. The history of science dates the birth of the probability calculus, the first attempt to bring the unpredictable under control – developed in the correspondence between Pierre Fermat and Blaise Pascal – to the year 1651.

The horror of ambiguity which was a hallmark of the hazardousness – the 'quixoticness' – of risk from the beginning, can still be felt today; indeed, it is more present than ever with the cutting-edge technologies in which the greatest promise and the greatest calamity are inextricably fused. Not only Descartes, but also Cervantes, not only philosophy and natural science, but also the novelist, explores the ambivalences of risk modernity. If Descartes conceived of the 'thinking ego' as the foundation of everything, with risk the acting ego defies the gods and a predestined future, an attitude that can be correctly characterized as 'heroic' in Hegel's sense. In the first modern novels, this heroism of risk is narrated as an awakening into an unknown world involving ever more unpredictability. At the beginning of Denis Diderot's *Jacques le fataliste et son maître*, we come upon the two heroes under way – where they are coming from or where they are going to we have no idea. They live in a time without beginning or end, in a space without limits, amid social landscapes whose future seems as present as it is infinite. One senses that, given the indeterminateness of risk, existential experimentalism is unavoidable. The experiential dimension of risk – the discovery, the suffering, the prediction of the unpredictable, the fear, the desire, the surprise, the occasional anticipation of death, which risk smuggles into everyday life – all of this can be summarized in the (of course ironical and playful) assertion *I risk, therefore I am*. I venture, therefore I am. I suffer, therefore I am. Who am I? Why am I? Why am I the person who I am and not the person I could also be, and thus also am?

The category of risk opens up a world within and beyond the clear distinction between knowledge and non-knowing, truth and falsehood, good and evil. The single, undivided truth has fractured into hundreds of relative truths resulting from the proximity to and dismay over risk. This does not mean that risk annuls all forms of knowledge. Rather it amalgamates knowledge with non-knowing within the semantic horizon of probability. Thus the category of risk reflects the response to uncertainty, which nowadays often cannot be overcome by more knowledge but is instead a result of more knowledge. Sometimes this inability-to-know [*Nicht-Wissen-Können*] is suppressed, sometimes it becomes the centre of attention, the horror scenario which is great for business and for playing power games. Through risk, the arrogant assumption of controllability – but perhaps also the wisdom of uncertainty – can increase in influence.

The history of the novel and the history of the social sciences can be described, in parallel though contrasting ways, in terms of the historical metamorphosis of risk. In Balzac's novels the dominant factor is no longer the existential hazardousness of a precarious human condition forsaken by God. Here modern social institutions – the police, the administration of justice, the world of finance or the world of criminals, of the military, of state authority – take centre stage. Risk is explored in the institutional forms which foster domination, as later in the almost Kafkaesque rationalization theory of Max Weber and Michel Foucault's theory of power. Balzac's novels no longer have any place for lucky new beginnings. Society is founded and administered on the basis of the ambiguity of risk. The promise of happiness still outweighs the premonition of the possible disaster. Such a perspective reaches its culmination in Kafka. Here the freedom promised by risk has metamorphosed into its opposite, into self-obstruction, self-accusation and self-subjection in the face of the all-pervasive court and castle. The impenetrability, omnipresence and undecidability of systemic risks are foisted onto the individual.[1]

Nowadays the semantics of risk is especially topical and important in the languages of technology, economics and the natural sciences and in that of politics. Those natural sciences (such as human genetics, reproductive medicine, nanotechnology, etc.) whose speed of development is overwhelming cultural imagination are most affected by the public dramatization of risks. The corresponding fears, which are directed to a (still) nonexistent future, and hence are difficult for science to defuse, threaten to place restrictions on the freedom of research. Under certain conditions, politicians feel compelled to impose such restrictions because public discourses concerning risk take on a dynamic of their own (which remains to be studied). Risk is thus a 'mediating issue' in terms of which the division of labour between science, politics and the economy in highly innovative societies must ultimately be renegotiated.

2   Risk society

In risk societies, the consequences and successes of modernization become an issue with the speed and radicality of processes of modernization. A new dimension of risk emerges because the conditions for calculating and institutionally processing it break down in part. Under such conditions a new moral climate of politics develops in which cultural, and hence nationally varying, evaluations play a central role and arguments for and against real or possible consequences of technical and economic decisions are publicly conducted. In the process, the functions of science and technology also change. Over the past two centuries, the judgement of scientists has replaced tradition in Western societies. Paradoxically, however, the more science and technology permeate and transform life on a global scale, the less this expert authority is taken as a given. In discourses concerning risk, in which questions of normative (self-)limitation also arise, the mass media, parliaments, social movements, governments, philosophers, lawyers, writers, etc., are winning the right to a say in decisions. The conflicts are leading to new forms of institutionalization and have even contributed to the emergence of a new field of law, risk law, which regulates responses to risks, above all those of scientific-technological provenance, and operates mainly at the level of administration, though already also increasingly at the level of research.

The struggle over blame and responsibility which is raging in social conflicts concerning the definition of risk, therefore, is not – as Mary Douglas (1966, 1986) asserts – an anthropological constant. Premodern threats also led to assignments of blame. Yet risks remained in essence 'blows of fate' that assaulted human beings from 'outside' and could be attributed to 'external' gods, demons or nature. The political history of the institutions of the developing modern society during the nineteenth and twentieth centuries can be understood as the conflict-ridden evolution of a system of rules for responding to industrial uncertainties and risks, hence those produced by decisions. That a 'risk contract' is a possible or necessary response to the adventure involved in opening up and conquering new markets and in developing and implementing new technologies is a social invention, an invention that goes back to the origins of intercontinental merchant shipping and that was extended to almost all social problem areas and gradually perfected with the emergence of national capitalism. Consequences that at first affect individuals become 'risks', that is, systemic, statistically describable and hence 'calculable' event types that can be subsumed under supra-individual compensation and avoidance rules.

This 'risk calculus' links the natural, technical and social sciences. It can be applied as much to highly diverse phenomena in public health – from the risk of smoking to the risk posed by nuclear power stations – as to economic risks, risks of unemployment, of traffic accidents, of ageing, and so forth. As François Ewald (1991) shows, by applying generalizable accident statistics and employing the exchange principle 'money for damage', the risk-insurance calculus makes it possible to institutionalize state promises of security in the face of an open, uncertain future.

Such a state-sanctioned risk contract involving precautions to curb the side effects and costs of industrial decisions and to ensure their 'just' distribution is situated somewhere between socialism and liberalism. For it recognizes the systemic origins of hazardous side effects while at the same time involving individuals in their compensation and prevention. Where this national risk contract is blatantly and systematically violated, the consensus which has sustained modernization at least in principle is open to challenge: this is the meaning of the category of *risk society*. It thematizes the process of problematizing the assumption that it is possible to control and compensate for industrially generated insecurities and dangers, an assumption which is central to the risk contract.[2] This means that the dynamic of risk society rests less on the assumption that now and in future we must live in a world of unprecedented dangers; rather, we live in a world that has to make decisions concerning its future under the conditions of manufactured, self-inflicted insecurity. Among other things, the world can no longer control the dangers produced by modernity; to be more precise, the belief that modern society can control the dangers that it itself produces is collapsing – not because of its omissions and defeats but because of its *triumphs*. Climate change, for example, is a product of successful industrialization which systematically disregards its consequences for nature and humanity. The global economy is growing too quickly, affluence is rising too sharply, which simply means that the greenhouse emissions of the industrial countries are steadily increasing – by 2.4 per cent since 2000, to be precise. And it has become clear that, faced with this global challenge, single-state solutions are like Stone Age answers to the questions of the industrial age. The uncontrollable impacts of global-ized financial flows for whole groups of countries, as suddenly transpired during the Asian crisis, are also an expression of the *radicalized* capitalist market principle which has cast off the fetters of national and supranational controls. Here political and institutional answers are still lacking.

The term *risk society* which I coined and made the title of my book in 1986 epitomizes an era of modern society that no longer merely casts off tradi-tional ways of life but rather wrestles with the side effects of successful modernization – with precarious biographies and inscrutable threats that affect everybody and against which nobody can adequately insure. From this I drew a number of conclusions:

- Risk possesses the 'destructive force of war'. The language of threat is infectious and transforms social inequality: social need is hierarchical, the new threat, by contrast, is democratic. It affects even the rich and powerful. The shocks are felt in all areas of society. Markets collapse, legal systems fail to register offences, governments become the targets of accusations while at the same time gaining new leeway for action.
- We are becoming members of a 'global community of threats'. The threats are no longer the internal affairs of particular countries and a country cannot deal with the threats alone. A new conflict dynamic of social inequalities is emerging.
- Scientific progress now consists in subverting the role of experts. The fundamental principle of science and its visualization technologies – 'I do not see any risk, therefore no risk exists' – is being challenged. More science does not necessarily translate into less risk but makes the percep-tion of risk more acute and risks themselves 'collectively' visible for the first time.
- Fear determines the attitude towards life. Security is displacing freedom and equality from the highest position on the scale of values. The result

is a tightening of laws, a seemingly rational 'totalitarianism of defence against threats'.
• The 'fear business' will profit from the general loss of nerve. The suspicious and suspect citizen must be grateful when he is scanned, photographed, searched and interrogated 'for his own safety'. Security is becoming a profitable public and private sector consumer good like water and electricity.

When I re-read *Risk Society* today, I find it touching. In spite of the dramatic tone, the world it describes is idyllic – it is still 'terror free'. Yet many structural features described in *Risk Society* read today like descriptions of the world after 11 September 2001, after the terrorist attacks in New York and Washington.

3 World risk society

In order to convey what is unfamiliar and novel about the category *world risk society* in contrast to that of *risk society*, here I will introduce and develop a whole series of conceptual innovations and differentiations – for example, the distinction between risk and catastrophe or between risk and culturally varying assessments of risk, whose importance is steadily increasing in the era of globalization. At the same time I will offer a typology of different 'logics' of global risks that makes it possible to define the new phenomena associated with transnational suicide terrorism (as compared with the national terrorism of struggles for independence or for political participation, such as that of the Irish or the Palestinians) and to compare it to environmental and economic global risks. Here I would like to mention by way of anticipation some of these conceptual innovations and the insights they open up.

Risk and catastrophe

Risk is *not* synonymous with catastrophe. Risk means the *anticipation* of the catastrophe. Risks concern the possibility of future occurrences and developments; they make present a state of the world that does not (yet) exist. Whereas every catastrophe is spatially, temporally and socially determined, the anticipation of catastrophe lacks any spatio-temporal or social concreteness. Thus the category of risk signifies the controversial reality of the possible, which must be demarcated from merely speculative possibility, on the one hand, and from the actual occurrence of the catastrophe, on the other. The moment risks become real, when a nuclear power station explodes or a terrorist attack occurs, they become catastrophes. Risks are always *future* events that *may* occur, that *threaten* us. But because this constant danger shapes our expectations, lodges in our heads and guides our actions, it becomes a political force that transforms the world.

One of the key questions which this book poses and seeks to answer shines a spotlight on this difference between anticipated risk and the really occurring catastrophe. How is the presence of future catastrophes 'manufactured'? Along what routes does risk acquire the predicate 'real' – in other words, how does it come to reign as 'believed' anticipation in people's minds and in institutions and indeed often across the boundaries between nations, regions, religions and political parties and between rich and poor? And why does the anticipation of catastrophe, of all things, prompt a reinvention of the political?

The answer, reduced to a formula, is: global risk is the *staging of the reality* [*Realitätsinszenierung*] of global risk. That is one of the essential perspectives in which *World at Risk* goes beyond the theses of *Risk Society*. 'Staging' here is not intended in the colloquial sense of the deliberate falsification of reality by exaggerating 'unreal' risks. The distinction between risk as anticipated catastrophe and the actual catastrophe forces us instead to take the role of staging seriously. For only by imagining and staging world risk does the future catastrophe become present – often with the goal of averting it by influencing present decisions. Then the diagnosis of risk would be 'a self-refuting prophecy' – a prime example being the debate on climate change which is supposed to prevent climate change.[3]

The emphasis on the perspective of staging makes it possible to highlight an aspect of the global terrorist conflict that has been largely neglected until now. To exaggerate somewhat: it is not the terrorist act, but the global staging of the act and the political anticipations, actions and reactions in response to the staging which are destroying the Western institutions of freedom and democracy. The restrictions on individual liberties discernible at many levels – from the increase in surveillance cameras to restrictions on immigration – are not simply effects of actual catastrophes (for example, acts of terrorist violence). They are a result of such experiences *and their globalized anticipation*, in other words, of the attempt to prevent the future occurrence of such events anywhere in the world. Bin Laden and his networks achieve global political prominence only when a whole series of further conditions are fulfilled that enable them to achieve global public resonance and presence. Whether it be the mass media broadcasting the images of bloodstained victims across the world, or American President Bush declaring war on terrorism, or NATO declaring a case of legitimate defence after 9/11: only when such reactions follow the deed does every terrorist's dream of a meteoric rise from obscure petty criminality to the 'number one enemy', the 'global danger' – in short, to 'terrorist world stardom' – become a reality.

Part of the success story of terrorism is that the US government, the European governments and the journalists working in the mass media have not yet grasped the importance of staging, i.e. how they unwittingly support the perpetrators by (contributing to) staging the anticipation of terrorism as global danger in the struggle for control over the images in people's minds – and in the process increase the terrorists' power. This involuntary complicity is reflected in the formula 'War on Terror': this scattered the terrorist seed over real battlefields where terrorism could achieve its greatest victories, namely, countless deaths and moral and political harm to the United States.[4]

The distinction between risk and cultural perception of risk is becoming blurred

A further moment follows from this difference between risk (as anticipated event) and catastrophe (as actual event). It does not matter whether we live in a world that is 'objectively' more secure than any that has gone before – *the staged anticipation of disasters and catastrophes obliges us to take preventive action*. This holds especially for the state, which is forced to take anticipatory precautionary measures because guaranteeing the security of its citizens is one of its pre-eminent tasks. This is true even if the relevant authorities (science, the military, the judiciary) do not have the corresponding instruments at their disposal (e.g. because their ability to respond to global risks is confined to the horizon of the nation-state).

This casts doubt on an often entirely unreflected 'rationalistic understanding' of risks, such as prevails in everyday life but is also formulated in disciplines such as the natural sciences, the engineering sciences, psychology, economics and medicine. On this interpretation, risk is assumed more or less without question to be an objective reality. Accordingly, risk research in these fields focuses primarily on the statistical-mathematical identification of risks, on formulating and testing causal hypotheses, on the resulting prognostic models for particular risks and on the answers of different groups to typical variations in perceptions of risk. These investigations in many disciplines are 'rationalistic' because they are guided by the assumptions that scientific methods of measurement and calculation are the most appropriate way to approach risks descriptively, explanatorily and prognostically, and importantly also politically.

This 'technical' science of risk rests on a clear separation between risk and perception which is underscored and supported by the parallel separation between experts and lay people. Correspondingly, the 'subjectivity' of risk, and hence the 'perception of risk', is delegated to attitude research. Here the perception of risk is viewed and analysed in turn largely as an individual reaction and response to 'objective' risks as measured by various 'heuristics' of individual judgement and understanding. It is clear on which side prejudices and mistakes are assumed to lie – namely, that of the lay people – and on which not – namely, that of the experts. The 'subjectivity of risk' is assumed to be pervasive among lay people, who are regarded as 'poorly informed' in comparison to the 'precise' and 'scientific' analyses of the experts. On this view, the irrationality of risk perception among large portions of the population is primarily a matter of inadequate information. If we succeeded in turning everyone into an expert, risk conflicts would resolve themselves – this, thought through to its conclusion, is the guiding idea. All complicating factors – such as different forms of non-knowing, contradictions among different experts and disciplines, ultimately the impossibility of making the unforeseeable foreseeable – are bracketed and dismissed as overrated problems.

The staging thesis generally contradicts this, especially in the case of global risks. The global anticipation of catastrophe for the most part resists the methods of scientific calculation. The less calculable risk becomes, however, the more weight culturally shifting perceptions of risk acquire, with the result that the distinction between *risk* and *cultural perception of risk* becomes blurred. The same risk becomes 'real' in different ways from the perspective of different countries and cultures – and is assessed differently. And the more the world contracts as globalization progresses, the more these clashing cultural perceptions stand out as mutually exclusive certainties. The 'clash of risk cultures', the collision of culturally different 'risk realities' (i.e. perceptions of risk), is developing into a fundamental problem of global politics in the twenty-first century (chapter 4).

Perceptions of risk clash in the global public arena of the mass media and are at the same time becoming an everyday conflict experience. In the global communications networks, all human beings, all ethnic and religious groups, all populations are part of a shared present for the first time in human history. Each nation has become the next-door neighbour of every other, and shocks in one part of the planet are transmitted with extraordinary speed to the whole population of the earth. But this factual common present is not founded on a common past and by no means guarantees a common future. Precisely because the world is being 'united' against its will, without its vote or agreement, the conflicts between cultures, pasts, situations, religions – especially in assessing and responding to global risks (climate change, terrorism, nuclear energy, nuclear weapons) – are becoming manifest. This means that it is increasingly difficult to make a clear and binding distinction between hysteria and deliberate fear-mongering, on the one hand, and appropriate fear and precaution, on the other.[5]

Many will regard the staging of risk as an abstract issue that has little or nothing to do with the experience of risk. But that would be a grave error, for such stagings always also have an *existential* aspect, an element of suffering. Global risk, through its omnipresence in the media, normalizes death and suffering, not just as an individual fate but also as a collective one, even though for most people suffering is synonymous with images of the suffering of others.

Does the 'staging' of risk therefore mean that risks do not exist at all? Of course not. Nobody can deny that the fears that an intercontinental airliner will explode as a result of a terrorist attack, that a nuclear power plant will be built, that an oil tanker will run aground or that London and Tokyo will be inundated as a result of climate change as some predict, are founded on objective realities. However, risk analysts in particular know that risk is not an objectively measurable quantity. What does the 'reality' of risk mean? The reality of risk is shown by its *controversial* character. Risks do not have any abstract existence in themselves. They acquire reality in the contradictory judgements of groups and populations. The notion of an objective yardstick against which degrees of risk can be measured overlooks the fact that risks count as urgent, threatening and real or as negligible and unreal only as a result of particular cultural perceptions and evaluations.

Risks are lurking everywhere. Some are accepted, others not. Are some risks rejected because they are more dangerous than others? Certainly not – but if so, then because the same risk looks like a dragon to some, but like a worm to others. Acceptable risks are those which are accepted. This apparent tautology goes to the heart of the matter: the greater and more objective a risk appears, the more its reality depends on its cultural evaluation. In other words, the objectivity of a risk is a product of its perception and its staging (also by experts).

To repeat, this does not mean that there are no risks, that risks are illusions, products of a widespread alarmism or the sensationalism of the mass media. However, it does mean that nobody can appeal solely to an external reality in dealing with risks. The risks which we believe we recognize and which fill us with fear are mirror images of our selves, of our cultural perceptions. And global risks become real in this antagonism of cultural certainties or against the backdrop of an emerging global solidarity.

Typology of global risks

I would first like to make a systematic distinction (without any claim to completeness and for purely pragmatic reasons of reducing complexity) between three 'logics' of global risks and explore their interrelations, namely, environmental crises, global financial risks and terrorist threats. A fourth dimension – biographical risks closely connected with the dynamics of individualization that play a prominent role in the risk society – I leave aside.[6]

An essential difference between environmental and economic dangers, on the one hand, and the terrorist threat, on the other, resides in the fact that in the latter case *purpose* takes the place of *chance*. Environmental crises and economic threats due to global financial flows, in spite of all their differences, exhibit a commonality: they must be understood in terms of the dialectic of *goods* and *bads*, and hence as contingent side effects of decisions in the process of modernization. This is not true of the new terrorism, which annuls the rational principles of former risk calculations because purpose replaces chance and maliciousness replaces good will.

Only in retrospect does it become apparent that the calculability of risks has a moral basis. It presupposes that a possible catastrophe occurs by chance and is not brought about with evil intent. This can be seen from a tiny but highly symbolic example, namely, air safety before 11 September 2001. The electronic airline ticket machine used for flights between Boston, New York and Washington asked the user in an electronic voice: 'Did you pack your bags yourself?' or 'Did anyone unknown to you ask you to carry anything on board?' And the answer which let you through could be given by pressing your finger on a particular part of the screen. This 'security machine' sums up the Western technical security strategy: it is founded on a kind of original civilizational faith in controllability that every terrorist threat subverts.

This entails (in the long term) a profound setback for the public legitimation of new technologies. Cutting-edge technologies – genetics, nanotechnology and robotics – are opening 'a new Pandora's box'. For this very reason, those responsible for well-intentioned research and technological development will in future have to do more than offer public assurances of the social utility and the minimal 'residual risk' of their activity. Instead, in the future the risk assessments of such technological and scientific developments will have to take into account, literally, intention as well as chance, the terrorist threats and the conceivable malicious uses as well as dangerous side effects.

The attacks on 11 September 2001 gave rise to a universal awareness of the vulnerability of the West, notwithstanding its economic and military superiority. At the same time this makes it clear that, whereas we are – more or less – insured against chance and accident, we are completely defenceless against suicidal terrorist attacks. This poses a dilemma for the sociology of risk and for risk society itself. On the one hand, they must anticipate the deed by thinking the unthinkable; on the other hand, in attempting to raise awareness they may alert possible attackers to new opportunities. The hazardousness of risk analysis, therefore, consists in the fact that imagining dangers that were previously unthinkable can inadvertently help to bring them about. However, in a world in which the imagination of the threats posed by civilization is freed from the reins of chance with the aim of prevention and is set upon the deliberate triggering of catastrophes, the foundations of freedom and democracy are in danger of being undermined.

Believed anticipation of catastrophe is transforming the concept of society in the twenty-first century

We are living in a world risk society not only in the sense that everything is being transformed into decisions whose consequences are unforeseeable or in the sense of risk-management societies or risk-discourse societies. Risk society means precisely a constellation in which the *idea* of the controllability of decision-based side effects and dangers which is guiding for modernity has become questionable. Thus it is a constellation in which new knowledge serves to transform unpredictable risks into calculable risks, but in the process it gives rise to new unpredictabilities, forcing us to reflect upon risks, as this book again shows.[7] Through this 'reflexivity of uncertainty', the indeterminability of risk in the present is for the first time becoming fundamental for society as a whole, which is why we have to overhaul our concept of society and the conceptual apparatus of social science.

At the same time, world risk society sets free a 'cosmopolitan moment' – for example, in historical comparison with ancient cosmopolitanism (stoicism), with the *jus cosmopolitica* of the Enlightenment (Kant) or with crimes against humanity (Hannah Arendt, Karl Jaspers) (chapter 3). Global risks force us to confront the apparently excluded other. They tear down national barriers and mix natives with foreigners. The expelled other becomes the internal other, as a result not of migration but of global risks. Everyday life is becoming cosmopolitan: human beings must lend meaning to their lives through exchanges with others and no longer in encounters with people like themselves.[8]

Both tendencies – the reflexivity of uncertainty and the cosmopolitan moment – point to a comprehensive meta-change of 'society' in the twenty-first century (chapter 11):

- The stagings, experiences and conflicts of global risk permeate and transform the foundations of social life and action in all spheres, national and global.
- World risk also exhibits the new way of coping with open questions, how the future is integrated into the present, what shapes societies assume as a result of internalizing risk, how existing institutions are changing and what previously unknown organizational patterns are emerging.
- On the one hand, (unintentional) large-scale risks (climate change) are gaining prominence; on the other hand, the anticipation of the new kinds of threats emanating from (deliberate) terrorist attacks represents a persistent public concern.
- A general cultural transformation is taking place: different understandings of nature and its relation to society, of ourselves and others, of social rationality, freedom, democracy and legitimation – even of the individual – are developing.
- A new, future-oriented *planetary ethics of responsibility* (Jonas 1984; Apel 1987; Strydom 2002; Linklater 2001; Mason 2005) is called for that finds its advocates among new cultural movements. By appealing to such a macro-ethics, social groups and firms coordinate their activities, offer competing assessments of risk and create new identities, laws and

international organizations in economics, society and politics. Even the military has transformed itself, at least in part, into an advocate of a post-national ethics of responsibility, as is shown by the foreign missions of the Bundeswehr in Afghanistan, Africa and Lebanon.

The overarching meaning of global risk has serious implications because it involves a whole new repertoire of ideas, apprehensions, fears, hopes, behavioural norms and religious conflicts. These fears have one particularly unfortunate side effect: people or groups who are (or are made into) 'risk persons' or 'risk groups' count as nonpersons whose basic rights are threatened. Risk divides, excludes and stigmatizes. In this way, new limits of perception and communication are developing, though also problems and undertakings that are for the first time subject to public pressure for cross-border resolution. As a result, the staging of global risk sets in train a social production and construction of reality. With this, risk becomes the cause and medium of social transformation. It is also closely connected with the new forms of classification, interpretation and organization of our everyday lives and the new way of staging, organizing, living and shaping society in light of the presence of the future – which is why it is decisive for a new definition of the basic concepts of sociology.

Max Weber and John Maynard Keynes or: Downplaying the central role of non-knowing

The leap from the risk society to world risk society can be clarified in hindsight by appeal to two witnesses: Max Weber and John Maynard Keynes, the modern classics of sociology and economics, respectively. In Max Weber, the logic of control triumphs in the modern response to risk, and so irreversibly that cultural optimism and cultural pessimism turn out to be two aspects of a single dynamic. The unfolding and radicalization of the basic principles of modernity, in particular the radicalization of scientific and economic rationality, threatens to give rise to a despotic regime, on the one hand in relation to the development of modern bureaucracy and on the other because of the victory march of profit-seeking capitalism. Hope and concern condition one another. Since the uncertainties and unseen, unintended side effects which are concomitants of risk rationality are repeatedly 'optimistically' mastered through an increase in and extension of rationalization and marketing, Weber's primary concern, in contrast to Comte and Durkheim, was not the deficiency of social order and integration. Unlike Comte, he was not afraid of the 'chaos of uncertainties'. On the contrary, he recognized that the synthesis of science, bureaucracy and capitalism transforms the modern world into a kind of 'prison'. This threat is not a marginal phenomenon but is the logical consequence of the *successful* rationalization of risk: when everything goes well, things get progressively worse.

Instrumental rationality depoliticizes politics and undermines individual freedom. At the same time, implicit in Max Weber's model is an idea that explains why risk becomes a global phenomenon, though not why it leads to world risk society. According to Weber, the globalization of risk is not bound up with colonialism or imperialism and hence is not driven by fire and the sword. Rather, it follows the path of the unforced force of the better argument. The triumphal procession of rationalization is based on the promised utility of risk and on the corresponding rational restriction of the side effects, uncertainties and dangers bound up with it. It is this self-application of risk to risk with the goal of perfecting self-control that globalizes 'universalism'. However, the idea that precisely the unseen, unwanted, incalculable, unexpected, uncertain, which is made permanent by risk, could become the source of unforeseeable possibilities and threats that effectively place in question the idea of rational control – this idea is inconceivable on the Weberian model. It provides the foundation of my theory of world risk society.

The sciences which concern themselves with risk modernity consistently sought and seek opportunities not only to analyse the unexpected but also to make it expectable. Here the crux is less the decision itself than the consequences of decisions. The key idea is that these risky consequences lurk and spread behind the mantle of non-knowing, of the inability-to-know, something about which we are only too ready to deceive ourselves. We project experiences of the past into the future and in this way become entangled in the snares of the past in the seemingly calculable future.

The reality of risk forces us to look the unexpected in the eye. But how can one expect the unexpected, the unexpectable? No frivolous faith in progress or frivolous pessimism can help us overcome this paradox. Frank Knight and John Keynes were the first to deal systematically with the uncertainty of all attempts to overcome uncertainty in a rational way. Already in his dissertation, which he completed at Cornell University in 1916 and published in 1921 under the title of *Risk, Uncertainty and Profit*, Knight made a clear distinction between risk and uncertainty:

But Uncertainty must be taken in a sense radically distinct from the familiar notion of Risk, from which it has never been properly separated . . . It will appear that a measurable uncertainty, or 'risk' proper . . . is so far different from an unmeasurable one that it is not in effect an uncertainty at all. (1921: 19–20)

With risk, chaos neither breaks out nor breaks down – any more than does disaster or threat. Rather, calculable uncertainty becomes a source of creativity, it makes it possible to allow the unexpected. The world of calculable and controllable risk sets free (perhaps even with the triumph of its claim to calculability) the moment of surprise.

When Keynes attempts to unravel the mystery of economic activity, his thinking ultimately turns on this irreversibility of uncertainty, which is a consequence of the claim of the mathematical models that uncertainty is insurmountable. Here there is first the difference between model Platonism and reality. The model assumptions of the economic sciences are postulates that by no means correspond to the actual decisions, their consequences and side effects of side effects, in economic, social and political reality. Keynes concludes that economic doctrines are misleading and can result in catastrophes if applied to the world of facts. In the idealized world of mathematical economic science, it was generally accepted that fluctuations in the economic cycle are regrettable, transitional phenomena that are not inherent in an economic system based on risk. The assumption was that you had only to modify some falsifying framework conditions for risk to unleash its power to create boundless happiness. The economic well-being of all lay just around the corner of the future, so to speak. Risk, by its inner logic, means uncertainty and accentuates uncertainty, and not only negatively in the shape of catastrophes (collapse of the global economy, etc.), but also positively: the experience of the everyday 'real world' is beyond the horizon of this risk-model science.

Against this Keynes objects:

By 'uncertain' knowledge . . . I do not mean merely to distinguish what is known for certain from what is merely probable. The game of roulette is not subject, in this sense, to uncertainty . . . The sense in which I am using the term is that in which the prospect of a European war is uncertain, or the price of copper and the rate of interest twenty years hence . . . About these matters there is no scientific basis on which to form any calculable probability whatever. We simply do not know. (1937: 213–14)

This straightforward insight – we simply do not know, perhaps we cannot know – conceals essential steps that point the way from risk to world risk society (chapter 7). This can be explained, first, in contrast to Max Weber's notion of the iron cage of bondage to rationality. The insurmountable uncertainty which lurks in risk from the outset, and may even increase with the claim to rationalization, *corrodes* the cage of calculable reason and – paradoxical as it may sound – liberates us. From a systematic perspective, one must even go a step further. Max Weber's model of rationality assumes that the uncertainty and ambiguity of risk can be 'rationalized' through self-application. Keynes contradicts this with good reason (even though he never formulated this idea in these terms). The controlling rationality of risk *cannot* be applied to the uncertainty of the effects, the side effects and the side effects of the side effects. The uncertainty of risk *cannot* be tamed by means of uncertain risk. Rather, the converse holds: all attempts at rational control give rise to new 'irrational', incalculable, unpredictable consequences. This is shown by the history of 'side effects' – for example, of climate change and the globalization of financial risks (LiPuma and Lee 2004) – and the associated research. Control of the control of control can become a source of threats and side effects of threats without end.

Risk is a reflexive notion because it balances benefits against harms and makes the future decidable in the present. Thus this anti-Weberian principle of the non-rationalizability of risk uncertainty also makes room for the ambiguity of world risk society. Behind the façade of non-knowing, the 'side effects', which were wilfully ignored or were unknowable at the moment of decision, assume the guise of environmental crises that transcend the limits of space and time.

At the beginning of the twenty-first century, we see modern society with new eyes, and this birth of a 'cosmopolitan vision' (Beck 2006) is among the unexpected phenomena out of which a still indeterminate world risk society is emerging. Henceforth, there are no merely local occurrences. All genuine threats have become global threats. The situation of every nation, every people, every religion, every class and every individual is also the result and cause of the human situation. The key point is that henceforth concern about the whole has become a task. It is not optional but the human condition. Nobody foresaw, wanted or chose this; nevertheless it represents the imperceptible summation of decisions and is now part of the human condition. Nobody can escape it. Thus began a transformation of society, politics and history that is not yet properly understood and which many years ago I conceptualized in terms of 'world risk society' (Beck 1992; 1999b). However, this concept is developed systematically for the first time in this book. What we now know is just the beginning. Elementary questions must be addressed anew: What constitutes 'society' within the horizon of global risk, hence of elementary manufactured uncertainty? What is 'politics', what is 'history', when these concepts can no longer be tied to nation and territory?

4   The argumentative architecture and divisions of this book

My aim in this book is not to provide an exhaustive typology of all possible risks of world risk society. Old risks (industrial accidents, wars) and natural catastrophes (earthquakes, tsunamis) overlap and are becoming associated with new risks (catastrophic climate change, global financial crises and suicide attacks) and thus can trigger in turn new, incalculable and unpredictable turbulences. It is scarcely possible to place limits on the apocalyptic imagination – and I have no ambition to become the Hieronymus Bosch of sociology.

My aim is to develop the existing theory and sociology of risk at least three steps further: first, through the *globalization perspective*, second, and connected with this, through the *staging perspective* and, third, through the *comparative perspective* of three risk logics, namely, environmental, economic and terrorist global risks.

Anyone who approaches world risk society from such a perspective is in danger of being overwhelmed by a flood of mostly undefined problems, indeed problems that can scarcely be solved with the existing methodological instruments, and must be careful not to drown in them. Once again: What is the new reality to be addressed in *World at Risk* twenty years after *Risk Society*? And how is this reflected in the argumentative architecture of this book? A number of essential new perspectives – for example, the distinction between risk and catastrophe and the differentiation between side effects catastrophes and intentional catastrophes (hence between environmental and economic global risks, on the one hand, and terrorist risks, on the other) – run through every chapter, in addition to the perspective of the staging of global risks which informs the book as a whole. Other vistas and insights are opened up, illustrated and developed in the respective chapters. To anticipate:

Chapter 2 takes up the guiding idea of the staging of risk by posing the question of the 'relations of definition' in the sense of the relations of domination which lend stagings collective validity and legitimation. Who decides in a world of manufactured uncertainties, in which knowledge and non-knowledge of risks are indissolubly linked, what is and is not a risk? Who decides on the compensation for injured populations – within nation-states and internationally? Here 'relations of definition' should be understood by analogy with and in contradistinction to 'relations of production' (Karl Marx). Strangely enough, the claim to rational control of institutions, which is currently breaking down in public conflicts over the definition of risk in the mass media, has prevented this background of domination from being thematized by the discursive, scientific community. At the same time, this chapter introduces the reader – step by step – to my theory of risk society which has been distorted by misunderstandings and inaccuracies (chapter 2: *Relations of Definition as Relations of Domination: Who Decides What is and is Not a Risk?*).

It may seem that anyone who studies how risks are staged must succumb to relativism. However, that is mistaken. Chapter 3 raises the question of the *normative horizon* of world risk society and the *normative frame of reference* of the sociology of world risk society. Global risks – this is the thesis – unexpectedly liberate a world-historical *'cosmopolitan moment'*. This involves a 'thick cosmopolitanism' (Dobson 2006). For global risks, because they make the anticipation of collective extinction into an everyday experience, release moral and political impulses by way of counterbalancing economic, political and cultural globalization across boundaries and divisions. They provide a basis of legitimation for political institutions and social movements that press for more humane forms of globalization, which does not preclude, of course, that this cosmopolitan moment can be instrumentalized for ideological purposes (chapter 3: *The 'Cosmopolitan Moment' of World Risk Society or: Enforced Enlightenment*).

This raises the question which will be addressed in chapter 4: How can we explain the *global political explosiveness* of global risks? Here I will consider two answers: it is a matter not, as Samuel Huntington asserts, of a clash of religiously based civilizations but of a *clash of risk cultures*. In the global public arena, in the controversies over global risks and the dangerous uncertainties to which they give rise, the most diverse – indeed diametrically opposed – cultural certainties encounter one another. Some people view the al-Qaeda terrorism through religious spectacles and see it as confirming prophecies of the Apocalypse; for others, risks enter the world stage only after God has made his exit. The awareness of global risks then becomes a secular awareness that ascribes the impending catastrophes to perpetrators and institutions. The other answer develops the hypothesis that the global political force of global risks is the result of the overlapping of the state of normalcy and the state of exception (chapter 4: *Clash of Risk Cultures or: The Overlapping of the State of Normalcy and the State of Exception*).

How or in what sense are staged risks 'real'? This question will be examined in chapter 5, where different variants of 'constructivism' and 'realism' will be contrasted with the aim of justifying the both/and position of a 'constructivist realism'. Two further key concepts and agents of the global staging of risk will be presented here: 'global public sphere' and 'global subpolitics' (chapter 5: *Global Public Sphere and Global Subpolitics or: How Real is Catastrophic Climate Change?*).

In chapter 6, two stages in the development of risk society will be distinguished; at the same time, I will explain how the pessimism concerning progress currently rife (at least in the West) becomes entangled in its own assumptions concerning linearity and thereby fails to grasp the fundamental indeterminacy – the surprise element – of global risk (chapter 6: *The Provident State or: On the Antiquatedness of Linear Pessimism Concerning Progress*).

The question of the relation between risk and non-knowing runs through the whole book. It is the focus of chapter 7. I will distinguish many forms of non-knowing, of which the 'unknown unknowns' are only an extreme form. Against the background of this typology of forms of non-knowing, various perspectives of 'reflexive modernization' will be developed and addressed (chapter 7: *Knowledge or Non-Knowing? Two Perspectives of 'Reflexive Modernization'*).

In *Ecological Politics in an Age of Risk* (2002), I introduced the *private insurance principle* as an operative distinguishing criterion between still controllable and no longer controllable threats. Not sociologists but private-sector insurance companies are supposed to decide, using criteria of economic rationality, whether a particular technological development can or cannot count as 'rationally controllable' in its effects at a particular moment in history. This principle has sparked lively debates and has been tested through case studies. These have established, for example, that, contrary to the insurance principle, a new insurance market for terrorist risks arose following 9/11. To what extent does insuring, for instance, against the risk of terrorism (which can stand in for other global risks) contradict this principle of private insurance protection? One could say that insurance companies [*Versicherungsgesellschaften*] are risk companies [*Risikogesellschaften*], for it is they who turn risk into a business. Thus in this chapter the *limits* of insurability will be explored by means of examples (chapter 8: *The Insurance Principle: Criticism and Counter-Criticism*).

The staging of *violence*, too, can and must be interpreted as the selective staging of the risk of violence, or so I argue in chapter 9. Martin Shaw (2005) speaks in this sense of 'risk redistribution wars'. On this conception, wars must be fought in such a way that they do not really disturb the 'felt peace' in the warring country. Hence, 'military operations' and 'peace interventions' call for spatial and social separation between felt peace and actual war using a particular pattern of staging and legitimation. These kinds of 'risk wars' reveal the identity of relations of definition and relations of domination within the global framework (chapter 9: *Felt War, Felt Peace: Staging Violence*).

In *Risk Society*, I highlighted the extreme case of equality in the face of global risks. The dynamics of risk society are 'beyond status and class', because global threats ultimately affect everybody, even those responsible for them. This remains true but is insufficiently differentiated. In chapter 10, I develop in a systematic way the *inequality dynamics of global risks* to which the understanding and analysis of *local vulnerability* is central. In this context, the distinction between methodological nationalism and methodological cosmopolitanism will be introduced and systematically developed. In the process it becomes clear that 'national sociology' confuses society with national society and is blind and makes us blind to the ruses, contradictions, strategies and social constructions of global unequal distributions of risk that remain, or are made, invisible to the inward-looking national gaze (chapter 10: *Global Inequality, Local Vulnerability: The Conflict Dynamics of Environmental Hazards Must be Studied within the Framework of Methodological Cosmopolitanism*).

The whole argumentative architecture of this book is summarized in chapter 11 under the heading '*Critical Theory of World Risk Society*'. Readers who are interested in social theory and would appreciate such an x-ray image should read this chapter first.

The final chapter recapitulates the thematic spectrum of this book in terms of the distinction between '*basic principles*' and '*basic intuitions*'. The insight which is examined here and which runs like a guiding thread through the whole book is that modern society is ailing not from its defeats but from its *triumphs*. Viewed in this light, mass unemployment is a sign of success not of failure; after all, increases in productivity are what make it possible to maximize production with constantly decreasing inputs of human labour. The successes of medicine mean that life expectancy has increased, with the result that retirement systems are breaking down. The hole in the ozone layer, too, and even the nuclear threat, are 'side effects' of scientific-technological triumphs. However, what does it mean if, in the course of radicalized modernization, it is not only basic institutions (full employment, welfare state, etc.) that are henceforth up for grabs but also the basic values and basic principles of modernity or of social life as such (chapter 12: *Dialectics of Modernity: How the Crises of Modernity Follow from the Triumphs of Modernity*)?

2

Relations of Definition as Relations of Domination: Who Decides What is and is Not a Risk?

In this chapter, I will present my concept of risk society once again in a systematic way. The point of departure is a series of objections and critical questions, including (1) whether risks are not timeless phenomena and hence not suited to characterizing a particular era. I will go on (2) to outline the 'risk calculus' as a response to the uncertainties generated by modernization. On a closer inspection of the basic institutions (science, law, the economy, etc.) which use their respective instruments to make these calculations in concrete cases, it becomes clear (3) that such controls are failing in the face of global risks – organized irresponsibility. This brings us to (4) the core argument of the present chapter. The actual staging of risks presupposes their social recognition: 'relations of definition' which – analogous to Marx's 'relations of production' – must be conceived as relations of domination in the staging of risk. Among the latter is (5) the legally defined power of experts. Following on this, (6) I will explore the social conflict over the environment and (7) explain how the terrorist risk is changing the foundations of international politics. Finally, (8) I will inquire into the 'counterforce of threat' and the chances of success of civic movements.

1 Are risks timeless?

Anyone who talks about risk society immediately faces a battery of questions, objections and counter-arguments. To mention just a few:

- Aren't risks at least as old as humanity?
- Isn't all life exposed to the risk of possible death at any moment – thus aren't and weren't all societies at all times 'risk societies'?
- Instead of speaking of a risk society, shouldn't we stress the opposite and emphasize the fact that, since the beginning of the industrial age, threats – of famines, plagues, etc. – have been consistently combated? For example, the decrease in infant mortality, the increase in life expectancy, the achievements of the welfare state, the advances in medical

technology – don't all of these point to how much more secure human existence has become?

- It is certainly true that 'new risks' have arisen, from global warming through financial crises and large-scale accidents in chemicals plants to terrorism. And no one can dispute that risks have enormous destructive potential when they lead to actual catastrophes. On the other hand, we also know that the probability of a catastrophe is negligible, a matter of fractions of fractions of per cents. Why all the excitement then? Aren't the new risks, on a sober analysis, less threatening than those to which we have already become accustomed and which are socially accepted – such as the countless fatal traffic accidents, for example?

- Isn't it a fundamental truth that human beings are denied ultimate security?

- Aren't the risks with which we are nowadays confronted unavoidable 'residual risks', the reverse side of the advantages (the almost unrestricted availability of the consumer goods affordable for many, mobility, etc.) which advanced industrial society provides on a historically unparalleled scale?

- Isn't risk an elementary 'driving force' (Giddens) leading to the discovery of new worlds and markets? Is progress without risks even possible?

- By dramatizing risks, aren't the media merely orchestrating a spectacle to drive up circulation and audience shares?

- And, finally, don't risks fall within the domain of expertise of technology and the natural sciences? What business does sociology have in this area?

2   The risk calculus: calculable security in the face of an open future

Whether the classical human disasters – plagues, natural catastrophes and famines – possessed as much destructive potential as modern large-scale technologies is not the central question in the present context. They must certainly count as threatening catastrophes. The key difference between classical and modern risks lies at another level. The risks generated by industrial and large-scale technologies are the result of conscious decisions, decisions which, first, are taken in the context of private and/or state organizations for economic gain and to seize the corresponding opportunities and, second, are based on a calculation for which hazards represent the inevitable downside of progress. Hence these hazards associated with industrialization do not become a political issue because of their scale but because of a social feature: they do not assail us like a fate; rather we create them ourselves, they are a product of human hands and minds, of the link between technical knowledge and the economic utility calculus. These kinds of risks also differ clearly from the impacts of wars, for they enter the world peacefully, they thrive in the centres of rationality, science and wealth and enjoy the protection of those responsible for law and order.

Correspondingly, the question of accountability always arises for large-scale industrial risks – the question of whom society makes accountable for the occurrence of the catastrophe (a question that arises even for events for which such an assignment of accountability is scarcely possible according to the rules of science and law).[1]

Nevertheless, the question remains: Don't we have to regard the past two centuries as an era of constantly increasing calculability and prevention in response to industrially produced uncertainties and destruction? In fact, it is a very promising and until now little explored path to trace the (political) institutional history of evolving industrial society as the conflictual development of a system of rules for dealing with manufactured risks (see Ewald 1991, 1993; Evers and Nowotny 1987; Lau 1989; Schwarz and Thompson 1990; Hildebrandt et al. 1994; Yearly 1994; Bonss 1995; Lash et al. 1996; Wynne 1996a, 1996b; van Loon 2002; Strydom 2002; Voss et al. 2006).

The triumph of the risk calculus would not have been possible if it did not have fundamental advantages. The first of these resides in the fact that risks create opportunities for documenting statistically effects that initially were always 'personalized', i.e. shifted onto the individual (for example, in the form of accident probabilities). In this way risk de-individualizes. Risks are shown to be systematic events that call for political regulation, something which has not yet been accomplished to a sufficient extent in the case of environmental diseases, such as mild croup, asthma and cancer. This opens up a corresponding field for political action; workplace accidents, for instance, are not blamed on those whose health they have already ruined, but are stripped of their individual origin and linked instead to the factory organization, inadequate safety measures, and so on. Thus the risk calculus permits a type of technological moralization that can dispense with ethical imperatives. For example, the place of the 'categorical imperative' is taken by the mortality rates associated with different levels of air pollution. In this way, the risk calculus symbolizes the mathematical ethics of the technological age.

A second advantage is closely associated with the first: insurance payments are agreed upon and guaranteed on a no-fault basis (setting aside the extreme cases of gross negligence or intentional damage). In this way, legal battles over causation become unnecessary and moral outrage is moderated. Instead, an incentive for prevention is created for businesses in proportion to the magnitude of the insurance costs – or not as the case may be.

The key point is that the industrial system is rendered capable of dealing with its own unforeseeable future through risk assessments. The revolutionary novelty lay in anticipating a state of the world that does not yet exist and in making this calculable. The completely normal marvel makes it possible to calculate the incalculable – with the aid of accident statistics, by generalizing settlement formulae, and through the generalized exchange principle disadvantages for all are compensated with money. In this way, a system of social rules of accountability, compensation and precaution, whose details are highly controversial, creates present security in the face of an open and uncertain future. The counter-principle of modernity, which imports uncertainty into every niche of life, is a *'social contract' against industrially produced insecurities and damages*, stitched together out of public and private insurance contracts, which prompts and renews *trust* in corporations and governments.

How, then, can we explain the prominence of the concept of risk? The concepts of risk and risk society bring together what used to seem mutually exclusive – society and nature, social science and material science, the discursive construction of risk and physical threats. The former British prime minister Margaret Thatcher once said, 'there is no such thing as society'. Most sociologists believe in a kind of 'inverted Thatcherism': there is nothing besides society. This nothing-but-society sociology is blind and makes us blind to the environmental, technological, materialized challenges of the second modernity (Latour 2004). The theory of risk society breaks with this self-centredness and modesty (Schillmeier and Pohler 2006). The ontology of risk does not privilege any particular kind of knowledge. It compels all different and often irreconcilable claims to rationality to combine and to argue and make decisions in view of 'contradictory certainties' (Schwarz and Thompson 1990).

3　Risk and threat: organized irresponsibility

Considering the challenges we are currently facing – changes in gene technology and human genetics, flows of information that are difficult to contain, breakdowns of financial systems, terrorism, environmental destruction – the foundations of the established risk logic tied to the nation-state are being undermined (Beck 2002, 2000b).[2] For, since the latter half of the previous century, industrial societies have been confronted with the possibility of the self-destruction of all life on earth due to human interventions which is without historical parallel. When a fire breaks out, the fire brigade comes; when a traffic accident occurs, the insurance pays. This interplay between before and after, between security in the present because provisions have been made for the worst conceivable eventuality, is nullified in the era of atomic, chemical, genetic and terrorist risks. Nuclear power stations, in all their dazzling glory, have cancelled the insurance principle, not only in the economic sense, but also in the social, medical, psychological, cultural and religious senses. *The 'residual risk society' has become an insuranceless society in which insurance protection paradoxically diminishes with the size of the threat.* For no institution, no real or presumably any conceivable institution could be prepared for the 'MCA', the 'maximum credible accident', and there is no social order that could guarantee its social and political integrity in such a situation.[3]

Large-scale threats are abolishing the three pillars of the risk calculus. They involve, first, often irreparable global harms that cannot be limited, so that the concept of monetary compensation fails. Second, precautionary aftercare [*vorsorgende Nachsorge*] for the worst conceivable accident is out of the question because it is impossible to gauge outcomes in advance. Third, the 'accident' has no limits in time and space, it becomes an event with a beginning but without an end, an 'open-ended festival' of creeping, galloping and overlapping waves of destruction (e.g. climate change). But this implies that norms, measuring procedures and hence the basis for calculating the hazards prove to be inapplicable. Incommensurables are compared and calculation turns into obfuscation, resulting in a kind of 'organized irresponsibility'. It rests on a 'confusion of centuries' (Günther Anders). The challenges of the beginning of the twenty-first century are being negotiated in terms of concepts and recipes drawn from the early industrial society of the nineteenth and early twentieth centuries. The threats to which we are exposed and the security promises which seek to contain them stem from different centuries. This explains both the periodic implosion of the highly organized security bureaucracies and the possibility of repeatedly normalizing these 'hazard shocks'.[4]

Is there an operational criterion for differentiating risks from threats? The economy itself defines the boundaries of what is tolerable with economic precision by refusing private-sector insurance.[5] If the logic of private-sector insurance disengages, if the economic risk of insurance coverage seems too great or too unpredictable for the insurance companies and they *de facto* increasingly exclude the relevant cases of damage under the guise of insurance protection, the boundary between 'calculable' risks and uncontrollable threats is breached on a large and a small scale (see chapter 6).

Thus two conflicting lines of historical development are clashing in Europe, namely, a high level of security founded on perfecting technical-bureaucratic norms and controls and the spread of historically novel threats that slip through all the meshes of law, technology and politics. This contradiction, which is not technical but social and political in character, remains hidden as long as the old industrial patterns of rationality and control hold up. It breaks out into the open to the extent that improbable events are becoming probable, as in the past couple of decades.

Thus large-scale risks have a social explosiveness over and above their physical explosiveness. Ever new promises of security are being squeezed out of the institutions with the emergence of threats for which they are responsible and at the same time not responsible, promises that they are completely incapable of honouring. On the one hand, they are exposed to unrelenting pressure to make even the safest things safer; on the other hand, this raises expectations to breaking point and heightens awareness, so that in the end not only real accidents but even the possibility of their occurrence can cause the façades of security assurances to collapse. The reverse side of the recognition of threats is the failure of the institutions which derive their justification from the non-existence of threats. This is why the 'social birth' of a threat is an event, as improbable as it is dramatic and traumatic, that sends shockwaves around the world.

However, gradually, accident by accident, the logic of institutionalized non-coping can turn into its opposite. What do probability assurances – and hence the whole diagnostic apparatus of the natural sciences – still mean for assessing an 'MCA' whose occurrence leaves the experts' theories intact but kills the experts themselves? What use is a legal system which regulates and prosecutes technically manageable small-scale risks in minute detail, yet which by its own authority legitimizes large-scale threats when they cannot be technically minimized and declares them to be tolerable for everyone, even for the many people who resist them? How can democratic political authority be sustained which must respond to the uncontrollable increase in the awareness of threats with emphatic assurances of safety, yet which in so doing puts itself permanently on the defensive and jeopardizes its whole credibility with every accident or indication of an accident?

4 Relations of definition as relations of domination: who decides what is and is not a risk?

In the community of Altenstadt in the Upper Palatinate, which has a lead crystal factory located in the vicinity, thumbnail size flecks of lead and arsenic fell on the town, and fluoride vapours turned leaves brown, etched windows and caused roof tiles to crumble. Residents suffered from skin rashes, nausea and headaches. No one disputed where it was all coming from. The white dust was spewing visibly from the smoke stack of the factory. In court it turned out to be an 'open and shut case', though in an unexpected sense. The court readily accepted the plaintiffs' insistence that the lead crystal factory was responsible. However, under existing law, there was an additional – mitigating! – factor, namely, there were three further glass factories in the vicinity emitting the same pollutants. This made it impossible to prove guilt since this required proof of *individual* responsibility. (An alternative would be a new legal position that proceeds from specific, definable correlations, for 'individual responsibility' is an antiquated concept given that industrial hazards have multiple sources.)

Such a situation is by no means the exception. With the increase in 'unseen and unwanted side effects', it is becoming impossible to ascribe harms suffered by many people – and at the extreme by everyone – to an author in conformity with valid legal norms and to assign responsibility. The institutional contradiction which follows from the interplay between industrialization and law and between industrialization and science is: *the more people who are poisoned, the less poisoning takes place*, at least on the social – in this case, legal – construction. It is even (here, in the national context) normal everyday visible injury and visible responsibility that are being transformed into an 'invisible side effect' by the prevailing legal norms and the social relations of definition they reflect. The legal and scientific relations of definition – hence the resources at the disposal of the protagonists in the struggle for the recognition of the risks and threats as well as the associated costs – boil down to the absurdity that the more generously the limits are fixed, the greater the number of smoke stacks, sewerage pipes, etc., through which pollutants and poisons are emitted, the smaller becomes the 'residual probability' of calling a perpetrator to account for the collective sniffling and wheezing, hence the less poisoning that takes place. And all the while the general level of contamination and poisoning increases – the one thing does not preclude the other. Welcome to the madhouse of the national definition of threats!

To recapitulate, a central contradiction of risk society results from the fact that the world is confronted with large-scale threats whose origin lies in the triumphs of modern society (more industry, new technologies), threats which, in view of the institutionalized state promise of security, can nevertheless neither be adequately confirmed nor attributed, nor compensated, nor (preventively) managed in accordance with prevailing legal, scientific and political principles. How is this contradiction, which is brewing within and between social systems and organizations, kept hidden and latent even in situations in which it re-erupts before the eyes of the (global) television public following a catastrophe? Because risks concern possible events that could but need not necessarily occur, they are marked by a high degree of unreality. *Risks are social constructions and definitions based upon corresponding relations of definition.* Their existence takes the form of (scientific and alternative scientific) knowledge. As a result, their 'reality' can be dramatized or minimized, transformed or simply denied according to the norms which decide what is known and what is not. They are products of struggles and conflicts over definitions within the context of specific relations of definitional power, hence the (in varying degrees successful) results of stagings. In such processes, we can observe how a multiplicity of antagonistic definitions clash on the basis of the competing rationality claims of different actors in struggles for national and international recognition. The key issue is how successfully social and legal constructions of the 'latent side effects' are upheld or undermined, and hence responsibility is manufactured, and thus to what extent a 'dense modernization' is successfully created in which perpetrators are directly confronted with the consequences of their actions.

This can be exhibited by the international relations between 'risk donor countries' and 'risk recipient countries'. In relations between countries (or continents), the hazards which are 'exported' count, on the established constructions, as 'latent side effects', albeit in this case for different, more fundamental reasons. Whereas, within the national sphere, legal norms based on the principle of individual authorship prevent an ascription of responsibility, in the cross-border traffic in risks the insensitivity to, and hence the irrelevance and unreality of, the threats and harm to others is typically a result of the *absence* of legal norms – or, more precisely, of the *limits of the validity* of legal norms. It is not only their character as side effects, but even the disappearance of side effects themselves (which, as stated, is associated with the national sphere of validity of law) that *facilitates* the 'invisible', 'latent' export of the threat. Of course, these threats cross the borders unrecognized – that is, provided they are not carried by the air or water but are transported by truck or ship. They are 'threat refugees', 'threat asylum seekers', that are difficult to identify and are often greeted with hospitality, and even complicity, in the affected countries. Of course, this can trigger international conflicts. For example, if China decides to produce a large part of its energy requirements using its highly sulphurous coal (employing primitive technology), that will have implications for the neighbouring countries in Asia and for the global environment. In Europe, the BSE pathogen also showed how risk management in the country of origin of a threat (in this case, Great Britain), and the export of the threat through trade and consumption chains, can plunge not only the transnational meat industry and the transnational consumption of meat but especially the political systems into chaos.

Since risks and the social definition of risks are one and the same, collective knowledge and lack of knowledge concerning the concrete injuries, possible injuries, standards, illnesses, diagnostic possibilities, and so forth, are an essential part not only of risk assessment but also of coping with risks. In cases of conflict it is becoming impossible to overlook how the national conditions of definition of risk represent special barriers to the monitoring of the transnational coming and going of threats. Since under the conditions of single-state sovereignty information is (at best) nationally organized, the recipient countries of threats often feel cut off from the necessary information.

In addition, conflicts between definition relations in different nations break out. What one country condemns as dangerous (according to the relations of definition and cultural perceptions pertaining in that country) can pass as more or less harmless in another country.

Thus there are two variants of 'organized irresponsibility': one exists within nation-states and is based on the legally founded non-ascribability of the threatening effects of decisions, the other is the result of the fragmentation of the legal spaces between nation-states. This explains why environmental destruction *and* the expansion of environmental law are advancing in tandem.

It is important for social theory that the concept of relations of definition be understood in a constructivist sense. *What 'relations of production' in capitalist society represented for Karl Marx, 'relations of definition' represent for risk society.* Both concern relations of domination (Beck 2002; Goldblatt 1996). Among the relations of definition are the rules, institutions and capabilities which specify how risks are to be identified in particular contexts (for example, within nation-states, but also in relations between them). They form at the legal, epistemological and cultural power matrix in which risk politics is organized (see chapters 9 and 10). Relations of definition power can accordingly be explored through four clusters of questions:

1   Who determines the hazardousness of products, dangers and risks? Where does the responsibility lie? With those who produce the risks, with those who benefit from them or with those who are potentially or actually affected by the dangers in their lives and their social relations? What role do the different publics and their actors play in this context? And how can these questions be answered within national spaces, between national spaces and globally?
2   What kind of knowledge or lack of knowledge of the causes, dimensions, actors, and so on, is involved? Who lays down the causal norms (or nomological correlations) which decide when a cause–effect relation is to be recognized? And who has the right to demand and get what information, and from whom?
3   What counts as 'proof' in a world where knowledge and lack of knowledge of risks are inextricably fused and all knowledge is contested and probabilistic?
4   Who is to decide on compensation for the afflicted – within one or several nation-states? How is the call for 'precaution' put into effect? To what extent are those most seriously affected by the 'latent side effects' involved in working out corresponding regulations?

Keeping these clusters of questions in mind, it becomes clear that risk societies, in virtue of the historical logic of their national and international legal systems, and scientific norms are prisoners of a repertoire of behaviours that completely misses not only the globality of environmental crises but also the specificity of manufactured uncertainties. Thus these societies find themselves confronted with the institutionalized contradiction according to which threats and catastrophes – at the very historical moment when they are becoming more dangerous, more present in the mass media and hence more mundane – increasingly escape all established concepts, causal norms, assignments of burdens of proof and ascriptions of accountability. As long as these relations of definition – ultimately with the aid of a critical theory of world risk society – are not uncovered and politically transformed (a truly Herculean task), the world will continue its fruitless search for its lost security.

What are the similarities and differences between 'relations of definition' and 'relations of production'?

Common to both is, first, as already suggested, that they are concerned with forms of domination, specifically in Max Weber's sense. In both cases institutionalized norms potentially equip specific groups with the power to impose their definitions and interests against the will of other groups. What is this potential power based upon in each case? In that of relations of production, it is a historical matter. The industrialist derives his power from ownership of the means of production, in contrast to wage labourers who have no share in the means of production. This control over the means of production enables the industrialist to decide who is hired and fired, what is produced, etc. 'Relations of definition' also rest on control over the 'means of definition', in other words, over scientific and legal rules. Here, too, there are 'owners of the means of definition' – namely, scientists and judges – and citizens 'bereft of the means of definition', who have the dependent status of 'laypersons' and are subjected to the power of definition and decision of experts and judges who decide on behalf of all which conflicting 'definitions of risk', and which liability and compensation claims derived from them, are recognized and which are not.

Underlying this is a clear hierarchy of knowledge. It lays down the superiority of the expert vis-à-vis the layperson. This presupposes that knowledge and non-knowing can be distinguished, so that in cases of doubt the monopoly over what constitutes knowledge resides with the experts. The complexes of issues outlined above – given the mixture of knowledge and non-knowing, who decides what counts as 'proof' and what not? – are ordered according to this hierarchical schema. Hence Sheila Jasanoff speaks of 'technologies of hubris': 'To date the unknown, unspecified, and indeterminate aspects of scientific and technological development remain largely unaccounted for . . . ; treated as beyond reckoning, they escape the discipline of analysis' (2003: 239f.).

A further commonality between relations of production and relations of definition resides in the fact that they occur in two stages, in two different 'aggregate states'. In the first, they count as unquestionably obvious. In the second, the founding rules lose their unshakeable obviousness and become disenchanted and politicized. The mechanisms regulating the transition from the first to the second stage are not known. However, the searing temperatures and strong winds of public conflicts play a crucial role. The one case involves class conflicts, the other conflicts over definitions of risk. In both cases the 'naturalness' of the rules of domination is dissolved in the public confrontation with alternatives and the rules in question turn out to depend on decisions and to be open to change.

How do 'relations of production' differ from 'relations of definition'? Jürgen Habermas's parallel distinction between 'labour' and 'interaction' provides the lineaments of an answer. Relations of production manifest themselves in the domain and language of business, labour and production, relations of definition, by contrast, in the domains and languages of tradition, publicity, science, law and politics. The former concern the 'conflict logic' of the labouring society, the latter the 'conflict logic' of the discourse society. In common with many of the advocates of the discourse concerning discourse society, however, Habermas largely overlooks the fact that public and scientific discourses rest on relations of definition power, especially in the areas of overlap.

It may seem obvious to seek a possible relation of determination between relations of production and relations of definition, for instance on the model of the Marxist schema of (material) base determining the (ideological) superstructure. The contrary thesis is more plausible, however, namely, that there is no relation of determination, and probably not even an affinity, between relations of production and relations of definition. But what certainly exists is a historical intermeshing of relations of production and relations of definition in the context of the first, industrial modernity of the nation-state.[6] To put it differently and more pointedly: *'green capitalism', such as is under discussion at present especially in Great Britain, is possible – in other words, a 'reform' of the relations of definition while holding relations of production constant.* However, it will become possible to test this hypothesis only when the political elites of the G8 countries champion the struggle against climate change, as demanded by the British government, the opposition included. It seems that the topic of 'global warming' has taken British public consciousness by storm. According to a September 2006 poll, Britons regard the greenhouse effect as 'the most serious threat to the future of the planet', far outstripping war and terrorism. Gordon Brown, at the time the chancellor of the exchequer and prime minister in waiting, captured this in rare unanimity with the then prime minister, Tony Blair, in the assertion that the 'progressive' capitalism of Europe, and in the future of the world, can no longer espouse the duality (the twin deities) of growth and full employment; it must raise concern for the environment 'to a new third founding principle guiding world politics' (*The Guardian*, 31 October 2006: 1; see also pp. 64ff.).

5   The role of technology and the natural sciences in risk society

The dominant relations of definition accord the engineering and natural sciences a monopoly position. They (i.e. the mainstream, not counterexperts or alternative scientists) decide without consulting the public what is tolerable and what is not given the menacing insecurities and dangers.

In order to avert unpredictable, inhuman effects of large-scale technological projects, a new research ethic is becoming the focus of a lively public debate and numerous national advisory boards are being created. Those who restrict themselves to such measures, however, fail to grasp the scale on which the engineering sciences are involved in producing hazards. An ethical renewal of the sciences, even if it did not get bogged down in the confusion of different standpoints, would resemble a bicycle brake on a juggernaut in the face of the autonomization of technological development and its interconnections with economic interests. (Moreover, the search for a research ethic loses sight of the logic of research and that the perpetrators and the judges (= engineering experts) in the technocracy of hazards are identical.)

An initial insight is key: when it comes to hazards, no one is an expert – especially not the experts. Predictions of risk are subject to a twofold fuzziness. First, they presuppose cultural acceptance yet they cannot produce it. The rejection and the acceptance of potential harms cannot be bridged by science. Acceptable risks are those which are accepted. Second, new knowledge can transform normality into threat overnight. Nuclear energy and the hole in the ozone layer are prominent examples. Therefore, the progress of science refutes its original security assurances. It is the successes of science that sow the seeds of doubt concerning its declarations about risk.

However, the converse is also true. The acute threat transfers the monopoly of interpretation to, of all people, those who caused it. In the shock of the catastrophe, people talk of becquerels, the hole in the ozone layer, avian flu, microscopic dust particles, etc., as if they knew what these words mean, and they must do so if they are not to lose their orientation in everyday affairs. This contradiction must be exposed. On the one hand, the engineering sciences unintentionally contradicted themselves through their confused risk diagnoses. On the other, they continue to exercise the monopoly accorded them in the nineteenth century to answer the most intensely political social question using their own internal standards, namely: How safe is safe enough?

The position of power which the relations of definition accord the engineering sciences is based on a straightforward administrative decision. They are granted the authority – binding for law and politics – to decide using their own standards what the 'state of technology' requires. If one asks, for instance, what level of exposure to artificially produced radioactivity the population must tolerate – i.e. where the threshold of tolerance separating normality from dangerousness is situated – then the German Atomic Energy Act provides the general answer that the necessary precautions must correspond to 'the state of technology' (§7 II, No. 3). Anyone who wants to know precisely how large a daily ration of standardized pollution citizens are supposed to tolerate need only consult the 'Ordinance on Large Combustion Facilities' or the 'Technical Instructions: Air Quality' and the like to discover the (literally) 'irritating' details.

Even the central claims of the classical instruments of political direction – statutes and administrative regulations – are empty. They juggle with the ominous 'state of technology', thereby undermining their own competence and in its place elevate 'scientific and technical expertise' onto the throne of the civilization of threats. Furthermore, the monopoly of scientists and technicians over the diagnosis of threats is being called into question by the 'reality crisis' of the natural and engineering sciences in their dealings with the hazards they produce. It has not only been true since Chernobyl that there is a world of difference between safety and probable safety; but with Chernobyl it became a reality for a broad public for the first time. The engineering sciences can assure at best probable safety. Thus their claims would remain true even if two or three nuclear reactors were to blow up tomorrow.

There was a time when science took place in the laboratory as a spatially and temporally limited empirical science. That time is past. The world has in the meantime become a laboratory. The mobility of genetically modified plants shows how difficult it is to restrict and monitor the experimental location and the possible consequences and dangers. Wolf Häfele, the doyen of the German reactor industry, wrote in a self-critical mood in 1974:

It is precisely the interplay between theory and experiment or trial and error which is no longer possible for reactor technology. . . . Reactor engineers take account of this dilemma by dividing the problem of technical safety into sub-problems. But even the splitting of the problem can only serve to approximate ultimate safety. . . . The remaining 'vestigial risk' opens the door to the realm of the 'hypothetical' . . . The interchange between theory and experiment, which leads to truth in the traditional sense, is no longer possible. . . . I believe it is this ultimate indecisiveness hidden in our plans which explains the peculiar sensitivity of public debates on the safety of nuclear reactors. (Häfele 1974: 317)

What this suggests is nothing less than the contradiction between experimental logic and atomic peril. Just as sociologists cannot force society into a test tube, engineers cannot let nuclear reactors blow up in order to test their safety. This means nothing less than the inversion of the logic of research as originally proclaimed. The sequence 'first laboratory, then application' no longer holds. Instead, testing *follows* the application, production *precedes* research. The dilemma into which large-scale threats have precipitated the scientific logic holds in general: science is hovering blindly over the abyss of threats.

6 Environmental conflict in society

Since the concept of risk society does not merely designate a technological challenge, we must ask: What political dynamics, what social structure, what conflict scenarios result from the legalization and normalization of global and uncontrollable systemic threats? The answer, reduced to an admittedly rough formula, is that, although need can be banished, global threats cannot be any longer. Hunger is hierarchical. Not everyone went hungry even during World

War II. Global warming, by contrast, is egalitarian and in that sense 'democratic' (although its impacts vary greatly from region to region). Nitrates in the groundwater do not stop at the general manager's water tap.[7]

All suffering, all misery, all violence inflicted by people on other people until now recognized only the category of the 'other' – workers, Jews, blacks, asylum seekers, dissidents, women, etc. – behind which those seemingly unaffected could retreat. The advent of global hazards marks the 'end of the other', the end of all our carefully cultivated opportunities for distancing ourselves. This is the source of their novel cosmopolitan force. Their power relates to the violence of threats, which eliminates all the protective zones and social differentiations within and between nation-states – and creates new ones.

It may be true that, in the storm tide of threats, 'we are all in the same boat', as the cliché goes. But here too there are captains, travellers, helmsmen, engineers and passengers overboard. In other words, certain countries, sectors and enterprises profit from the production of risk, whereas others suffer public health problems and at the same time their economic existence is threatened. At the front line of the future, industrial civilization is being transformed into a kind of 'World Cup' within world risk society (chapters 7 and 8). Destruction of nature and the destruction of markets coincide. It is not what one has or can do that determines one's social position and future but rather where and from what one lives and to what extent others are permitted, with a prearranged impunity, to pollute one's possessions and abilities as an 'environment'.

The greenhouse effect, for example, will raise temperatures and sea levels around the world as a result of the melting of the polar ice caps. The interglacial period will submerge entire coastal regions, turn farmland into deserts, shift climate zones in unpredictable ways and dramatically accelerate the extinction of species. *The poorest people in the world will be the hardest hit.* They will be the least able to adapt themselves to the changes in the environment. But those who are deprived of the basis of their economic existence will flee the zone of misery. An exodus of eco-refugees and climatic asylum seekers will flood across the wealthy North; crises in the so-called Third and Fourth Worlds could escalate into war.

A lot of things would be easier here if the industrializing countries could avoid the mistakes of the highly industrialized countries. However, the unchecked expansion of industrial society is still regarded as the *via regia* that promises the mastery of many problems – not only those of poverty – so that the prevailing misery often overshadows the seemingly abstract consequences of environmental destruction.

'Threats to nature', therefore, are not only that; their proof also poses a threat to property, capital, jobs and trade union power, undermines the economic foundations of whole sectors, countries and regions, and destroys the structure of nation-states and global markets. Thus there are 'side effects' on nature and 'side effects of side effects' within the basic institutions of the first modernity.

Although it may still be possible to speak of the 'environment' at the level of an individual company, such talk becomes fictitious at the level of the economy as a whole, because here a type of 'Russian roulette' is actually being played with the 'environment'.

However abstract the threats may be, their concretizations are nonetheless irreversible and regionally identifiable. What is denied collects in particular regions, in 'loser zones' that have to pay the price for the damage and its organized 'unaccountability' with the basis of their economic existence. This 'environmental expropriation' represents a historically novel devaluation of capital and achievement, while relationships of ownership, and sometimes even the characteristics of the commodities, remain constant. Sectors that have nothing or very little to do with the production of the hazards – agriculture, the food industry, tourism, fisheries, but also parts of the service economy – are especially affected worldwide.

When the global economy splits into risk winners and risk losers, this polarization also leaves its mark on the occupational structure. First, new types of country- and sector-specific antagonisms arise between occupational groups and hence within and between trade union interest groups. Second, these are third-hand antagonisms, derived from those between capitalist interests, which turn the 'destiny of workers' in a further, fundamental dimension into 'fate'. Third, with the heightened awareness of the lines of conflict, a sector-specific *alliance* of the old 'class opponents', capital and labour, may come about. This could lead to a confrontation between this union–management block and other mixed factions, over and above the class divisions which lose their urgency under the pressure of 'environmental politicization'.[8]

What form could an environmental labour movement take? The production and definition of hazards occurs largely at the product level, almost completely outside the influence of the works councils and workers' groups and entirely within the jurisdiction of the management. However, workers must expect to lose their jobs if the worst comes to the worst.

Moreover, the latent risk definition strikes at the heart of their pride in achievement, their sense of usefulness. Labour and the workforce can no longer understand themselves as the source of wealth, but must also conceive of themselves as the motor of the threat and of destruction. The labour society is not only running out of labour, the only thing that lends life meaning and solidity in such a society, as Hannah Arendt ironically put it; it is also jeopardizing this residual meaning.

To summarize rather roughly: what the polluting industries dismiss as 'environment' is the basis of the economic existence of the affected loser sectors and regions. The result is that the large-scale geographical environmental conflicts which affect many different nation-states lead to 'geopoliti-cal' shifts that expose the domestic and international structure of economic and military blocks to completely new stresses, though they also open up new opportunities. The current politics of risk society must accordingly be conceived in cosmopolitan terms because the social staging and mechanics of threats extend far beyond the nation-state (on this see chapters 7 and 8). In this sense, apparently iron-clad political, military and economic constella-tions are becoming mobile. And this also necessitates and makes possible a new global domestic policy.

7   The terrorist risk is transforming the foundations of international politics

Suicide terrorism has also reached this cosmopolitan level, though in a new guise. This form of terrorism exploits the difference between (possible) threat and (actual) catastrophe. Without the brutal evidence of the consciously produced catastrophe and its staging in the mass media, the anticipation of the catastrophe – which constitutes the heart of the terrorist risk – always remains merely more or less improbable. For example, an expert commission warned President Bush of the imminent terrorist attacks in the United States and described their consequences a couple of months before they occurred. This warning was dismissed as 'too hypothetical', as completely untrust-worthy. Following the trauma of violence and helplessness broadcast by the global mass media, the fear that further terrorist attacks could occur is sud-denly omnipresent. The catastrophe itself is spatially, temporally and socially fixed, it has a well-defined beginning and end. This is *not* true of the terrorist risk, i.e. the staging and expectation of the catastrophe.

   Thus the globalization of the terrorist threat first manifests itself as the globalization of the expectation of possible terrorist attacks almost anywhere in the world at any moment. It is this expectation which has far-reaching consequences for law, the military, liberty, everyday life and the stability of the political system throughout the world, because it corrodes the security guarantees formerly provided by the basic institutions of the nation-state.

   Following the collapse of the bipolar global order, we are in transition from a world of enemies to a world of threats and risks. The state-centred paradigm for justifying security according to which states threaten states is by no means obsolete; however, the threats of world risk society, which are now being increasingly staged and perceived, spring from a different, post-state security paradigm for which a suitable conceptual analysis, and even a social and political grammar, are lacking (Kaldor 2007; Daase et al. 2002). Intentional terrorist catastrophes cannot be correlated with any spatially and temporally localizable actor or with any classical, clearly defined military capability. Rather than being direct and certain, the risk is indirect and uncertain. In short, terrorist acts lack what is a matter of course for classical enemies, namely, military predictability. The suicide attacker does not run any risk because his action is dead certain. Deterrence does not deter him. By dying, he makes himself invincible. The radicalization of the resolve to use suicide as a means of committing mass murder, and thus to stage and globalize its expectation, renders the powerless powerful, indeed for a brief moment even more powerful than the greatest military power in human history. Although clearly inferior in a military sense, for a short time the attacker can create a balance of horror; he can even provoke the expectation of catastrophe within world risk society and make it a permanent condition, by ensuring through his action that the more or less futile anticipation and defence becomes the reorganizing principle of society. Even the fantastic arsenal of possible side effects catastrophes is magnified by the expectation of targeted destruction which plays diabolically on the threat imagination of world risk society.

What differentiates the old nation-state security agenda of the first modernity from the new postnational security agenda of the second modernity is thus the *regime of non-knowing*, even worse, not just of known, but above all of unknown non-knowing – of 'unknown unknowns' (see chapter 7) – and hence the collapse of ontological security. This is lost when at least one factor in the classical security equation – agent, intention, potential – becomes an unknown. In the case of terrorist networks, all three factors become unknowns. The murky terrorist agent networks are, as it were, 'violence NGOs'. Like non-governmental organizations in civil society, they operate independently of territory, without an organizational centre, hence at once locally and transnationally. Whereas Greenpeace, for example, denounces environmental risks and Amnesty International the human rights violations of states, terrorist NGOs target the states' monopoly on violence. They suddenly attack where, until then, nobody had expected them to. They demonstrate their power of destruction by transforming civic social spaces into potential death zones. Their terror is indiscriminate, aimless and unpredictable. No battle takes place. The threat is in the most radical sense asymmetrical. For the victims, whether in uniform or not, have no opportunity to resist. Courage is as futile as cowardice. The terrorists' primary weapon is fear. They do not want to gain a victory but to create panic. They devalue the national grammar of the military and war by spreading the antisocial, anti-human condition of horror across borders. Their goal is to transform the peaceful symbols of civil society into instruments of dread. In this respect, the terrorist world risk society must be conceived as an anti-national threat constellation in which the state of exception is normalized, and *hence* states are at once disempowered (because their established means are becoming useless) and empowered because the call for lost security drowns out everything and justifies everything – ultimately to the detriment of freedom, equality and democracy.

Unintended side effects catastrophes (e.g. climate change) contradict the state guarantees of security; and they may even make its guarantees appear as threats to public safety and undermine the authority and legitimacy of states. This also holds in a different way for the terrorist risk posed by intentional catastrophes. An indication of this is the helplessness with which the United States and its president placed itself at the forefront of the movement for the global propagation of freedom and human rights, while simultaneously undermining the validity of these rights in order to wage a preventive war on the militarily unpredictable terrorist risk. Some try to generate the impression that the American government is acting like a gang of pathologically violent torturers. However, this view ignores the experience of literally boundless impotence of the greatest military power on earth in the face of the attacks. The so-called war against terror makes the weakness of the strongest power manifest to all. The destructive force of the military fizzles out without effect. World risk society compels the nation-state to admit that it cannot fulfil its self-declared constitutional promises, namely, to guarantee its citizens what is arguably the highest legal good, namely, their security.

The only answer to global terror – but also to global financial risks, climate change and organized crime – is transnational cooperation. To achieve this, the *de facto* disempowered nation-states must overcome themselves and the fiction that they are autonomous if they are to reap the political benefits of the new, pooled sovereignty in dealing with national and global problems.

Global risks necessitate a new politics of uncertainty. They compel us to make a distinction between *theoretical* and *factual uncontrollability*. National and international politics (under certain circumstances also transnational economic enterprises) are not liberated from all need to act by the fate of theoretical uncontrollability; rather, the global public discourse of risk puts the screws on them to justify themselves and to take action. They are condemned to respond. This expectation of responses presupposes the counterfactual hypothesis of controllability even when all available response models fail. To do nothing in the face of acknowledged risks is politically out of the question, regardless of whether acting minimizes the risk, increases it or achieves nothing, as seems to be particularly true of the terrorist risk. The anonymity of risks must be overcome and global risks must acquire an identifiable face. Bin Laden's face is the face of the terrorist risk. The uncertainty of recognized global risks – 'fortuna' in classical political theory – which cannot be politically influenced, is translated into 'virtù' for which political instruments and institutions must be invented. In the process, a particular value hierarchy of forms of political action simultaneously arises: pre-active politics is attached a high value, whereas re-active politics is devalued.

8   Political reflexivity: the counterforce of threat and the opportunities of social movements

Risk conflict is certainly not the first conflict which modern societies have had to master, but it is one of the most fundamental. Class conflicts or revolutions change power relations and replace elites, but they hold fast to the goals of technological and economic progress and clash over universally recognized civil rights. The Janus face of 'self-annihilating progress', however, generates conflicts that are capable of corroding the social basis of rationality – science, the military, the police, law and democracy. Society thereby comes under constant pressure to negotiate foundations without a foundation. It is exposed to an institutional destabilization in which all decisions – from local government regulations on speed limits and parking, through the details of the manufacture of industrial goods, to the foundations of social security and military security, of the provision of healthcare and the energy supply, of rights of equality and liberty – can be drawn into fundamental political conflicts.

In spite of the apparently unaltered operation of the basic institutions, quasi-governmental power positions arise in research laboratories, genetic factories, editorial offices, courts, non-governmental organizations, military units, and so on, in connection with hazards that depend on staging and are responsive to publicity. In other words, systems become vulnerable to action and subject-dependent as a result of the contradictions of the security state. The courageous Davids of this world get their chance, just as do social movements. The colossal interdependence of threat definitions gives rise to key positions and media of 'risk staging' that are at odds with political and professional hierarchies. (However, this holds in a completely different way for terrorist risks and environmental-technological risks; thus we will be concerned exclusively with the latter in what follows.)

One can, on the one hand, use all of one's powers of conviction to assemble arguments for the institutional non-existence of suicidal threats, one need not strip the institutional hegemony of one iota of hope, and one can even add the distraction of the social movements and the limitations of their political effectiveness; and yet one can nevertheless recognize with equal realism that all this is thwarted by the counterforce of threat. It is constant, permanent, independent of the interpretations which deny its existence, and it even remains present where exhausted demonstrators have long since left the scene. The probability of improbable accidents increases with time and with the number of large-scale technologies that have been implemented. Every 'event' evokes memories of all the others, everywhere in the world.

Different types of revolutions have been contrasted: *coups d'état*, class struggles, civil disobedience, and so forth. Common to all is that they empower and disempower social subjects. Revolution as a self-perpetuating process, as a hidden, latent, permanent condition, in which social conditions turn against themselves and their own interests while political structures or property and power relations remain unchanged – this possibility has not even been entertained until now, let alone thought through.

This figure of thought is the *social power of the staged threat* (even if, in the case of environmental crisis, it favours completely different actors than in the case of terrorist violence). As a side effect threat, it is the product of a deed that does not need to be authorized or authenticated. Once in existence, however, public awareness of it endangers all institutions – from the economy to science, from law to politics – which have produced and legitimized it.

Everyone asks: Where will the opposing forces come from? Presumably it would not be very promising to place a missing ad for the 'revolutionary subject' in the most abstruse publications. Of course, it feels good, and hence is harmless, to appeal to reason with all the means at one's disposal because, viewed realistically, it leaves few traces behind. One could found yet another circle for solving global problems. It is indeed to be hoped that political parties will get the message.

Should it transpire that all of this is not sufficient to stimulate political countermeasures, however, then there remains the insight into the activatable political reflexivity of the threat potential.[9] The global experiment of nuclear energy (toxic chemistry, genetic engineering, 'virtual reality' technologies, etc.) has itself in the meantime taken over the role of its own critics, perhaps even more convincingly and effectively than the political countermovements could ever have managed on their own. This becomes apparent not just in the worldwide, unpaid negative advertising at peak news times and on the front pages of newspapers, but also in the fact that everyone in Germany – from Halligen in the North to the alpine meadows of the South – now suddenly understands and speaks the language of the critics of atomic energy. Under the dictate of necessity, people have undergone a kind of crash course in the contradictions of threat management in risk society, in the arbitrariness of threshold values and calculation procedures or the unimaginability of the long-term consequences and the possibilities of rendering them anonymous through statistics. In the process, they have learned more, and more vividly and clearly, than even the most critical critique could ever have taught them or demanded of them.

The most tenacious, convincing and effective critics of nuclear energy (or the genetic technology industry, etc.) are not the demonstrators outside the fences or the critical public (no matter how important and indispensable they may be). The most influential opponent of the threat industry is the threat industry itself.

In other words, the power of civic movements is not founded on themselves alone but is also a function of the nature and scope of the contradictions in which the hazard-producing and -administrating industries become entangled in risk society. These contradictions are made public and scandalous by the needling activities of the social movements. Thus, there is not only an automatic suppression of threats, but there are also countervailing tendencies to uncover the suppression, even though they are much less pronounced and always depend on the moral courage of individuals and the vigilance of social movements.

This oppositional power of the involuntary revelation of threats depends, however, on social framework conditions that until now have been fulfilled only in a couple of countries: parliamentary democracy, (relative) independence of the press, and an advanced production of wealth in which the threat of cancer or AIDS is not outweighed for the majority by famine.

In the interplay between inside and outside across the boundary-lines separating subsystems, therefore, there are also symptoms of strength which have until now passed almost unnoticed. The socially most disconcerting, surprising and probably least understood phenomenon of the past decades, not only in Germany, is *individualization*, the unexpected renaissance of an 'enormous subjectivity' – within and outside of institutions. It is no exaggeration to say that *the civic networks and movements have taken the initiative*. It was they who put the global threat on the agenda from the 1970s onwards against the resistance of the established parties. The issues which are now on everyone's lips did not spring from the farsightedness of governments or from parliamentary debates – and certainly not from the cathedrals of power in business, science and the state. They were put on the global political agenda against the concerted resistance of this institutionalized ignorance by the muddled, moralizing groups and groupuscules fighting over the correct path while fractured and plagued by doubts. *Democratic subversion has won a quite improbable thematic victory.*

The environmental extension of democracy means playing off the concert of voices and powers, the increase in the autonomy of politics, law, the public sphere and daily life against the dangerous and false security of a society 'conceived in the abstract'.

My proposal involves two interconnected principles: first, the imposition of the division of powers and, second, the creation of a public sphere. Only a strong, competent public sphere 'armed' with scientific arguments is capable of separating the scientific wheat from the chaff and of reconquering the power of independent judgement from the institutions for regulating technology, namely, politics and law.

This means that, in all controversies and committees of broad social relevance, dissenting voices, counter-experts, interdisciplinary diversity and, not least, systematic new alternatives must always be brought together. The public sphere would have the role of acting in tandem with a kind of 'science of publicity' as a second locus of 'discursive examination' of scientific laboratory results in the cauldron of conflicting opinions. Their particular responsibility would comprise all major lines of development and dangers of scientific civilization, which are chronically excluded in standard science. The public would play the role of a kind of 'open upper chamber'. It would apply the standard 'How do we want to live?' to scientific proposals, results and threats.

This presupposes that research will take the public's questions into account and will be addressed to the public rather than merely multiplying shared problems in an economic short-circuit with industry. Perhaps through these two steps – the opening up of science from within and the filtering out of its professional blinkered vision in a public practical test – a sharpening of the steering and monitoring instruments on the side of politics and laws (which are currently largely ineffective) would become possible.

The cultural blindness of daily life in the civilization of threats is irreversible; but cultural 'perception' is filtered through the symbols of the mass media. The images of the victims of the Asian tsunami catastrophe in December 2004 in the evening news opened people's eyes (as the cliché goes). Making the threats publicly visible and awakening attention within one's own living space – these are cultural eyes through which 'blind citoyens' can perhaps regain their autonomous judgement.

To conclude with a question: What would happen if radioactivity itched? Realists, also known as cynics, will answer: people would invent something, for example an ointment, to 'suppress' the itching – a profitable business with a good future. Certainly, explanations would promptly be offered with great public impact claiming that the itching was unimportant, that it was possibly correlated with other factors besides radioactivity, and that in any case it was innocuous – unpleasant perhaps, but demonstrably harmless. If everyone ran around with skin rashes scratching themselves and photo sessions with fashion models and management meetings of the united institutes of denial were accompanied by universal and incessant scratching, it must be assumed that such explanations would have a poor chance of survival. In that case, the mode of dealing with modern large-scale hazards would confront a completely different situation: the controversial issue being negotiated would be culturally visible.[10]

This is also decisive for the future of democracy: Do we depend on experts and on counter-experts in all details of life-and-death issues – from our everyday lives to global transformations – or are we regaining the capacity for independent judgement through a visibility of threats that must be culturally created? Is the only remaining alternative one between an authoritarian and a critical technocracy? Or is there a way to counteract the incapacitation and expropriation of daily life in the age of risk?

Sociologists talk a lot about and conduct extensive research on insecurity, though they generally mean by this social insecurity. They thereby overlook what a dramatic decline of ontological security now confronts lifeworlds, even in the peaceful corners of the earth. The three pillars of security are crumbling – the state, science and the economy are failing to provide security

– and are naming the 'self-conscious citizen' as their legal heir. But how are individuals supposed to accomplish what states, sciences and economic enterprises are unable to achieve? Sociology at least must reveal the self-delusion of the second modernity and ask: What does life in world risk society mean and how does it become possible?

3

The 'Cosmopolitan Moment' of World Risk Society or: Enforced Enlightenment

In this chapter I will explore the normative horizon of world risk society or the normative frame of reference of the theory of world risk society.[1] This normativity should not be posited in a philosophical and ethical manner but should be developed out of the real evolutionary dynamic of world risk society and its ambivalences.

Anybody who confronts global risk from this perspective must appreciate unintentional irony. The grand (and the local) narrative of the learning history of risk and its social and political effects is replete with irony. It tells of the unintentional satire and the optimistic futility with which the basic institutions of modern society – science, the state, the economy and the military – seek to anticipate what cannot be anticipated. We had to await the events of the second half of the twentieth century to learn what Socrates meant by his puzzling statement 'I know that I know nothing'. Ironically, our continually perfected scientific-technological society has granted us the fatal insight that we do not know what we do not know. But this is precisely the source of the dangers that threaten humanity. The perfect example of this is the debate over the coolant CFC (Böschen et al. 2004). In 1974, around forty-five years after its discovery, the chemists Rowland and Melina put forward the hypothesis that CFCs destroy the ozone layer of the stratosphere and that as a result the world is increasingly exposed to ultraviolet radiation. Their conclusion was that a chain of unpredictable side effects would lead to a dramatic increase in the cancer risk among human beings. When this substance was invented, however, nobody could have known or even suspected that this 'miracle agent' would have such devastating effects.

Those (like the US government) who believe in non-knowing aggravate the threat of a climate catastrophe. Or, in more general terms, the more emphatically world risk society is denied, the more it becomes a reality. The disregard for the globalizing risks aggravates the globalization of risk. (Avian flu is another striking example: the failure to acknowledge its global spread is accelerating the global spread of the risk of infection.)

The greatest military power in history constructed a defence system costing countless billions of dollars to protect itself against missile attacks. Must it not also count as a bitter irony when the sense of security and the self-confidence of the United States are deeply shaken by an attack which, by any risk logic, was extremely improbable – namely the use of commercial passenger aircraft piloted by suicide attackers as missiles – since this action destroyed the symbols of American world power? The irony of risk here is that rationality – which means past experience – misleads us into measuring risks against completely inappropriate standards and into treating them as calculable and controllable, whereas catastrophes always occur in situations of which we know nothing and which as a result we cannot anticipate. One could extend this list of bitter risk ironies almost indefinitely, for example by citing the ever tighter restrictions on individual rights and liberties by the government in order to protect the populace against terrorism, in the process damaging society without averting the terrorist threat. The grim irony here is that the doubts concerning official government assurances to protect the citizens which are nourished by general risks provoke criticism of the incompetence of scientific and state authorities, criticism which disregards the possibility that this fundamental inability could be exploited to justify an authoritarian state.

It may now be clearer how I wish to explore the normative horizon of world risk society in the present chapter. Risk is synonymous with ambivalence. In the modern world, taking risks is inescapable for individuals and governments. At the turn of the twenty-first century, all actions must confront global risks. But against the view that we are helpless in the face of obscure powers, I want to ask: What is the ruse of history which also belongs to world risk society and comes to light with its realization? In a word: Does world risk society have an *enlightening function* and what form does this take? Does the dynamic of world risk society – contrary to the secular apocalyptic interpretation expressed in the social sciences – set free a 'cosmopolitan moment' and how could this be understood and justified?

The experience of being at the mercy of global risks represented a shock for the whole of humanity. Nobody predicted such a development. Nietzsche had a premonition when he spoke of an 'age of comparison' in which different cultures, peoples and religions can enter into relations to each other and live side by side. Even though he did not say as much, he was aware of the historical irony that not only physical but also ethical destructive power made it possible for modern human beings to overcome the nation-state and the international order and thus to go beyond the heaven and hell of modernity.

When risk is perceived as omnipresent, three reactions are possible: *denial*, *apathy* or *transformation*. The first is a hallmark of modern culture, the second finds expression in postmodern nihilism, the third constitutes the 'cosmopolitan moment' of world risk society. What this means can be explained by appeal to Hannah Arendt. The moment of existential threat – herein lies the fundamental ambivalence of global risks – unintentionally (and often also imperceptibly and ineffectually) opens up the (mis)fortune of a possible new beginning (which is no excuse for false sentimentality). How can and should one live in the shadow of global risks? How can one lead one's life when old certainties come to naught or prove to be lies? Arendt's answer anticipates the irony of risk: the expectation of the unexpected means that the taken-for-granted can no longer be taken for granted. The shock of danger is a call for a new beginning. Where there is a new beginning, there are new possibilities of action. For example, people forge relations across established borders. Freedom means strangers acting in concert. Freedom is founded on this ability to make new beginnings.

Hannah Arendt writes: 'Politics rests on the fact of human plurality' and hence its task is to organize and regulate the cultural coexistence of people who encounter one another as equals. Drawing on the customary interpretation of human beings as a *zoon politikon* (Aristotle) according to which the political is an intrinsic part of human nature, Arendt stresses that politics does not have its source *in* the human being but *between* human beings – more precisely, between human beings who belong to different worlds and who create a joint space of action through their actions. In view of the catastrophic experiences of the twentieth century – indeed, almost as a response to them – Arendt emphasizes that 'human beings themselves, in a most miraculous and mysterious way, are endowed with the gift of performing miracles', namely, they can act, take initiatives, make a new beginning. 'The miracle of freedom resides in this ability to make new beginnings, which resides in turn in the fact that every human being, by being born into the world which existed before him and continues to exist after him, is himself a new beginning' (Arendt 1993: 34).

Arendt thought that the republican idea of a new beginning under conditions of freedom was realized at just a few historical moments, in the Athenian *polis* and with the American founding fathers, though also following the Holocaust. I go a step further by focusing on the cosmopolitan moment of world risk society. Paradoxically enough, sociology – a child of the first modernity – does not share this sceptical self-confidence in the possibility of a new beginning against the background of the expectation of catastrophic risks, a confidence that makes possible a wholesale reinvention of the basic institutions of the modern national society (Beck 1997a). On the contrary, a certain nostalgia which has never disappeared is built into the foundations of European sociological thought. Perhaps this nostalgia can be overcome through the theory of world risk society. My aim is a new, non-nostalgic critical theory whose task is also to reconceptualize the past of modernity from the standpoint of the threatened future (see chapter 11). It is not correctly described as 'utopianism' or 'pessimism'; only the concepts of 'irony' and 'ambivalence' accurately describe it. Instead of an either/or, I am looking for a new both/and: a way of bringing two contradictory postures, self-destruction and the capacity for a new beginning, into equilibrium. I would like to present this in two steps: (1) in terms of the difference between old threats and new risks and (2) in terms of the 'cosmopolitan moment' or the ruse of history. To what extent are global risks a force in present and future world history that escapes any control while simultaneously opening up new opportunities for action for states, NGOs, and the like?

1   Old threats – new risks: what is new about world risk society?

Modern society has become a risk society because it is increasingly engaged in debates over self-generated risks in an attempt to manage and to prevent them. A possible objection to this statement might be that the current situation is a result of hysteria and a politics of fear instigated and continually stoked by the mass media. Furthermore, wouldn't an external observer of European societies be forced to conclude that the risks we are getting worked up about are exclusively luxury risks? After all, our part of the world seems a lot safer than the war-torn regions of Africa and the Middle East, for example, or Afghanistan and Iraq. Aren't modern societies distinguished by the fact that they have been more or less successful in bringing contingencies and uncertainties, such as accidents, violence and illness, under control? However, the year 2005 reminded us once again, with the tsunami catastrophe, the destruction of New Orleans by Hurricane Katrina, and the devastation of extensive regions of South America and Pakistan, of how limited the claim to control of modern societies remains in the face of natural forces. But even natural hazards occur less randomly than in earlier times. Even though human interventions may not be able to prevent earthquakes or volcanic eruptions, these can be predicted with reasonable accuracy. We anticipate them in order to take preventive structural measures against them.

Why should it not also be possible to 'manage' the manufactured uncertainties of the second modernity?

Managing manufactured uncertainties

In fact, the pressing issue in world risk society is to anticipate and prevent self-inflicted catastrophes, in short, to deal with manufactured uncertainties. Of course, such necessities create large and growing markets for technologies, experts, counter-experts and products – world risk society is big business! Conventional studies of uncertainty, whether in business, the financial sector or the social sciences, take their orientation from the so-called Gauss curve. The curve is shaped like a bell that falls off sharply at both ends. In the case of the distribution of intelligence, most human beings are located somewhere in the middle, close to the point at which the curve reaches its highest value, and only a few close to the extremes. Successfully employed by the mathematician Carl Friedrich Gauss in the nineteenth century to describe deviations in astronomical measurements, the bell curve or Gauss model has permeated our scientific culture, the economy and the self-image of modern society in general. It is more than a technical description. It shapes our thought. We think in terms of Gaussian distributions. The problem, however, is that measurements of uncertainty using the bell curve fail to take into account or attach any importance to the possibility of abrupt peaks or discontinuities. Employing such a measurement procedure in world risk society would be like concentrating completely on the grass and ignoring the (gigantic) trees. But in fact the occasional and unpredictable large deviations, even though they are seldom, cannot be dismissed as 'outliers' because their cumulative effects are dramatic.

Traditional instruments of risk management concentrate on normal procedures and regard extremes as inconsequential. This approach is misleading in world risk society, which necessitates a turn towards a non-linear approach: *the exceptions that only apparently confirm the rule must be the primary focus of attention.*

These two perspectives correspond to two mutually exclusive types of chance, namely, *linear* or soft and simple chance, on the one hand, and *non-linear* or wild and reflexive chance, on the other (Taleb 2004, 2007; Voss et al. 2006). Whereas body weight, height or calorific intake conform to the 'soft' form of randomness, wealth exemplifies 'wild' randomness. Income, profits on the financial markets, the numbers of fatalities in wars or victims of terrorist attacks also belong to the 'wild' category. Almost all variables created by human beings are 'wild' (= non-linear reflexive modernization). Moreover, natural science continues to discover further examples of 'wild' uncertainty, for instance the intensity of earthquakes, hurricanes and tsunamis.

The same is true in the world of global capitalism, where the motto 'the winner takes all' holds:

Consider, for example, how Google grabs much of internet traffic, how Microsoft represents the bulk of PC software sales, how 1 per cent of the US population earns close to 90 times the bottom 20 per cent or how half the capitalisation of the market (at least 10,000 listed companies) is concentrated in less than 100 corporations . . . We are living in a world primarily driven by random chance, and tools designed for random walks address the wrong problem. It would be like tinkering with models of *gases* in an attempt to characterize them as *solids* and call them 'a good approximation'. While scalable laws do not yet yield precise recipes, they have become an alternative way to view the world, and a methodology where large deviation and stressful events dominate the analysis instead of the other way around. We do not know of a more robust manner for decision-making in an uncertain world. (Mandelbrot and Taleb 2006: 2)

Every modelling of uncertainty remains under the spell of the tradition of risk analysis and risk management which has its roots in classical security research and is driven by the concern to achieve a socially acceptable and efficient 'managing' of uncertainty. From the perspective of sociology, a paradigm shift is now called for. The primary focus for the present must be on the global social constitutive conditions of risk and not on coping with their consequences.

What is the hallmark of global risks?

The theory of world risk society makes a distinction between old and new risks and argues that the new types of risks that are prompting the global anticipation of global catastrophes rock the foundations of modern societies. Such global risks exhibit three characteristic features:

1   *Delocalization*: their causes and consequences are not limited to one geographical location or space; they are in principle omnipresent.
2   *Incalculability*: their consequences are in principle incalculable; at bottom they involve 'hypothetical' risks based on scientifically generated nonknowing and normative dissent.
3   *Non-compensatability*: although the dream of security of the first modernity did not exclude harms (even major harms), these were regarded as compensatable so that their destructive impacts could be made good (by money, etc.). If climate change is irrevocable, if human genetics makes possible irreversible interventions in human existence, if terrorist groups already possess weapons of mass destruction, then it's too late. Given this new quality of 'threats to humanity', argues François Ewald (2002), the logic of compensation is breaking down and is being replaced by the principle of *precaution through prevention*. Moreover, attempts are being made to anticipate and prevent risks whose existence has not yet been demonstrated.

The delocalization of incalculable, interdependent risks occurs on three levels:

a)   *spatial*: the new risks (e.g. climate change) are spreading over national borders, and even over continents;
b)   *temporal*: the new risks have a long latency period (e.g. nuclear waste), so that their future effects cannot be reliably determined and restricted; moreover, knowledge and non-knowing are changing so that the question of who is affected is itself temporally open and remains disputed;
c)   *social*: since the new risks are the result of complex processes involving long chains of effects, their causes and effects cannot be determined with sufficient precision (e.g. financial crises).

The incalculability of risk is an implication of the overriding importance of the inability-to-know. At the same time, however, the claim to knowledge, control and security of the state had to be renewed, deepened and extended. This results in the irony of having to control something even though one does not know whether it exists. But why should a science or a discipline concern itself with something that it does not even know? Sociology offers a conclusive answer to this, namely, because the priority which modern society accords security is not annulled, but, on the contrary, is activated and dominated, by non-knowing (as is shown in particular by the terrorist risk). Manufactured uncertainties make society more reliant than ever on security and control. The combination of knowledge and non-knowing of global risks, in particular, destabilizes the established systems of national and international 'relations of definition' (see chapter 2). It may sound ironic, but it is precisely the unknown unknowns which provoke the major conflicts over the definition and construction of political rules and responsibilities – with the aim of preventing the worst.

At present, the most recent and striking example is the second Iraq war, which was – at least also – conducted in order to prevent what we cannot know, that is, whether and on what scale terrorists are getting their hands on chemical and nuclear weapons of mass destruction.

As this example shows, world risk society is confronted with the awkward problem (here one can no longer speak of irony) of having to make decisions about life and death and war and peace on the basis of a more or less frank lack of knowledge. The dilemma is rendered especially apparent by the fact that the option which relies on there being no danger in a particular area is also based on non-knowing and is equally high-risk, because terrorists really could acquire weapons of mass destruction, and precisely because we think that we cannot know and hence do nothing. Here the irony of non-compensatability is driven to a tragic extreme.

If we anticipate catastrophes whose destructive potential threatens everybody, then the risk calculation based on experience and rationality breaks down. Now all possible, to a greater or lesser degree improbable, scenarios must be taken into consideration; to knowledge drawn from experience and science we must add imagination, suspicion, fiction and fear.

François Ewald writes:

the precautionary principle requires an active use of doubt, in the sense Descartes made canonical in his *Meditations*. Before any action, I must not only ask myself what I need to know and what I need to master, but also what I do not know, what I dread or suspect. I must, out of precaution, imagine the worst possible, the consequence that an infinitely deceptive, malicious daemon could have slipped into an apparently innocent enterprise. (2002: 285)

Given their task of averting dangers, politicians, in particular, may easily find themselves compelled to proclaim that the observance of security standards is assured even though such guarantees are impossible. They do so nonetheless because the *political* costs of omission are much higher than those of an overreaction. It is not going to be easy in future, therefore, given the state's promise of security and a mass media hungry for catastrophes, to prevent a diabolical power game with the hysteria of non-knowing. I do not even venture to think about calculated attempts to instrumentalize the situation.

From trustee to suspect

Global risks reflect a new form of global interdependence to which national politics or the established forms of international cooperation do not do adequate justice. All past and present practical experiences in dealing with uncertainty can claim equal justification; however, for that very reason they do not offer a solution to the resulting problems. More than that, key institutions of modernity, such as science, business and politics, which are supposed to guarantee rationality and security, are confronted with situations in which their apparatus no longer has any purchase and the basic principles of modernity no longer hold automatically. As a result, these institutions are being judged completely differently – no longer as trustees but as suspects. They are no longer seen as *managers* of risk, but also as *sources* of risk.

Tragic individualization

As a result, a new stage of individualization is becoming discernible in the everyday life of world risk society. Faced with the uncertainty of the globalized world, individuals have to make their own decisions. This new form of individualization is the result of the failure of experts in the management of risks. Neither science, nor the reigning politics, nor the mass media, nor business, nor the legal system, nor even the military, is in a position to define or control risks in a rational way. The individual is forced to mistrust the promises of rationality of these institutions. Hence, people are thrown back upon themselves: *disembedding without embedding* is the ironic-tragic formula for this dimension of individualization in world risk society. Thus, for example, responsibility for deciding on genetically modified foods and their unpredictable and unfathomable long-term effects is foisted onto the so-called responsible consumer. The institutions cynically whitewash their own failure by appealing to 'responsibility'. However – and this is also part of the tragic irony of this process of individualization – individuals, whose senses fail them in the face of unfathomable threats to civilization and who, thrown back upon themselves, are blind to dangers, are at the same time unable to escape the definitional power of expert systems whose judgement they cannot, and yet must, trust. Maintaining individual integrity in world risk society is indeed a tragic affair.

To summarize, global risks are the main triggers of an explosive transformation that is rendering visible the contours of society in the twenty-first century. The theory of world risk society addresses the increasing ubiquity of globally manufactured uncertainty. The key institutions and actors of the first modernity, who are responsible for judging and controlling manufactured uncertainties, are being undermined by the growing awareness that they are ineffective, indeed that their measures are counterproductive. This does not occur haphazardly, but systematically. The radicalization of modernity gives rise to this irony of risk: the sciences, the state and the military are becoming part of the problem they are supposed to solve. This is the meaning of the expression 'reflexive modernization': we are not living in a *post*-modern world but in a *hyper*-modern world. It is not the crisis but the *victory* of modernity which is undermining the basic institutions of first modernity due to unintended and unknown side effects (chapter 12).

The concept of world risk society signifies a historical era. It refers to the new historical social arrangement of modernity which made its first tentative experiences in the 1960s and especially in the 1970s, which is at present undergoing a further development and which will probably achieve its breakthrough over the next thirty to fifty years. It is a concept of social theory that makes sense only in the context of the theory of reflexive modernization as a theory of the self-transformation of modern society. From the preface to *Risk Society*, my first book, up to my most recent publications, my main concern has been to offer a diagnosis that enables us to take the measure of the future that is beginning to take shape and to grasp the signature of the present era. This can succeed only by breaking with the normative horizon of 'methodological nationalism' and by replacing this with a normative framework derived from the dynamics of world risk society.

2 The 'cosmopolitan moment' of world risk society or: The cunning of history

I have described the ambivalence, the bitter and tragic irony, which achieves world-historical significance with the advent of global risk. But what forms does the alleged enlightening function (see also chapter 2) of global risk take? Which empirical indicators speak for it and which against it? Is it pure cynicism to attempt to seek a final spark of hope in the collective distress over uncertainty? Is this merely wishful thinking?

I will try to counter this well-founded scepticism by means of six conceptual components that constitute the 'cosmopolitan moment' of world risk society, namely, enforced enlightenment, communication across all divides and boundaries, the political power of catharsis, enforced cosmopolitanism, risks as a wake-up call in the face of the failure of governments, and the possibility of alternative forms of governance in a globalized world.[2]

What is meant by the 'cosmopolitan moment'?

What is 'cosmopolitan' about the 'cosmopolitan moment'? Is it a normative or a descriptive concept? As already explained, through the increased awareness of the dynamics of world risk society, all people have become the immediated neighbours of all others, and thus share the world with non-excludable others, whether they like it, or want to recognize it, or not. Hence the cosmopolitan moment resides in the first instance in this compulsion to include cultural others which holds for all people throughout the world.

This amounts to the claim that this *sociological* concept of cosmopolitanism (Beck 2006; Beck and Grande 2007) refers to a particular social way of dealing with cultural difference – in contrast, for example, to hierarchical exclusion (as encountered in past and present racist thought and practice), to the *universalism* which declares the dissolution of differences, to the *nationalism* which levels differences and at the same time excludes them in conformity with national antagonisms, and to the *multiculturalism* which is understood and practised as plural monoculturalism (mostly within the national framework). Cosmopolitanism differs from these forms by virtue of the fact that, as we have seen, it makes the inclusion of others a reality and/or its maxim.

Of course, there is a world of difference between cosmopolitanism as 'reality' and as 'maxim'. In the normative sense (of 'maxim'), cosmopolitanism means *recognition* of cultural otherness, both internally and externally. Differences are neither hierarchically ordered nor dissolved but are accepted as such, and even regarded positively. However, nowhere in the world at the beginning of the twenty-first century are such conditions anywhere near being accepted. But what can unite human beings of different skin colour, religion, nationality, location, pasts and futures if not recognition? The answer proposed by the theory of world risk society is: by the traumatic experiences of the enforced community of global risks that threaten everyone's existence. However, the recognition of the reality of the threat by no means includes the recognition of otherness.

Hence, we must make a clear distinction between a world in which the plurality of others is denied, ignored or condemned, even though it can no longer be expunged from the world, and a world in which this plurality is *recognized* and in which all share in the commonality of difference. The 'cosmopolitan moment' of world risk society means, first, the *conditio humana* of the irreversible non-excludability of those who are culturally different. We are all trapped in a shared global space of threats – without exit. This may inspire highly conflicting responses, to which renationalization, xenophobia, etc., also belong. *One* of them incorporates the *recognition* of others as equal *and* different, namely, normative cosmopolitanism.

World risk society forces us to recognize the plurality of the world which the national outlook could ignore. Global risks open up a moral and political space that can give rise to a civil culture of responsibility that transcends borders and conflicts. The traumatic experience that everyone is vulnerable and the resulting responsibility for others, also for the sake of one's own survival, are the two sides of the belief in world risk.

One can make two diametrically opposed kinds of assertion: global risks inspire paralyzing terror; or: global risks create new room for action. Neither of these statements is true and neither is false. Both are correct. But under certain conditions both are also wrong. That is what I mean when I speak of the ambivalence of the 'cosmopolitan moment' of world risk society.

From this perspective, the 'cosmopolitan moment' has both a descriptive and a normative meaning. In the first place, it is a matter of grasping the *reality* of non-excludable plurality which is driving the dynamic of world risk society, regardless of whether this reality is ignored and demonized or embraced and transformed into active global policy. Thus at the same time clues and principles become visible concerning which kind of cosmopolitan thought and action is possible and could and should be realized.

Enforced enlightenment: representations of danger in the mass media can lend the underprivileged, the marginalized and minorities a voice

It is a commonplace that the Greek *polis* knew only face-to-face communication and that it was both elitist and exclusive because it excluded women, slaves and the underprivileged. Danger globalized via the mass media can lend the poor, the marginalized and minorities a voice in the global public arena. Hurricane Katrina was a horrifying act of nature. As a global media event, it also performed an involuntary and unintended *enlightening function*. What no social movement, no political party, and certainly no sociological analysis, no matter how brilliant and well founded, could ever have achieved occurred within the space of a couple of days: America and the world were confronted with the voices and images of the repressed *other* America, the racist face of poverty in the sole remaining superpower. American television does not care for images of poor people, but they were ubiquitous during the coverage of Katrina. The whole world saw and heard that the black districts of New Orleans were destroyed by the storm tides because of their social vulnerability. The hurricane was a natural occurrence. Thus it does not seem to fit with the conceptual scheme that attributes catastrophes to human decisions rather than to nature. In fact, however, the scale of events such as the 2004 tsunami rests on social differences and previous developments. Thus the lack of information and early warning systems contributed to the monstrous abruptness of the tidal wave. This also led to many people losing their lives because they ran helplessly in the wrong direction. The deforestation of the islands and beaches and deficiencies in the location and construction of hotels, slums, etc., contributed to aggravating the threat posed by tidal waves. Is climate change already reflected in the rise of the sea level, so that the force of the 'giant wave' and the defencelessness of the population were further magnified by the effects of civilization? In this sense, 'pure' natural occurrences are also 'risks', because decision-making in world risk society ensures that nature and society are intermeshed.[3]

Thus, the television images of the tsunami disaster brought the first law of world risk society – namely, that *the risk of catastrophes haunts the poor* – into every living room. Global risks have two sides, namely, the probability of possible catastrophes and the social vulnerability as a consequence of catastrophes (chapter 10). There are good grounds for the prediction that climate change will cause devastation especially in the poor regions of the world, where the problems of high population growth, poverty, water and air pollution, inequalities between classes and genders, AIDS epidemics and corrupt, authoritarian governments all overlap.

A further aspect of the ambivalence of risk, however, is that with the globalization of compassion – as reflected in the unprecedented willingness to donate to the relief effort – the tsunami victims were simultaneously categorized, and became the focus of political debates, in accordance with their *nationality*. Moreover, the many other catastrophes that go completely unreported, or are reported only fleetingly, in the West are indicative of the egoistic selectivity with which the West responds to the threats of world risk society.

Which moments or principles of publicity are operative here? And which theoretical proposals can help us to understand them? I just mentioned one principle: there is an imperative which creates an at least fleeting 'voting right', not necessarily in their municipalities but in national and global media publics, especially for the underprivileged and the excluded 'regardless of status and class'. Of course, this should not be idealized. The mass media do not follow the principles of enlightenment but those of market rationality and profit. There are also good reasons for doubting whether the voice of the voiceless really acquires argumentative and political influence and shapes judgements and decisions. And yet the individualized and anonymous individual destinies are bundled in a powerful way through the dangers and harms that blamelessly befall them in the exemplary stories of suffering narrated by television images and reports (which used to be possible only through protest marches) and in this way they are forged into a political event that cries out for identifying those responsible, for rethinking and for policy changes.

The principle of almost *boundless inclusion*, as regards both groups and topics, is reminiscent of analyses of the public sphere such as those offered by Hannah Arendt, Jürgen Habermas and most recently Roger Silverstone (2006). Interestingly, this cosmopolitan moment engages with the social hierarchy both towards the top and towards the bottom: not only the voiceless but also powerful people who do not vote are included and called to account. Correspondingly, with the declaration of 'imminent danger' the light of publicity is shone, irrespective of topic, into even the darkest corners of power and the most hermetic spaces of decision.

However, global risk public spheres have a completely different structure from the 'public sphere' explored by Jürgen Habermas. Habermas's public sphere presupposes that all concerned have equal chances to participate and that they share a commitment to the principles of rational discourse. The threat public sphere is founded on involuntariness and is emotionally and existentially determined. Here it is terror that breaks through the armour of anonymity and indifference, even if for most people it is images of terror that become the source of terror. This is as little a matter of commitment as it is of rationality. Potential bearers of responsibility who hide behind 'systemic constraints' are hauled before the court of global public opinion via the media. Without mercy and without regard for their social status, they are confronted with objections and are convicted of self-contradiction. The images of horror do not produce cool heads but they do give rise to cross-border compassion. False alarms, misunderstandings, condemnations are part of the story. In these risk public spheres, too, the pressure reaches volcanic proportions. Threat publics are impure, they distort, they are selective and stir up emotions and anger. They make possible more, and at the same time less, than the public sphere described by Habermas. They resemble more the picture of 'Mediapolis' so minutely and sensitively painted by Roger Silverstone (2006) and the picture sketched by John Dewey in *The Public and its Problems* (1946). There Dewey defends the thesis that it is not actions but their *consequences* that lie at the heart of politics. Although he was not thinking of global warming, BSE or terrorist attacks, his theory can be applied perfectly to world risk society. A global public discourse does *not* arise out of a consensus on decisions, but rather out of *disagreement* over the *consequences* of decisions. Modern risk crises are constructed out of just such controversies over consequences. Although some insist on seeing an overreaction to risk, risk conflicts do indeed have an enlightening function. They destabilize the existing order but can also be seen as a vital step towards the construction of new institutions. Global risk has the power to confuse the mechanisms of organized irresponsibility and even to open them up for political action.

Enforced communication across divides

Egoism, autonomy, autopoiesis, self-isolation, improbability of translation – these are key terms for describing modern society in sociology and in public and political debates. The communicative logic of global risk must be under-stood on precisely the opposite principle. World risk is *the* unwanted, unin-tended obligatory medium of communication in a world of irreconcilable differences in which everyone is turning on their own axis. Hence the public perception of risk forces people to communicate who otherwise do not want to have anything to do with one another. It imposes obligations and costs on those who resist them, often even with the law on their side. In other words, large-scale risks cut through the self-sufficiency of cultures, languages, reli-gions and systems as much as through the national and international agenda of politics; they overturn their priorities and create contexts for action between camps, parties and quarrelling nations that know nothing about each other and reject and oppose one another.

For example, the anticipation of catastrophic side effects means that large companies increasingly meet with anticipatory resistance to their decisions. No power plant can be built without protests from nearby residents, no oil-field can be explored without critical scrutiny by transnational NGOs, no new medicine can be hailed without listing the associated known and unknown risks. In other words, global risks ensure an involuntary democratization.

However, they also ensure unexpected alliances. Thus US industry wants far more climate protection and is forming alliances with environmental groups against the Bush administration, which has consistently rejected inter-national agreements to limit environmental pollution (such as the Kyoto Protocol). The heads of the major US corporations agree that an active climate policy is absolutely indispensable and want to sway the government in this direction. This ecological conversion is the outcome of an intensive cooperation between environmental groups and the industry lobby since 1999. Of course, it is also a matter of securing an early advantage in the global competition for the massive business in environmental technology on the road to green capitalism.

Political catharsis

'Who would have thought that tears would become our common language?' exclaimed a Turkish television reporter in Athens into his microphone. These words were his commentary on the unbelievable occurrence that, at the end of the twentieth century, two major earthquakes in succession had reconciled the two 'sworn enemies' who had been feuding for 180 years. Peace in Banda Aceh, public spirit in New Orleans, the opening of the border in Kashmir: the catastrophes of 2005 reflected across the world how global events also possess the power of political catharsis (at least for a historical moment). But this is not a one-way street to more freedom, democracy and peace. The world-historical power of global risks is ambivalent in principle. The cunning of history need not be a cunning of reason, it can also become a cunning of unreason or anti-reason, and often it is all of these at once (for example, the 'War on Terror').

Enforced cosmopolitanism

Perhaps even global risks can be rationally explained, anticipated and controlled through appropriate action. The assumed ability to isolate individual strands of risk, however, is contradicted by the trans-systemic, transnational and trans-disciplinary dynamics of world risk society. The history of risk resembles the story of the race between the hare and the hedgehog (or was it a tortoise?). The risk that was here just a moment ago and had a specific face is now already over there and has taken on a completely different aspect in different cultures, systems, regions and scientific disciplines. It is the 'fluidity' (Bauman), that is, the permanent transformation, accumulation and multiplicity of different, often transitory risks – ecological, biomedical, social, financial, symbolic and informational – that constitutes the ambivalence and incalculability of world risk society.

'Enforced cosmopolitanization' means that global risks activate and connect actors across borders who otherwise don't want to have anything to do with one another. Hence I want to make a clear distinction between the philosophical and normative notions of cosmopolitanism, on the one hand, and 'impure', real cosmopolitanization, on the other. The key point is that cosmopolitanism cannot become a reality deductively by applying philosophical principles but can only enter through the back door of global risks, unseen, unintended and under duress. Down through history, cosmopolitanism bore the taint of elitism, idealism, imperialism and capitalism. Today it has unexpectedly become an everyday affair. Cosmopolitanism in this narrower sense[4] does not mean – as it still did for Kant – a value or the task of ordering the world. Cosmopolitanism in world risk society opens our eyes to the uncontrollable vulnerability, to something that happens to us or befalls us, but at the same time prompts us to make new beginnings that overcome boundaries. The insight that the dynamics of world risk society involve an enforced cosmopolitanization robs 'impure' cosmopolitanism of much of its ethical appeal. If the cosmopolitan moment of world risk society is at once deformed and unavoidable, then apparently it is not a suitable object for sociological and political reflections. But to draw this conclusion would be a serious mistake.

The birth of a global awareness of risk is a human trauma; it combines the experience of an anthropological shock and a shared cosmopolitan destiny with the premonition of the possibility of a collapse and a new beginning. This need not imply that 'Where there is danger, salvation grows too.' For when people are confronted with the alternative 'Freedom or security', a large majority of them seem to prefer security, even if that means curtailing or even suppressing civil liberties. As a result of the experience of the terrorist risk, there is an increasing readiness, even in the centres of democracy, to break with fundamental values of humanity and modernity – for example, with the principle 'Torture should be abolished' or 'Nuclear weapons must not be used', and that means globalizing the practice of torture and threatening the so-called terror states with a preventive nuclear strike.

The return of state responsibility or: Why the neoliberal state is a failure

Whose task is it actually to arrest climate change? For a long time it seemed that this is a challenge that everyone must tackle, as *individuals*. In this way, the struggle against climate change was transformed into a green lifestyle choice (cycling instead of driving, hiking at home instead of flying on holiday). But be careful, climate change is much too big a problem to be dealt with solely through the concerted actions of individuals – on the motto 'Bus instead of car' (Jonathan Freedland). Here governments must take the lead. But even they, taken 'individually', are pretty helpless.

By now it is almost a commonplace that carbon dioxide knows no boundaries and that any attempt that does not operate transnationally, hence at once locally and globally, is doomed to failure. Since it will surely be quite some time before humanity is united in this aim, we need an interim solution for the foreseeable future. Even the most dyed-in-the-wool Eurosceptic must acknowledge that the EU is the ideal agent for a policy against climate change. The multibillion-Euro EU budget can give a boost to innovations, from alternative energy sources to energy-efficient technologies.

In the same cosmopolitan vein are cooperation agreements – with China, for instance – from which both sides profit, for example agreements on carbon dioxide-free technologies, regions and markets. The staging of global risks points to the possibility of creating 'compulsory markets' in which products that are useful to humanity must be consumed, and hence also produced and bought. The Europeans could, let us say, design an ultra-efficient, environmentally friendly refrigerator; the Chinese could manufacture it cheaply and, through their global market networks and strategies, sell it worldwide – to the benefit of everyone; only climate change would finally be the loser. Forging such a global alliance between states and business could provide new legitimation for both sides.

At this point, at the latest, a heretical thought is unavoidable: governments cannot do this because they long ago ceased to have control over economic decisions. One can, of course, place one's trust in the magical market forces. But even assuming the greatest conceivable success, it would be a very slow process. The time is terribly short. It is not governments but nature that is setting the 'deadline'.

It is true that there is no way back to a planned state economy. But equally important is the realization that, if ever the 'sovereignty of the market' represented a deadly threat, then it is now, with the impending environmental collapse and the unimaginable costs associated with this.

Thus global risks serve as a wake-up call given the failure of nation-states in the globalized world. There is a surprising parallel between the 1986 Chernobyl reactor catastrophe and the 1991 Asian financial crisis, on the one hand, and 11 September 2001 and the consequences of Hurricane Katrina in 2005 for the self-image of America, not to mention the reignited debate over climate change, on the other. In each case they led to worldwide discussion over how far the dynamic of world risk society must count as a historical refutation of the neoliberal conception of the minimal state. For example, one result of the shock triggered by the revelation of the hidden Third World face of the United States was that, despite the sceptical attitude of many Americans towards the state, the question of the appropriate role of government was addressed much more openly.

In this way, the old opposition between left and right is finding new expression. The one side emphasizes that the task of the US federal government is to minimize the threats and risks to which individuals are exposed; the other side dismisses this conception of the state as false and misguided. There is an interesting exception, namely, military security. Whereas individuals are expected to bear the costs of their social security themselves and to make their own provisions for the event of a catastrophe, the importance of external security, and with it the need to expand the military apparatuses, is dramatized. A social contract? A public good? At best an option, by no means a duty. President Bush's campaign manager argued that the appropriate reaction to Hurricane Katrina could be described as an 'oversized entitlement programme' that 'would squander money and required programmes that would be better delivered by organizations like the Salvation Army.' Barack Obama, who has conducted a successful campaign within the Democratic Party for the next presidential nomination, and is himself an African American, responded: 'The ineptitude was colour blind. Whoever was in charge', he went on, 'appeared to assume that every American has the capacity to load up their family in an SUV, fill it up with $100 worth of gasoline, stick some bottled water in the trunk, and use a credit card to check in to a hotel on safe ground.' This scepticism towards the state which – in the face of global dangers – propels the individualization of its citizens, particularly the weakest, is difficult to comprehend from a European perspective.

However, other voices are also making themselves heard in the United States. They are not only convinced of the fatal consequences of a man-made climate change, they also seem to have discovered the 'cosmopolitan moment' of a global staging of the environmental catastrophe, the political 'sleeping giant' of global risk.

One reason President Bush has failed to become the leader of the West is because he has failed to lead on green, which has become so important to all our allies. I doubt that he'll redefine U.S. policy in his last two years, but the issues around climate change and energy conservation are now rising so fast it's impossible to imagine that his successor won't – whoever it is. And once that happens, it is impossible to imagine that living green, instead of fighting reds, won't become the new glue of the Atlantic alliance. (Friedman 2006: 7)

The new glue of the West and of the world – this expresses a cosmopolitan opportunity for world risk society, namely, to refashion global risks into realistic utopias for an endangered world, utopias that make it possible to revive the state and politics and to lend them new legitimacy.

Historical alternatives of cosmopolitan action or: The positive-sum game of global threat politics

A further peculiarity of global risks resides in the fact that they compel political action across borders, not – and this is the key point – as a result of a universal consensus on values that is in any case impossible (and in the meantime is the exception in a divided world, even around the family table), but because the faith in the secular religion of threat forces everyone into concerted action. This of course requires a major missionary effort, namely, that all really believe in it. As we know, religions already failed in this regard. Should it succeed, the credit for this secular religion is owing to the looming threats which human beings have brought upon themselves.

This cosmopolitan component, formulated in terms of a realistic political theory, asserts that the secular character of this faith in global risk is founded on the fact that the religion of risk makes it possible to maximize national self-interest through the deliberate creation of interdependencies across all borders. In forging interdependencies, self-obligation and the obligation of others presuppose and reinforce one another. Dependencies are created that force states – though also economic actors! – to take the interests of others into account if they are not to harm themselves and if they want to enhance their own utility. The result is a positive-sum game because in the process each must simultaneously contribute to enhancing the utility of others.

The rhetoric of world risk society – the reference to the 'planetary state of emergency', the 'economy of climate change' ('climate change is the greatest market failure the world has seen, greater than the two world wars and the Depression put together'), the 'foreign policy of climate change' (the prevention of wars over resources, especially in the zones of the planet which are already politically unstable), the 'hazards of the proliferation of nuclear weapons', etc. – all of this shapes international relations, alliances and communities in a qualitatively completely different way from what is even considered possible within the national understanding of politics.

The collapse of the Berlin Wall gave rise to enemyless states in search of new enemy avatars. Some people fear or hope that terrorism will take over the role of communism as an enemy image capable of uniting the West. However, this assumption was refuted by the fiasco of the Iraq War, if not before. At the same time, a historical alternative is materializing. The shared nature of the challenges posed by the threat of environmental crises could provide the glue to hold the West together in future without recourse to negative enemy images. For there is no greater threat to the Western way and quality of life than the combination of climate change, environmental destruction, dwindling energy and water resources and the wars they could spark. As the German foreign minister, Frank-Walter Steinmeier, put it recently: 'Energy security will be the key factor determining the global security agenda in the twenty-first century.' Here the contours of the hyper-modern model of a cosmopolitan world domestic policy which could replace the outdated model of national foreign policy are becoming discernible: postnational, multilateral, acronymic, economistic, highly peaceful in all respects, preaching interdependencies on all sides, everywhere seeking friends, nowhere suspecting enemies, only enemy images to be dismantled. In this rhetorical world, 'national interests', like shapely thighs, remain discreetly hidden beneath the heavy fabric into which the new discursive threads of 'climate protection', 'cosmopolitanism', 'human rights' and 'humanity' are woven.

Underlying this are two premises. First, world risk society fosters a new historical logic. No nation can cope with these problems alone. Second, in the age of globalization a realistic political alternative that counteracts the loss of the power of command of state politics vis-à-vis globalized capital becomes possible. The precondition is that globalization must be understood not as economic destiny but as a strategic game for world power (Beck 2005).

A new global domestic politics, which is already in part effective beyond the national–international divide, has become a meta-power game whose outcome is completely open. It is a game in which boundaries and fundamental orientations are being renegotiated – not only those between the national and international spheres, but also those between global business and the state, transnational civic movements, supranational organizations and national governments and societies. No single player or opponent can win on their own; everything depends on alliances. This is how the immanent antagonisms of the diffuse power game of global domestic politics are being played out. The first alternative, which is currently the dominant one, gives pride of place to global capital. The goal of the strategies of capital is, in simplified terms, to merge capital with the state in order to open up new sources of legitimacy in the guise of the *neoliberal state*. Its article of faith is that there is only one revolutionary power capable of rewriting the rules of the global power order – namely, capital – whereas the other actors – nation-states and the civil society movements – remain in thrall to the forms of action and power characteristic of the national and international order. This coalition of capital and the national minimal state is not only incapable of responding to the challenges of world risk society but is also losing any remaining credibility in the experiential space of global risks.

The strategies of action opened up by global risk are abruptly overturning the order brought forth by the neoliberal coalition between capital and the state. Global risks *empower* states and civic movements because they uncover new sources of legitimation and options for action for these groups of actors; on the other hand, they *disempower* globalized capital because the consequences of investment decisions give rise to global risks, destabilize markets and awaken the power of the sleeping consumer giant. Conversely, the goal of a global civil society and its actors is to connect civil society with the state, and that means bringing about what I call a *cosmopolitan form of statehood*. The forms of alliances into which the neoliberal state has entered instrumentalize the state (and the theory of the state) in order to optimize and legitimize the interests of capital throughout the world. Conversely, the goal of the idea of a cosmopolitan state in the guise of a civil society is to outline and realize a resilient diversity and a postnational order. The neoliberal agenda gives itself an air of self-regulation and self-legitimation. The agenda of civil society, by contrast, surrounds itself with the aura of human rights, global justice and the struggles for a new grand narrative of radical democratic globalization.

This is not wishful thinking; on the contrary, it is an expression of a *cosmopolitan realpolitik*. In an age of global crises and risks, we need a politics of 'golden handcuffs' – the creation of a dense network of transnational interdependencies – if we are to regain national autonomy, not least vis-à-vis a highly mobile global economy. The maxims of a nationally grounded realpolitik, which holds that national interests have to be pursued by national means, must be replaced by the maxims of a *cosmopolitan realpolitik*, namely, the more cosmopolitan the political structures and activities, the more successful they will be in promoting national interests and the greater will be the weight of national structures in the global age. It is, of course, important to consider the unwanted and unforeseen side effects of this cosmopolitan vision. Appeals for justice and human rights are being used to legitimize invasions of other countries. How can one advocate a cosmopolitan form of legitimation when it leads to crises and wars and hence to the bloody refutation of the idea itself? Who will rein in the side effects of a cosmopolitan moral principle that speaks of peace while promoting war? What does 'peace' mean when it universalizes the possibility of war? We must make a clear distinction between *true* and *false* cosmopolitanism; and yet such clarity is difficult to achieve because it is cosmopolitanism's comparatively high degree of legitimacy that makes it so tempting to instrumentalize it for national-imperial purposes – the Iraq War being only the most recent example.[5]

4

Clash of Risk Cultures or: The Overlapping of the State of Normalcy and the State of Exception

After exploring the normative horizon of world risk society in the last chapter, in the present chapter I will focus on the symbolic and material staging of the reality of global risks. I will approach this topic in four steps:

1 Risk is synonymous not with catastrophe but with the anticipation of the catastrophe – this is what I established in my initial treatment of the staging of risk. Does this mean that catastrophe is the new thing-in-itself? No, we must also pose the complementary question concerning the *staging of the catastrophe*: how do local catastrophes become global catastrophes? Or, more precisely: how should we decipher the 'symbolic code' of 9/11, the tsunami catastrophe, etc.?

2 The more manifestly global risks elude the scientific methods used to predict them, the more the influence of the perception of risk grows. The result is that the contradictory certainties of religious, secular and political cultures confront one another in evaluations of global risks: *clash of risk cultures*.

3 How can the conflictual and subversive potential of global risks be explained in political theory? My thesis is that the global political potential of global risks stems, in all of its ambivalence, from the *overlapping of the state of normalcy and the state of exception*.

4 Finally, I will examine the consequences for the legitimation of state authority [*Herrschaft*]. Here we must distinguish between the increase in authority and the increase in its inefficiency: global risks produce authoritarian 'failed states' – even in the West.

1 The cosmopolitan event or the 'symbolic code' of 9/11

The mode of existence of risks does not consist in being real but in becoming real. Becoming real, the globally shared *expectation* of catastrophe, however, proceeds from the staged and globalized real experience of the catastrophe itself. How? Seldom has an image captured so clearly the instant of global transformation, the shock-birth of a global threat. One of the most massive structures erected by human beings collapsed within 14 seconds in a monstrous cloud of whirling and swirling dust – a hundred-floor giant was transformed into a rising plume of white smoke. The end of the World Trade Center gave the Americans an idea of what it means to awaken suddenly in the strange new world risk society. On the fateful day, two airliners were detached from their socially defined context of use and 'converted' into weapons, partly into weapons of mass destruction, partly into weapons of symbolic destruction.

'Staging', the deliberate production of the real possibility of the global terrorist threat, captures and circumscribes this deconstructive and reconstructive real and symbolic destructive unity. This destructive force was directed at the Twin Towers of a, in a literal sense, materially constructed and simultaneously profoundly symbolically imbued social authority, namely, the World Trade Center. The resulting fireball consumed everything around it, including thousands of human lives. It exploded everywhere, in every living room in the world. In the process, the deed destroyed deeply rooted cultural assumptions. The television images of the twin cathedrals of global capitalism collapsing suddenly in a giant cloud of dust exerted such a fascination because of their traumatic obscenity. The belief in the invulnerability of the greatest military power on earth was executed before a live audience. The eruption transformed the site into a dark crater that swallowed up life, dignity, compassion and military security.

These material and symbolic explosions brought forth something spatially and temporally removed from them, namely, the *expectation* of terrorism. They created the taken-for-granted belief that, however improbable it may seem, such a thing is really possible, which means that it can reoccur anywhere at any time. And because expectation is the medium and goal of staging, the boundary between justified concern and hysteria is becoming blurred. In this form, the future of possible attacks exists in the present and the traumatic experience prompts the cry 'Never again!'

Faced with the incomprehensible, US President Bush declared that the terrorists were the 'heirs of all murderous ideologies of the twentieth century': 'By sacrificing human life to serve their radical visions – by abandoning every value except the will to power – they follow in the path of fascism, and Nazism, and totalitarianism.' Bush is mistaken. The al-Qaeda 'fighters' are neither Nazis nor Soviet communists. Al-Qaeda does not control any state and does not send a regular army to fight. Its members have embraced guerrilla tactics, a form of spectacular, highly symbolic terrorism that was driven to a level of apocalyptic brutality that the world had never before experienced. The result, though not the main aim, was mass murder, for the 'point' of such terror is to destroy the self-confidence of the modern world through *the symbolically mobilizing and (de-)constructing global anticipation of terrorist attacks* – something in which it has been quite successful. The terrorists understand very well the meaning of civil insecurity, threat and vulnerability for the collective consciousness and their symbolic effects. At the same time, al-Qaeda was transformed into al-Qaedaism by the armed engagements of the Americans and their allies. In this way, a relatively small conspiratorial organization has managed to transform itself into a worldwide political movement with thousands of followers who are only waiting for the opportunity to adopt these methods. It could be called 'viral al-Qaeda', and it is being transmitted by the highly motivated next generation of followers who are downloading their terrorist manuals from the virtual training camp of the Internet.

What, then, constitutes the symbolic code of '9/11' – and that of the countries and places, such as Tunisia, Bali, Istanbul, Madrid, Beslan and London, whose names stand for similar terrorist attacks – or the symbolic code of the 2004 tsunami, of Hurricane Katrina, of avian flu, to mention only the most recent and well-known catastrophes? Why and in what sense can and must the 'becoming real' of the terrorist (etc.) risk be understood as a 'cosmopolitical event' (Michael Schillmeier)? Which moments can be distinguished here?

- *The becoming of the catastrophe in the mass media:* How can the indifference be overcome and the distance be bridged? The sheer number of the dead is not sufficient. It requires, in addition, *the deaths of huge numbers in real time on a global scale with the active presence and participation of the whole of humanity.* It is this traumatic shock experience, this breaking of taboos, this real-life thriller in everyone's living room that tears down the walls of national indifference and overcomes the greatest geographical distances. Humanity is present as a witness in London, in New York, in Beslan, in Madrid, and so forth. The tsunami, or the tsunami of images of the tsunami (which amounts to the same thing), forbids apathy:

The clips of the amateur filmmakers depicting the terrifying wave come to us, the wave successively washing away the rows of deck chairs on the beach, the blue pool with the bathers and the restaurant deck. Moving images come to us of a man who reaches out to a drowning person in the flood but in the end fails to reach him or her. Images of coffins. Of children. Of mounds of corpses. And thus we stand before this sea of images recorded with jerky, panic-stricken camera movements and we are projected into the midst of the flood. The horror has a face for us . . . , it has many faces and all of them look like our own. (*Der Spiegel*, 1 (2005): 98)

- *The planetary sense of pain:* It is faces such as these that break the world's collective heart:

As the first wave receded into the ocean, the inhabitants ran to the train and left their children behind. Then a second and a third wave crashed into the train and flung the wagons into the surrounding houses and trees. The rescue teams think that only a handful of the fifteen hundred people in the train survived. Among the dead were five children whose father had put them in the train because he believed they were safe there. (Ibid.)

We all know that *the face of the tragedy could have been our own*. A planetary sense of pain grips everyone. The old-fashioned word 'collective fate' has acquired a new aftertaste of reality, as a cosmopolitan, traumatic experience that shocks and unites the hyper-individualized world risk society.

It is not only that the 'tectonic plates' that have become interlocked but the social continents – Asia, Europe and the United States – are also overlapping and interpenetrating in the labour markets and the ghettos of the poor, above all in *mass tourism*. The latter (one of the least appreciated yet most far-reaching ways in which the world has contracted over the past twenty years), in tandem with modern communications technologies, makes the catastrophe into an extremely personal matter for those who live thousands of kilometres distant from it. Television, e-mail messages and satellite telephone enable people to remain in contact with their loved ones and make horrifying images and videos available at the click of a mouse.

- *The for-us*: Global risks are not the result of any catastrophes whatsoever, but rather of anticipated catastrophes *for us*. In order to become a cross-border reality, this for-us presupposes numerous *national* tragedies, for example, German eyewitnesses, German victims, missing Germans, the nation of German holidaymakers. In the case of the tsunami catastrophe, European foreign ministers spoke of the 'national tragedy' and did not mean Sri Lanka, India or Thailand. They meant Germany or Sweden or Denmark, etc. Only because it was also a national event in domestic politics could it become a cosmopolitan event. Only because the dead and missing were also, or even solely, counted in national terms, did the 'for-us' of the tsunami become an inclusive for-us, namely, *both* national *and* international.
- *The anthropological shock experience of the vulnerability of the foundations of the civilized world*: It is not only the deaths of human beings in huge numbers but also the death of deeply rooted cultural norms and taken-for-granted assumptions of civil life that is transformed into a live event that nobody can elude. 11 September also destroyed the certainty that the security of citizens increases with the extent of military superiority. When it comes to anticipating this kind of catastrophe, the controlling institutions, not only of the military, but also of science, fail. The prediction of an earthquake remains, notwithstanding instrumentation costing billions and much effort, as uncertain as one's own death – all that is certain is that it will happen sometime. Thus 'cosmopolitan events' are highly mediatized, highly selective, highly variable, highly symbolic local

and global, national and international, material and communicative reflexive experiences and blows of fate that transcend and efface all social
boundaries and overturn the global order that holds sway in people's
minds. They are unthinkable until they occur, and their cosmopolitan
empathy, reality and authenticity must be symbolically produced (and
reconstructed accordingly) in step with the gradual unfolding of the catastrophes. However, new commonalities and new conflicts have the same
source, namely, the experience of global risks.

2   Belief in God or in global risk: clash of risk culture

In chapter 3, I introduced and explained the idea of the 'cosmopolitan
moment' of world risk society. There the power of belief in threat played a
central role beyond consensus on values and mutual recognition in the face
of the planetary predicament of how to force cross-border communication
and cooperation. Put differently, the brutal 'reality' of the mass-mediatized
danger is giving rise to a post-normative 'commonality' that transcends all
borders. In this section I will explore the opposite movement, namely, that
risk is taking on the character of radical religious conflicts, secular wars of
religion, on account of its explosive linkage of uncertainty and threat. One
could easily dismiss this contradiction with the standard claim that it is a
matter of the famous 'two sides of the same coin'. But that would be too
easy.

Nevertheless there is a relatively simple explanation for the contradictory
consequences of global risks. Threats do not exist as such any more than
do catastrophes. Thus the experience of the 'reality' of catastrophe need not
lead to an enforced unification at all. Since it goes without saying that the
'brutal reality of the threat' remains a manufactured, interpreted threat – a
'highly mediatized, highly selective, highly variable, highly symbolic local
and global' cosmopolitan event (see above) – it can also lead to splits and
extreme polarization, and this for the very reason that this experience is
refracted in the world's cultural, religious, national, ethnic and economic
antagonisms.

When and to what extent this 'reality experience' unites or splits, however,
is a function of the specific type of staging of global risks. Thus a stubborn
abstractness clings to the threats and anticipated effects of climate change (in
contrast to the terrorist threat), for it involves a global risk that rests on scientific models and calculations and is difficult to prove or refute on the basis
of everyday experience. Even if it should become a regular occurrence that
New Yorkers can walk around in bikinis at Christmas and that the Mediterranean winter ruins the ski business for the Bavarians, climate research consistently offers the same explanation which fails to satisfy the profound
human need for simple cause–effect relationships: individual extreme weather

occurrences, the experts declare, do not provide proof, but at most circum-
stantial evidence, of the existence of climate change. Thus at the very moment
when weather occurrences are beginning to open people's eyes to impending
climate change, climate researchers have to attenuate the felt climatic catastrophe with mathematical objectivity. The scientifically correct relation
according to which storms, floods and droughts are becoming statistically
more frequent, even though individual weather events cannot be causally
attributed to the change in the climate, uncouples the interpretation in principle from everyday experience. By contrast, the belief in the terrorist risk is
being collectively instilled as a global media event. However, this is by no
means the case for climate change. Thus there is a striking discrepancy
between the material destruction being wrought by climate change, which is
irreversibly transforming conditions of life on the planet, and its *suitability
for staging in the mass media*. Whereas the 'reality' of the terrorist risk is the
product of missionary self-promotion in the mass media and the omnipresence of the obscene images of violence (even though irreversible material
relations are not involved), the 'reality' of the climatic catastrophe is more
the result of a 'top-down staging' due to the power and skill of an alliance of
scientists, politicians and social movements (the most recent expression being
the film on the impact of climate change by the former vice-president Al
Gore). It is not local catastrophes and their globalization through the mass
media that produce the 'experienceability' and 'reality' of this global risk but
above all the successful proselytizing of people to adopt a particular expert
conception, though one always marked by uncertainty. For only those who
have the climatic catastrophe 'in their heads' can 'see' that specific natural
transformations – for example, the mounting once-in-a-century flooding of
the rivers, receding glaciers, summer temperatures during the winter in
Europe – 'are' concrete manifestations of the global climate risk. For those
sectors of the global population that do not or cannot afford to share this
belief, the climate catastrophe is a nothing, a non-thing, a hysteria or a new
strategy of Western imperialism. And as with any religion, in the case of the
global climate risk there are also heretics, agnostics, mystics, unbelievers, the
ignorant and also radical secularists who don't want to have anything to do
with this kind of I'm-saving-the-world faith.

Finally, in the cultural turmoil and exchange of world risk society a previously scarcely noticed competitive relation between the secular belief in
global risks and the religious belief in God is emerging. Risk enters the global
stage after God has made his exit. When Nietzsche pronounced that God is
dead, this had the – ironic – consequence that human beings must henceforth
find their own explanations and justifications for the impending catastrophes.
Those who believe in a personal God can try to win favour and forgiveness
through prayers and good works and in this way actively contribute to their
own salvation as well as to that of their families and their community. For
those who believe in God, risk is not risk because it is also or in essence

ascribed to God's (or the devil's) transcendence and does not spring (only) from human action. In this sense, there is a close connection between secularization and risk. Risks presuppose human decisions. They are in part positive, in part negative, Janus-faced consequences of human actions and interventions and *not* the work of transcendent powers. This does not preclude the fact that religious traditions have always confronted the most diverse risks, judged them and warned against or accommodated themselves to them.

In contrast to the national industrial society of the first modernity, which was marked by socio-economic conflicts between labour and capital, and in contrast to the international constellations in the East–West conflict, which was marked by the antagonism between political systems, the cleavages within world risk society are of a *cultural* nature. To the extent that global risks cannot be calculated in accordance with scientific methods and prove to be objects of non-knowing, the cultural perception of global risk – that is, the post-religious, quasi-religious *belief* in its reality – acquires central importance.

However, contra Huntington, it is not traditional, religiously founded 'civilizations' that are at the heart of the global cultural conflicts over values but conflicting 'religions' of risk faith or risk belief and of faith in God. We are confronted with a *clash of risk cultures and risk religions*. Thus there are wide divergences between the prevalent risk faith of most Europeans and that of the current US government. For Europeans, risk (faith) issues, such as climate change and the threat posed by global financial movements for individual countries, are much more important than the threat posed by terrorism. Whereas many Americans think that Europeans are suffering from environmental hysteria and 'Frankenstein food' hysteria, in the eyes of many Europeans many Americans are afflicted with terrorism hysteria.

Likewise the inversion of the concepts of secularism and religiosity is striking. It seems that religious cultures are characterized by a 'risk secularism'. Those who believe in God are risk atheists. Correspondingly, the contradictory certainties of a religious and a secular understanding of the world clash in the conflict over risk. What is at stake here is not which concrete global risk – terrorism or climate change – merits the crown of futility in the world ugliness contest. For the religious outlook, the more far-reaching issue is that al-Qaeda terrorism 'is' not a 'risk' at all but conclusive proof of the advent of the prophesied Apocalypse. From the perspective of the religious fundamentalists, the talk of 'world risk society' shrinks to a European phenomenon. For it is an expression of the *secularization of the Apocalypse* which is now entering its post-secular menopause when viewed in global terms. In other words, in the eyes of the religious fundamentalists, the phenomenon 'global risk', which bothers mainly the Europeans, does not even exist. *That* is the 'religious' core which demonizes wars of risk religion. In these conflicts, incompatible, indeed incommensurable, *certainties* clash –

paradoxically in dealing with uncertainties. They are literally a matter of life or death, of risk, of human existence and of our status in the eyes of God.

The collision of risk cultures is a central characteristic of second modernity:[1]

- It is a matter of life and death, not of individuals and of individual nations, but potentially of everyone.
- The decisions which are at the core of the physical and moral survival of humanity must be taken within a horizon of more or less acknowledged and controversial non-knowing and cannot be imputed to specific social actors.
- In many fields the empirical logic of trial and error is breaking down. It is not possible to allow only a small amount of genetically modified foodstuffs, only a small amount of nuclear energy or only a small amount of therapeutic cloning.

The cultural differences in perceptions of risk invite the question: How much tolerance of the ignorance of others can 'we' afford? Or: How can binding regulatory procedures and standards gain acceptance if we assume cultural differences in the perception, and ignorance of the consequences, of decisions which are transforming the anthropological character of the human race? Here two contradictory basic principles of risk evaluation come into conflict, namely, *laissez-faire* – something is safe until it has been proven dangerous – and *precaution* – nothing is safe until it has been proven harmless.

Ultimately, the ongoing controversy over genetically modified foodstuffs is an explosive example of how risk atheism, risk religion and global market interests are on the one hand merging and on the other colliding, and which strategic power and counterpower options are emerging as a result. The coalition of the US government and transnational corporations regards the Europeans' risk awareness either as hysteria or as protectionism – in fact, as both together. America, as a fundamentalist risk atheist regarding genetically modified foodstuffs, developed a master plan for how these should be foisted on the world. The United States cited Europe for its prohibition on the import of such foodstuffs before the World Trade Organization (WTO) in 2004 with the goal of opening up lucrative new markets.

In February 2006, three judges of the WTO Dispute Settlement Body publicly declared after years of secret consultations that Europe had imposed a *de facto* ban on the import of genetically modified foodstuffs between 1999 and 2003 in violation of WTO rules. The Dispute Settlement Body declared further that Germany, France, Italy, Luxembourg and Austria did not have the requisite legal statutes to impose unilateral import prohibitions. 'Europe found guilty!' was the triumphal headline in the US press.

In reality, the United States above all won a host of new enemies. Europe believes rather in the principle of precaution: nothing is safe until it has been proven harmless. If anything, the rejection of genetically modified foodstuffs seems to have increased since the dispute was brought before the WTO. Europe, its member states and its consumers unanimously rejected the regulations, which seems to confirm the supposition that the WTO has lost its connection to the people, and with it its authority to make decisions in areas such as the environment, public health or consumption.

The European Commission, which had attempted to force genetically modified plants on Europe against the will of the member states, declared that the WTO decision was 'irrelevant' because in the meantime EU law had been changed. Individual countries have declared that they are no more willing to take directives from the EU than from the WTO concerning what they should eat and what they should plant and that they would resist all attempts to force them to accept genetically modified foodstuffs.

Thus Hungary announced that it had a financial interest in remaining GMO-free and Greece and Austria declared their total opposition to these plants. Italy described the WTO regulations as 'unbalanced' and the Polish prime minister plead for keeping his country GMO-free. The opposition of local parliaments and assemblies is even more pronounced: more than 3,500 elected assemblies in 107 European regions have declared their territory to be GMO-free.

Faced with this coalition of the unwilling, the WTO, the EU and the United States can do very little. If the United States tries again to force its genetically modified products on Europe, as it did during the 1990s, it will backfire. Europe's biotech industry can now try to force the EU to implement the WTO ruling and bring these five countries to repeal the laws against GMOs through import bans; but it will meet with much stronger and more determined resistance.

In reality, Washington and the US companies do not need to be particularly concerned about the predictable European reaction. Europe has certainly not disappeared from the map of the global spread of GMOs. The companies and supermarkets know that there is little or no demand for genetically modified plants and Europe's state-subsidized farmers are reluctant to alienate the public even further by cultivating such plants.

Thus it is obvious in retrospect that the real reason why the United States brought Europe before the WTO Dispute Settlement Body was to make it easier for its own firms to break down trade barriers in China, India, Southeast Asia, Latin America and Africa – in those global regions to which the bulk of US exports go. Millions of tons of US foodstuffs end up in those regions to which American GMO companies are trying to gain access at any price by buying up seed companies and courting presidents and prime ministers.

More than two-thirds of US corn exports which formerly went to Europe now go to Asia and Africa. As an employee of the American firm Monsanto said of the WTO decision: 'Our impression is that it is important for countries outside the EU to have scientifically based guidelines.'

Like the tobacco industry, the GMO companies are now concentrating on the developing countries. But there too the industry is meeting with the resistance of powerful unions and farmers' groups. Brazil has capitulated but Bolivia could soon become the first Latin American country to ban GMOs completely. Some Indian states are against genetically modified food in principle, and there have been large-scale demonstrations in the Philippines, Korea, Indonesia and other countries.

The United States claims to have won a major victory for free trade with the help of the WTO and to have set a milestone on the path 'to making genetically modified plants acceptable throughout the world'. Perhaps, but the battle is far from won, and in the meantime everyone who is against these plants will be dismissed as an enemy of the United States.

As it happens, this shows that the national perspective on the dynamics of risk conflicts in world risk society is outdated. A cosmopolitan outlook is required if we want to understand the global dynamics of risk conflicts in general and at the national or local level in particular. But we are only at the beginning. Thus the decoding of the human genome in the summer of 2000, for example, has clearly become one of the most important foundations of world risk society. The exploration of the associated possibilities – not to mention the requisite cultural, social and political forms – will take decades. The further development of the technologies of the future – genetic technology, nanotechnology and robotics – is opening up a Pandora's box. Genetic manipulation, communications technology and artificial intelligence, which are now also being combined, are sapping the state monopoly on power and are opening the door to an individualization of war – unless prompt and effective global countermeasures are taken.

3   Risk society is a (latent) revolutionary society in which a state of
normalcy and a state of exception overlap

How can one explain this global political conflict and revolutionary potential of global risks, which is, if at all, at best inadequately recognized and understood by the conventional sociology of risk? One answer is: *in dealing with catastrophic risks, the present of the future planetary state of exception, which can no longer be contained and managed at the national level, is being negotiated.* The state of exception no longer holds within a nation but on a 'cosmopolitan' scale, and thus gives rise to new conflicts, new commonalities and opportunities for action for diverse groups of actors. Here we must distinguish two variants of central importance for the theory of world risk society: on the one hand, the anticipation of side-effects catastrophes, such as those associated with the successes of the new cutting-edge technologies, but also with climate change, and so forth; on the other, the anticipation of *intentional* catastrophes, with transnational suicide terrorism being the prime example. It is in fact a matter of developing the theory of risk society in the light of this key distinction between the anticipation of *un*intended and *intended* catastrophes.

Side effects catastrophes (climate catastrophe, etc.) are *conditional* in a *bivalent* sense: they are a mixture of *goods* and *bads*. They give rise to a particular combination of utility and more or less probable destruction and havoc, usefulness for some, havoc for others, varying from one time and place to another. This intertwining and antagonism of socially unequally distributed hopes and fears does not hold for the anticipation of intentional catastrophes, because the perhaps remote probability of terrorist attacks is not counterbalanced by any compensatory benefits. In the side effects world risk society, grim eventualities (of climate catastrophe, of reactor breakdowns, of poisons in the food chain or of global financial crises) are consistently made more palatable by a promise of secular bliss (at least for some). The terroristic world risk society, by contrast, is the deliberate attempt to create hell upon earth. Side effects risks and intentional catastrophes even reinforce one another: terror, climate catastrophe and wars intermingle.

Side effects catastrophes involve the expectation of a *negligent* state of exception that places state, scientific and economic authority in question and hence favours the *disem*powerment of the state and the *em*powerment of social movements. Correspondingly, state, scientific and technical power and legitimacy may implode. In the terrorist world risk society, by contrast, the conceptual axes which have kept the catastrophic potential of radicalized modernization in check are collapsing. The notion of intentional catastrophes makes a mockery of the classical distinctions of the first modernity. This is especially true of the distinctions between state of normalcy and state of exception, war and peace, military and civilian, enemy and criminal, national and international, us and them. Perhaps the outstanding feature of terrorist risk society is that the clear demarcation of the state of exception is replaced by its *unlimited* social, spatial and temporal *extension*.

The state of exception becomes *socially* unlimited because the decision concerning its declaration lies no longer in the hands of state actors but in those of globally and anonymously operating non-state violence NGOs, which thus cannot be controlled by nation-states. The terrorist networks are 'cosmopolitan' agents of violence in a negative sense whose omnipresence is a result not of their actions but rather of the anticipation of their actions as staged by states and the mass media. The traditional instruments of national armies, police and legal systems have difficulty in coping with this. In this sense of 'unfathomability' (as measured by the institutionalized answers), it is in the first place a matter of an *enforced* state of exception. It is the inadequacy of the responses by individual states that confirms the impotence of even the global superpower in the state of emergency. Of course, this does not preclude that this state may be used to promote an active policy of the same superpower because it offers governments the option of state authoritarianism.

The state of exception has become *spatially* unlimited because it takes hold of all nations and recasts the taxonomy and hierarchy of international relations.

Finally, its *temporal* unlimitedness is shown by the fact that no end of the so-called war against terror is in sight. There is no identifiable subject of terrorism with whom peace negotiations could be conducted, and the global power of the terrorist networks is founded upon this organized anonymity. They are, as it were, '*un*-insurance companies', which nevertheless have one thing in common with their adversaries the insurance companies – they profit from the spread of the awareness of danger in spite of relatively few catastrophes. They know the 'insecurity business'. Someone who acts in especially random, blind and barbaric ways can plunge whole populations (continents) into fear and terror. The terrorist networks know how to prompt the call for security and heighten it into escalating appeals for security and in this way achieve what they could never achieve through their actions, namely, the strangulation of freedom and democracy.

One might initially think that Carl Schmitt anticipated the political potential of the state of exception induced by global risks (cf. Grande 2004). However, in his theory of sovereignty, Schmitt (2005) associates the state of exception exclusively with the nation-state. A transnational or even a cosmopolitan state of exception that, quite to the contrary, transcends the distinction between friend and foe is utterly unthinkable for Schmitt. 'The exceptional case reveals the essence of state authority most clearly. Here the decision detaches itself from the legal norm and (to put it paradoxically) authority proves that it does not have to be within the law in order to make law.' In the exceptional case, which means for Schmitt 'in the most grave emergency, the threat to the existence of the state', the state power first proves itself by defending the state of normalcy against the state of exception. Since the globalized, intentional terrorist risk is threatening to annul the principle of statehood (the guarantee of security for one's own citizens), it is no longer simply a matter of what Schmitt took to be the core of state authority. 'Sovereign is he who decides on the exception' (ibid.: 11). Contrary to Schmitt, the disempowerment of the state is a direct result of the empowerment of the terrorist risk, something for which states that declare particular terrorist groups to be the 'number one global enemy' are in no small part to blame (see above p. 10 and below pp. 146ff.).

As Giorgio Agamben observes, 'in conformity with a continuing tendency in all of the Western democracies, the declaration of the state of exception has gradually been replaced by an unprecedented generalization of the paradigm of security as the normal technique of government' (2005: 87–8). However, this thesis also overestimates the sovereignty of the state. It fails to recognize that state authority is simultaneously restricted and extended at the national and transnational levels and, in general, underestimates the complex meta-power game of global actors whose strategies, courses, impacts, paradoxes and contradictions are obscured by a state-fixated perspective (Beck 2005).

4   Global risks produced authoritarian 'failed states' – even in the West

It is obvious that taking the national frame of reference for granted – i.e. what I refer to as 'methodological nationalism' – prevents sociology from analysing the dynamics and conflicts, ambivalences and ironies of world risk society. This also holds, at least in part, for the two most important theoretical approaches and the two most important empirical research programmes which deal with risk, namely, the tradition of Mary Douglas, on the one hand, and that of Michel Foucault, on the other. These traditions undoubtedly yielded important and detailed results when it comes to understanding definitions and politics of risk, studies that nobody can ignore. Their achievement and their persuasiveness lies in having decoded risk as a struggle to redefine state and scientific power.

Their fundamental error, however, resides in viewing risk in varying degrees – or even exclusively – as an ally of the powerful rather than as an *unreliable* ally or even as a potential antagonist, as a hostile force confronting the power both of the nation-state and of global capital. This inability is a function of the theoretical premises of their respective approaches. Douglas and Foucault define the problem in such a way that the struggle over risk is always viewed within the perspective of a reproduction of the social and state power structure. In this way they fall prey to the manifestly ineffective surveillance state, to its false self-image.

Everyone is searching for lost security. But the nation-state, which tries to deal with global risks on its own, is like the drunk on a dark night who tries to find his lost wallet in the beam of a streetlamp. When asked 'Did you really lose your wallet here?', he answers 'No, but at least I can look for it in the light of the lamp'!

In other words, global risks produce authoritarian 'failed states' – even in the West. The state structure which arises under the conditions of world risk society could be characterized in terms of inefficiency and post-democratic authoritarianism. Hence we must make a clear distinction between authority and inefficiency. The final result could indeed be the depressing prospect that completely ineffective and authoritarian state regimes will emerge (even within the Western democracies). The bitter irony here is that manufactured uncertainty (knowledge), insecurity (welfare state) and the sense of insecurity (violence) undermine *and* confirm the power of the state beyond the scope of democratic legitimation. Given the intolerable conditions of world risk society, the older critical theory of Foucault runs the risk of affirmation and antiquatedness, as do large parts of the sociology which focused on class relations in the welfare state. It underestimates and castrates the communicative cosmopolitan logic and irony of global risks.

However, a cosmopolitan sociology that focuses on the challenges posed by global risks must also abandon its political quietism. Society and its institutions are incapable of adequately analysing risks because they remained captive to the concepts of the first modernity, the modernity of the nation-state. And it must ask itself: How can non-Western risk society be understood by a sociology that until now assumed as self-evident that its object – Western modernity – is both historically unique and universally valid? How should we understand the internal relation between risk and race, risk and foe image, risk and exclusion?

Everywhere the question burns like a beacon: How should we live in times of uncontrollable risks? How are we to live our lives when the next terrorist attack is already haunting our thoughts? How troubled should we be? Where is the boundary between prudent precaution and overwhelming fear and hysteria? And who defines it? Perhaps scientists, whose results are often mutually contradictory, who change their opinions so fundamentally that the pill which one can 'safely' swallow today can turn out to be a 'cancer risk' in a couple of years? Can we believe the politicians and mass media when the former declare that there is no risk, while the latter dramatize risk in order to increase circulation and viewing figures?

Even I know that I do not know how I should answer these questions. Insight into the irony of risk suggests responding to the omnipresence of risk in everyday life with sceptical irony. Perhaps scepticism and irony are at least homoeopathic, practical, everyday antidepressants against the omnipresent intimidations and stagings of world risk society.

5

Global Public Sphere and Global Subpolitics or: How Real is Catastrophic Climate Change?

To draw an interim conclusion: risk society, thought through to its conclusion, means world risk society. For its basic principle is that humanly generated, anticipated threats cannot be restricted either temporally, spatially or in social terms. This annuls the framework conditions and basic institutions of the first, industrial modernity – class conflict, national statehood and the notion of linear, technical-economic progress.

This chapter will focus on one – but only one among others – of the key dimensions of the dynamic of world risk society, namely, *environmental* crises, in particular *climate change* and its diverse consequences. It will have little to say about 'nature' or the 'destruction of nature', or about 'ecology' or 'environmental destruction', but all the more about 'world risk society'. This concept is chosen with systematic intent. For I want to propose a concept for the sociological analysis of environmental questions that allows us to grasp them, not as problems of the *environment* in the sense of the surrounding world [*Umwelt*], but as problems affecting the *inner world* [*Innenwelt*] of society. In place of the seemingly self-evident key concepts of 'nature', 'ecology' and 'environment', which underline the difference from the social, I propose a conceptual framework that goes beyond the opposition between society and nature and shifts the focus to the *uncertainty fabricated* by human beings: risk, catastrophe, side effects, insurability, individualization and globalization.

It is often objected that the concept 'world risk society' encourages a kind of neo-Spenglerism and hinders political action. Precisely the opposite is the case. As world risk society, society becomes *reflexive* in a threefold sense.[1] First, it itself becomes an issue: global threats found global commonalities, indeed a (virtual) global public sphere is taking shape. Second, the perceived globality of the dangers produced by civilization itself triggers a politically manipulable impulse towards the revitalization of national politics and the development of cooperative international institutions. For example, the then British prime minister, Tony Blair, and his successor Gordon Brown discovered and awakened the 'political giant' lurking in climate change at the end of 2006 when they proclaimed their vision of a 'green Great Britain' and 'green capitalism'. This was made possible by the so-called *Stern Review* (Stern 2007) which offers eloquent warnings against the dire *economic* consequences of irreversible climate change (see below). Third, politics is losing its sharp contours: constellations of a global and direct 'subpolitics' are forming which relativize and circumvent the coordinates and coalitions of national politics and could lead to worldwide 'alliances of mutually exclusive convictions'. In other words, a 'cosmopolitan society' can take shape in the perceived danger confronting world risk society.

1   Elements of a theory of environmental world risk society

The indeterminacy of the concepts of 'nature' and 'ecology'

The concept of 'ecology' has enjoyed an impressively successful history. Nowadays, responsibility for the condition of nature is laid at the door of ministers and managers. Evidence that the 'side effects' of products or industrial processes pose a threat to human life or to its natural bases can cause markets to collapse, destroying political confidence as well as economic capital and faith in the superior rationality of experts. This (in many respects highly subversive) success disguises the fact that 'ecology' is an utterly vague concept; everyone offers a different answer to the question of what should be preserved.[2]

'Once again I realized what humbug nature is', writes the German poet Gottfried Benn.

Even when snow does not melt, it provides hardly any linguistic or emotional themes: you can fully grasp its indisputable monotony without leaving the house. Nature is empty and desolate; only philistines see anything in it, poor devils who have to keep going on about it. Forests, for example, lack any thematic potential and everything below 1500 metres is old hat since you can see Piz Palü in the cinema for a mark . . . Steer clear of nature! It confuses your thoughts and is notoriously bad for your style! *Natura* – female, of course! Always looking to tap the male's semen, to copulate with him and exhaust him. Is nature even natural? It begins something and then lets it drop, as many interruptions as beginnings, changes of direction, failures, desertions, contradictions, flashes, meaningless deaths, experiments, games, appearances – the textbook example of the unnatural! And it is also uncommonly laborious, uphill, downhill: ascents that cancel each other out, vistas that become blurred, previously unknown lookout points that are immediately forgotten – in short, idiocy. (Benn 1986: 71ff.)

The use of the word 'nature' immediately invites the question: What *cultural model* of 'nature' is being assumed? Nature in its current state, driven to exhaustion by industry? Or the country life of the 1950s (as it now appears in hindsight or as it appeared to country dwellers at the time)? Mountain solitude before the appearance of the book *Hiking in the Solitary Mountains*? The nature of the natural sciences or the longed-for nature (in the sense of silence, mountain streams, inner peace) as extolled in the tourist brochures of the supermarkets of global solitude? The 'hard-headed' image of nature of businessmen for whom industrial operations on nature can always be rectified or the image of 'hypersensitive' individuals stirred by nature for whom even the most insignificant changes cause irreparable damage?

Nature – especially nature – is not nature but is more than ever a concept, a norm, a recollection, a utopia, an alternative plan. Nature is being rediscovered and pampered at a time when it has ceased to exist. The ecological movement is a reaction to the global condition of a contradictory fusion of nature and society that has superseded both concepts in a relationship of mutual connections and violations of which we do not as yet have any notion, let alone a concept. Attempts in the environmental debates to use a natural condition as a standard against its own destruction rest, and always rested, on a *naturalistic misunderstanding*. For the nature invoked no longer exists (Beck, 1992, 2002; Oechsle, 1988). What do exist, and what cause such a political stir, are different forms of socialization and different symbolic mediations of nature (and the destruction of nature), *cultural concepts* of nature, conflicting notions of nature and their (national) cultural traditions, which determine ecological conflicts throughout the world beneath the surface disputes among experts, the technical formulae and threats.[3]

But if nature 'in itself' cannot form the analytic point of reference for the environmental crisis and for a critique of the industrial system, what can play this role? There are a number of possible answers to this question. The most common is: the *science* of nature. Technical formulae – levels of toxins in the air, water and food, climatological models or the cybernetic conceptions of feedback loops in the science of ecosystems – are supposed to decide how much damage and destruction are tolerable. This approach, however, has at least three drawbacks. First, it leads directly to 'ecocracy', which differs from technocracy only in its greater intensity – namely, global management – crowned with a robust good conscience. Second, it ignores the meanings of cultural perceptions and of intercultural conflict and dialogue. Third, scientific models themselves involve ecological questions, implicit cultural models of nature (for example, that of systems theory, which contrasts with the understanding of nature of early natural conservation).

Thinking in natural scientific terms is a precondition for perceiving the world as ecologically endangered in the first place. Thus environmental awareness is the exact opposite of a 'natural' attitude; it is an extremely scientific view of the world, in which, for example, the abstract models of climatologists influence everyday behaviour. And the question of what kind of staging, indeed 'visualization', is necessary and possible in order to overcome this abstractness and render climate change and its apocalyptic consequences 'visible' is particularly urgent (see pp. 71ff.).

Yet no expertise can ever answer the question of how we want to live – what people are and are not prepared to accept cannot be deduced from any technical or ecological diagnosis of threats. It must instead be made the topic of a global dialogue between cultures. This is the aim of a second perspective, that of *cultural* sciences. It states that both the scale and the urgency of the ecological crisis fluctuate in accordance with intracultural and intercultural perception and evaluation. What kind of truth is it, one might ask with Montaigne, that is accepted in Europe but is regarded in the United States as deception and illusion? From this perspective, dangers do not exist 'in themselves', independently of our perceptions. They become a political issue only when everyone becomes aware of them; they are the products of social stagings which are strategically defined, covered up or dramatized with the aid of scientific materials. It is no accident that two Anglo-American social anthropologists – Mary Douglas and Aaron Wildavsky – presented this analysis as early as 1982 in their book *Risk and Culture*. Douglas and her co-author argue there (in a deliberate affront to the emerging environmental consciousness) that there is no effective difference between the dangers of early history and those in developed civilization, except in how they are culturally perceived and how they are organized in world society.

However correct and important this view may be, it remains unsatisfying. First, it highlights the (mistakes of a) sociology which reduces everything to society and ignores the characteristic 'both/and' quality of the immateriality (social staging) *and* the materiality of risk (physical change and destruction). Second, we know that people in the Stone Age did not have the capacity for nuclear and ecological self-destruction and that the threats posed by lurking demons did not exhibit the same political dynamic as the man-made risks of climate change.[4] *Act now or the world as we know it will be lost forever!* – this is the conclusion drawn by the *Stern Review*, which provides very concrete and dramatic illustration of the apocalyptic impacts of climate change:

If global warming increases by 1 degree Celsius (by comparison with the pre-industrial temperature of the earth) – in 2000 it had already reached 0.8 degrees – small glaciers (for example, in the Andes) will melt; the water supply of 50 million people will be in jeopardy; 300,000 human beings will die annually from malaria, diarrhoea, etc.; 10 per cent of animal species will become extinct.

An increase of 2 degrees Celsius could mean an unimaginable 60 million malaria fatalities in Africa alone; the sea level will rise by 7 metres.

If the temperature of the earth rises by 3 degrees, 40 per cent of all animal species will become extinct and Southern Europe will be threatened by a devastating drought.

If 4 degrees are reached, agriculture will collapse, first in Australia and Africa but in other regions of the world as well.

Finally, if the temperature increases by 5 degrees, London, New York and Tokyo are in danger of being inundated by the sea, the glaciers in the Himalayas will disappear, and there will be mass migrations and movements of refugees. (Stern 2007: 57, table 3.1)

What timescale are we dealing with here? Since 1980 alone, global warming has increased from 0.2 to 0.8 degrees. Some studies conjecture that the temperature will rise by 5 or 6 degrees if emissions continue to increase at their present rates, and the warming effect may even be accelerated by the escape of CO_2 gas from the ground.

This report by the former World Bank economist Nicholas Stern is undoubtedly an extremely skilful piece of staging. In order to counteract the abstractness of climate change and render the invisible visible, the anticipation of catastrophes is heightened in thematic and geographical terms by means of empirical indicators which touch cultural nerves (malaria, water shortage, dying agriculture and animal species, not to mention the demise of London, New York and Tokyo). Yet this is not all. The point of the message is that climate change represents the greatest market failure ever, greater than the economic costs of two world wars and the Great Depression of the 1920s put *together*! This impending *economic* catastrophe can only be averted at great cost. But this is relatively small, and the money in question is a good investment, because it will avert the threatened economic catastrophe. Is this a representation of 'reality' or a work of 'fiction'? Is it 'realist' or 'constructivist'? After all, 'climate change' is not (yet) a reality. It is a risk, something which threatens to become a reality, a future projected into the present, an *anticipation* bearing all the hallmarks of uncertainty, whose aim is to change present actions, specifically those of governments and managers, and ultimately of all human beings throughout the world. What, then, is meant by 'reality' when we speak of the 'reality of the impending catastrophe'?

The realism–constructivism debate

This is the starting point of the theory of world risk society. There are two possible answers to the question of the justification for this concept, a *realist* one and a *constructivist* one (for an interpretation and critique, see Szerszynski et al. 1996 and Wynne 1996a). In the *realist* view, the consequences and dangers of developed industrial production 'are' now global. This 'are' is supported by natural scientific data. In this view, the development of productive forces is interlinked with the development of destructive forces, and together they are giving rise to the novel conflicts dynamic of a world risk society – in the shadow of latent side effects. Aside from the 1986 Chernobyl reactor disaster, this dynamic is reflected at the beginning of the twenty-first century in global warming which is an ideal-typical illustration of the fact that environmental destruction 'knows no boundaries'.

The realist perspective conceives of world risk society in terms of global socialization which is enforced by man-made threats. The new situation enhances the importance of international cooperation and institutions. To global dangers, therefore, correspond – 'realistically' – global modes of perception, fora of public debate and action and, finally, assuming the supposed objectivity generates sufficient practical impetus, transnational actors and institutions.

The strength of realism can be seen in its clear historical sequential model, in which industrial society has gone through two distinct phases. In the first phase, class or social questions were paramount, in the second phase, ecological questions. Yet it would be a gross simplification to assume that the environmental question is supplanting the class question. Clearly, environmental, labour market and economic crises overlap and may well aggravate one another. Such a phase model becomes more persuasive, however, if it represents the globality of ecological questions as following upon the issues of poverty and class which dominated the national phase of industrial capitalism. Often suspected of naïvety, this realism thus represents – or even generates – a considerable power stimulus to carry through a policy that counteracts the catastrophic impacts of global warming.

Yet even a superficial examination of such realist justifications of world risk society reveals how untenable they are. In the first place, the unreflected realist viewpoint forgets or suppresses the fact that 'realism' is nothing other than sedimented, fragmented, mass-mediated collective consciousness. Of course, as Brian Wynne has shown, public knowledge concerning risk is often not expert but lay knowledge that was denied social recognition.[5] Nevertheless ecological images and symbols are by no means scientifically confirmed as intrinsically certain knowledge. They are culturally perceived, constructed and mediatized; they are part of the social knowledge 'fabric', with all of its contradictions and conflicts. The catastrophic consequences of climate change must, as we have seen, be *made visible*, that is, they must be effectively staged in order to generate pressure for action. The explanatory power of realism is a function of the exclusion of all considerations that support the interpretative superiority of constructivist approaches. How, for example, is the borrowed self-evidence of 'realistic' dangers actually *produced*? Which actors, institutions, strategies and resources are key to its *fabrication*? These questions can be meaningfully posed only from a constructivist perspective.

On the social-constructivist view, world risk society is not a function of the globality of problems (as diagnosed by science) but of '*transnational discourse coalitions*' (Hajer) that place the global threat to the environment on the public agenda. These coalitions were forged and became powerful only in the 1970s and 1980s. In the 1990s, and especially since the Rio Earth Summit, they began to reshape the discursive landscape around global planetary pro-blems and now, at the beginning of the twenty-first century, are reaching a new acme with the green turn of the New Labour government, the EU and perhaps the United States. Necessary preconditions are the institutionalization of the environmental movement, the construction of networks and transnational actors, such as the IUCN, WWF and Greenpeace, the establishment of environment ministries, national and international laws and treaties, and the elevation of environmental industries and 'big science' to the task of global management of world problems. Moreover, these actors must also be *successful* and continually assert themselves against powerful opposing coalitions.

Thus far, the diagnosis of a world risk society has met with three kinds of counter-arguments. First, it is argued that the relevant (lay and expert) knowledge concerning global risks is far from clear. It appeals to future events that have not yet occurred and hence uses assertions that can at present be neither proven nor refuted. Thus critics repeatedly refer to discrepancies between the actual state of expert knowledge and the public dramatization of threats and crises.

Second, the global definition of environmental problems is criticized as a kind of Western *ecological neo-imperialism*, especially by actors and governments in the so-called Third World. The claim is that Western states thereby assure themselves of a lead in knowledge and development over poorer countries, while at the same time covering up their own primary responsibility for the global civilizational threats.

This is why, in conceptualizing the dynamics of inequality in world risk society, it makes sense to distinguish between *self-endangerment* and *endangerment by others* (Beck and Holzer 2004; see below chapters 9 and 10). In Europe, environmental crises are perceived in the first instance as a creeping change that takes the form of a latent *self-endangerment* through the impacts of industrial modernization. For Third World countries it is nothing new that, within the context of a world system that systematically (re)produces inequality (Wallerstein 1974; Frank 1969), modernization in the so-called First World hinders their development. However, such theories reflect a reductive economistic analysis of the interrelations. Regions are unequally affected not only by the impacts of failed modernization but also by the 'side effects' of *successful* modernization, as the theory of world risk society emphasizes.

Third, it is objected that the global character of ecological questions leads to a perversion of 'nature conservation' into its opposite, a kind of global world-management. In this way new monopolies of knowledge are established, the hi-tech 'global climate models' (the 'global circulation models' of the International Panel for Climate Change, IPCC), with their inbuilt policies and claims to interpretation and control (specifically, those of the natural and computer sciences).

Furthermore, it is becoming apparent that world risk society is by no means synonymous with overcoming ethno-national conflicts of perception and evaluation. On the contrary, it seems to herald the outbreak of new antagonisms (for example, in disputes over 'levels' of danger, or who is 'responsible' for them and over the need for countermeasures), which in turn give rise to national winners and losers (see chapters 9 and 10).

However contradictory the essentialist-realist and constructivist approaches may be in their points of departure and their methods and basic assumptions, in their diagnoses they agree on a central issue. They both justify speaking in terms of world risk society. This certainly should not lead us to play down the differences. It is particularly striking that realism places the emphasis on *world risk* society, whereas constructivism, by contrast, stresses world risk *society* (where the concept 'society' in this context is indeterminate). In the constructivist optic, transnational actors already have to have *imposed* their discursive politics if the globality of environmental issues is to determine social perceptions and calls for action. On the 'realist' view, by contrast, this globality is grounded *solely* in the assumed intrinsic power of objective dangers. One could say that realism conceives of the ecological problematic as 'closed', whereas constructivism stresses its *openness* in principle. For some, the *dangers* (the doomsday scenarios) of world risk society are the central focus; for others, it is the *opportunities*, that is, the contexts in which actors can operate. For some, global dangers must first give rise to international institutions and treaties, for others, talk of global environmental dangers already presupposes successfully operating supranational discourse coalitions. However, realism recognizes something that constructivism easily loses sight of, namely, the *irreversibility of the damage and destruction* which stand in an inverse relation to their public thematization, on the motto 'those who deny climate change contribute to its acceleration' (see pp. 127f.).

Table 5.1 Theoretical and epistemological positions

Epistemology	Theory	Theorists
Strong (naïve) realism	Human ecology	Catton, Dunlap
	Environmental sociology	Huber, Jänicke, Spaargaren
	Ecological modernization	and Mol
Weak (critical/ reflexive) realism	Green social theory	Dickens
		Burns and Dietz
Weak constructivism (constructivist realism)	Reflexive modernization	Beck, Giddens, Eder
	Actor network theory	Latour
Strong (naïve) realism	Rational choice theory	Esser
	Cultural theory	Douglas
	Autopoietic systems theory	Luhmann
	Governmentality	Ewald, Rose, Ericson

Source: adapted from Strydom (2002: 47).

But a further, indeed a farther-reaching, question arises here: Are realism and constructivism mutually exclusive in every respect in their approaches to world risk society? This is true only if *naïve* versions are assumed on both sides. For just as there is belief in nature and reality as they really exist, so too there is belief in a purely constructivist form of constructivism. As long as we remain at this level, we will fail to recognize the interpretative content of *reflexive realism*, and hence its potential role in *strategies of power*. Such a reflected form of realism highlights sources which first make 'constructions of reality' into a 'reality'; it examines how self-evidence is generated, questions are curtailed, alternative interpretations are shut up in 'black boxes', and so on.

Thus, if one mistrusts simple oppositions, one can oppose a 'naïve' constructivism to a 'reflexive' realism or situate them on the same level. Naïve constructivism fails to recognize the different varieties of constructivist realism and as such remains rooted in a 'realist' self-misunderstanding of its strict constructivism. It fails to appreciate that durable stagings of reality that are supposed to guide action must repudiate their constructed character because otherwise they will be conceived as *constructions* of reality and not as *reality tout court*. Furthermore, naïve constructivism underestimates the materiality or the 'natural', scientifically diagnosed inherent constraints of global threats, which are by no means inferior to the materiality of economic constraints. Constructivist analyses that lose sight of the difference between destruction as *event* and *discourse* concerning this event can downplay dangers in a cognitivist manner.

In a 'realist constructivism', by contrast, the essentialist meaning content in discourse concerning 'nature' and the 'destruction of nature' is replaced by *expert and anti-expert knowledge* (as in Brian Wynne and Maarten Hajer). The latter, in criticizing mainly Anglo-American discourse and cultural theory, developed a politically and analytically more radical approach to this dimension of knowledge. In the process, the naturalist-essentialist content of discourse concerning 'the destruction of nature' takes an – only apparently paradoxical – turn towards the *action-related theory of actors and institutions*. *'Discourse coalitions'* that stretch across the boundaries of classes, nation-states and systems now take centre stage. They are, as it were, discursive landscape architects: they create, design and alter 'cognitive maps', 'narrative frameworks' and 'taboos'. Reality becomes the project and product of action, with an until now unclarified ambiguity in talk of the 'production' [*Herstellen*] of reality assuming major importance. This may be meant primarily in a *cognitive* sense, thus referring *only* to the construction of knowledge, or it may include *action* (decision, work, production) and thus refer to material change through production or the purposeful shaping of realities. Although it is often difficult to demarcate these two aspects of the meaning of production from one another, nevertheless they refer to different modes of the 'creation of reality' or of the 'shaping of the world'. The point is no longer merely how realities are created in world risk society (for example, through corresponding reports concerning threats in the mass media); there is also the question of how reality 'in itself' is (re)produced through discourse politics and coalitions within institutional contexts of decision, action and work.

Consequently 'constructions of reality' can be distinguished as to whether they are more or less 'real'. The closer they are to and in institutions (understood as institutionalizations of social practices), the more powerful and closer to decision and action they are, and the more 'real' they become or appear. Essentialism, when scrutinized and analysed by the sociology of knowledge, turns into a kind of strategic institutionalism geared to power and action. In a world risk society dynamic that reduces everything to decisions, reality 'in itself' arises out of structures of action, ingrained decision and work routines, in which modes of perception are 'realized' or redrawn. The way in which people continue to speak of 'nature' and the 'destruction of nature' may be an indicator of the paradoxical strategy of the construction of deconstruction. The appearance of construction is thereby (more or less) reflexively and powerfully destroyed and the appearance of the 'in itself' is produced.

Institutional constructivism

With these points in mind, we can make the theory of world risk society more concrete. It shares in the rejection of the dualism of society and nature which Bruno Latour (1995, 2004), Donna Haraway (1991) and Barbara Adam (1995) effect with such intellectual flair.[6] The only question is: How do we deal with nature *after* it ends? This question is answered in the theory of world risk society along the lines of an *institutional constructivism*. 'Nature' and the 'destruction of nature' are institutionally produced and defined (in conflicts between lay people and experts) within industrially internalized nature. Their essential content correlates with institutional power of action and organization. Here production and definition are two aspects of the material *and* symbolic 'production' of '(the destruction of) nature'; they refer, if you will, to discourse coalitions within and between fundamentally different, global action networks. It remains to be examined in detail *how*, and with what discursive and industrial resources and strategies, these differences in the 'naturalness' of nature, its 'destruction' and 'renaturalization', are produced, suppressed, normalized and integrated within institutions and in the conflict between cognitive actors.

The theory of world risk society translates the question of the destruction of nature into another question: How does modern society deal with self-produced uncertainties? The point of this formulation is to distinguish between decision-dependent *risks* that can in principle be brought under control and *threats* that have escaped or neutralized the control requirements of industrial society, in at least two forms (see also chapter 2).

First, the norms and institutions developed within industrial society – risk assessment, insurance principle, the concept of an accident, disaster prevention, preventive aftercare (Ewald 1991; Bonss 1995) – can fail. Is there a convenient indicator of this? There is, for the controversial industries and technologies are often those which either do not have private insurance or have only inadequate private insurance (more on this in chapter 7). This holds for atomic energy, for genetic engineering (including research) and also for other sectors of high-risk chemical production. What goes without saying for motorists – never use your car without insurance protection – has apparently been suspended for whole industrial branches and cutting-edge technologies, where the dangers involved present too many problems.

Second, the pattern of decisions in industrial society and the globality of their aggregate side effects belong to two different eras. Whereas decisions bound up with the scientific, technical-economic dynamic are organized at the national level and at the level of individual enterprises, the resulting threats make us all members of a world risk society. The task of ensuring the health and safety of citizens can no longer be performed at national level in the developed system of danger-industrialism.

This is the 'cosmopolitan moment' (see pp. 56ff.) of the ecological crisis. With the appearance of ecological discourse, the end of 'foreign policy', the end of the 'domestic affairs of another country', the end of the national state is becoming an everyday experience. At the same time, a central strategy in the production of difference and indifference becomes discernible. The established rules for allocating responsibility – causality and blame – are breaking down. This means that their indefatigable application in administration, management and the administration of justice now produces the opposite result: dangers grow *as a result of* being made anonymous. In other words, the old routines of decision, control and production (in law, science, administration, industry and politics) cause the material destruction of nature *and* its symbolic normalization. The two complement and aggravate one another. To put it more concretely, it is not the rule violation but the rule itself which 'normalizes' the death of species, rivers and lakes.

This circular movement between symbolic normalization and permanent material threat and destruction is captured by the concept of 'organized irresponsibility'. The state administration, politics, industrial management and research work out the criteria of what is 'rational and safe', with the result that the hole in the ozone layer grows larger, allergies become endemic, and so on.

Alongside (and independent of) the material explosiveness, discourse-strategic action potentially renders *politically* explosive the dangers which are normalized in the circuits of legitimation of administration, politics, law and management and spread uncontrollably on a global scale. To speak with and against Max Weber: purposive-rational bureaucracy transforms universal culpability into acquittal, and as an unintended side effect threatens the very basis of its claim to rational control.

The key idea of the theory of world risk society, therefore, is: the transformation of the unseen side effects of industrial production into global ecological flashpoints is not strictly a problem of the 'environing' world – it is not a so-called environmental problem – but instead *a radical institutional crisis of the first (national) phase of industrial modernity*. As long as these new developments are understood within the conceptual horizon of industrial society, they continue to be seen as negative side effects of seemingly justifiable and calculable action ('vestigial risks') and their tendency to subvert systems and delegitimize basic principles of rationality goes unrecognized. Their central political and cultural significance becomes apparent only within the conceptual horizon of world risk society and they underscore the need for reflexive self- and re-definition of the Western model of modernity.

During the phase of the discourse of world risk society, it gradually becomes apparent that the threats triggered by technological-industrial development are neither calculable nor controllable as measured by existing institutional yardsticks. A prime example of this is the climate change debate. It requires crass ignorance or decidedly selective vision to overlook the link between an ominously rising temperature curve and increasing greenhouse gas emissions, notwithstanding the uncertainty of the correlation. That the established national institutions have no answer to this is also in the meantime a truism. This forces us to reflect on the bases of the democratic, national, economic model of the first modernity and to examine existing institutions (for externalizing the effects in the economy, law, science, and so on) and the historically devalued bases of their rationality. This is a truly global challenge, out of which new global flashpoints and even wars – though also supranational institutions of cooperation, conflict regulation and consensus building – can emerge.

The economy is also undergoing radical change. Once upon a time, in the entrepreneurial paradise of early capitalism, industry could launch projects *without* submitting to special controls. Then came the period of state regulations when business activity was subject to labour legislation, safety regulations, tariff agreements, and so on. In world risk society, all of these agencies and regulations can be observed without this guaranteeing security. Even managers who observe the regulations may suddenly find themselves placed in the dock of global public opinion as 'environmental polluters'. Manufactured insecurity thus appears in the core areas of action and management founded on economic rationality. The normal reactions of industry and politics are to block demands for effective change and to condemn as 'irrational' or 'hysterical' the storm of protest that breaks out in spite of official assurances. The way is now open for a series of errors. Proudly confident of representing reason in a sea of irrationalism, people tumble headlong into the trap of extremely heated risk conflicts (see Lau 1989; Nelkin 1992; Hildebrandt et al. 1994; Holzer and Sørensen 2003; Voss et al. 2006).

In world risk society, business projects become *political* matters, in the sense that large investments presuppose long-term consensus. Such consensus, however, is no longer guaranteed – indeed it is jeopardized – by the old routines of simple modernization. What could formerly be negotiated and implemented behind closed doors under the guise of 'practical constraints' (for example, waste disposal, and even production methods or product design) is now in danger of being exposed to the crossfire of public criticism.

The most important consequence is the politicization of formerly taken-for-granted presuppositions and institutions. Who has to 'prove' what under conditions of manufactured uncertainty? What should be regarded as sufficient proof? Who should decide on compensation? The legal system does not found social peace any longer because it generalizes and legitimizes threats to life – and at the same time political threats (see pp. 31ff.).

2 Indicators, conditions of emergence and forms of expression of a global subpolitics

On the concept of global subpolitics

Anyone who speaks of world risk *society* must also address how global threats lead to action. Here two arenas or actors can be distinguished: first, globalization *from above* (for example, through international treaties and institutions) and, second, globalization *from below* (for example, through new transnational actors operating outside of the system of parliamentary politics who challenge established political organizations and interest groups). There is compelling evidence for the existence and operation of both arenas. Thus the majority of international accords on the environment were reached over an extremely short period, i.e. over the past three decades.

Richard Falk identifies a number of political arenas in which globalization from above is pushed through:

The response to threats against strategic oil reserves in the Middle East, the efforts to expand the GATT framework, the coercive implementation of the nuclear nonproliferation regime, the containment of South–North migration and refugee flows . . . The legal implications of globalization-from-above would tend to supplant interstate law with a species of global law, but one at odds in most respects with 'the law of humanity'. (1994: 137)[7]

It is repeatedly objected that global environmental politics represents, at best, the proverbial drop in the ocean. However, we must also consider whether in years to come we will witness an ecological conversion and whether policy on climate change will be raised to the level of 'serious politics' because governments whose hands are tied by the institutions of the nation-state discover new opportunities for strategic action and an unexpected source of legitimation in a global alliance around climate change. Already over the past decade a number of spectacular global boycott movements operating across cultural borders have made clear that the impotence of official policy when faced with industrial interests is an impotence vis-à-vis the classical institutional divisions. For in the meantime agencies of a globalization *from below* have also appeared on the scene in the shape of non-governmental organizations (NGOs) such as Robin Wood, Greenpeace, Amnesty International and Terre des Hommes. Here one can discern the initial contours of a 'global citizenship' (Richard Falk and Bart van Steenbergen) – or, as we would say, a new constellation of global subpolitics is emerging. The principal conclusion is that this constellation can give rise to a differentiation between governance and the nation-state. The first concrete indicators of this are new alliances between civic groups and national governments which are seizing their chance and are sweeping everything else (opposition, their own errors and omissions) away in the name of 'Save the World'. In this respect, the concept of global subpolitics deepens the cosmopolitan moment of world risk society (chapter 3). We must now explain how this is possible.

The victory march of industrial modernity heralds the universal success of a purposive-rational form of political administration. The common sense of this era is supported by an everything-under-control mentality, which extends even to the uncontrollability that it itself produces. However, the imposition of this form of order and control brings about its opposite, namely, the return of uncertainty and insecurity. Global climate problems arise as 'second-order dangers' (Bonss). In this way, society opens up into the *(sub)political* as a result of the 'side effects' of global dangers. All fields of action – the economy and science, private life and the family and politics – face a decisive turning point: they need a new justification, they must be renegotiated and rebalanced. How should this be conceptualized?

'Crisis' is not the right concept, any more than 'dysfunction' or 'disintegration', for it is precisely the *triumphs* of unbridled industrial modernization that call it into question. This is what is meant by 'reflexive modernization': theoretically, self-application; empirically, self-transformation; politically, loss of legitimacy and a power vacuum. This can be clarified by a figure of thought of Thomas Hobbes. As is well known, he argued for a strong, authoritarian state, but he also specifies *one* individual right of civil resistance. If the state creates or permits life-threatening conditions, with the result that a citizen must 'abstain from the use of food, ayre, medicine, or any other thing, without which he cannot live', then, according to Hobbes, 'hath that man the Liberty to disobey' (1968: 269).

Analysed in terms of social policy, therefore, the ecological crisis involves a *systematic violation of basic rights,* whose long-term socially destabilizing effects can scarcely be overestimated. For dangers are being produced by industry, externalized by economics, individualized by the legal system, legitimized by the natural sciences and downplayed by politics. That this is undermining the power and credibility of institutions only becomes apparent when the system is put to the test by Greenpeace, for example, and, in a completely different way, by al-Qaeda. The result is the subpoliticization of world society.

The concept of 'subpolitics' refers to the *decoupling of politics from government*; it underlines that politics is also possible beyond the representative institutions of the nation-states. This holds for transnational corporations as much as for the managers of global uncertainty in international organizations, social movements or, in the opposite sense, the terrorist network which breaks the state's monopoly on violence. Thus the concept of 'subpolitics' directs attention to indicators of a global self-organization of non-state politics that has the potential to mobilize all areas of society. Subpolitics means 'direct' politics – that is, *selective* intervention, sometimes even individual participation in political decisions, bypassing the institutions of representative will-formation (political parties, parliaments), often without legal backing or in deliberate violation of all law. In other words, subpolitics means the shaping and transformation of society from below irrespective of the political aims of this intervention. The state, business, science, law, the military, occupation, everyday existence, the private sphere – in short, the basic institutions of first modernity – become caught up in the storms of global political controversies. Interestingly, this differentiation between state politics and subpolitics does not lead automatically or exclusively to depoliticization, as is often assumed. Rather, it now becomes possible to forge new transborder alliances in order to implement highly legitimate civic goals that afford governments new opportunities for action in domestic policy against the opposition, business, the mass media and the electorate. Accordingly, in a future 'cosmopolitan doctrine of government' the overlapping of domestic and foreign policy – in particular, the extension of the state's domestic room for manoeuvre through its involvement in global affairs (climate change policy) – must assume central importance. Such alliances do not fit into the traditional spectrum of party-political differences, however. Thus the subpolitics of world society can certainly find expression in *ad hoc 'coalitions of opposites'* (of parties, nations, regions, religions, governments, corporations and social movements) (see p. 60). The decisive point is that, in one way or another, subpolitics sets politics free by changing the rules and boundaries of the political so that global politics becomes more open and more amenable to new goals, issues and interdependencies.

In what follows, I will illustrate this, first, with an example of a symbolically staged mass boycott, second, with the subpolitics of climate change and, finally, by way of contrast, with the subpolitics of terrorism.

*Subpolitics from below: symbolically staged mass boycott –
a case study in global subpolitics*

In the summer of 1995 Greenpeace, the latter-day crusader for good causes, first succeeded in getting Shell to dispose of a scrapped oil rig on land rather than sinking it in the Atlantic. This multinational activist concern then tried to halt a resumption of French nuclear tests by publicly pillorying President Jacques Chirac for a deliberate breach of international treaties. Many asked whether it signalled the end of fundamental rules of (foreign) policy when an unauthorized actor such as Greenpeace could conduct its own world domestic policy without regard for national sovereignty or diplomatic norms. Tomorrow it could be the turn of the Moonies and then some other private organization that wants to bring happiness to the world in this way.

What such jibes overlooked was that the multinational oil company was brought to its knees not by Greenpeace but by a mass public boycott set going by a worldwide televised indictment. Greenpeace itself did not rock the political system; rather it revealed the resulting vacuum of power and legitimacy.

Everywhere there are signs of this coalition model of global subpolitics or direct politics. Alliances of forces 'totally' incapable of allying with one another are coming into being. Thus the then German chancellor, Helmut Kohl, joined the protest as a citizen who also happened to be the head of government and supported the Greenpeace action against the then British prime minister, John Major. Suddenly political elements in everyday action were discovered and put into effect – for example, in the act of filling one's car with fuel. Car drivers banded together against the oil industry (which is really something to savour). In the end, the state joined in with the illegitimate action and its organizers. In this way the state used its power to legitimize a deliberate, extra-parliamentary rule violation, while for their part the protagonists of direct politics explicitly sought to escape – through a kind of 'ecological self-administered justice' – the narrow framework of indirect, legally sanctioned authorities and rules. Finally, the anti-Shell alliance marked a scene change between the politics of first and second modernity. National governments sat in the audience while the unauthorized actors of second modernity orchestrated the events.

In the case of the worldwide movement against President Chirac's decision to resume nuclear testing, a spontaneous global alliance arose between governments, Greenpeace activists and the most diverse protest groups. The French miscalculation was reflected in two aspects of the situation: (a) the Mururoa decision coincided with commemorations of the fiftieth anniversary of the dropping of atomic bombs on Hiroshima and Nagasaki; and (b) it was unanimously condemned by a meeting of the ASEAN Forum, in which to top it all the United States and Russia took part. All this pointed to a fleeting alliance of direct politics spanning national, economic, religious and political-ideological differences. The result was a global coalition of conflicting symbolic and economic forces. A special feature of this politics of the second modernity is that in practice its 'globality' does not exclude anyone or anything – not only in a social sense, but also morally and ideologically. It is, thought through to its conclusion, a politics *without opponents or opposing forces*, a kind of 'enemyless politics'.

The political novelty, therefore, was not that David had beaten Goliath but that David *plus Goliath*, acting at a global level, successfully joined together, first against a multinational and then against a national government and one of its policies. What was new was the worldwide alliance between extra-parliamentary and parliamentary forces, citizens and governments for a cause that is legitimate in the higher sense: saving the world or the environment.

Something else also became apparent. The post-traditional world only appears to be dominated by individualization. Paradoxically, the challenges posed by global threats provide it with a source of new global morality and activism and of new forms (and forums) of protest – though also of new hysterias. Status or class-consciousness, belief in progress or decline – all of this could be replaced by the humanity-wide project of saving the world environment. Global threats found global risk communities, at least *ad hoc* ones at particular historical moments.

This is also new. Politics and morality are acquiring priority over expert rationality. Whether one can go beyond single issues to constitute a coherent environmental politics through such politicization is quite another matter. This probably marks the limits of global subpolitics. Conversely, the trend towards subpoliticization should not be considered as irrational at all because it bears the hallmarks of republican modernity in contrast to the representative, national-parliamentary democracy of parties. The activities of multinationals and of national governments is being exposed to the pressure of a global public opinion. Striking and decisive here is the individual–collective participation in global action networks: citizens are discovering that the act of purchasing can function as a vote that they can always use in a political way. In boycotts, the active consumer society thus links up and forms an alliance with direct democracy, on a global scale.

In this way, the cosmopolitan society constitutes a global nexus of responsibility in which individuals, and not only their organizational representatives, can participate directly in political decisions. This explains the discussions of and calls for 'technological citizenship' in the United States. The issue is the recovery of basic democratic rights in the face of the 'anonymous rule' of technological developments. In Andrew Zimmerman's view (1995: 88), social autonomy is being hollowed out by technological autonomy, whereas in the first modernity, the well-being and 'freedom' of the citizen were a function of the well-being and freedom of technical systems.

Philip Frankenfeld's contrasting approach attempts to justify the demand for technological participation:

The status of technological citizenship may be enjoyed at the national, state, local, or global level or at levels in between. Hence one can be a technological citizen of . . . the Chernobyl ecosphere, of the plastic explosives production and use 'noosphere' – which is global in scale – of a particular nuclear-free zone in the non-contiguous network of them, of the realm covered by the non-proliferation treaty. . . . However, one *would* be a technological citizen of *any* of these spheres of impact *if* their inhabitants deigned to create a set of agencies, a cocoon of protections or benefits, or a cocoon of rights and responsibilities granting subjects status in relation to impacts of technologies with a specific overarching purpose. (Frankenfeld 1992: 463f., quoted in Zimmerman 1995: 89; see also van Steenbergen 1994; Archibugi and Held 1995)

As normatively overarching goals of citizenship, Frankenfeld cites: '(1) autonomy, (2) dignity, (3) assimilation – versus alienation – of members of the polity.' It therefore includes: '1. rights to knowledge or information; 2. rights to participation; 3. rights to guarantees of informed consent; and 4. rights to limitation on the total amount of endangerment of collectivities and individuals' (Frankenfeld 1992: 462, 465).

But where are the sites, and what are the instruments and the media of this direct politics of a 'global technological citizenship'? The political site of world risk society is not the street but *television*, the Internet – in short, the old and the new media. Its political subject is not the working class and its organization, the trade union. Its function is assumed by the *staging of cultural symbols in the mass media*, where the accumulated bad conscience of the actors and consumers of industrial society can be assuaged.

This thesis can be illustrated from three directions. First, destruction and protest are symbolically mediated in the abstract omnipresence of dangers. Second, in acting against ecological destruction, everyone is also their own enemy. Third, the ecological crisis is breeding a cultural Red Cross consciousness. Those who inscribe this on their banner are admitted into the ecological nobility and rewarded with an almost unlimited credit of trust – which has the advantage that, in case of doubt, one's information and not that of the agents of industry is believed.

Herein lies a crucial limitation of direct politics. Human beings are like children wandering around in a 'forest of symbols' (Baudelaire). In other words, we have to rely on the symbolic politics of the media. This holds especially because of the abstractness and omnipresence of destruction which keep world risk society going. Tangible, simplifying symbols, in which cultural nerve fibres are touched and alarmed, here take on central political importance. These symbols have to be produced or forged in the open fire of conflict provocation, before the strained and terrified public of television viewers. The key question is: Who discovers (or invents), and how, symbols that disclose the structural character of the problems while at the same time fostering the ability to act? The latter should be all the more successful the simpler and neater is the staged symbol, the fewer are the costs of public protest actions for the individual, and the more easily everyone can thereby relieve their conscience. In this way, even errors in information, such as those committed by Greenpeace in the anti-Shell campaign, can be glossed over.

Simplicity has many meanings. First, *transmissibility*: we are all environmental sinners; just as Shell wanted to dump its oil rig in the sea, 'we all' itch to toss cola cans out of the car window. This is the everyman situation which makes the Shell case (as socially constructed) so 'transparent'. However, there is the essential difference that the size of the sin seems to increase the likelihood of official acquittal. Second, *moral outrage*: 'the big shots' can sink an oil rig filled with toxic waste in the Atlantic with the approval of the government and its experts, while 'we small fry' – especially in Germany – have to divide every teabag into three – paper, string and leaves – and dispose of them separately in order to save the world. Third, *simple alternative actions*: in order to damage Shell, you had to and could fill up your car with 'morally clean' petrol from one of its competitors. Fourth, *sale of ecological indulgences*: the bad conscience of the original inhabitants of industrial society lent the boycott importance because it meant that a kind of personal *ego te absolvo* could be granted at no personal cost.

Far from aggravating a general sense of meaninglessness in the modern world, global ecological threats give rise to a horizon of meaning dominated by avoidance, resistance and assistance, a moral climate that intensifies with the scale of the perceived danger and in which the roles of hero and villain acquire a new political significance. The perception of the world within the coordinates of environmental and industrial self-endangerment combine morality, religion, fundamentalism, desperation, tragedy and tragicomedy – always connected with their opposites: salvation, assistance and liberation – into a universal drama. In this worldwide tragicomedy, business is free to assume the role of the villain of the piece or to slip into the role of the hero and rescuer. This is the very background which enables Greenpeace to hog the limelight with the cunning of weakness. Greenpeace practises a kind of *judo politics* whose goal is to mobilize the superior strength of environmental miscreants against themselves.

The Greenpeace people are multinational media professionals who know how self-contradictions between pronouncements and violations of safety and surveillance norms can be presented so that the great and powerful (corporations, governments), blinded by power, stumble into the trap and thrash around telegenically for the entertainment of the global public. Henry David Thoreau and Mahatma Gandhi would have been delighted to see Greenpeace using the instruments of the media age to stage worldwide mass civil disobedience. Greenpeace is at the same time a veritable forge of political symbols in which cultural transgressions and symbols of transgression are produced with the artificial means of black-and-white conflicts, which can concentrate protests and turn them into a lightning rod for the collective guilty conscience (see Beck and Grande 2007: 211). This is how new certainties and new outlets for rage are constructed in the enemyless democracy of Europe after the end of the East–West conflict. This is and remains part of the global fairground of symbolic politics.

Isn't all this an absurd distraction from the central challenges of world risk society?

If we focus not on single issues, however, but on the new political constellation, then the stimulus provided by a success experience becomes apparent. In the playful merging of opposites into transcultural global resistance, cosmopolitan society feels its direct power. Everyone knows that nothing is as infectious as success. Anyone who wants to track down what is exciting or thrilling soon discovers that here mass sport and politics fuse with one another on a global scale. It is a kind of political boxing match with active audience participation, all around the world. No normal television entertainment can compete with that; it lacks not only the extra kick of the real, but also the ecological aura of world salvation that no longer meets with opposition. At any event, *this* case study makes clear that the widespread talk of the end of politics and democracy or of the demise of all values – in short, the whole canon of cultural criticism – is foolish because it is blind to history. People only need the slightest touch of the coat-tails of 'tangible' success and they are swept away.

As awareness of the risks spreads, world risk society becomes self-critical. Its foundations, coordinates and ready-made coalitions are thrown into turmoil. Anyone who wants to understand why must inquire into the cultural and political significance of manufactured risks. Risk too is externalized, concentrated subjectivity and history. It is a kind of collective obsessional memory of the fact that our decisions and mistakes are behind what now confronts us. Global risks are the embodiment of the errors of the whole industrial era; they are a kind of collective return of the repressed. In their conscious investigation may lie an opportunity to break the spell of industrial fatalism. If someone wanted to build a machine to counteract the mechanization of society, they would have to use the blueprint of ecological self-endangerment. It is a reification that cries out to be overcome. This is the admittedly tiny chance for global (sub)politics in world risk society (see pp. 180f.).

If the need for a worldwide environmental politics from above is also included, then it becomes apparent that we are condemned to reinvent the political.

*Subpolitics from above: global climate policy and
the potential emergence of the 'cosmopolitan state'*

The global character of risks (climate change) is giving rise to uncertainty – the framing of the global problem, possible organizational responses, legal underpinnings, global economic preconditions and implications, etc. – which is being processed by a whole ensemble of institutions such as the International Monetary Fund, the World Bank, the WTO and the OECD. The directors of these institutions, who represent the incarnation of 'globalization from above', know each other and often move from one organization to the other. They have close contacts with the national think-tanks and decision-making bodies from which they are mainly recruited. Thus a good nickname for such 'experts in matters global' would be 'Mr or Mrs Network'. They are embodiments of the global interdependence and 'discourse coalitions' of which we spoke above. Viewed from the one angle, they sit between the stools in their professional activity but, from the other, they sit 'on several stools'. Under conditions of indeterminate global risks, they are constantly confronted with the contradictions between the different national definitions of their work or the various definitions in terms of global regions. This sets them free from the 'national framings' and enables them to define the shared goals of their work pragmatically and in an ongoing mutual dialogue. It is they who also decide whether what they do explodes the national premises, while for that reason perhaps also being in the global *and* national, hence cosmopolitan, interest. This means that here it is possible (though not necessary) that conceptual factories for forging a cosmopolitan subpolitics may emerge that escape the constraints of the national definition relations of risk politics. The climate report of the former head of the World Bank, Nicholas Stern (2007), written at the behest of the British government, which presented it with great pomp, is an outstanding illustration of this point.

Its major accomplishment as a work of 'stage management' is not only that it transformed the 'rationale' of the climate problem but that it made it into an economic and political policy issue. For years scientists have been presenting compelling reasons why global warming must finally be met with decisive action. Nicholas Stern's study has now added the decisive economic argument. Not so long ago, the associated rational construct – i.e. the way in which catastrophic climate change was 'framed' – boiled down to the alternative of balancing high costs today against a vague risk in the distant future. How much of our current prosperity must we sacrifice to prevent our planet from possibly overheating some time in the future? That was the *staging of a dilemma* that permitted chauvinistic national politicians and sceptical voters to do nothing. The *Stern Review* turns the argument from its head onto its (economic) feet. The costs of taking measures against global warming today are minor in comparison to the costs of doing nothing. In future doing nothing could rob the global economy of 20 per cent of its performance – annually. Thus the new rationale is that what the world invests in climate protection today will be repaid with compound interest in the future. This robs the opponents of the cost argument – there's no excuse left.

If the newly staged 'rationale' is to acquire historical force, however, we need more than a successful demonstration of the lack of economic alternatives to preventive climate protection. In addition, an alliance of global economic actors must be forged, one of whose major goals is to commit the nations and governments who are anxious about their sovereignty to the new vision of multistate cooperation. The lingering doubt concerning one's own argument must be shielded against internal critics. Let us begin with this last point.

Definition relations are relations of domination that confer collective validity and legitimation on the stagings of risk (see pp. 31ff.). In the national constitution of the first modernity they are geared to 'progress'. This means that, in the distribution of the burdens of proof, *laissez-faire* – something is safe until it has been proven dangerous – enjoys priority over the principle of *precaution* – nothing is safe until it has been proven harmless. The Stern Report substitutes the principle of precaution for the laissez-faire distribution of the burdens of proof, not as the result of an official pronouncement and debate or a vote among scientists but through the power of publicly staged arguments. Thus the relations of definition were 'revolutionized' in that now, when faced with manufactured uncertainty and the threat to the planet, the principle which had previously held – 'When in doubt, opt for doubt' – was replaced by the opposite principle – 'When in doubt, opt against doubt.' In view of the threat facing humanity, the irreducible uncertainty of any catastrophe prognosis is played down, as it were, and the option of hiding behind the protective shield of burdens of proof that cannot be satisfied is removed.

The *anticipation dilemma* of self-endangering civilization is either to succumb, because the feared decline regrettably could not be proved, or not to succumb but to expose oneself to the scornful mirth of a scientifically staged global panic echoing through the centuries.

Stern stage-manages the magical power of large numbers. Economists, being economists, will expose his calculations to scrupulous doubt. But the methodology of uncertainty – namely, presenting ranges of possible scenarios rather than absolute prognoses – has in the meantime won the agreement of renowned colleagues.[8]

In general, we should expect methodological misgivings from within the profession gradually to lose their countervailing staging power to the extent that the global economy itself sees decisive political action to counter climate change as a source of new opportunities for markets and growth, as is clearly increasingly the case. The one-time major adversaries of the ecology movement – the oil multinational Shell and the energy companies, etc. – have long since wrapped themselves in a green cloak and are busily looking for ways out of the carbon dioxide business. These are not born again do-gooders who are acting out of humanitarian interest. Business continues to pursue short-term goals that threaten long-term harm to human beings and the environment as (shall we say?) 'acceptable costs of doing business'. Yet the global consensus on climate protection which is now within reach is also creating new markets, 'enforced markets', as can typically occur in the context of acknowledged global risks. The economic attraction here is that safety and precautionary principles prescribed by the state enforce the (ultimately even worldwide) 'consumption' of carbon dioxide-free and energy-efficient technologies. Under a regime of 'green capitalism' composed of transnationally structured ecological enforced markets, ecology no longer represents a hindrance to the economy. Rather the opposite holds: ecology and climate protection could soon represent a direct route to profits.

Ultimately, state politics can be reinvented by actively embracing a policy of climate protection in an alliance with civic groups. In the first place, the attribute 'global' and the honorific term 'climate protection' promise elevated status and weighty responsibility and entice heads of government, ground down in the mills of domestic politics, with the prospect of statesmanlike stature. In the case of Great Britain, there is the additional factor that the term 'global climate protection' revives pleasant memories of the past glories of the 'British Empire' in a humanitarian guise.

The cosmopolitan state has internalized the cosmopolitan outlook in institutional form to the extent that it has ceased to invoke the national outlook and, by actively cultivating connections with other states and civic movements, has taken advantage of the room for manoeuvre opened up by the globalization of the economy and culture (Beck 2005: 217f.). This means in concrete terms that the cosmopolitan room for manoeuvre of the state must be conceptualized and explored at both the conceptual and the political level independently of the received notions of sovereignty and autonomy. In that case the 'sovereignty' or the 'autonomy' of the state would no longer be the primary focus but instead its *practical capacities* in the broadest sense, hence the ability of states to cooperate in solving global problems (Grande and Risse 2000: 253).

To put it even more concretely, the state's recovered cosmopolitan scope for action *extends* its influence in the domestic *and* the foreign domains through action and governance in transnational networks to which other states – but also NGOs, supranational institutions and transnational corporations – belong. Thus the cosmopolitan state, freed from scruples concerning sovereignty, uses the unrecompensed cooperation of other governments, non-governmental organizations and globally operating corporations to solve 'national' problems.

Hence the room for manoeuvre of cosmopolitan states which could be generated by overcoming climate change can no longer be derived from the institutional capacities of national governments. The 'doctrine of government' trapped in methodological nationalism is becoming false because, and to the extent that, it ignores the cosmopolitan extension of power in the national political domain and is incapable of conceptualizing 'national' governance as stomping ground, shunting station and unpaid cooperation and resistance of multinational actors. Reduced to a formula, the scope for action of the cosmopolitan state would be the *sum* of the scopes for action of the national governmental institutions and bureaucracies *plus* the deliberate use of the cooperative capacities of transnational networks.

Of course, this optimistic construction could easily collapse under its own weight. It is fragile because the costs and benefits of an active climate change policy are not equally distributed, either internationally or nationally, and because the burning question of justice in a radically unequal world is at the heart of the distribution conflicts. The costs will hit existing generations hardest whereas the benefits will fall to the grandchildren of our grandchildren. The wealthiest countries must demonstrate the greatest willingness to compromise even though they are not the most vulnerable to the impacts of global warming. In order to strike the required 'global deal', the agreement of the United States is most urgently needed, even though it would have to pay China, its arch-rival, gigantic sums in order to make that country carbon dioxide-free – at a historical juncture when this huge country is preparing to overtake the United States economically and to become the centre of world power. The counter-argument is easy to foresee: the poor must pay for the highflying dreams of rescuing the world. Thus there are many reasons for resignation. But a large-scale political experiment of historic dimensions has begun that will exert a great fascination, as a global drama or also as a global comedy, and probably both.

The subpolitics of terror

A series of key features (aside from the general difference between intentional and side effects catastrophes) differentiates the terrorist risk society from the environmental risk society: What lends the subpolitics of terror the power to stage 'felt war' (see pp. 146ff.)?

Ecological risks are *hidden* risks which for the most part escape everyday perception, often rest on abstract scientific models and calculations (climate change) and are correspondingly controversial; but above all they cannot be locally circumscribed. This is the precise point of application of the Greenpeace method of dramatizing invisible processes on the global stage. By contrast, acts of terrorism rip arbitrary groups of people to pieces in a particular place at a particular time, and the global images and echoes staged in the mass media worm their way into people's heads as an omnipresent terrorist risk. In the former case, the expectation of the catastrophe must first be fabricated against the evidence of everyday life, in the latter, the generalized expectation of the catastrophe springs from the traumatic evidence of the intentional catastrophe.

In the end nobody can be made responsible for ecological destruction on the prevailing relations of definition. The terrorist who indicts and convicts himself as perpetrator through his insane act poses a direct and profound challenge to the citizens' interest in, and the state's promise to provide, security through the deliberate unpredictability of his action. Hence, anticipating intentional catastrophes becomes as necessary as it is difficult, if not impossible.

In this general situation everyone must invest in prevention. At first sight, prevention always represents the superior option because it frustrates the insane act; and the pressure towards pre-active alertness grows with the insanity of the anticipated terrorist attacks. The greater the threat – or the greater it is made – the more easily democratic majorities can be won for restrictions on freedom. Faced with the alternative between freedom and security, the majority of the population would presumably always opt for security. The prevention state doesn't need publicity, or, more precisely, the terrorist attacks, whose expectation is an ubiquitous everyday presence, are the best advertisement for the prevention and security state which is threatening the foundations of the constitutional state.

This priority of prevention means that society as a whole is transposed into the *subjunctive mood* by the anticipation of terrorism. What *could* happen? This transformation of society means, in turn, that mistrust of 'aliens' and condemnation in advance increases not only in the perception of the population but also in the legal and institutional practices of the police, the secret services and the administration of justice. Since the passage of new anti-terrorism laws in Great Britain, the security authorities have at their disposal the power arsenal of a police state. They can eavesdrop on the telephone conversations of 'presumed' suspects and plant bugs without court permission. The police can also take 'suspected' terrorists into custody and hold them for four weeks without accusing them of any specific offence.

As far as society's way of dealing with the terrorist risk goes, there are only *dead* terrorists or *suspected* terrorists. The former have paid for the proof of their guilt with their lives. The latter group, by contrast, is difficult to narrow down. 'Racial profiling' refers to the practice of exposing a whole group of people to general suspicion on the basis of their race or religion. Such practices used to be frowned upon in democratic societies. If there was no evidence, then at least concrete incriminating factors had to be cited in order to trigger investigations. In the could-be society, unearthing sources of danger is becoming a frantic, suspicionless quest. Everyone must count on becoming a victim of surveillance, not only in the public domain but also especially in the private sphere, with all the attendant violations. This tendency is growing to the extent that the profile of the perpetrators does *not* coincide with alien stereotypes, such as conspirators from Palestinian refugee camps or from poor Pakistani families. They are much more likely to be 'nice boys from the neighbourhood' who were born in our country and grew up in good middle-class and well-integrated immigrant families. The most conspicuous thing about the members of this perpetrator group is their inconspicuousness. Which also means that everyone is conspicuous. This, of course, prompts general unease.

The paucity of evidence is increasing in the could-be society. Since both the paucity of evidence and the threat are increasing, the probability that the lack of evidence will be subject to revaluation and that evidentiary norms will be relaxed is growing (Hudson 2003). As stated, the investigative authorities face the dilemma that the auto-conviction of the attackers comes too late, whereas, by contrast, the earlier they intervene to prevent an insane attack, the more difficult it becomes to convict these potential, suspected terrorists of their crime in accordance with existing criteria of evidence. In the could-be society, where the logic of possibility is undermining the logic of reality, it may in the end only be necessary to prove the possibility of the crime – whatever that may mean – in order to justify a conviction. The conclusion here, too, is that the generalized terrorist risk is threatening to weaken the presumption of innocence – that everyone is innocent as long as he cannot be proven guilty – and to transform it into its opposite: when in doubt, the *presumptive* terrorist, hence everybody, must in the end prove their innocence. One can only hope that the leader of the extreme right-wing British National Party was more or less alone when he demanded a general prohibition on air travel for male Muslims aged between fifteen and fifty. Yet the warning of human rights experts that 'racial profiling' would affect Muslims disproportionately, and hence would be discriminatory, is becoming increasingly ineffectual. After all – goes the sarcastic counter-argument – suicide attackers are also recruited disproportionately among Muslims. The anticipation of intentional catastrophes unleashes waves of aggravated imputation. Being different and being dangerous are entering into (not so) new relations. Everywhere people are hastening to classify – either dangerous or not dangerous – in accordance with the tried and trusted 'us and them' stereotypes.

This leads to amplification effects. The trend towards excluding risk corresponds to the trend towards auto-stigmatization. People increasingly conform to the stereotype that the Islamophobe prejudice sees in Muslims: more headscarves, more external signs of difference. People are excluding themselves. With the Internet and satellite television, the globalization of the media is making it easier for immigrants never even to arrive where they live and work but to remain instead in the virtual present of their countries of origin. The old scare word 'identity' has regained its power: because we are different, the others cannot understand us. Under these conditions, the ideology of resistance to 'globalization', political Islamism, is becoming increasingly attractive. With the fiction of the world-spanning umma living in conformity with sharia, it offers the prospect of an anti-modern counter-globalization.

How far the terrorist attacks have already pushed the West in the direction of the could-be society is shown by the impacts of the *frustrated* terrorist attack in London in August 2006. Although nothing happened (because the plan to blow up American passenger aircraft could be prevented), the anticipation of the terrorist attacks transformed the institutional conditions of this anticipation profoundly. Henceforth, no liquids (e.g. shaving cream) can be taken on board aeroplanes in carry-on bags; exceptions such as baby food must be meticulously checked before boarding. In Dulles Airport in Washington, carry-on bananas had to be peeled under the suspicious eyes of security personnel. The result is that the additional costs for security in airline travel, which are now set to increase, operate like a tax on the international division of labour, and this, as a side effect of the side effect, can promote a policy of climate protection by reducing airline traffic. The subpolitics of terrorism – the 'recruits of madness' (*Der Spiegel*) – do not conform to the image of military organizations according to which there is a 'leader' (Bin Laden) who devises the strategy which is then implemented by the lower ranks. Here the operative organizational model is the transnational model of *hierarchy-free, horizontal terrorism* in which potentially everyone who satisfies the necessary preconditions – namely, hatred and an Internet connection – can become or turn themselves into 'do-it-yourself terrorists'. Just as transnational corporations increasingly rely upon 'self-entrepreneurs', there are also self-entrepreneur terrorists specializing in religious war.

'Today al-Qaeda does not stand for the decentralization of killing but for its individualization. Every poorly integrated, failed or disappointed Muslim can feel himself called to lend his botched existence an ostensibly higher meaning' (*Der Spiegel* 33 (2006): 96).

The subpolitics of terror means the *individualization* of war. The individual suicide attacker is the David versus Goliath rebellion in its most radical form. By sacrificing himself as an instrument of mass murder, the individual can endow his insignificant life with a heroic meaning precisely because he traps the gun-slinging superpower in the autoparalysis of anticipation. Conversely, it is the *glamour of terror* as staged in the West which transforms terrorism into a power drug. One need only entertain the thought experiment of what would happen if the Western states and the mass media were to agree on a ban on information on terrorist attacks; first, the threat (expectation) of terrorism would collapse and, second, the offence would lose much of its world-historical halo of terror.

Those who, as happens in the West, reduce the terrorist rebellion at the centre of the centre solely to a security problem are playing into the hands of the terrorists. For – hard as it may be to conceive from a parochial Western point of view – the overt or latent support which the terrorists enjoy in the so-called Third World is essentially bound up with the fact that terrorist subpolitics constitutes the most illegitimate and effective means conceivable to pose a key problem in the global public arena and to direct it against economic globalization: How can *justice* and *dignity* be realized simultaneously in the global age? To put it differently and more pointedly: because the West with its one-dimensional globalization both taboos and sabotages the justice question, terrorism finds a sympathetic response, and often even tacit approval, in a radically unequal world as a last-ditch ideology of resistance in the eyes of those who are overrun and put in the shade by Western modernity. Thus it would be a fatal error even to entertain the idea that it is the method of madness – and not a renewed Enlightenment for the global era – which places the question of justice on the global political agenda. For the Arab public, the West often stands for cultural decadence and economic imperialism whose fragile arrogance must be countered with the anti-modernity of political Islamism.

The so-called Third World feels inferior precisely because it adopts so much from the West – science, mobile phones, the Internet, fashions, national sovereignty, a profit-oriented mindset, individualism. They hate what is steamrollering them and making them dependent. The hatred of Western modernity is a product of its *triumph*. Terrorism is the response to the dilemma of those who have long since become part of the West while at the same time being unable to reconcile themselves to the fact that the West is shaping the world according to its image. *That* is the global context in which terrorist subpolitics develops its world-political aura.

6

The Provident State or: On the Antiquatedness of Linear Pessimism Concerning Progress

As explained elsewhere in this book, industrial society can be described as a form of society that produces its negative effects and self-endangerments systematically but *without* thematizing them publicly as political conflicts.

A completely different situation exists when the hazards produced by industrial society dominate public, political and private debates. The institutions of industrial·society create and legitimize risks that they cannot control. Industrial society then sees and criticizes itself *as* risk society.

The concept of 'reflexive modernization' can be introduced as a consequence of these two stages. This does *not* signify *reflection* (as the adjective 'reflexive' seems to suggest), but above all *self-confrontation*. The transition from the industrial to the risk era of modernity takes place *un*intentionally, *un*seen and under duress in the course of a self-perpetuating dynamic of modernization, on the model of *unintended side effects*. One can say that constellations of the risk society are created because the self-evident truths of industrial society (the consensus on progress, the abstraction from environmental consequences and hazards) dominate the thinking and behaviour of people and institutions. Risk society is *not* an option that could be chosen or rejected in the course of political debates. It arises through the self-propelling process of modernization which is blind and deaf to consequences and dangers. Cumulatively and latently these produce self-endangerments that invalidate the principles of industrial society.

Risks always rest on decisions; they presuppose the possibility to make decisions. They are the result of the transformation of uncertainties and threats into decisions (and they necessitate decisions, which in turn generate risks).[1] The incalculable threats are transformed into calculable risks by industrial society. This leads to the emergence of a variety of insurance systems; indeed society comes to be understood by insurers as a risk community – as a *provident state* [*Vorsorgestaat*] and a *providing state* [*Versorgungsstaat*] (Ewald 1993). The unpredictable is transformed into something predictable; what has not yet occurred becomes the object of present (precautionary) action. The dialectic of the risk and insurance calculus furnishes the requisite cognitive and institutional instruments.

The entry into risk society occurs at the moment at which the manufactured risks undermine or annul the provident state's prevailing risk calculations. Those who ask for an operational criterion for this transition find their answer here: *the absence of private insurance protection.* To be more precise, industrial, technical-scientific projects are *uninsurable* (on this, see chapter 8). Industrial society, which has involuntarily mutated into risk society through the manufactured threats, teeters *beyond the domain of private-sector insurance.* The rationality which led to this boundary being drawn springs from the rationality at the core of this society, namely, *economic* rationality. It is the private insurance companies which patrol the frontier of risk society. By insisting on the logic of economic action, they contradict the protestations of safety made by the technicians and the companies in the danger industry. They state that in the case of 'low probability but high consequences risks' the technical risk may tend towards zero; nevertheless the economic risk tends towards the infinite. A straightforward mental experiment reveals the extent of the normalized state of neglect. Anyone who today makes private insurance protection, such as is taken for granted by every car owner, a precondition for establishing an advanced and dangerous industrial production apparatus simultaneously proclaims the demise of major sectors of so-called cutting-edge technologies and large research organizations, which all operate without any, or any adequate, insurance cover.

Paradoxically, risk society also tends to be a *self-critical* society. Insurance experts contradict safety engineers. Where the latter diagnose zero risk, the former declare it to be uninsurable.

1   The end of linear technocracy?

One prognosis can be derived from the foregoing: the decisions and the 'objective laws' of scientific-technological progress are becoming political issues. This invites the question: Is the growing awareness of risk society synonymous with the *invalidation of the linear models of technocracy* – whether they are optimistic or pessimistic concerning progress – which have fascinated society and its science for the past hundred years?

In the 1960s, Helmut Schelsky (drawing on Max Weber, Thorstein Veblen, Arnold Gehlen and many others) argued that the modern state has to internalize technology with progressive technologization and the penetration of science into all spheres of life in order to preserve and expand its power. It thereby pursues normative or political state goals less and less but responds to technological constraints – it is becoming a 'technological state'. In other words, the instrumental rationalization and the encroachment of technology are consuming the substance of a society in the grip of modernization. Increasingly it is experts who are governing where politicians are nominally in charge.

Technical-scientific decisions cannot be subjected to any form of democratic decision-making; otherwise they would become ineffective. If the political decisions of government leaders are made in accordance with scientifically sanctioned causal laws, then the government has become an organ for administering objective necessities, and the parliament a body for monitoring the correctness of expert opinion. (Schelsky 1965: 459)

Jost Halfmann points out that, from the perspective of the sociology of risk, Schelsky assumes 'a development of society in the direction of zero risk' (1990: 21). In this way, the explosive force of a development of modernity that transforms everything into decisions, and hence into risks, remains completely unrecognized.

[High-]risk technologies flatly contradict technocratic theoretical expectations. . . . The central position of the state in the material promotion and political regulation of technological progress has enabled political institutions to assume an important role in the 'liability' for the consequences of progress vis-à-vis society. Technological progress and its consequences have thereby taken on the character of collective goods. (Ibid.: 26)

When society has become a laboratory (Krohn and Weyer 1989; Beck 2002), decisions concerning, and the monitoring of, technological progress become a collective problem.

Science is no longer an experimental activity without consequences, and technology is no longer the low-risk application of secure knowledge. Science and technology generate risks by performing their experiments and thereby burden society as a whole with the task of managing the risks. . . . Depending on the risk culture, quite different strategic consequences result for dealing with risk. Industrialists assess risks according to cost–benefit principles; market failure becomes the main focus of risk avoidance. Bureaucracies assess risks according to hypothetical definitions of the common good and look for redistributive solutions in coping with risks; here the main problem is the institutional integrity of the administrative apparatus. Social movements measure risks according to the potential for catastrophe involved and try to avoid risks which could entail a threat to present and future quality of life. The effective irreconcilability of these various risk assessments transforms concrete decisions over acceptable risks into struggles for power. 'The issue is not risk, but power' (Charles Perrow). (Ibid.: 28; see above pp. 29ff.)

What is at stake in this new risk conflict, as Christoph Lau demonstrates, is not so much the avoidance of risk as its distribution, which means that it is about the *architecture of risk definition* in view of the growing competition among overlapping discourses of risk (e.g. nuclear power versus the hole in the ozone layer):

Debates over risk definitions and their consequences for society take place essentially at the level of public (or quasi-public) discourses. They are conducted with the aid of scientific arguments and information which serve as the scarce resources of the collective actors, as it were. The scientifically permeated public sphere then becomes the symbolic location of conflicts over distribution, even if this is disguised by the objectifying, scientistic logic of expert arguments concerning risk. (Lau 1991: 254)

Thus risk definitions trace boundary lines within society by attempting to define factors such as the size, position and social characteristics of the groups responsible for or affected by the risks in question. As such, they become the target of controversies.

Whereas, within the context of the 'old' distribution conflicts, the success of strategic action can be identified and measured by differentiated media (money, ownership of the means of production, wage settlements, vote counts), such symbolic media, which could clearly represent risk gain and risk loss, are scarcely available. All attempts to establish yardsticks of risk, such as probability estimates, threshold values and calculations of costs, etc., founder in the case of late industrial risks on the incommensurability of threats and the problem of the subjective assessment of probabilities of occurrence. This explains why conflicts essentially break out at the epistemic level around problems of definition and causal relationships. Primary resources in this struggle over risk justice are not directly strikes, vote counts and political influence but above all information, scientific findings, assessments and arguments. (Lau 1991: 254)

Niklas Luhmann takes this pattern of risk conflict as his point of departure. In Luhmann the distinction between risk and danger coincides with the opposition between *decision-makers* and those *affected* by the decision. Agreement between the two is difficult, though not impossible. Nevertheless, no clear lines of conflict develop because the confrontation between decision-makers and those affected varies according to topic and situation.

We talk of risks if possible future injury is attributable to one's own decision. If you don't board an aeroplane, you cannot crash. Dangers, by contrast, are a matter of external harms. If, say, to stay with the example, you are killed by falling aircraft wreckage. . . . The familiar dangers – earthquakes, volcanic eruptions, aquaplaning and marriages – become risks insofar as it becomes known through which decisions one can avoid exposing oneself to them. . . . But this clarifies only half of the situation. For, with the decisions, the dangers also increase once again, specifically in the form of dangers resulting from the decisions of others. . . . Thus today the distinction between risk and danger cuts through the social order. One person's risk is another person's threat. The smoker may risk cancer, but for others it is a danger. The car driver who makes a risky overtaking manoeuvre behaves in just the same way, the builder and operator of nuclear power stations, genetic engineering research – there is no shortage of examples. (Luhmann 1991: 81)

The impossibility, or at any rate the sheer insurmountability, of the barriers to agreement results from the perception and evaluation of catastrophes. Here the yardstick of the 'rationality' of the probability of occurrence fails.

> It may indeed be true that the danger emanating from a nearby nuclear power station is no greater than the risk involved in deciding to drive a couple of extra miles per year. But who will be impressed by this argument? The prospect of catastrophes represents a barrier to calculation. We want to avoid it at all costs – even if it is extremely improbable. But where does the catastrophe threshold lie beyond which quantitative calculations are no longer convincing? Clearly this question cannot be answered independently of further variables. It is different for rich and poor, for those who are dependent and those who are independent. . . . The really interesting question is what counts as a catastrophe. And this is presumably a question that will be answered very differently by decision-makers and victims. (Luhmann 1991: 91; on this, see below chapters 9 and 10).

This may be true, but it fails to recognize the systemic yardstick of economic insurance rationality. Risk society is the *uninsured* society in which insurance protection *decreases* with the scale of the danger – and this in the historic milieu of the 'welfare state' that includes all areas of life and of the comprehensive insurance society. Only both together – uninsured *and* comprehensive insurance society – explain the explosive political force of risk society.

2   On the antiquatedness of linear pessimism concerning progress

The ancestral gallery of profound and dogged critics of modernity is long and includes many hallowed names. The best thinkers in Europe have taken this side, including during the twentieth century. In these overpowering analyses one can read how the authors are themselves spellbound by the process they describe. Sometimes a hopeful little chapter is tacked on at the end which is like a deep sigh at the decline of the world in the face of the general hopelessness, and then the author makes his exit leaving his shattered readers stranded in the veil of tears portrayed. Hopelessness is ennobling, to be sure, and affords the considerable advantage of wallowing in superiority while being relieved of all responsibility for action. If the proposed diagnosis of the ambivalence of world risk society is correct, however, then the theorists of doom can begin to rejoice because their theories are *false* or will become so.

In a discussion of the English edition of my book *Risk Society*, Zygmunt Bauman offered a further brilliant summary of the arguments which encourage people to sit back and do nothing. The problem is not only that we are confronting challenges on an undreamt of scale but, more problematically, all attempted solutions contain the seeds of new, more difficult problems.

[T]he most fearsome of disasters are those traceable to the past or present pursuits of rational solutions. Catastrophes most horrid are born – or are likely to be born – out of the war against catastrophes. . . . Dangers grow with our powers, and the one power we miss most is that which divines their arrival and sizes up their volume. (Bauman, 1992b: 25)

But even where risks are taken up, it is always only the symptoms that are combated, never the causes, because the struggle against the risks of unrestrained business activity has itself become

a major business, offering a new lease of life to scientific/technological dreams of unlimited expansion. In our society, risk fighting can be nothing else but business – the bigger it is, the more impressive and reassuring. The politics of fear lubricates the wheels of consumerism and helps to 'keep the economy growing' and steers it away from the 'bane of recession'. Ever more resources are to be consumed in order to repair the gruesome effects of yesterday's resource consumption. Individual fears beefed up by the exposure of yesterday's risks are deployed in the service of collective production of the unknown risks of tomorrow . . . (Bauman 1992b: 25)

Bauman explicitly takes up the idea of reflexive modernization:

Beck has not lost hope (some would say illusion) that 'reflexivity' can accomplish what 'rationality' failed to do. . . . What amounts to another *apologia* for science (now boasting reflexivity as a weapon more trustworthy than the rationality of yore and claiming the untried credentials of risk-anticipating instead of those of discredited problem-solving) can be upheld only as long as the rule of science in the past and present plight of humanity is overstated and/or demonized. But it is only in the mind of the scientists and their hired or voluntary court-poets that knowledge (*their* knowledge) 'determines being'. And reflexivity, like rationality, is a double-edged sword. Servant as much as a master; healer as much as a hangman. (Bauman 1992b: 25)

Bauman speaks of 'reflexivity' but fails to recognize the peculiar relation between reflex and reflection within risk society. What is meant is precisely not more of the same – science, research into effects and self-steering. Rather, in reflexive modernity the forms and principles of the industrial society are dissolved.

Bauman, the social theorist of ambivalence, conceives of modernity in much too linear terms. The banal possibility that something unforeseeable could emerge from the unforeseeable (and the more incalculable, the more surprising) is lost from view. Yet it is with this adventure of decision-based unpredictability that the social history is being rewritten at the start of the twenty-first century (chapters 11 and 12).

7

Knowledge or Non-Knowing? Two Perspectives of 'Reflexive Modernization'

1 Point of departure

Living in world risk society means living with ineradicable non-knowing [*Nichtwissen*] or, to be more precise, with the simultaneity of threats and non-knowing and the resulting political, social and moral paradoxes and dilemmas. Because of the global character of the threat, the need and burden of having to make life-and-death decisions increase with non-knowing. Talk of the 'knowledge society' is a euphemism of the first modernity. World risk society is a *non*-knowledge society in a very precise sense. In contrast to the premodern era, it cannot be overcome by more and better knowledge, more and better science; rather precisely the opposite holds: it is the *product* of more and better science. Non-knowledge rules in the world risk society. Hence, living in the milieu of manufactured non-knowing means seeking unknown answers to questions that nobody can clearly formulate.

To forestall the most serious misunderstandings, I distinguish between 'knowledge' and 'truth' (cf. Wehling 2006) as an initial conceptual guideline. I do not speak of 'knowledge' or 'non-knowing' in the cognitive sense common in philosophy, in the theory of science or in natural science, but in the sociological sense, which construes 'knowledge' as *expectation*, as social attribution and construction. Thus, the sociologist of knowledge – or, to be more precise, the sociologist of non-knowing – can mount, classify and systematize the diverse species of non-knowing much as an entomologist would butterflies or greenflies: provisional non-knowing, unacknowledged non-knowing, wilful ignorance [*Nicht-Wissen-Wollen*] and – a particularly striking and interesting specimen – conscious and unconscious inability-to-know [*Nicht-Wissen-Können*].

Non-knowing permeates and transforms human conditions of life and suffering, expert and control systems, the notions of sovereignty and state authority, of law and human dignity. The theory of world risk society both compels and enables the reconceptualization of the basic constants, concepts and institutions of the modern world.

Manufactured non-knowing as existential condition: On 26 April 1986, a nuclear reactor exploded in Chernobyl. This catastrophe not only destroyed human immune systems and the genetic structure of human cells and contaminated the soil, rivers and plants; it also contaminated social life and political action, indeed almost all public institutions – expert systems, hospitals, the social security system, political parties and the national self-understanding – with different forms of more or less controversial non-knowing. The nuclear explosion was accompanied by an explosion of non-knowledge, and this inextricable intermeshing of nuclear contamination and non-knowledge constitutes the strange, symptomatic, thoroughly Kafkaesque character of the post-Chernobyl world.[1]

First we must highlight a basic feature of life in world risk society, namely, the expropriation of the senses, and hence of common sense, as an anthropological precondition of self-conscious life and judgement. Human life is thereby jeopardized to its very core and individuals are robbed of their power of judgement. For the 'affected' lifeworlds (and to what extent it is 'affected' is not known because that is part of the non-knowledge), the inability-to-know has become an ineradicable part of their lamentable condition. Hence those who are robbed of their senses and judgement must use the knowledge and non-knowing which they accumulate concerning their lamentable condition as a 'currency' to negotiate their biological, social, economic and political survival in their struggle with the controlling authorities.

Of course, there are different, competing theories of radiation. One such theory asserts, for example, that radioactivity would – possibly – trigger genetic illnesses only above a specific dose. Others hypothesize that any dose, even the most minute, is harmful, which is why illnesses are destined to become more frequent, often with a time lag and at a spatial and social remove, as the dose increases. New research brings forth new results and new hypotheses. Generalizations arrived at by different methods, even those based on attempts of victims to derive evidence from their own suffering, are dismissed as speculative and as symptoms of 'radiation phobia'. But the 'truth' changes. What used to count as knowing is becoming non-knowing, and non-knowing is acquiring the status of knowledge. Biological definitions change, in part as a result of 'technological progress', in part as a result of political guidelines. People suffering from genetic disorders are then suddenly cured and healthy people are stricken with genetic illnesses. In the process, the statistical principles for classifying 'casualties' and 'fatalities' are changed. Then human suffering, medical controls, the extent of the risk and of the 'population at risk', the illness and the resulting welfare claims have to be reassessed in geographical and political terms. Depending on the specific battle array of non-scientific and medical knowledge and non-knowledge, old indicators of suffering lose their meaning and validity. Constantly and rapidly changing statistical knowledge is increasingly succumbing to the domination of non-knowing.

Since governments and authorities must continually reaffirm and re-establish their control over uncontrollable risks, people are exposed to a barrage of shifting forms of more or less (acknowledged) non-knowledge of scientific standards, biochemical categories and welfare state compensation claims. Estimates of the number of victims of the Chernobyl reactor catastrophe fluctuate between 31,000 and hundreds of thousands of deaths. 'Contaminated' geographical areas and those declared 'safe' also shift. But who is willing to rely on such distinctions? Unofficial maps of the contamination are produced alongside the official maps, state maps, revised state or internationally authorized maps, or ones circulated by NGOs. These related forms of hushed-up, conscious or unconscious non-knowing give rise to the strangest paradoxes.

Such paradoxes seem to be the exception but the normal case is not much different. In its cover story on 'Living with Risk' (28 July 2003), *Time* magazine described in detail how inescapably people in the advanced countries have become entangled in indistinct risks and in irreducible, scientifically generated non-knowledge. Scientists can determine the risks posed by genetically modified foods, mobile phones and the everyday use of chemicals at best through probability calculations; but that says nothing about whether they are genuine risks and how the consumer can make a 'rational' choice in a given situation. Which concerns should one have and in what situations? Where are the boundary lines between prudent concern, crippling fear and hysteria? And who should decide – scientists, whose results often contradict each other at a particular moment and change radically over longer periods of time? Take BSE, SARS or avian flu. The schema – the link between non-knowledge and threat – is everywhere similar. Here the lack of knowledge extends, among other things, to the source of the illness, to the paths of transmission and to the latency period following an infection. And depending on whether one understands this lack of knowledge as a reason for doing nothing or, on the contrary, as a reason for prompt, preventive action in view of the catastrophic threat which can be avoided only in this way, one arrives at radically divergent worldviews and conclusions.

The greater the threat, the greater the gap in knowledge, the more urgent and more impossible is the decision (decision paradox). Expectations were high when industrial production of chlorofluorocarbons (CFCs) began in the United States in 1930 (Böschen et al. 2004). It all seemed perfect: the chemical properties – non-toxic, non-flammable, odourless – opened up undreamt-of possibilities for the refrigerator market. Who could have dreamt that, of all things, a general-purpose chemical also used in hairsprays and deodorants would lead to an almost irreversible thinning out of the ozone layer, which protects human beings against skin cancer, among other things? It was only scientific hypotheses formulated during the 1970s and the discovery of the hole in the ozone layer over the Antarctic in 1985 that revealed one of the most dramatic and far-reaching examples of environmental non-knowledge.

The threat posed by CFCs is that, in future, the ozone layer could be broken down so that the sun would become a threat to life instead of its source. The boundary between knowledge and the lack of knowledge is becoming blurred. This is becoming paradigmatic because, for more than forty years, science did not even know what it did not know. Thus the issue is not the traditional problem of what is not yet known but unconscious or unacknowledged non-knowledge; and it is the inability-to-know in this form that must be regarded as the 'cause' of the threat to the human race. It is a case of *un*intended inability-to-know, at any rate at the moment of decision.

The ongoing controversy over the release of genetically modified organisms exhibits clear parallels to the ozone case. For to date there has also been little or no knowledge concerning the long-term effects of the production, release and utilization of trans-genic plants and animals. The situation has changed, however, to the extent that the 'risks of non-knowledge' (Krohn), and also and especially of unrecognized non-knowledge, have now themselves become a focus of controversy between supporters and critics of genetic engineering, not least as a result of the CFC case. How much lack of knowledge can one 'afford' without conjuring up uncontrollable hazards? Which suppositions and hypotheses concerning our lack of knowledge seem to be relevant and which can one 'safely' ignore? 'Which mixture of knowledge and lack of knowledge and which mixture of control and chance is tolerable for responsible action?' (van den Daele). A major source of controversy in this context is which social authorities and institutions are both legitimate and in a position to answer such questions and what criteria should be employed in the process. (Wehling 2006: 11f.)

Intentional non-knowing must be carefully distinguished from this, however. One might say that the essence of al-Qaeda terrorism resides in organized non-knowledge. Since it is impossible to know where and when it will attack, al-Qaeda has dissolved into a cloud of al-Qaedaism. From the beginning al-Qaeda was a flexible organization, a complex, worldwide network of shifting alliances and marriages of convenience with other shadowy groups. Following the attacks in the United States, al-Qaeda's 'centre of gravity' shifted to anywhere and nowhere. Methods for making the terrorist risk calculable either focus on studying the motivations of terrorist groups or try to narrow down and estimate the probability of a nuclear ter-rorist attack, for example (or they combine both methods). Common to both is a failure to grasp the aims of these terrorist networks and the basis of their extremely successful mode of operation, namely, the distinction between actual catastrophes and the globalized *expectation* of catastrophes, hence the terrorist risk or, more precisely, the organized conscious ignorance concern-ing the next terrorist attack.

In the case of both unintended and intentional non-knowing, one can compensate for normal catastrophes, but not for the greatest possible catas-trophes. They *have to* be prevented. The compensation principle is replaced by the precautionary principle. However, compensation and precaution obey different logics. Compensation rests on the mathematical craft of calculating possibility and probability. Taking precautions against the worst case scenario, by contrast, must rely on more or less fictive suppositions, hypotheses and imaginary scenarios because it *cannot* and *must not* rest on corresponding experiences. It is too late when weapons of mass destruction fall into the hands of terrorist groups. Averting such greatest possible catastrophes through precautionary measures, therefore, changes the meaning of risk. The precautionary principle contains the injunction to relativize analyses of probability and to give free rein to the imagination of threats, and hence to base decisions on dubious hypotheses or mere suspicions. Again, what cannot be known must be prevented. In this way, danger itself becomes a source of danger. The preventive measures against catastrophic risks themselves trigger catastrophic risks, which may in the end be even greater than the catastrophes to be prevented. The Iraq War is a textbook example of this. This was presented, among other things, as a war against terrorism but has had the effect of transforming Iraq into a playground for terrorists.

2   Two perspectives of 'reflexive modernization'

Starting points: institutional reflection, reflexive community, side effects

It is difficult to avoid misunderstanding the concept of 'reflexivity'. Anthony Giddens, Scott Lash and I developed the concept and theory of reflexive modernization in two distinct and yet overlapping directions. In the first view (represented by Giddens and Lash), '*reflexive*' modernization is associated primarily (in keeping with its literal meaning) with *knowledge* (reflection) concerning the foundations, consequences and problems of modernization. In the second, represented by my thesis (at first sight apparently at odds with the literal meaning), reflexive modernization is primarily the result of *side effects* of modernization. In the first case, one could speak of *reflection* (narrowly construed), in the second, of the *reflexivity* (in the wider sense) of modernization – in the wider sense because reflexivity, in addition to reflection (knowledge), also involves the idea of a 'reflex' in the sense of the (preventive) effect of *not* knowing. (However, this terminology is unfortunate because it invites misunderstandings.)

A particular difficulty of this distinction is that it is not really sharp. Thus, in speaking of the 'century of side effects' without contradicting oneself, one cannot appeal to absolute, but only to relative non-knowing, and the interesting issue is the nature of this relativity. Who knows what, why and why not? How are knowing and non-knowing constructed, acknowledged, problematized, denied, asserted and excluded? Thus the idea of 'side effects' does not contradict the understanding of knowledge in reflexive modernization; instead it opens up a wider and more complex scenario that includes non-knowing as well as the various forms and constructions of knowledge (Böschen et al. 2006). Thus, when I explain reflexive modernization with reference to Anthony Giddens and Scott Lash, I am also speaking in a certain sense of my own understanding of this concept. Whereas all three of us include the knowledge aspect, Giddens and Lash fail to recognize the importance of side effects and non-knowing.

Reflexive modernization says something about late modernity, reflecting on the limitations and difficulties of modernity itself. That relates to key problems of modern politics, because simple or linear modernization still predominates in some parts of the world, most notably in South-East Asia, at least up until recently. In the West and the developed industrial societies, there are conditions of reflexive modernization, with the key problem of modernization being what modernization itself is all about. (Giddens and Pierson, 1998: 110)

Giddens's approach to knowledge under conditions of reflexive modernization can be summarized as follows:

- The more society modernizes, the more knowledge it generates concerning its foundations, structures, dynamics and conflicts.
- The more knowledge about itself it possesses and the more it applies it, the more expressly is tradition-guided action replaced by a knowledge-dependent, scientifically mediated global reconstruction of social structures and institutions.
- Knowledge compels decisions and creates new contexts of action. Individuals are liberated from structures and they must redefine their situation of action under conditions of manufactured insecurity in forms and strategies of 'reflected' modernization.

A difficulty with this approach to knowledge is that *some* form of knowledge, consciousness, reflection, communication and self-observation is relevant not only for all modern but also for all *traditional* societies. In fact, as all schools of sociology have stressed, from Max Weber through Georg Simmel to Erving Goffman and Harold Garfinkel, it is a basic feature of *every* social interaction. There is a beautiful image for the idea of reflection which has been so central since the Enlightenment, namely, seeing which is equipped with an 'eye' of its own (Fichte). Alvin Gouldner speaks of 'reflexive sociology' and Jürgen Habermas of the 'communicative society'. Emphasizing the 'self-referentiality of systems' (Niklas Luhmann), by contrast, shifts the focus to a very different aspect of self-referentiality. In the opposition between consciousness and unconsciousness, Pierre Bourdieu takes a mediating position. He conceives of 'reflexivity' as systematic reflection on the unconscious preconditions (categories) of our knowledge.

The universality of the concept of reflection represents a problem for any epistemology of reflexive modernization. Either one clings to an undifferentiated concept of reflection, in which case the term 'reflexive modernization' becomes a mere pleonasm, a more or less grandiose tautology; or one distinguishes between different species and types of knowledge and associates statements concerning late, and hence reflexive modern societies with *particular* types of knowledge and reflection. The latter path is the one taken by Anthony Giddens and Scott Lash. Giddens speaks of 'institutionalized reflexivity' to describe the treatment of scientific and expert knowledge concerning the principles of social action. This authorized knowledge deflects social conduct from its prescribed courses and integrates it into new contexts; in other words, it is the motor of change in structures and forms of social action.

To illustrate this view with an example: the reflexive appropriation of information tends to increase the instability of financial markets – they can develop in unexpected directions, become chaotic, be used by free riders and lead to herd behaviour. For the financial wizard and multimillionaire George Soros, the financial markets must be classified among those momentous global risks which are influenced by information about and perceptions of these risks. One could even hazard the assertion that the global reflection of these global financial risks may be one of the triggers of a total economic collapse.

What we are finding now is that the world isn't quite as the Enlightenment thinkers assumed. Increasing our knowledge about the world, the drive to produce information, create new forms of risk for which we have little prior experience – and which can't be calculated on the basis of established time-series, for the data don't exist. Risk in financial markets is also problematic and complicated because it becomes more reflexive . . . What I call 'manufactured uncertainty' is bound up more with the advance of knowledge than with its limitations. (Giddens and Pierson 1998: 104–5)

The more dominant the 'reflexive appropriation of knowledge' becomes in the interaction between the institutional dimensions, the more uncontrollable become the global interrelations in a world that is increasingly merging into a single planetary unit. Giddens uses the concept of 'trust' to explain the relation between the internal dynamics of systems and human influence. Whereas the relations between people and their environment in traditional social systems were determined by standardized rules of behaviour and action that guaranteed something like an 'ontological security', all that is left to members of modern societies is the hope that the functional systems might fulfil expectations. Yet underlying this is the knowledge of their instability and fragility, which grows as the reflexive dynamism of modernity increases.

Trust originally becomes generalized from some of the same contexts as risk, in commercial relationships. . . . The noun form of trust comes from that source as well, as when you talk about a bank as a trust, or holding things in trust and so on. If you think of trust as something relevant to the future rather than to the past, that's the basic difference. Previous forms of trust were much more deeply involved with more traditional forms of commitment and morality, such as kinship obligations. Trust involves a more directly future-oriented relationship with whomever or whatever you are trusting. . . . Trust has to be mutual to be effective, and it offers security in the face of future contingencies. That's why I relate it to the idea of basic security in personality, as well. . . . To survive in life at all you need a generalized notion of trust, and that's essentially something people get from their early emotional experiences. If you don't have that, you're in big trouble. But to repeat, to be effective trust is always reciprocal – it never rests upon *blind* faith. (Giddens and Pierson 1998: 108–9)

Scott Lash also identifies reflexive modernization with modernization of *knowledge*, with questions of the distribution, circulation, consumption and enhancement of the form and content of knowledge and the resulting conflicts. In his view, reflexive modernization is a modernization of knowledge through which the foundations of social action (and hence the foundations of sociological thought and research) become questionable and open to reorganization and restructuring. In contrast to Giddens, however, Lash stresses the emergence of new conflicts through different types of knowledge, which are at the same time types of certainty. Drawing on Kant, he makes a distinction between *cognitive, moral* and *aesthetic* reflection. He focuses on the emotional peculiarities of '*aesthetic* reflection' which cannot be reduced to emotional, cognitive or moral elements and give rise to '*reflexive communities*'. He connects this with the objection against Giddens and me that our arguments rest on a narrowly cognitivistic understanding of reflection (and hence of reflexive modernization). Against the background of advanced individualization and of Anglo-American 'cultural theory' and trends towards a 'new communitarianism', Lash places his primary emphasis on 'reflexive communities'. These are conceived as a second, elective world of aesthetic symbols. They include the international markets, mobility, consumer habits and local symbolic universes and life-worlds and at the same time make possible what seemed to be impossible, namely, social, personal and global identities that are mobile, interchangeable and elective, and yet are also fixed and suited to being lived out in standardized ways.

What distinguishes my conception of reflexive modernization from those of Giddens and Lash? To put it briefly and pointedly: *the 'medium' of reflexive modernization is not knowledge, but – more or less reflexive – non-knowledge.* I will develop this idea in the following three steps: (1) in contradistinction to non-knowing as denial; (2) by means of the distinction between linear and non-linear theories of knowledge; and (3) through a typology of forms of non-knowing.

Non-knowing as denial

In this outline, the (terminologically unhappy) distinction between reflection (knowledge) and reflexivity (side effects) of industrial modernization is replaced by the distinction between knowledge and non-knowing. This would amount to replacing one unclear concept with an even less clear one. For the concept of 'non-knowing' (and the overlap and possible magnification of forms of knowledge and non-knowing) opens up not only new horizons of questions, but an unexplored jungle of interpretations, meanings and misunderstandings as well. 'Non-knowing' can be conscious or unconscious, concrete or theoretical, it can signify wilful ignorance or an inability-to-know, and so on.

Screening out, shutting one's eyes, isolating oneself, not wanting to know, only seeing what one wants to see – these are all forms of denial (Cohen 2001). Alcoholics in denial about their condition; US President Bush refusing to admit his defeat in Iraq; scientists who suppress their lack of knowledge in the face of growing threats to civilization: do these phenomena have something in common? When we deny our lack of knowledge, are we aware of what we are denying? Or is this an unconscious defence mechanism? Are there cultures of denial also, and especially, of non-knowing? How can environmental movements break down these walls of silence? By denying their own lack of knowledge and pretending to know what they cannot know? Or by revealing the general lack of knowledge and by giving expression to the resulting predicament that, in view of this inability-to-know and the growing threats, we are compelled to make decisions concerning the uncertain future?

In his book *But is it True? The Relationship between Knowledge and Action in the Great Environmental and Safety Issues of our Time* (1994), Aaron Wildavsky turned these questions against the environmental groups (drawing on empirical studies) and pointed out that knowledge of the side effects of natural devastations and health risks that upsets the public also involves a large amount of non-knowing – wilful omissions, mistakes, errors, exaggerations, dogmatisms:

Looking back at the array of environmental and safety issues, many of which, like Love Canal [near Niagara Falls] and global warming, have become imprinted on the public consciousness, we can discern a clear pattern: The more that is known, the less reason there is to fear the worrisome object and the weaker the rationale for preventive measures. The single partial exception is CFCs leading to ozone depletion. (Wildavsky 1994: 24)

Wildavsky and his associates drew this conclusion from an analysis in which they compared scientific results and their public presentation (on television and in newspapers) for numerous issues of 'environmental protection' and 'health risks'. The authors frequently uncovered errors in how surveys were conducted (for example, the restriction to *one* source of information) or the bare supposition of the 'existence' of risks that apparently do not need any further justification. According to the authors, investigating risks is a necessary condition for uncovering 'hazardous side effects' of industrial activity but by no means a sufficient one. Moreover, the (in Giddens's terms) 'active citizens' need to practise suitable ways of acquiring information and to react to and process this information actively.

It is striking, however, that even Wildavsky and his associates, in posing the instructive question 'But is it true?', still assume a clear and unambiguous distinction between knowledge and non-knowledge. They assume that this is something established by expert rationality. They do not inquire into forms of (involuntary) self-problematization of expert knowledge, for instance through the contradictory risk diagnoses of different institutes based on different methodologies or work environments. 'Non-knowledge' in the sense of the falsification of expert knowledge by public media and 'translators' is therefore just *one* dimension of non-knowledge.

Wildavsky's main fear is that the suppression of error probabilities in calculations of risk could result in overestimating threats and hence in overreaction and overregulation of all spheres of social action in the shape of a policy of preventive risk avoidance. Thus his demand is: 'Reject the precautionary principle, annul the environmentalist paradigm, stop regulating minor causes with even more minor effects!' That is worth serious consideration, but it once again follows in a highly selective way the progressivistic notion that the most serious and most frequent errors are committed, not by the experts, but by their critics.

Corresponding to the dogmatic understanding of expert knowledge to which Wildavsky falls prey is a dogmatization of counter-expertise to which many social movements fall prey (with the 'good intention' of politicizing issues and conditions). Uncertainties in one's own (risk) knowledge, many activists seem to think, *block* political action:

Effective management of highly publicized risks such as nuclear power and storing nuclear wastes, global warming and the greenhouse effect depends heavily on public trust in science, in technology and in managing institutions. . . . Institutional legitimacy rests to a considerable extent on trust. (Short and Clarke 1992: 12)

This points to the fact that, within the horizon of modernity, non-knowing is viewed as a shortcoming or a failure even by counter-experts.

If we cannot (yet) know anything about the effects of industrial research, activity and production (as is overwhelmingly true at present in the areas of genetic engineering and human genetics), if neither the optimism of the protagonists nor the pessimism of their critics rests on knowledge, then should

we give a green or a red light to the large-scale industrial utilization of technology? Does the inability-to-know represent *carte blanche* for action, therefore, or a reason for *slowing down* action, for moratoria or perhaps for doing
nothing? How can maxims of action or refraining from acting be justified by
the inability-to-know?

Linear and non-linear theories of knowledge

It is possible and necessary, therefore, to make a distinction between *linear*
and *non*-linear theories of knowledge of 'reflexive' modernization, where
this difference depends essentially on the distribution and defence of
non-knowledge.

Linear theories postulate (usually tacitly as the reverse side of their core
assumption) that non-knowing is *not* relevant (or central) to reflexive modernization. Non-linear theories affirm the opposite: types, constructions and
effects of non-knowing constitute a key problem in the transition to the
second, reflexive modernity.

Whereas linear theories of knowledge assume (more or less) *closed* circles
of formally responsible expert groups and epistemic actors, non-linear
theories see an open, *diverse* field of competing epistemic actors marked by
conflict. In the limiting case, there are two contrasting scenarios: the expert-
monopoly or *technocratic* decision model, on the one hand, and the 'palaver
model', in which it is unclear who may *not* contribute to the discussion, on
the other. In the zone of overlap of the two models, the problem arises of
how rules of admission and procedure can be simultaneously agreed upon
and practised, whether consensually or through dissent.[2]

Linearity means *consensual expert* knowledge: limited numbers of recognized and authorized practitioners in research institutes and organizations
and corresponding explicit sites for producing, accrediting and implementing
knowledge linked in cooperative networks. Non-linearity means *dissent* and
conflicts over rationality and hence over principles, that is, confused, unco-
operative, antagonistic networks of epistemic actors and coalitions (Hajer
1995) engaging in conflicts over (at the limit) contradictory certainties (images
of nature and human beings) in subsidiary public spheres employing opposed
strategies and with complementary chances of prevailing.

The distinction between and distribution of knowledge and non-
knowledge is thus based on a social structure, a power differential between
individuals, groups, authorities, monopolies and resources (institutes, research
funding, and so on), on one side, and those who challenge them, on the other.
This distinction, expressed in concrete, sociological terms, corresponds to the
scenario of a conflict over rationality that is very difficult to circumscribe.
The talk of 'side effects' signals a stage in the conflict in which homogeneous
expert groups are *still* in a position to exclude other epistemic actors and

modes of knowledge as unqualified. Its gradual breakdown marks the end of linear modernization and the beginning of non-linear modernization (in *my* sense of 'reflexive').

Thus the operative criterion is closed versus open, consensual versus dissenting agent networks, queries, methods, guiding hypotheses, scenarios, assessments and evaluations of risks and threats. Why is this distinction so central? Because, on the one hand, this is how the questions of non-knowing (in the twofold sense of the *inability*-to-know and of wilful ignorance) arise *for everybody*; on the other hand, this very state of affairs generates a compulsion to open oneself to 'external knowledge', to the external perspective. In this way the foundations of the (economic, technical, political, scientific, etc.) monorationality characteristic of linear modernization, which is oblivious to consequences, begin to crumble. This very monorationality is still advocated today in the guise of systems theory (with the suggestion that functionality and autonomy depend on screening out the external perspective). Both factors – the question of *our own* inability-to-know and the ability to adopt the perspective of alien rationalities – mark the transition to the second modernity of (self-)uncertainty that is simultaneously manufactured by civilization and known. Only then can we pose the general question of how these antagonisms and differences of *known non-knowledge* can be interconnected, played out and combined into decision-making procedures in new forms and forums.

Typology of forms of non-knowing

The introduction of non-knowing as a key conflict of 'reflexive' modernization entails a number of distinctions.

First, until now the talk was mainly of opening up the epistemic agenda through conflicts concerning *selective assumptions* that scale the ladder of credibility from non-knowing to knowledge.

From this we must distinguish, second, wilful ignorance [*Nicht-Wissen-Wollen*] and, third, *reflected non-knowing*. It follows the pattern: one knows that and what one does not know. Here knowledge and non-knowing mark a separation *within knowledge*.

This gives rise, fourth, to zones of the *conscious inability*-to-know. The issue of how knowledge of the inability-to-know should be assessed, whether it justifies a green or a red light for technological development, for example, is hotly disputed among the uncertainties of the self-endangering modernity.

By contrast, repressed or *unconscious non-knowing* points, fifth, to the limited horizon of a form of knowledge that does not reflect on its own limits. One does not know what one does not know. This is encountered among experts and counter-experts and in new (and old) religious and social movements.

Finally, from this we must distinguish, sixth, the figure of the *unknown inability-to-know*, i.e. those 'unknown unknowns' in which there lurks the ineradicable element of surprise.

The epistemological concept of side effects involves a certain combination of knowledge and non-knowledge.[3] It is a well-known fact (independently of the gradations of knowledge and non-knowing in concrete cases) that unseen, screened-out 'side effects' do not eliminate the self-endangerment to which they point, but rather intensify it. This is due, among other things, to the fact that side effects presuppose *actions*, hence subjects, practices and institutions. The practice of these subjects does not end with lack of knowledge of side effects; on the contrary, their practice fosters non-knowledge. The lack of knowledge of side effects has an inhibiting effect on existing routines of action that is cancelled when we know more about the side effects. Thus *theoretical* knowledge of side effects involves the supposition that side effects have a paradoxical intensifying effect *in virtue of* not being known. This supposition is connected with specific (more or less verifiable) effects, as is implied by the metaphor of 'the dying out of forests' [*Waldsterben*]. The prerequisite, however, is that the side effects – here, the 'dying out of forests' – become known and that this knowledge is recognized. Then active wilful ignorance will not halt the death of forests and the extinction of species, for example, but may *accelerate* it because it does not halt or correct the dynamic of industrial self-endangerment which operates independently of knowledge.

Thus the concept of 'side effects' signifies a paradoxical figure of (non-) knowing in which (under certain conditions) non-knowing, as an intensification of self-endangerment, is *known*, assuming that knowledge of the side effects exists and is believed, regardless of the specific basis of this belief. This is the basis of the power of counter-definition of social movements and of the public sphere informed by scientific knowledge. The more emphatically accepted knowledge concerning industrial self-endangerments is negated, the more threatening becomes the '*actual*' potential for endangerment (increasing under the cover of wilful ignorance), such as the destructive potential of climate change, which cannot be halted simply by denying its existence. The knowledge contained in knowledge of industrial side effects even permits or forces us to distinguish between *known* and *actual* threats. More pointedly, it rests on the epistemic construction of an 'in-itself', an 'objective' world of manufactured threats independent of our knowledge or ignorance of them.

This social construction of a knowledge-independent and hence 'objective' threat, however, is not true in and of itself. Instead, it calls for well-focused studies and appropriate empirical indicators. For the question concerning the *social construction* (and sociological reconstruction) of '*objective*' empirical indicators of threats and destruction arises. My answer is based on two stand-points: the 'objective' indication of the self-endangerment is linked back to the mutual criticism of social agents. The supposition is that, wherever established expert rationalities contradict each other, indicators of an as it were *institutional constructivist* 'objectivity' of the empirical indicators of threats is to be found (see above, pp. 85ff.).

The central example of this in my view is the *principle of private insurance*.

8

The Insurance Principle: Criticism and Counter-Criticism

1 Non-knowing, drama and sociology

The dramatist Friedrich Dürrenmatt appended *21 Points* to his play *The Physicists* (1982), which was first staged in 1962. They read like an anticipation of the key theses of the world risk society and mark commonalities and differences in argumentative architecture between drama and sociology:

1. I don't start out with a thesis but with a story.

I too start out with 'stories', such as those conveyed by the scare words 'Chernobyl', 'BSE', '9/11', 'Beslan', 'Istanbul', 'Madrid', 'London', 'Tsunami', 'Hurricane Katrina'.

2. If you start out with a story you must think it through to its conclusion.
3. A story has been thought out to its conclusion when it has taken its worst possible turn.
4. The worst possible turn is not foreseeable. It occurs by accident.
5. The art of the playwright consists in employing, to the most effective degree possible, accident within the action.

Indeed, the 'stories' of world risk society must be thought through to their conclusion. They have been thought through to their conclusion with the *attempt* to *anticipate* the worst possible turn. The worst possible turn is not foreseeable. It is founded on the inability-to-know, it occurs by accident. However, non-knowing does not preclude, but rather includes, anticipation and makes stagings possible. The task of the sociologist is to trace the conflicting anticipations of the worst possible turn in their effects on human action.

8. The more human beings proceed by plan the more effectively they may be hit by accident.
9. Human beings proceeding by plan wish to reach a specific goal. They are most severely hit by accident when through it they reach the opposite of their goal: the very thing they feared, they sought to avoid (i.e. Oedipus).

This echoes – to a T – the core assertion of the theory of world risk society, as is increasingly confirmed by risk management. The unknowable risks of the risk models hide behind the façade of controllability. Since modern forms of risk management for the most part maximize mathematical precision, they systematically underestimate *unforeseen* and *improbable*, but not therefore *impossible*, occurrences, as regards both their frequency and the extent of the damage they cause. This apparently slight difference between 'improbable' and 'impossible' involves a world of difference. The unfortunate combination of the frequency and extent of damage constitutes the 'insecurity trap' into which many industries fall. On the one hand, they must base their decisions in a pragmatic and optimistic way on rational probability calculations. Accordingly, they take their orientation from the most frequent – and sometimes also the worst – *probable* risks but not from the worst *possible* risks; for how else should they make decisions if they want to do business with the non-existent and not expectable future? At the same time, however, the rationality conflict becomes more acute because the possible – and not just probable – risks unsettle the public and undermine their trust in business and science.

10.   Such a story, though it is grotesque, is not absurd (contrary to meaning).
11.   It is paradoxical.

Grotesque, not absurd but paradoxical – this is the *irony* of risk dealt with in this book.

12.   Playwrights, no less than logicians, are unable to avoid the paradoxical.

The fact that this also holds for sociologists is, of course, nothing to get excited about.

14.   A drama about physicists must be paradoxical.

This holds for 'science' in general, not just for science with a big 's' (which Bruno Latour describes as the theory and philosophy of natural science) but also for science with a small 's' which, according to Latour, determines the actual *practice* of physicists, disconnected from the epistemological superstructure.

15.   It cannot have as its goal the content of physics but its effect.

This is pure Latour.

16.   The content of physics is the concern of physicists, its effect the concern of all men.

As it happens, this is the side effects theorem of world risk society.

17. What concerns everyone can only be resolved by everyone.

The principle of cosmopolitan *realpolitik* (see chapter 11).

18. Each attempt of an individual to resolve for himself what is the concern of everyone is doomed to fail.

Critique of political and methodological nationalism.

19. Within the paradoxical appears reality.
20. He who confronts the paradoxical exposes himself to reality.

This – also understood in methodological terms – runs through the whole sociology of world risk society.

21. Drama can dupe the spectator into exposing himself to reality, but cannot compel him to withstand it or even to master it.

Even this negation, whether expressed by the dramatist or the sociologist, does not go far enough. But at least it raises the question of how far the 'truth' of both drama and sociological analysis first manifests itself in a pragmatic sense in the consequences for action drawn by the 'audience.'[1]

2 The insurance principle: objections

If one views the panorama of threats and the new uncertainties of world risk society through the spectacles of the first modernity, one sees only negative side effects of imputable, rational decisions – that is, 'vestigial risks', that can be progressively reduced through cost–benefit analyses and the continual development of techniques of control in companies, the economy and science and technology. Seen through the spectacles of the second modernity, these new uncertainties and dangers delegitimize institutional authority and erode scientific rationality. Distrust of Dürrenmatt's 'physicists' is spreading (meanwhile, of course, it has also spread to human geneticists, specialists in reproductive medicine, designers of genetically modified foods, etc.). The four pillars of the risk calculus – compensation, restriction, safety and classification – are crumbling. As a result the discourse of manufactured uncertainty is permeating all social life worlds and regulatory institutions.

Even the pragmatic distinction between first and second modernity contradicts the relativism and contextualism concerning perceptions and definitions of risk which prevails in the sociology of culture. I can almost see the frowns – representative of so many others – running through Gabe Mythen's 2004 book and summed up by David Goldblatt: 'It almost seems as if Beck assumes, we agreed with his assessment of the threats we are confronted with – surprisingly Beck somehow skates over the knowledge of the relative and controversial character of risk perception and definition' (1996: 158).

But in fact it is this relativism that is inconsistent. It conflicts with points 2 and 3 of Dürrenmatt's risk dramaturgy: it doesn't think 'the story' through to its conclusion, it shirks the worst possible turn. This is a 'naïve' relativism. It remains within the nation-state frame of reference and fails to recognize that, beyond this specific context, tracking the distinction between self-endangerment and external threats, new, non-relativist collective definitions of risk and threat shape the anticipations and actions of individuals and organizations (see above pp. 85ff. and chapters 9 and 10). Hence, naïve, so to speak, relativist relativism fails to recognize that constructivist assumptions are by no means incompatible with the binding character of threat perceptions that polarize people. This is especially true if we accord primary importance to the institutional constraints and guidelines – the relations of definitional power – under which the staging of risks and threats occurs. Viewed in this way, self-confident relativism turns out to be a kind of intellectual laziness that is satisfied with an answer to a question that it is not even able to pose, namely, in spite of cultural relativism concerning risk, haven't global perceptions of the hazardousness and uncertainty of civilization acquired a new historical character to which the mono-relativist view is blind? Does the plurality of cultural risk definitions preclude the existence of institutional conditions, criteria and processes, which – especially in dealing with unacknowledged ignorance – force us to negotiate risks in the antagonism between national, international and transnational risk alerts and risk-regulating institutions? Aren't precisely the scare words and events of world risk society proof that global, cultural norms and institutionalized demands for control exist that lend local catastrophes such as 9/11 the character of a 'global risk'?

This is why I sought (beyond the domain of sociological expertise, but nevertheless with a sociological awareness of the institutionalized definitional power of risks) a kind of 'frontier barrier' that marks the transition from still controllable to no longer controllable, manufactured uncertainties. The answer I came up with is the *insurance principle*. It asserts that the absence of adequate *private* insurance protection is *the* institutional indicator of the transition to the uncontrollable risk society of the second modernity.

In my view, this hypothesis has three advantages. First, it can be empirically operationalized and refuted; second, it does not absolutize sociological or cultural theoretical relativism but is perfectly compatible with it, because it directs the spotlight onto the global insurance industry and treats it as an (involuntary) border guard; and, third, this principle of private non-insurance has major political implications. At any rate, it highlights the fact that it is often the most advanced technologies and product generations that do not have any, or at best inadequate, private insurance protection. The *economic* calculations of the insurance industry can be made the chief witness for a *politically charged* practice: the bigger the threat, the more limited the private insurance protection. This practice in turn flatly contradicts the zero-risk pronouncements of politicians and engineers and the judicial practices based upon them, so that, all things considered, this is a prime example of the (undetected) self-critique of risk society.

I am in the lucky position that this line of argument has been subjected to a systematic empirical examination in a brilliant case study by Ericson and Doyle (2004) that focuses on the example of the terrorist risk. The authors asked to what extent 9/11 overextended the insurance industry and whether since then the terrorist risk has been insured or not. The authors use their findings to criticize my hypotheses: '9/11 was a "major break" and the insurance industry nevertheless functioned relatively well in paying out compensation. In this case at any rate a modernization risk was perfectly within the capacity of the insurance industry to master' (ibid.: 169).

Beck concedes that insurers sometimes continue to insure catastrophic risks under conditions of extreme insecurity, but he sees these efforts as desperate attempts to feign control over things that they believe to be uncontrollable. Our case study shows that although newly discovered catastrophes raise completely new kinds of problems for knowledge and control, insurers nevertheless do not shy away from their insurance course but are turning threats into market opportunities. (Ibid.)

The authors also demonstrate that the growing risk to which the risk insurers are exposed is reflected in a trend towards catastrophic losses that is rocking the insurance industry to its foundations (Froot 1999; Bougen 2003). However, what should have occurred according to my principle of private non-insurance – namely, the withdrawal of insurance providers from uninsurable uncertainties – is not confirmed at any rate by this key example, on the contrary:

1 Insurance companies have always excluded certain aspects of risks from their insurance protection; thus selective non-coverage is nothing new.
2 The rational scientific bases of the insurance calculation were always incomplete and questionable when measured against the standard formula of the frequency and extent of anticipated accidents. *Incalculability* does not imply *uninsurability* because the insurance providers are routinely able to translate uncertainty and ignorance into their own capital-risk logic, in part by drawing on non-scientific forms of knowledge (O'Malley 2003; Ericson and Doyle 2004).
3 Anyone who wants to find out how insurance providers bring new risks and uncertainties under control with the means available to them

must first determine the variety and variability of the types of threat and examine how they are perceived and dealt with by private insurers and state institutions, respectively, and the interrelations between them.

There can be no doubt that the results of this study *refute* the hypothesis that there is a *sharp* dividing line – an either/or relation – between insurable and non-insurable risks. However, the case study *confirms* my thesis insofar as it proves that the *private* insurance industry runs up against its limits in the case of catastrophes and must rely on *public* co-insurance (i.e. subsidies). At the same time the study reveals the extreme internal fragility of the private sector insurance system within world risk society: 'The way in which insurers perceive risks and make decisions with respect to uncertainty leads to crises in the settlement capacities of insurance providers and to new forms of inequality and exclusion' (Ericson and Doyle 2004: 135).

In this sense the authors in many respects confirm the basic hypothesis that reflexive modernization erodes the foundations of traditional risk management. They agree with Dürrenmatt: 'The more human beings proceed by plan, the more effectively they may be hit by chance.' Or as Ericson and Doyle put it:

Insurance insiders describe 9/11 as risks which were inconceivable before they triggered catastrophic losses and which now, after these losses, have two consequences. The first concerns the immediate costs of unexpected compensation payments. The second is the effort to find out how unknown risks can set in motion a learning process, only to discover that with the accumulation of knowledge the uncertainty increases. (2004: 149)

Viewed in this way, we can turn the tables: to what extent can the empirical findings of the study be reinterpreted from the perspective of the theory of world risk society?

3   Counter-questions, counter-objections

(1) The authors gloss over the central distinction between damage and risk, between terrorist catastrophe and its *anticipation*, which is constitutive of the terrorist *risk*. On closer examination, the result of the study is not really surprising: it is not the terrorist *risk* that can be and is insured, but the *spatially and temporally limited catastrophe which occurred in New York on 11 September 2001*. This case involves neither open-ended, creeping catastrophes – such as the impacts of climate change – which can and will have completely different repercussions in different regions, nor the *expectation* of intentional catastrophes which is neither spatially, temporally nor socially fixed.

The study and reflection on its results have made one thing clear to me: the terrorist risk is a hybrid of the first and the second modernity. It manifests itself, on the one hand, in horrific events that are spatially and temporally *limited* and are in a classical sense 'accidents' and 'cases of damage'. At the same time, if we focus on intent, these are not accidents at all, since they embody what was previously unthinkable. This hybrid of accident and catastrophe can be insured provided that the damage remains within limits. It is uninsurable to the extent that it (a) represents the spatially, temporally and socially unlimited anticipation of such incalculable, catastrophic losses and their economic, social and political consequences and (b) shatters the established conceptual logic no longer merely 'by chance' but intentionally, in a 'paramilitary' way.

The authors commit a kind of category-mistake when they fail to make a clear distinction between catastrophe (loss) and risk (anticipation). Terrorism here reveals its Janus-faced character: the *un*limited risk of terrorism can trigger both *limited* losses and *un*limited catastrophes. These components are completely different from the perspective of insurance but it is difficult or impossible to draw a boundary between them. To conclude from the paradoxically limited, intentional terrorist 'accident' of 9/11 that the terrorist *risk* is limited, insurable and insured would be to fail to understand the logic of anticipation and ambivalence in the world risk society.

(2) The scope of the terrorist risk can be determined at best *ex post*, but not *ex ante*. Between these two points in time there is an abyss of known and unknown non-knowledge that hinders, and may even preclude, a rational approach to insecurity. In other words, it is impossible to predict the actual course of what retrospectively appears as the realization of an uncircumscribable risk. Ultimate risks do not have a definitive end through which the truth is discovered and limits are stabilized. The absence of past experience means that, *in the context of manufactured uncertainties, the subjunctive has replaced the indicative mood*. Possibility can claim the same importance as reality, also because the past has to be continually rewritten in the light of new, catastrophic experiences. Many cases where we were completely certain that we had an overview of all of the effects and side effects and the side effects of side effects proved to be fatal. Once we apply this knowledge to the present and the future, we lose our grip on (practically) all certainties. Virtual risks do not have to exist to be perceived and taken seriously as facts. The cause and effect relations are for the most part unclear, especially in cases of globally produced uncertainties, and the assessment of these threats is correspondingly controversial. What the insurance providers and other organizations charged with managing this insecurity fail to appreciate is that being controversial like this is itself a risk, an economic risk for insurers and companies and a political risk for governments.

(3) In fact, a proper understanding of how risks are produced must also reveal to what extent the decisions of organizations specialized in controlling the uncertainties, such as the insurance companies, lead to new, unforeseen

consequences and hazards. The separation between production and management of risks becomes untenable when risk management can itself become a source of risks. The latter need not rest on 'mistakes' but are rather a result of the operation of financial markets, for example. More precisely, the application of perfect, rational and promising risk strategies is itself a source of second-order risks. Actuarial risk assessment in financial markets must cope with the problem of reflexivity. Models *of* the market do not include the *application* of these models *in* the market. The more these models become general practice, the more likely are the principles on which their application is based to be annulled and their effects to become uncontrollable and unpredictable. Here, too, Dürrenmatt is right: 'They are most severely hit by accident when through it they reach the opposite of their goal: the very thing they feared, they sought to avoid [i.e. Oedipus].' Even if this seems absurd and grotesque, it is neither nonsensical nor unreal, just 'paradoxical'. In this sense, the risks of risk management are paradoxical consequences of the increased attempts to make financial risks controllable by refining and quantifying them.

(4) My error is the (paradoxical) result of the quasi-ontological attempt to draw a sharp boundary between either being insured or not being insured, thereby ignoring a central research result in the context of reflexive modernization, namely, that a new kind of both/and holds in an increasing number of fields of social action that must be carefully differentiated (Beck and Lau 2004). Applied to the insurance business this means that we must distinguish between the specific forms of 'being both insured and uninsured' and reinterpret the findings of the case study accordingly.

(5) First, there is the strategy of *selective exclusion* of terrorist risks in particular contexts or, as an insurance expert put it:

Rules of exclusion must be applied, in order to ensure that we are not drawn on for every kind of terrorism . . . That of course constitutes an element of uncertainty . . . Of course, we cannot insure against terrorism in every respect . . . We exclude certain forms of terrorism on the basis of a specific catalogue of criteria. That means, for example, the office of a director or a senior employee at an airport or a large office building which organizes share trading, for example – we would exclude terrorism in this sense as a matter of course. (Ericson and Doyle 2004: 32)

The various attempts to define and operationalize terrorism and to negotiate these kinds of exclusion conditions when drawing up contracts tend to support this kind of limitation and exclusion. Here this maxim holds: 'In order for us to be able to exclude something, we need to redefine it' (ibid.: 33). Thus the local confinement of the catastrophic potential, as represented by 9/11, was made the basis of exclusion strategies. Nuclear, biological and chemical terrorist attacks were excluded, as were the particularly endangered upper storeys of skyscrapers. Threat and insurance stand in an inverse relation to one another: the greater the threat, the less the insurance coverage. In other words, the globalization of the terrorist risk is limited to the compensation model of 9/11.

The study brings something curious to light in this connection. Often the policy holders exclude the most vulnerable parts of buildings, the upper storeys, from the insurance coverage and insure only the less threatened lower storeys. The study nevertheless shows

(6) how the private (re)insurers shift strategic risks onto *the state as reinsurer of last resort*. Here the debate concerning preventive insurance protection against transnational terrorist attacks coincides with the end of *private* insurance – and that is precisely what my insurance principle asserts. 'In fact, given the risk of terrorist attack, the reinsurance industry insisted that the US government took over the guarantee of ultimate reinsurance.' Such state reinsurance programmes were also negotiated in other countries, such as France and Germany.

As the interviews confirm, the threat by the private reinsurers to withdraw from insuring against terrorism unless there was major state involvement also had a strategic significance. It touched on a sore point by revealing the limit in principle of insurability in the face of the potential threat of terrorist attacks, which would have had profound reverberations for the ontological security of modernity with repercussions in all areas of social life and action. On the other hand, given the prevailing fear of the impact on business and politics, they were able to make highly effective use of their intimidation potential vis-à-vis the neoliberal self-image of the governments.

The government is the risk manager of last resort because it has unrivalled capacities for intervening in imperfect markets and hence is in a position to influence, distribute and reduce the direct effects of risks . . . Compared to the private sector, governments have quite a number of advantages when it comes to risk management. (Ericson and Doyle 2004: 54)

The study describes the full extent to which, after 9/11, the US government developed and extended the function of the reinsurer of last resort in dealing with terror risks (ibid.: 54–5). Viewed in this light, its findings refute the naïve notion of the private insurance business abandoning at one fell swoop the insurance coverage of terrorist catastrophes. But they also emphatically confirm how fragile and selective the modes and forms of 'being both insured and not insured' actually are. This raises a number of counter-questions which are not, or only inadequately, treated in the study:

(7) Don't the findings also suggest that the manufactured, more or less global uncertainties have a similar effect on insurance companies and on states in that they simultaneously empower and disempower them? Aren't

there now also '*failed insurances*', just as in the world risk society there are 'failed states', even in the West (see pp. 79ff.)? And isn't the distinguishing characteristic of this 'failing insurance business' that it is very well able to distinguish between 'good' (profitable) and 'bad' (expensive, loss-making) risks?

In what sense is the private sector insurance business in this way erecting a 'Potemkin village called insurance protection', a '*Potemkin insurance protection*'? How far do the promises of insurance protection still hold good there, to what extent are 'bad' risks increasingly excluded from it? To what extent is insurance protection being systematically *hollowed out* in the world risk society and, thus, to what extent are the uninsured risks and uninsured groups increasing behind the façade of continuing insurance coverage? Is it the inefficiency, the exclusion policy, of private insurance – more pointedly: the dismantling of insurance protection, the increase in non-coverage behind the façade of insurance – that opens up new markets for private business? And shouldn't research on insurance in the social sciences make it one of its central aims to abandon this unspoken functional premise of private insurance protection and to develop its own critical perspective on the simultaneous collapse and expansion of private insurance coverage? Perhaps the insurance principle, which assuaged the anxiety over the impacts of modernization of a whole era, ends in a macabre irony in world risk society: we insure each individual, and humanity as a whole, against everything but they have to bear the risks themselves, in particular those that threaten their collective existence.

(8) The insight into the simultaneity of the removal of the world's insurance protection and ongoing Potemkin insurance protection can be taken further. The category of risk exhibits an expansive logic. Risk embraces everything, permeates all spheres and all distinctions, true and false, good and evil, guilty and innocent. The moment a group or a population becomes a risk, risk overshadows all other characteristics and the group becomes just this: a risk to others. For a whole era, the space of expansion of risk seemed to coincide with the space of insurability. But, as François Ewald (1993) argues, risk, in virtue of its expansive logic, escapes the boundaries of insurability in two directions: first, in the micro-sphere of infinitely small risks (e.g. toxins in foodstuffs) and, second, in the macro-sphere of infinitely large risks (e.g. catastrophic climate change, nuclear contamination). What do micro- and macro-risks have in common? In all of these cases the risk concerns not only the immediate victims, but *life itself*. This means that it alters the reproductive conditions of human existence. It escapes biological and genetic, and hence also temporal, spatial and social, restrictions (Adam 1998).

This makes it clear that the uninsurability of world risk society (with the concurrent expansion of private-sector insurance policies) is the result not just of the limits of insurance but also of the expansionist logic of risk, which, with the triumph of decidability, transforms the reproductive conditions of human existence in unpredictable ways.

(9) This uncoupling of insurance protection and the expansion of risk can be further illuminated from another perspective, that of social theory. What kind of risks can be compensated *for whom* – for individuals, for whole societies, for humanity, including future generations? The era in which risk and insurance spread more or less congruently was based on the principle of the *individualizability* of cases of damage. It is always individuals – persons or organizations – who take out insurance policies and whose limited damages and losses are financially compensated. The risks of world risk society, however, make a mockery of the principle of individualizability. The anticipation of damages affects whole societies and global regions and in the end includes even the unborn generations. Neither private nor state insurance protection is a match for this apocalyptic dimension of world risks, as is becoming evident in the wake of climate change and of global economic crises.

(10) Above (p. 31) I made a distinction between two kinds of 'organized irresponsibility'. One arises in the national legal domain from the unimputability of precarious decisions, the other emerges in the international legal domain as a result of the fragmentation into national legal spheres which evade global risks. Here it becomes apparent that this national/international legal system, which obscures global risks, represents the unquestioned background against which the private insurance principle still seems valid. In fact, however, global risks retreat beyond the horizon of insurance protection and confirm the principle of uninsurability.

Insurance protection (whether private or state-organized) had a twofold function from the perspective of social theory, namely, *neutralizing damage* and thereby *neutralizing fear*. To the extent that the expansion of risk outstrips insurance protection, the latter loses its function of neutralizing fear at both the social and the political level, behind the still intact Potemkin façade of insurance protection. Free-floating fears are being set free, especially within the (full coverage) milieu of the European welfare states, which are open to political instrumentalization by all kinds of actors and groups.

9

Felt War, Felt Peace: Staging Violence

This chapter will examine two issues, first, the *antagonism of risk* and the *difference* between those who make the decisions and the groups and populations who are affected and tormented by the risks taken by others. Examination of the risk of passive smoking will show that this difference between situations and perceptions of risk depends, in turn, on stagings. Second, the example of *'risk wars'* will be used to demonstrate the importance of international relations of definitional power for how violence is actually staged at the global level.

1 The antagonism of risk is grounded in its logic

Anyone who wants to discover the relation between risk and social inequality must reveal the kernel of the sociological concept of risk, namely, that risk does not exist beforehand only to be distributed in socially unequal ways later. Risk and social inequality – indeed, risk and domination, risk and power – are two sides of the same coin. It is part of the *logic* of risk to polarize, to exclude and to stigmatize. This asymmetry and the conflict of perspectives it involves are not something additional and external but (to put it in old-fashioned terms) constitute the essence of risk. Risk involves a staging of the *dichotomization* of situations of risk and risk classes that is becoming ever more apparent with the evolution of risk society into world risk society.

Why? Risk is not a thing, not something that you can hear, smell, see or taste. Nor is it a fact that can be investigated objectively in such a way that, as the risk experts would wish, all errors miraculously accumulate on the side of laypersons and all knowledge on the side of the experts. On the contrary, the same thing that some regard as a 'risk', others regard as a 'danger'.

Risk presupposes a decision, hence a decision-maker, and produces a radical asymmetry between those who take, define and profit from risks and those who are their targets, those who must experience directly the 'unseen side effects' of the decisions of others, who may even have to pay for them with their own lives, without being able to take part in the decision-making process.

The relation between risk and inequality resides in this split. The potential profits and advantages fall to the 'we' of the decision-makers, apart from the fact that, in virtue of their position of social power, they are able to make such decisions in a (relatively) autonomous way (thanks to freedom of investment, freedom of research and science and/or their superior economic and military power). The 'we' of the 'living side effects', by contrast, consists in and springs from a double exclusion: these people are excluded from the potential benefits of the decision and from the conditions under which the decision is made, and often even from the information concerning the effects on their health or chances of survival against which they are helpless.

Why are there cross-border risks? What is the source of the utility and appeal of the 'globalization' of risks for whom? Here the relation between risk and risk inequality, risk and domination, also becomes apparent. It is often the case that the threat is *exported*, either in space to countries whose elites see this as an opportunity, or in time to still unborn future generations (chapter 10). Far from having to be removed for this export of threats to flourish, it presupposes the existence of national frontiers. Only because these barriers to vision and relevance are erected in people's minds and in the law does conscious action remain 'latent' and a 'side effect'. Money is saved when the risk is transported to places where safety standards are low and the reach of the law, in particular of national law, is inadequate. This holds as much for the export of torture as for the export of rubbish, of dangerous products and of controversial research. The hazards are 'deported' across the frontiers – into low-security countries, low-wage countries, low-law countries and low-ethics countries. In the cosmopolitan outlook, the allocation of the 'latent side effects' conforms to the pattern of the exploitation of law-deficient, marginal and peripheral regions, because there civil rights are an alien concept and the political elites maintain their position because their country is seen as a largely compliant 'side effects country' and they accept the 'threat-maximization' which is kept 'latent' with the goal of maximizing profits.

The failure or unwillingness to perceive the risks grows as human existence is stripped of alternatives. The risks are shifted to places where they are not recognized or are not taken seriously. Acceptance of hazards in these countries should not be equated with consent; their suppression and the associated secrecy are driven by need. In other words, hazards are imposed rather than accepted. This happens unnoticed, through the power of staged non-staging [*inszenierten Nicht-Inszenierung*].

The disdain for risks in states in which poverty and illiteracy rates are especially high, therefore, is by no means an indication that these societies are not integrated into world risk society. In fact, the opposite is true: they are the worst hit because of the scarce resource of *silence*, which they offer in abundance. A fateful magnetism exists between poverty, social vulnerability, corruption and the accumulation of hazards. The poorest of the poor live in the blind spots, and hence the most precarious lethal zones, of the world risk society.

Seen through the lens of individualization, they are to cap it all themselves to blame for their 'misfortune' because they move to where all are fleeing and, driven by necessity, expose themselves to the (foreseeable) natural catastrophes. It is not surprising that the numbers of such victims are increasing at the fastest rate in the poor regions of the world.

As we have seen, risk, as a matter of its conceptual logic, represents the *negation* of equality, justice and consensus. However, this should not be misunderstood in such a way that the existing global inequalities of risk (as I have pointed out) are necessary and hence justified and unalterable. The antagonistic conflict dynamic implicit in the social risk structure between the 'we' of the decision-makers and the 'we' of the living side effects becomes intelligible as a socially conditioned, alterable relation of domination and power at the latest when the 'risk class position' of the decision-makers coincides with the *power over the relations and means of defining risk* and this becomes public knowledge. Risks can and must be socially and politically defined and produced, can be hidden or revealed, be played down or writ large, become known and acknowledged in accordance with the highly mobile norms of science and law, or not, as the case may be, depending on who has control over the relations and means of definition (see pp. 31ff.).

If one understands risk, as I have here, as an inescapable structural condition of reflexive modernization, one must subject the 'mathematical morality' of expert thought and the public discourse concerning 'risk profiles' to systematic critique. Even the most precise and moderate objectivist form of risk expertise remains bound to a hidden morality, politics and domination. Risk cannot be reduced to the product of the probability of an event multiplied by the intensity and scope of possible losses. Given the power relations of global society, risk is instead a socially constructed and staged phenomenon through and through in which some have the capacity to define risk and others do not.

Not all actors benefit from the reflexivity of risk. The class divide runs between those who have the power to define their self-produced risks and those who are exposed to, or at the mercy of, risks over which others decide. This risk-based difference increasingly overlays, aggravates or replaces the old class division as the original and intrinsic form of inequality. Thus risk is another word for power and domination. This is especially true of the world risk society in which the Western governments and powerful economic actors determine the risks for others, for the underdogs of the world risk society.

Pluralization as self-defusing of risk conflicts

Beginning with the same figure of argument, Niklas Luhmann (2003) worked out 'preventively', as it were, two counter-tendencies and counter-arguments that are likewise implicit in the logic of risk against the dichotomous structural conflict dynamic of risk: first, the *pluralization* and, second, the *universalization* of risk conflicts. Taking Luhmann's position, one could object that the dichotomy between the 'we' of the decision-makers and the 'we' of the side effects to which I attach central importance is permanently thwarted by the likewise system-determined *pluralization* which turns decision-makers into side effects victims, depending on the context and issue at stake, and, reversing the relations, side effects victims into decision-makers, and so on. Since risks increase with the frequency of decisions, since all issues are becoming dependent on decisions in principle, there cannot be any zero- or non-risk. In this way Luhmann's concept of threats bundles the side effects for others in an anti-collective, plural, non-dichotomous manner: the threat side of risk disintegrates in the unlimited diversity of decision-makers and people affected. On the one hand, according to this thesis risk conflicts pose irrevocable questions of accountability because the consequences are imputed to decision-makers. On the other hand, this is excluded because of the immanent plurality and mobility of decision-makers, impacts and perceptions of threats. Thus Luhmann defends an agnostic point of view regarding the social and political definition of risk. His agnosticism concerning risk *depoliticizes* risk conflicts by universalizing them: meanings are always unavoidably plural and relative. The result is that the distinction between the decision-maker 'we' and the 'we' of the living side effects is becoming obsolete as risk spreads.

Luhmann's position is reinforced by the *universalization argument*. There is no risk-free behaviour, hence none that is free of danger. The refusal to accept risks has itself become risky. Risks are unavoidable, assuming that one is in a position to decide at all. Hence one must renounce the hope of, for example, regaining security through further research (Luhmann 2003: 93ff., 119ff.). From this perspective, all attempts to refer to the self-endangerment of modernity, or even to look for new institutional answers, seem to be part of the problem. Every diagnosis, every proposal is subject to the laws of the multiplication of risk which the critic is trying to counter. Whatever proposals I, for example, have put forward – be it the inversion of self-destructive into self-critical tendencies, the reversal of the burden of proof through new principles of accountability and recognition, alternative institutions and networks that facilitate reciprocal controls, increased opportunities for opposition and veto, etc. – on this relativist and sceptical view of risk, all efforts succumb to the unavoidable dilemma of risk politics, namely, by multiplying risk instead of minimizing it. According to Luhmann, we are currently living in a society that has no choice but to take risks, yet which, in virtue of this universalization and the exponential increase in the variety of risks, defuses their political explosiveness in a fatalistic way.

There can be no doubt that these three models in political theory – my dichotomization scenario and Luhmann's pluralization and universalization scenarios – are implicit in the structure of the logic of risk and represent theoretically possible and empirically observable developments in the world risk society. Contra Luhmann, however, one must assert that *all three* scenarios are operative and that they relativize and permeate one another. To what extent this occurs and how is an empirical historical question that I will explore in this chapter and the following.

The dichotomization of smokers and non-smokers

Individualization and anonymization: To smoke or not to smoke seemed (as the globally powerful cigarette industry implied) to be a purely individual matter, although it has long been known that death from smoking represents an individual fate shared by masses of others with enormous economic costs. The smoker (it has been possible to speak of the 'we' of smokers only since the emergence of the opposition to the 'we' of non-smokers) enjoys the pleasure of smoking, yet bears the possible resulting costs, namely, death through lung cancer. Hence the smoker is at once a decision-making beneficiary and a side effects victim. Accordingly smoking is staged in terms of the responsibility schema of *self*-endangerment rather than that of the endangerment of others. Thus on the other side of the divide was only the non-community of non-smokers.

This individualization and pluralization of the distribution and perception of risk came to an abrupt end, however, once the staging in terms of self-endangerment was replaced by staging in terms of the endangerment *of others* using scientific and legal arguments, and thus non-smokers were transformed into *passive smokers*, i.e. side effects victims of the decision to smoke. Suddenly something for which before nobody had been made socially accountable – the involuntary inhalation of the blue plumes of smoke which the cigarette smokers lustfully exhaled like miniature smokestacks – represented a potential legal, social and political offence that transforms all others into the 'we' of non-smokers. Non-smokers are no longer non-smokers but passive smokers, whose health and well-being appears to be collectively jeopardized by the heedless pleasure of smoking.

The disadvantages piled up on the side of this increasingly well-defined 'we' group of non-smokers, while they remained excluded both from the pleasure and from the decision over who ignites cigarettes, cigars or any other weed for egoistic reasons in public (and where and when). From this transition from self-endangerment to the endangerment of others, and thus from a non-conflict to a dichotomizing conflict, from the individualized risk scenario of generalized smoking to the polarizing 'we'-consciousness of smokers and non-smokers, one can read off all of the characteristics and dynamics of the dichotomizing effect of risks and their political intensification as under a microscope.

Risk antagonism: This arises with the transition from self-endangerment to the endangerment of others, something which is discernible not in objective changes in behaviour but in how behaviour is socially staged. The behaviour remains the same – smoking and non-smoking – but how it is socially perceived, evaluated and processed (at the levels of public health, the economy, law, etc.) changes radically. Within the horizon of risk antagonism, the social conflicts are relativized, at least for a historical moment, under the spell of this intensification; to smoke or not to smoke – that is the Hamlet question which is posed (more or less systematically) at all levels of society. The 'we' of smokers and the 'we' of non-smokers transcend and permeate social relations from top to bottom, left and right, male and female, old and young, black and white, religious and atheistic, inside and outside national borders.

Relations of definition: How is it possible that, notwithstanding the concerted attention paid to risks in the mass media and elsewhere, certain risks remain anonymous and as a result can increase to a point where they are suddenly described as 'serious problems' and set alarm bells ringing? The 'objective' character of the threat does not explain this process. For until recently the fact that cigarette smoke kills was proclaimed by various health ministers, in tacit complicity with the tobacco industry, after every cigarette advertisement in the cinema, while nevertheless shamelessly profiting from the duty on tobacco. A possible answer is that, on the one hand (following Luhmann), alarmism over risk permanently sabotages itself as a result of the pluralization and universalization of risks (the alarmism is drowned out by the general din of the alarm bells); on the other hand, this mechanism suddenly no longer works. On closer inspection, it is quite implausible that an increasingly extreme dichotomous risk class conflict between smokers and non-smokers should divide and disrupt the world in opposition to, of all things, the globally powerful cigarette industry, state tax revenues, the sacrosanct freedom to consume, etc. (Luhmann overlooks the *relations of risk definition power* and the *staging of collective situations* that result from this.) The definitional pointers can be set to anonymization and individualization or to the staging of collective threats by others that are triggered by economic definitions of harms and for which collective accountability can be assigned by scientific and legal means. The anonymization construction holds up as long as the relations of definition remain invisible and stable. By contrast, if, as occurred in the United States in response to the exponential increase in costs within the healthcare system and in the context of an ingenious liability law that potentially empowers consumers, the non-group of non-smokers becomes transformed into a collective of disenfranchised passive smokers and side effects victims, the pluralization, individualization and universalization scenario collapses.

Inversion of values: It is true that risk conflicts presuppose and liberate a plural, argumentative handicraft of risk definition and redistribution. Among its practitioners are experts and publicity specialists from a variety of social sectors, as well as scientists, politicians, lawyers, social movements and, of course, the mass media. Here an exhibition fight is conducted between a plurality of antagonistic definitions based on competing and conflicting rationality claims, where the various actors, depending on their situation, enter the fray with the foil of the law, the rapier of public accusations or the sabre of boycott. If the non-smoker 'we' of living and suffering side effects is successfully constituted by legal and social means, as occurred in the case of the smoking conflict, then the process of dichotomization takes its course.

Suddenly smokers no longer endanger only their own health but also that of everyone else. Rich and poor, great and small, black and white are brought together under the collective category of 'smokers', just as on the opposite side the collective of 'non-smokers' emerges across all social boundaries as the conflict escalates. In this matter, the two sides are irreconcilably opposed, and may even have incompatible worldviews. The well-being and self-image of the smokers splits off from the suffering assigned to the non-smokers who, with the new sense of power conferred by public attention and recognition, seize upon the possibilities for exclusion and stigmatization also afforded by the logic of risk. Thus the smokers, who not long ago fuelled the locomotive of growth as free consumers, find themselves devalued and stigmatized as 'drug-addicted social vermin'. The public authorities are mobilized ('public safety is threatened') to arbitrate this risk conflict, not by prohibiting smoking, but by isolating it. The solution is a kind of legally sanctioned apartheid of the smokers that permanently institutionalizes this 'otherness' introduced by the risk dichotomization – i.e. the opposition between smokers and non-smokers – while, on the other hand, arbitrating it through a spatial compromise. It is obvious that, in the case of many risk conflicts, this state-imposed geographical compromise is completely out of the question.

2   Risk wars or: Staging organized violence in the world risk society

World society becomes world risk society as the logic of dichotomous global risk situations intensifies. Amazingly enough, at the level of world society the trends towards the pluralization and individualization of risk situations seem less pronounced than their dichotomization (at any rate under certain conditions). This may have something to do with the fact that global risks remain in principle diffuse and hence provide material for the renewal or redefinition of cultural stereotypes and conflicts. I alluded to this earlier when I described global risk conflicts in terms of a quasi-religious 'clash of risk cultures' (see chapter 4). In what follows I will develop this thesis using the example of 'risk wars'. In this I take up a remark of Martin Shaw: 'Surprisingly, sociological risk theorists have not generally paid much attention to risk in war' (2005: 97).

The transformation and pluralization of war

A *transformation* and *pluralization* war is taking place in the world risk society, i.e. the emergence, differentiation and combination of forms of organized violence that resemble war or go beyond it (Beck 2006, chapter 5). These can be differentiated, at least for the sake of analysis, according to which aims, which means and which actors play the decisive role,[1] into (a) *old* war, (b) *new* war or privatized violence, (c) *virtual* war and (d) *globalized terrorist risk*.

(a) The 'old' wars of the twentieth century pitted states against states and armies against armies. This form of confrontation is in principle 'symmetrical' also in the sense that the actors – the states (governments, armed forces) – behave in predictable ways as regards the political goals and the threat potential (the military means).

The Cold War is an example of how the most extreme reciprocal threat potential – the nuclear stalemate – can be compatible with a form of calculability that fosters peace. Each side knew that the other did not want to jeopardize its own survival or that of the species. But that meant that neither side could launch a first strike attack against the other as long as the side targeted was in a position to strike back. No one wanted a double suicide. A system of treaties of reciprocal disarmament and even of 'interpersonal support' [*menschliche Erleichterungen*] that bridged ideological divides could be built on this basis.

(b) In a parallel development 'new wars' arise, that is, organized forms of *privatized violence* that displace the violence exercised by the state and challenge, undermine and replace the state's monopoly on violence. The actors who give the orders here are unofficial commanders and local dictators. They are often religious or nationalist fundamentalists and rapacious violence entrepreneurs all in the same person, who build Mafia-like networks while living off arms smuggling, drug-trafficking and protection rackets, theft and plunder. In regions in which such forms of asymmetrical, unpredictable violence take root, 'islands of civility' (Kaldor 2007: 174) surrounded by barbed wire develop amidst omnipresent violence.

What bothers and frightens people in the Middle East is not war between well-equipped armies, as in 1967 and 1973. The Palestinians do not have an army and the Arab states with good reason no longer become involved in traditional wars. What the Palestinians can muster in terms of privatized violence remains well below the threshold of war. But the very fact that violence is no longer under state control is making peace impossible. This already shows that privatized violence escapes the distinction between war and peace. Where it holds sway there is no peace. But there is no war either. Because of this, military superiority does not have the final say either. (Eppler 2002: 47)

Israeli governments are fooling themselves if they think that sooner or later the Palestinians will have to succumb to Israel's vastly superior military power. Winning a conventional war is one thing, putting an end to privatized violence something different.

(c) Michael Ignatieff introduced the idea of 'virtual war' in his book on Kosovo (2001), where 'virtual' has two meanings: the strategy of conquest employing ground troops is replaced by the strategy of aerial bombardment; in this way, the losses among Western troops could be kept to a minimum. For Western societies, war becomes a pure 'spectator sport' (ibid.: 191). The mass media become *the* decisive platform, *the* production script from which the operative strategies of the military take their direction.

Because virtual wars are fought on camera ... Western military commanders know that success is now contingent on public acceptance. In fact, there is no such thing as purely military success: a success which takes out a target but leaves behind moral or political debris is a strike which has failed. The Western military's response to sharpened moral and political exposure has been to call in the lawyers. (Ibid.: 197).

The concept of security has changed fundamentally in the twenty-first century. It is still a matter of preventing wars in the classical sense (for example, between North and South Korea, India and Pakistan, Iran and Israel). Security is also increasingly understood against the background of a worldwide solidarity (reflected in a UN mandate), as a matter of safeguarding elementary human rights in regions in which elementary human rights are severely threatened, where states are collapsing, where privatized, commercialized, lawless and brutal violence tyrannizes and plagues human beings, where terrorists threaten to employ weapons of mass destruction, etc.

(d) Whereas the realization of *humanitarian goals* is cited as the goal of virtual war (which, of course, is sustained by all sorts of national and material interests), the new forms of suicidal terrorism à la bin Laden are driven by the radically opposed goal, namely, to defeat Western modernity with its own instruments in the name of Allah and to stage the Apocalypse. Religious warriors, people who believe they are fulfilling God's will upon earth, have always stood out for their unimaginable brutality. Terrorist violence, however, is an extreme form of the privatization of violence. It does not conform to the profit principle or the market principle, it does not serve the personal enrichment of the terrorists or the satisfaction of their private hatreds, however much the latter provide the motive for the attackers and are the driving force of their deeds. The national terrorism of the first modernity is also categorically different from the transnational, global terrorism of the second modernity, even though this difference is often blurred. Islam as such is not terroristic, nor is transnational terrorism necessarily confined to radical Islam. Perhaps the radical Islam represented by the Egyptian thinker Sayyid Qutb and the al-Qaeda network which puts his ideas into practice are merely the beginning and this plague of violence is spreading to other global religions and regions.

'Old' terrorism, whether nationally or ethnically motivated, is geared to establishing a national and ethnic state of one's own (and its success is measured accordingly). The national terrorist elites of today are potentially the heads of government and ministers of tomorrow. This all-or-nothing game, this career leading from illegality to legality, from control over terrorist violence to control over the state monopoly of the means of violence, belongs to the old, national terrorist motivation and ideology.

All this holds for the transnational terrorism à la al-Qaeda only up to a point. The perpetrator groups and their 'backers' are neither bound to nor motivated by a territory or a state; they are not fighting for their own state, which is one of the main reasons for the failure of the measures employed by the global hegemon to control them. For the power of the state rests both internally and externally on the logic of deterrence, which is based in turn on the threat and fear of death. But these kinds of terrorists cannot be deterred. How can you threaten suicide bombers with death? The use of state power presupposes control or conquest of a territory. This type of terrorist does not control *any* territory and, unlike the state, is not rooted in a territory, hence is not bound by any state and accordingly is everywhere and nowhere – a poor starting point for military deterrence and military interventions.

What are *analytically* differentiated here – old, new and virtual wars and the anticipation of global terrorist attacks – mingle, overlay and blend in the military conflicts of recent years, for example, the Iraq War and the war in Lebanon. We are dealing with a confused mixture of new and old wars, of virtual wars and nationally and transnationally operating terrorism.[2] I will refer to them as 'risk wars'.

The concept 'risk war' has a twofold meaning. On the one hand, it designates – as it is understood by the governments who employ the military means, at any rate – military interventions in foreign (not hostile), more or less unstable (both collapsing and stable) states with the goal of minimizing and controlling a 'global risk' (transnational terrorism, the proliferation of atomic, chemical and biological weapons of mass destruction, etc.). What is involved is a kind of global risk management with military means, though one which presupposes and/or replaces other diplomatic, police, judicial, economic, etc., initiatives.

At the same time, the concept 'risk war' refers to *'risk-transfer war'* (Shaw 2005, on whom I draw here). By this is meant the new risk redistribution wars in which war is planned and conducted in such a way that, under the primacy of controlling risk and minimizing casualties, the threat to one's own troops is minimized and the threat to others is maximized. This leads to strategies of warfare (e.g. bombing instead of using ground troops) that shift the risk of deaths and casualties onto those who are attacked.

Both aspects of risk war are paradoxical and systematically interrelated, for in a certain sense what is involved is war to prevent war, where this mode of legitimation necessitates the spatial and social decoupling of war from casualties. At most only 'invisible deaths' are permitted, at any rate on one's own side. The risk of dying must be 'exported'. The whole war strategy has to be geared to this 'risk transfer' or 'risk export'. To the extent that this is brought to light or fails (as in the Iraq War in 2006), the legitimation crumbles.

The fact that the transformation of wars into risk wars is becoming the norm is a classical instance of the thesis that the social risk structure does not pluralize but gives rise to a conflict over domination. Those who want and take the risk must have the means of power and violence to foist the consequences and costs of their decision onto others. They must be able to do this but also to stage and legitimize this before a global public. The one thing concerns the military, economic and scientific productive power of the risks, the other, their power of legitimation and definition. The unity of the power to produce and define is the source of the superiority of the global overdog over the global underdog.

The question of legitimation

Risk wars depend in the highest degree on legitimation. This means that the widely held notion that, when in doubt, law and legitimacy spring from the 'biggest club' is being falsified, indeed it is becoming counterproductive, in the world risk society. In the latter, the use of military force can no longer be legitimized exclusively at the level of the nation-state (through the consent of parliament or the euphoria of the population), but calls instead for *cosmopolitan* legitimation. Risk wars can be planned and conducted in ways that are legitimate for a global public only in the context of a UN resolution; hence they presuppose the authorization of the UN Security Council or must serve to avert a 'global risk' or a present or imminent crime against humanity. Based on the systems of human rights which emerged in response to the military and genocidal horror of the twentieth century (Levy and Sznaider 2004), wars are no longer conceived and undertaken in a positive sense as a national *opportunity* to expand the power of a particular state or empire, but rather in a *negative* sense, re-actively and pre-actively. They give effect to avoidance imperatives on the motto 'Never again!' (at least as the central point of reference for their legitimation before a global public).

Peaceful war

When risk or, what amounts to the same thing, perceptions of risk dominate, society as a whole finds itself *'forcibly transferred' into the sphere of possibility*. The 'could-be' reigns and 'being' withdraws. 'Possibility' is too weak a concept here because it has lost its opposite pole, namely, reality. Thus the domain of possibility of the threat solidifies into a becoming-real, into belief in the reality of a possible becoming-real that must be prevented. In this sense, the threat is a *reigning expectation*, it takes possession of the mind, thinking is open for stagings, a product of staging, a future, that, as still to come, is omnipresent and derives from this its mobilizing force for prevention in the present.

The key question is: How can the distinction between war and peace be overcome, on the one hand, and what would a new combination look like, on the other? An unexpected sunny day in January in Munich makes the difference between *felt* and real temperature as clear as an unexpected snowy day in August. In an analogous and more profound way, it makes sense to distinguish between *felt* war and *real* war, *felt* and *real* peace, in order to explore the strategic spaces of the material and symbolic staging of violence.

The excessive violence of terrorism follows the script of *felt war*, whereas risk redistribution war, by contrast, follows the script of *felt peace*. The dramaturgy of the felt war (in which both hostile parties are engaged) is, in turn, the presupposition for conducting war 'elsewhere' within the staged milieu of the felt peace. Thus US President Bush and his government exploit every opportunity to 'milk' every single terrorist story for their politics of fear. In the meantime, Bush has cried wolf so often – especially to drown out the bad news emanating from Iraq – that alarmism has the effect of an unintentional joke even in the United States. In other words, to link war and peace as though they were interchangeable faces makes it possible to wage war under conditions of felt peace and to normalize it under the guise of risk redistribution war. However, the attendant contradictions can destroy the credibility of the staging.

A direct implication is that the internal legitimation of risk war must not disturb the felt peace in one's own country – only then is it 'successful', only then is it 'legitimate'. In other words, risk war must be fought as an *incidental war* [*Nebenbei-Krieg*]. This construction of latency and side effects holds, of course, only for domestic purposes. Thus it is radically hierarchical and intrinsically paradoxical. For a military intervention is, of course, an *intentional* catastrophe, at any rate an intentional catastrophe for *others*, which must not be greeted with acclaim within the domestic spheres of the belligerent nations (as in the past) but must be rendered invisible. The incidental war, which is not supposed to disturb the felt domestic peace, must not disturb the normal workings of the economy, of politics and of social life. Even modest downturns in rates of economic growth must be regarded as 'jeopardizing the war effort' – not to speak of the dead, whose faces and stories are broadcast by the media and whose distraught mothers, wives and children protest before the world's cameras. A risk war, therefore, is a war that not only does not take place 'among us' but rather takes place as invisibly as possible among the 'others' and leads to 'losses' there, not here. Arguing in terms of the sociology of risk, the point is to uncouple the national 'we' of the decision-makers spatially, socially and in the mass media from the 'we' of the threatened or dead side effects victims. The war, which is *virtual* only in the sense of being invisible in the West, must be fought in such a way that it can be largely integrated into the normality of Western societies and macro-economies. What does this mean? In order to prevent the risk war from becoming an electoral risk for the belligerent governments, for example, it must not take place during election campaigns. But how can this be organized multilaterally when, as in the case of the NATO mission in Yugoslavia and Kosovo, a *single* military campaign has to be coordinated with ten or more elections and electoral campaigns?

Virtual war

One might say that the achievement of the French social theorist Jean Baudrillard resides in the radicality of the assertion that the first Iraq War, in 1990–91, did not take place. One must add, however, that the weakness of his theory resides in the fact that the Gulf War did take place. The two statements are not mutually exclusive: the war took place for the *others*, *not* in the country of the belligerent nation. Felt peace and actual war coexisted; they were spatially and socially separate and connected with one another according to a specific pattern of staging and legitimation in the *selective* virtuality of war. As it happens, it is the *Western* outlook which is expressed in Baudrillard's overstatement, one which is blind to the victims of the others.

However, this stunted virtuality has to be deliberately manufactured. This succeeds only insofar as the war is something which takes place 'over there', in which the war dead are not 'our' dead, in which 'our' dead remain or are rendered largely 'invisible' by preventing their representation in the mass media. This fabricated unreality of the war demands a radical hierarchy, the decoupling of the place and the state in which the decision is taken from the place and the state in which the 'side effects' occur. It presupposes, in addition, that the wars are executed as *quickly* as possible and as *bombing* wars, that the risk of death is shifted from our soldiers onto the civilian population of the other side, etc.

Thus the dividing line between felt peace and real war coincides exactly with the dividing line between reality and virtuality which the Western armed forces and governments must erect and maintain on account of their superiority if they want to minimize the risks of war for themselves and maximize them for the other side. 'Legitimate' and 'successful' is ultimately the zero-deaths war – correction, the zero-*own*-deaths war – which blots out the countless deaths on the other side, in particular among the civilian population, thereby rendering the war virtual for the Western nations and all the more brutally real for the victim populations.

So there is a *transfer* of life-risks from Western personnel to civilians, and this transfer is well understood by all concerned. In this sense, the 'minimizing' of risks to civilians is highly relative: these risks are not minimized as much as those of Western personnel, nor is their minimization an equal priority. To this extent, the consistent overall pattern of greater losses of life among civilians than among Western militaries is intended. (Shaw 2005: 86)

Ignatieff (2001: 197) also draws the conclusion that virtual wars involve the West in an open contradiction with its own values. Or, as Paul W. Kahn (1999) puts it succinctly: 'Riskless warfare in pursuit of human rights is . . . actually a moral contradiction.'

Cosmopolitan publics

Erhard Eppler describes the cosmopolitan moment of the world risk society (chapter 3) as it manifested itself following the terrorist attacks on New York and Washington:

Never before was it so uncontroversial that the organs of state, ministries, secret services and public prosecutors' offices of the various countries should cooperate. Never before was there so little opposition to the necessity of armed intervention – in more or less sovereign states. Never before was the idea of something like a global police force more popular, at any rate outside the United States. Never before was the latter's opposition to a world criminal court so hard to comprehend. Never before was the determination to crack down on privatized violence or to subject it to law as pronounced. The world risk society is what could force a world domestic policy. (2002: 101)

Governments, armed forces and parliamentarians generally appeal to national legitimacy. Politicians in general think mainly in terms of national control. They thereby fail to appreciate the power and possibilities of control of transnational authorities, actors and publics. By this is meant not only the reliance upon a kind of cosmopolitan legitimacy such as that which the UN Security Council can generate. No less central is the fact that the element of reflexive observation and surveillance is already mediated by the intersecting news reports and commentaries within the international and global space of discourse. National public arenas reflect a multiplicity of voices, the criticisms and support of friendly countries, but many other voices are also registered, at least in part. Thus, in all of the apparently nationally confined public arenas, there arise new mixtures of inside and outside, of friend and foe, of us and them. These voices express their standpoint, and hence the legitimacy of some decision or other, mainly against the backdrop of a postulated postnational legitimation that must always be organized and articulated transnationally and must secure a hearing for the voices of the others in the assumed ideal case. Here, too, the notion of national public spheres as islands misrepresents the reality that national public spheres mirror one another and that a global public opinion is articulated at least in how they mutually refract one another. National public spheres in the West, in particular, are integrated into the global media, institutions and public opinions, something which also strategically influences the relations of power in the respective theatres of war. Parallel to the physical wars, therefore, symbolic proxy battles are fought in the interconnected public arenas with the participation of peace movements, UN observers, members of the Security Council and the images and voices of the victims on the various sides.

In the West, the idea of 'dialogue' is endlessly propagated as an answer to the intensification of the conflicts in the world risk society resulting from the simultaneity with which geographical distances are being effaced, universal interdependencies are increasing, and the mutually exclusive world situations and interpretations are colliding. However, this idea of a polite conversation between 'civilizations' ignores the rigorously hierarchical global (dis)order which is especially pronounced in the military relations of violence and definition of the reproduction and definition of risk through war. Hence, every reference to the 'global civil society' is immediately subject to ridicule – isn't it precisely 'incivility' that is driving the dichotomization of the world risk society into 'the West and the rest'?

The fiction of a harmonious cosmopolitan community that feels bound together by norms and rules obscures the fact that the logic of risk is leading to the establishment of a dichotomous conflict structure and dynamic. At the upper pole, the shortcomings and harms (up to the killing of human beings) are regarded as the unavoidable consequences of a self-authorized decision to take certain risks for the sake of advantage and profit. At the other pole of the hierarchy are located the mass of those who perceive and experience the losses as externally caused, imposed alien threats. The subaltern, excluded side effects 'we' can only refuse or evade the well-meaning offer of dialogue. The global *anticipation* of the clash between the 'class' of 'risk giver' states and the resulting class of 'risk receiver' states disrupts the dialogue, not least because the 'historical wounds' and traumas of the colonial period are repeatedly reopened.

However, the war against a global risk confuses the twentieth-century wars between states with the threats of the world risk society at the beginning of the twenty-first century. In this way, a war against the 'terrorist risk', which was announced and led by the US president, becomes a textbook example of how the most powerful state defeats itself.

3 The terrorist risk: the global staging of felt war

With the figure of the suicide attacker and its social spread, the antagonism of the risk logic undergoes a transformation. Granted, we must make a distinction between the perspective of the perpetrators and the perspective of the victims, where one of the outstanding features of the case is that the perpetrator is his own victim. From the perspective of the perpetrator, the distinction between risk and threat collapses. The difference between those who take risks that they can in principle avoid, and those who are exposed to the threat against their will, collapses: the suicide attacker wants to be a mass murderer who uses his willingness to die deliberately as an instrument of mass murder. The short-circuiting of risk and threat magnifies the (staging of the) threat beyond comprehension.

From the perspective of the victim, this amounts to a strategy of threat maximization because the space of possibility of the deeds becomes boundless and the institutions of prevention, calculability and control are circumvented. With still relatively 'low' numbers of victims and deeds, the *felt violence* and *felt war* are maximized and explode in the centres of the felt peace, both literally and in the mass media.

Side effects catastrophes are distinguished by the fact that individual decision-makers and decisions cannot be identified. This problem of 'organized irresponsibility' is annulled or, more precisely, is inverted into its opposite. The problem of accountability no longer arises in the case of deliberate catastrophes triggered by suicidal attacks. The act itself is what produces the self-attribution of responsibility by the agent. But now the opposite problem arises: if the perpetrators are identified and judged by their own act, what remains for the authorities and governments, courts, soldiers and police to do? For their social existence derives its justification from the fact that such catastrophes *do not* occur. How can the authorities responsible for control and prevention justify their existence when what they were supposed to prevent is destined to become even less preventable in the future and threatens to render them superfluous? Tough security laws are of only limited use against 'home-grown terrorists'. If we want to filter out possible perpetrators early on we must start keeping tabs on all well-off, upper-middle-class teenagers with British or German passports. The specialists in pat political remedies suggest that Islamist terrorists are a body of men who merely have to be disarmed or extradited. We are dealing with a different kind of 'enemy' whose most conspicuous feature is its inconspicuousness, with a 'different war' that does not speak its name and spreads felt violence throughout the world. Perhaps we should invade distant countries – 'risk states' – in which the 'backers' are assumed to be holed up? Doesn't this also happen because it is unbearable, indeed politically intolerable, to be at the mercy of threats, especially for those who are responsible for security? Or are various forms and strategies of *symbolic* prevention *invented*, precautionary measures (e.g. detecting shaving cream in the carry-on baggage of airline passengers) that conform to national self-attributions of responsibility, even though they are useless against this kind of danger. The result, in other words, is *a systematic confusion and transposition of risk and threat*. Terrorist threats have to be treated and negotiated as politically controllable terrorist risks that can be prevented through constitutional legal norms – reinforcing the police, video surveillance, deploying the armed forces in the domestic arena, etc. The restless search for the lost security begins through measures and strategies that lend the appearance of control and security instead of guaranteeing them and exacerbate the general feeling of insecurity and endangerment.

As we have seen, risk means risk conflict. Since, as a general rule, risk givers and risk receivers belong to separate camps, opposed standpoints of observation and evaluation arise, thus leading to a pluralization of rationalities. But even this is not strictly true of the terrorist threat, at least not in the extreme case. The perception of threats also founds a wide-ranging *solidarity* that transcends class, national and regional antagonisms and a *consensus* over legitimate defence against threats that violate the fundamental principles of humanity (which does not preclude that there are also advocates, patient sufferers and sponsors, or that the community of solidarity and consensus can be instrumentalized for completely different interests). If the immanent plurality of risk perception is a way of neutralizing the exclusive assignment of threats (as Luhmann argues), then the converse holds, namely, the wrath and outrage over inhumanity gives rise to political explosiveness. In this way a contradictory complementarity develops between the risk-transfer wars and the global political significance of terrorist attacks.

Vulnerability

As we have seen, there has been a renaissance of war as limited high-speed warfare under the condition that the danger is externalized. The criterion of success is, among other things, the suppression of the extreme vulnerability of Western civil society. The felt peace makes possible the normalization of war. The presupposition is the successful integration of the state of exception of war into the normalcy of Western society (the 'anti-Schmitt principle'). This high-speed war conforms to the myth of the 'clean', 'surgical' no-casualties-*on-our-side* war. This is precisely the Achilles heel of the West.

The terrorist attacks aim at this place in that they follow the opposite logic and make clear to the whole world the vulnerability of the supposedly in all respects superior West. The Middle East has now found an answer to the

Western Way of War. For centuries the political dominance of the West, from Asia to Africa and into the New World, was founded upon military power, technology and discipline. Now, however, the Arab world has learned how to compensate for the advantages of conventional high-tech weaponry and to strike at the heart of the superpower without using tanks and bombers. The secret is: *it is not the terrorist act that destroys the West, but the reaction to its anticipation*. It ignites the felt war in the minds and centres of the West.

This means that war must be internalized. Insane acts that mimic war must explode, both really and in the mass media, with predictable unpredictability at the vulnerable heart of Western civil societies. Terrorist attacks must accordingly be placed in such a way that business, politics and social life are struck in the heart of the felt peace.

The globalization of the terrorist risk

The scope of the threats against which the armed responses of the West seem to be justified has undoubtedly increased. National interests, general Western interests and global interests are seen as fused, which also means, among other things, that national interests can be defended *as* global interests. An important expression of this unlimited expansion in the scope of Western interventions is US President Bush's talk of the 'axis of evil' which places the security of individual countries, and hence of whole global regions, in question because the latter must anticipate becoming the targets of possible surprise wars.

The globalization of the *expectation* of terrorist attacks (with all of its drastic implications for the compulsory internalization of war in the civil metropoles of the West) also depends on the structure of the multi-local choice of the scenes of terror. The more terrorist attacks with spectacular impacts in the mass media potentially affect all countries and continents, the more arbitrary and unpredictable they appear and the more shamelessly they violate the basic principles of humanity, the more probable it is that the anticipated space of threats of possible terrorist attacks will be at once globalized and institutionalized, that is, that it will become a part of everyday and increasingly 'watertight' reactive routines that are accepted with universal regret. The anticipation is ultimately what drives the globalization of terror. Indeed, it is the West itself that – albeit as an unwanted side effect – ignites the felt war in people's heads, raises the costs of escalation and pushes its own power system into a state of crisis.

The military imperative

The Western strategy of minimizing risks for us and maximizing them for others follows, on the one hand, the *risk aversion* of the West. In societies in which death is tabooed and human rights enjoy a high priority, the outbreak of belligerent violence is especially shocking. In the 'total' wars of earlier times, the military imperative permeated all domains of social action. Governments could nationalize companies, control production, postpone elections and impose news censorship. This no longer holds for the war of the (seemingly) controlled risk. It becomes possible to redistribute risk only if militarism can be successfully confined to the professional ideology of the armed forces. However, this is what opens up the option of rapid war for the political elites.

The religiously motivated *totalization of risk* confronts the Western aversion to risk. Suicide is perfected as a weapon for the mass murder of innocent civilians. Violence is sanctified as counterviolence, dissociated from the military and political rules founded on the laws of war. The intentional character of the catastrophe unleashes a post-military and postnational apocalyptic threat that transports the fear of mass murder into even the most sheltered corner, into every living room of vulnerable civil society. In short, it maximizes the felt war.

Images and stories

The images and stories of the mass media represent a central theatre of war on account of their (de)legitimizing power. Whereas in the Western risk avoidance wars the global media serve to redistribute the 'burdens', to keep the despair over the dead and the devastation for the most part *in*visible, for terrorist attacks the exact opposite maxim holds: to globalize the images of suffering and horror.

The Western strategy of media management is geared less to imposing the official line than to

> ensuring that events do not fundamentally disrupt it. Of course, many things happen in war which journalists and audiences find uncomfortable, and today's Western governments expect criticism and questioning. What they fear is a single incident that is so challenging that it threatens to 'break' the established narrative, suggesting to journalists, readers and viewers the need for a radically different understanding. (Shaw 2005: 93)

Thus the *internal* dangers for political elites spring from the linking of images and stories. As long as the images of the suffering of the other side do not sabotage the bases of the official why-story of the war, they do not jeopardize the felt peace. This boundary was clearly transgressed by the cynical violence of the scornfully brutal images of torture from the US prison in Iraq, no less than by the news reports and pictures from the Guantánamo prison camp with its contempt for the Geneva Conventions and human rights. These two global public scandals destroyed the official legend because they revealed to the whole world that the US campaign against terrorism and for human rights is violating human rights. Seven years after 9/11 it is less clear what the West means by 'Western values': the construction or the dismantling of the Guantánamo prison?

In this respect, too, the staging of the risk war has also been undermined by its contradictions. The refrain of the US government that Iraq is the central battlefield in the 'war against terror' has proven not only to be false but also to be self-destructive. In a poll conducted and published by CBS in the summer of 2006, only 9 per cent of the population still agreed with the statement that the Iraq War was helping to combat terrorism. And on its fifth anniversary, 9/11 was far surpassed by the death toll in Iraq: the number of Iraqi civilian fatalities in one month was greater than those who died as a result of the attack on America.

Global Inequality, Local Vulnerability: The Conflict Dynamics of Environmental Hazards Must be Studied within the Framework of Methodological Cosmopolitanism

In the previous chapter I outlined the dichotomizing logic of risk according to which risk *per se* does not exist; rather there exist two mutually exclusive and more or less irreconcilable worldviews concerning the same risk. To the extent that the cognitive schema of risk marks not only how people interpret their experience and understand their world but also how they orient their actions, reality begins to disintegrate into opposing worlds (something which is also reflected in different understandings of risk in different scientific disciplines). On the one hand, the world of modernity is framed and cultivated as 'opportunity', and the gaze is directed to the potential advantages for the decision-maker as individual or as enterprise, state or region. These decision-makers view the negative effects on others as a 'side effect'.[1] On the other hand, modernization appears as a problematic, questionable and even unacceptable jeopardization of one's own social existence by the decisions of others. The latter are prepared to take risky decisions because they see risks primarily as a measure of the probability and scale of occurrences whose admittedly dangerous side effects are outweighed by their advantages, and hence by the significant promise of gain from which they will benefit. To others the same decisions appear as life-threatening, where the decisions and practices that go hand in hand with scientific-technical industrialization and its globalization jeopardize not only the organic foundations of all life forms but also the majority of human beings, without any public debate or consensus. Of particular importance for sociological research in this regard are the illusions of experts, the illusory promises of safety of business, science and state inspectors; however, the illusions of social movements and of the public arenas of the mass media also belong here. This means that risk has become the central way of constituting and organizing society. Hence, the competition, contestation and dichotomous conflict logic associated with social definitions and discourses of risk cannot be confined to the economy or to politics, and certainly not to the national domain. At stake is the simultaneity of cultural and political antagonisms and material destruction and harms which are rooted in the central nervous system of world society.

In the final section of chapter 9, I attempted to trace this basic idea of a dichotomous dynamic of risk conflict in two dimensions: first, the practices of minimizing risks for oneself and the shifting of dangers into the manufactured latency of the suffering, killing and material destruction of others, as organized in the new way of staging violence of risk transfer war; and, second, the intentional catastrophes whose goal is to maximize and globalize the 'felt violence' and 'felt war', in conformity with the cultural symbolism of the morally and legally uninhibited escalation of terrorist violence. The present chapter will develop in a third dimension the logic of *environmental hazards and conflicts* as the anticipation of side effects catastrophes.

Threats to the environment as social threats

The globalization of environmental problems [*Umweltproblemen*] as social problems [*Innenweltprobleme*] obeys a twofold logic. As we have seen, environmental and technical dangers initially spring from the inexorable triumphs of a linear industrialization that is oblivious to its consequences and which consumes its own natural and cultural foundations. Hence environmental hazards are constructions of the 'latent side effects' of industrial decisions (of economic enterprises and of states and also, of course, of consumers and individual persons). During the first modernity, in the latter half of the nineteenth and the first half the twentieth century in Europe, these 'side effects' had to be rescued from institutionalized irrelevance by corresponding social movements and instructive and inflammatory writings (such as *Silent Spring*, etc.). The regulatory energies of states were traditionally directed to mundane, *visible* problems (such as the combined smog of smoke stacks and automobile exhausts). Only gradually were less visible problems (such as toxins in food) taken up. Similarly, companies initially concentrated their risk management efforts on the industrial security of their own factories and workers and are only gradually beginning to regard the long-term effects of the violation of health standards of distant populations as 'their' problem.

This is precisely what is presupposed and prompted by *global* environmental hazards: *the decoupling of the social location and the social decision-making responsibility from the places and times at which other, 'foreign' populations become (or are made) the object of possible physical and social injuries.* Thus perceiving global risks calls for a cosmopolitan outlook that makes it possible to transpose ways of dealing with familiar everyday accidents for which routines and empirical data exist by analogy with rare but catastrophic accidents, of which we have little or no experience and whose 'possible reality' has to be visualized through technological simulation and corresponding scenarios.

In the case of global environmental hazards, scientific progress again plays an important role in prompting collective awareness of the invisibility and the spatio-temporal (de)coupling of decisions and side effects.

The newer they are, the more unfathomable become the problems posed by hazards. These global hazards are marked by complex interactions across national frontiers and – especially difficult to grasp – global sources, dynamics and effects (destruction of the ozone layer in the stratosphere, climate change, global warming, etc.); by long latency periods between activities and changes in global interrelations between energy and material; and by geographical divisions into 'cause regions' and 'side effect regions' where the effects transpire, i.e. complex interrelations between human and physical systems and the slow accumulation of material disruptions and destruction. At the same time, the crises of the future, and the political dynamic of mastering them, are increasingly likely to proceed from these global hazards (chapter 3).

Thus the social latency is in part a result of the everyday 'cultural blindness' vis-à-vis these risks and in part a consequence of their unfathomability and exclusively scientific constitution. This construction of 'latent side effects' is also bound up with the fact that managing them collides with the national outlook and the national logic of political institutions and political action. Global environmental risks are at once latent and ultimate hazards. What is at stake is the survival of the planet; at the same time, these ultimate hazards cannot be politically processed with the traditional institutions through which they are socially perceived.

How can global awareness – and, in particular, the awareness of the developing world – of these hazards be awakened? As regards the role of the social sciences (which can scarcely be underestimated), this cannot be accomplished through global threat analyses or national risk profiles but through comparative analyses of transnational and regional risk constellations in their immanent interrelations with, and their status within, the world risk society, i.e. through the institutionalization of a cosmopolitan outlook on the dynamic of conflict and inequality that unfolds with global risks. This is precisely the topic of this chapter.

As is shown by the political turbulence regularly caused by the protests of social movements at meetings of the World Trade Organization, the international regimes regulating trade, finance and the distribution of resources are acquiring ever greater importance in the distribution of global risks. International risk management is even acquiring increasing influence over national risk policy. An example of this development is how the European Union is extending its key role in the risk management of the European nation-states, for instance, with its January 2007 plan for a European climate policy with painful consequences for the automobile industry. The weakening of national structures and the strengthening of transnational non-governmental organizations of global civil society point in the same direction.

The key questions concerning the framework and norms of cosmopolitan accountability and responsibility crystallize out in these contexts. Andrew Linklater (2001) speaks of 'cosmopolitan harm conventions', by which he means intergovernmental agreements and treaties that transform the inflicting of cross-border injuries and damages into prosecutable and punishable crimes. Here, too, initial proposals for a cosmopolitan law of risk as part of international law are being developed (Strydom 2002; Mason 2005; Apel 1988). As Linklater (1998: 84) puts it, condemning 'transnational harm requires a commitment to regard insiders and outsiders as moral equals . . . Transnational harm provides one of the strongest reasons for widening the boundaries of moral and political communities to engage outsiders in dialogue about matters which affect their vital interests.'[2]

Thus those who cannot dismiss global risks but instead make them into the historical touchstone of theory-construction and research in the social sciences (chapter 11) must create a new agenda for sociological theory. First, it must uncouple society from the nation-state; second, it must abandon the notion that society could be controlled by anybody; third, it must no longer conceive of modernization as a self-perpetuating process of functional differentiation, but as a process that bears within itself the kernel of the self-dissolution, self-endangerment and self-transformation, but also the self-renewal, of the basic institutions of the nation-state and industrial society; and, fourth, as regards global risks, it must accord central importance to the temporal, spatial and social uncoupling of the 'we' of the decision-makers from the 'we' of the side effects.

These are precisely the themes of a historical-empirical social theory of the world risk society which are to be sketched in the following two combined steps. The issue is, on the one hand, *methodological problems*, that is, how the equation of society and the nation-state, which has become the main hindrance to research on the world risk society, can be overcome; on the other hand, it is a matter of a parallel typology of global risk inequalities that makes it possible to concretize the dynamic of risk conflicts according to theme, area and dimension. Both presuppose the distinction between the national, the international, the transnational and the cosmopolitan.

How can the inequality dynamic of world risk society, with its repercussions for regional, national and local spaces, be introduced into theory and research on inequality in sociology? What role is played, in particular, by nation-states, international organizations, social movements and transnational corporations in rejecting and assigning, defining and redistributing, global risks? What role is played by the distinction between 'self-endangerment' and 'endangerment of others' and by the manufactured latency of 'side effects'? What is the importance of the category 'social vulnerability' for understanding 'glocal' risks? How can it be defined and operationalized?

Let us begin with a simple model proposal: why are anonymity, imputability, decision-making autonomy and vulnerability to threats distributed in

Table 10.1 Critical theory of world risk society: paradigm shift in the sociology of social inequalities

		Methodological perspective	
		National	*International*
Transformation of boundaries: (in)congruence of territorial, political,	Congruence of boundaries (either national or international)	I Methodological nationalism (contextualism)	II Methodological internationalism
economic and social boundaries, as well as boundaries between risk decision-makers and those affected by dangers	Incongruence of boundaries (both national and international)	III Methodological transnationalism (regionalism)	IV Methodological cosmopolitanism

radically unequal ways across national borders? For the purposes of illustration, it makes sense to make a paradigmatic distinction between two polar opposite models of global risk inequality: *hierarchy* and *reciprocity*.[3]

Hierarchy: This model can be best illustrated by the pattern of transborder downriver–upriver inequalities. Countries that undergo industrialization upriver of other countries find themselves in the advantageous 'risk-donor situation' of being able to dispose of their 'side effects hazards' in a natural way by exporting them downriver. In this way, downriver countries 'invisibly' and 'unintentionally' become 'receiver countries', hence countries in which what giver countries like to treat as 'invisible' and 'unintentional' is transformed into an often all-too-visible accumulation of medical problems and natural disasters. Two elements – the 'natural' direction of flow and the national hiatus in responsibility, law and co-determination – render the social construction of the 'latent side effects' invisible, making it seem like a matter of fate.

Upstream countries have little incentive to establish and acknowledge hazards and to take corresponding precautionary measures. Downstream countries, by contrast, being isolated by the sovereignty of the other countries, have no control over the hazards to which they are exposed and few possibilities of influencing the decisions which trigger them; likewise they have little negotiation power (at least as regards this risk hierarchy alone). Ultimately they must rely on displays of good will and on international cooperation to pressurize the countries which threaten their basic living conditions into taking action.

Methodological nationalism:

Type 1: *Methodological nationalism* (contextualism)

Type 2: *Hierarchy of international inequalities in risks and threats*

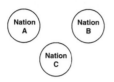

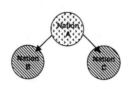

Global risks do not really exist; risks and hazards are defined, distributed and individualized in contextual, national terms (individualization of global risks)

Examples: Chernobyl; centre–periphery; self-endangerment; endangerment of others

Methodological cosmopolitanism:

Type 3: *Transnational actor-networks for defining and distributing risks*

Type 4: *Cosmopolitan inequalities of global risks*

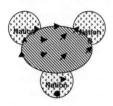

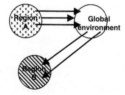

Example: probability and vulnerability of/to BSE, SARS, avian flu, etc.

Social vulnerability; social construction of 'latent side effects'; reflexivity of global risks

Diffusion of decision-makers and those affected	Source nation/region of decision-makers and risks	Nation/region affected by hazards

Figure 10.1 Typology of unequal dynamics of risk and conflict in world risk society

Source: Adapted from Kasperson and Kasperson (2005: 223).

Reciprocity: In this opposing model, the benefits and costs (harms) of decisions involving risks are distributed more or less equally among different countries and regions, including the countries where the risky decisions are made. The opportunities are correspondingly greater to discover and organize shared interests in cross-border prevention and control of risks and to implement them in institutionally binding ways (the North Sea littoral states being an example). Insofar as cultural perceptions of risk diverge against a backdrop of national stereotypes, however, it is difficult to translate this theoretical commonality of transnational communities of risk destiny into practically effective regimes (as is shown by the example of Asia).

The hazards threatening the world show no respect for borders, sovereignty, political authority or government. At the same time, their social and political definition conforms surprisingly to the international order of nation-states. Taking the key methodological question of which unit of investigation is assumed or defined in each case, I would now like to present the typology of unequal risk situations and dynamics of conflict (Table 10.1).

Type 1: methodological nationalism

A first and fundamental criticism concerns how (inequality-)sociology defines its unit of investigation (as should be clear from the parallel methodological and substantive distinctions presented in table 10.1 and figure 10.1). What is analysed here using the example of the production, definition and distribution of risk (and, to be more precise, only in the dimension of *environmental*, not of *economic* global risks) can and must also be analysed in the various dimensions of the distribution of wealth and poverty, hence the classical themes of the sociology of global inequalities. The methodological schema of argument is similar in both cases (see Beck 2005: 20–34). There are different ways of sharpening the sociological perception of transnational and global constellations of conflicts. The systematic differentiation of various inequality and conflict scenarios – national, international, transnational and cosmopolitan and, corresponding to this, methodological nationalism, hierarchy of international inequalities in risks and threats, transnational actor-networks for defining and producing risks, and cosmopolitan inequalities of global risks – is already sufficient to refute the unreflected monopoly claim of methodological nationalism (on this see, among others, Beck 2006; Beck and Sznaider 2006, including its bibliography).

However, if I may add a terminological remark, the concept of methodological nationalism must not be confused with an *explicitly* national methodology. The concept 'methodological' is used here more in a metaphorical sense. It involves a set of *implicit* historical premises whose analysis and critique is a task for a sociology of sociology. Two (non-mutually exclusive) variants of methodological nationalism must be distinguished: a *historical* concept (that points to the nineteenth-century genesis of sociology) and a *logical* concept (that reflects the internal connection between individual background assumptions; see Chernilo 2006).[4]

How does this methodological nationalism construe inequality? 'Society', as organized and limited by the nation-state, is presupposed as the unit of investigation of the empirical and theoretical sociology of inequality (regardless of whether society is defined in terms of class, stratification or individualization, or in terms of inequalities of age, gender, town and country or region). Two variants of methodological nationalism can be distinguished here: national-sociological *self-analysis* (social structural analysis of Germany by German sociology or of Great Britain by British sociology, etc.) and *comparative studies* (comparison of national societies).

To be more precise, methodological nationalism rests on a twofold congruence assumption: first, of congruence between territorial, political, economic, social and cultural boundaries and, second, of congruence between the actor perspective and the perspective of the social scientific observer. As a consequence, the premise of the actors' normative-political nationalism is unreflectively adopted as the premise of the observer perspective of social science. These two congruence assumptions are mutually reinforcing.

The research problems, the social and political questions and conflicts thrown up by the incongruence of borders, cannot be posed, let alone answered, within the framework of methodological nationalism, whether in empirical, theoretical or political terms. Although territorial, state, economic and social boundaries continue to exist, they no longer coexist. This triggers an avalanche of questions, concerning the *ambivalence* of co-national or multinational contexts of action and life situations; concerning the *contingency* of incongruent border constructions that must be deciphered as the result of individual and collective decisions; and concerning the production and reproduction of *transnational* spaces of action (translevel and transborder interaction networks).

Thus what is decisive is the *extension of risks across borders* and the *social constructions of latency*. Methodological nationalism prevents these two issues from being thematized. As a consequence, the change in the meaning of borders in world risk society remains unrecognized. Asserting an abstract and general 'globalization of risk' does not go far enough. Overcoming borders often takes the form of a deliberate export of threats by shifting them onto others. In such cases, overcoming borders must be understood as a strategy that seeks to transform the lax safety standards in other political jurisdictions or continents into economic profit. Border-transcending strategies also exploit zones of least resistance, and hence follow the power hierarchy both within national borders and in the international domain (see above pp. 140ff.).

Thus the freeing of threats from boundaries does not annul national borders but instead presupposes and exploits them. Because national borders are at the same time boundaries of vision and relevance, they can be used to produce latency and side effects constructions. In this way, the spatial separation between the places in which the risks are produced – between the 'decision-maker regions' and the 'victim regions' in which human beings and nature are exposed to the potentially and really destructive side effects – makes it possible to cause global risk inequalities to *disappear*. This occurs in a *twofold* way in the methodological nationalism of inequality and risk sociology. It confirms the non-existence of global inequalities, not because it explicitly denies them (based on empirical research) but because its unit of investigation and the corresponding questions and theoretical assumptions remain focused exclusively on national societies to the exclusion of the 'side effects' for others. This does not change even when comparative studies of national risk profiles are presented that fail to take account of the cross-border interdependencies and interactions and the 'glocalizing' moments of world risk society.

The result is that the spatial segregation between the contexts of producers and of those affected and its doubling in the methodological-national outlook of social science leads to an *intensification* and unequal accumulation of risks across the borders that render them invisible. Those who, beholden to methodological nationalism, concentrate on the national context, therefore, fail to appreciate the distinction between those affected by hazards who, within the nation-state in question, can at least *in principle* influence the decisions whose impacts threaten their health, and those who are denied *any* such possibilities.

The victim nations or victim regions become collection points of risks and harms not least because of the prevailing lack of knowledge or wilful ignorance (chapter 8). The more extensive is non-knowledge or partial knowledge concerning the possibility and reality of unexpected threats, the greater is the communicative and political turmoil before, and especially during, the catastrophe. Because nothing is known, or nothing precisely, cultural and political problems pile up, rumours run wild and hostile stereotypes are revived. This is what makes cross-border distributions of risks and hazards so politically explosive. Once a catastrophe occurs, the strict demarcations of legal classification and responsibility, but also of information, take hold, with the result that an unholy confusion of safety standards, technical knowledge, defensive and preventive norms, affected markets and political elites breaks out between states (a paradigmatic case being the BSE crisis). Here again a paradox emerges. The political explosiveness of transnational risks is based on the national responsibilities for defining and preparing for risks. Hence, responsibility, conceptions of justice, distrust and inveterate cultural stereotypes clash with one another in the case of hazards affecting a plurality of nations – and which hazards do not in the world risk society? However, methodological nationalism in sociology – this is the refrain – blinds us to all of this. Why?

Insofar as society disintegrates on the methodological nationalist outlook into demarcated, territorially bound national societies organized as states that are inward-looking and closed off from the outside, global risk inequalities are fragmented into domestic national risk issues. The latter are easily disguised by the pluralization and anonymization of risk and threat standpoints, whereas international hierarchies and inequalities remain beyond the field of vision. If risk inequalities are located exclusively within the national horizon of observation, they appear diffuse and ambiguous because the risk issues change and in the process so does the accountability for their consequences (see pp. 143ff.).

On the one hand, the decision-maker region and the threat-receiver region remain interrelated according to the social logic of risk. On the other hand, political-methodological nationalism severs this connection insofar as politics and research concentrate on the national context. For the global hierarchies between centre and periphery to remain invisible, they must count as *incomparable*. On this approach, what is politically necessary within nation-states – namely, comparing inequalities – becomes politically irrelevant between states.[5]

The export of threats to non-developed countries and the import of labour from these countries means that the countries in which the global threats are accumulating are being stripped of the people and professional skills required to deal with these threats (see UNFPA 2006). For example, more Malawian doctors now work in Manchester than in the whole of Malawi, a southeast African country with a population of 13 million people. If 20,000 people with medical training continue to emigrate from Africa per annum, the developmental goals for HIV/AIDS and infant and maternal mortality will remain beyond reach. According to the United Nations Population Fund, the problem will become more acute because of the 'huge demand' for nurses in the ageing societies of the developed countries.

However, methodological nationalism also obscures the fact that the migration so demonized in the West has become an important source of private developmental aid and poverty alleviation in the Third World. According to World Bank estimates, in 2005 migrant workers transferred a total of $232 billion of their foreign earnings to support relations in their native countries; $167 billion went to developing countries. This sum is considerably greater than all developmental aid together ($106.5 billion, of which $75 billion were donated by states). The largest part of these contributions went for healthcare and the education of children. Experts assume that the total sum of transfers to native countries is twice this level because many migrants send cash to avoid bank fees.

Conversely, methodological nationalism leads or misleads to an *individualization of global risks*. In combination with neoliberalism, the individual becomes his own 'moral entrepreneur' and thus holds the fate of civilization in his hands. The result is a new 'categorical imperative': act as though the fate of the world depends on your action. Separate your waste, ride a bicycle, use solar energy, etc. The key contradiction which is both obscured and revealed here is that the individual is condemned to individualization and self-responsibility, even vis-à-vis global threats, despite the fact that he is severed from the decision contexts which escape his influence.

Type 2: hierarchy of international inequalities in risks and threats

Here the focus of investigation is no longer on national social units but on binational constellations that build on the difference between the national and international. This differentiates these types of transnational constellations which overlay the national/international dichotomy. The question of who are the agents of risks and who the victims, who the winners and who the losers, is not obscured at this level by a general blurring and mixing of decision-makers and those affected; it follows the schema for allocating responsibility and the national-cultural stereotypes and hostile stereotypes in relations between nations: *self-endangerment* and *endangerment of others*. Individualizations are possible (perhaps even probable) within the schema of self-endangerment within states. Threats to others that extend across national borders, by contrast, conform to collective stereotypes in perceiving and imputing threats – they follow the opposition 'us versus them'. This way of structuring international relations has two consequences: on the one hand, the national spaces permeate one another in accordance with the risk conflict between decision-makers and those affected; on the other hand, the context of the decision-makers who determine the causes and the context of the hazardous consequences of these decisions coincide with the boundaries and conflicts of national spaces of perception and action.

Because risk inequalities permeate and split national spaces, national antagonisms can be intensified and aggravated socially and politically by a whole range of situations and perceptions of risks and threats. The national stereotypes and the easily inflammable antagonisms and emotions conserved in them function like sounding boards. Even relatively minor threats that can be ignored and rendered anonymous in the national sphere can take on a life of their own and trigger public uproar in conflicts between nations. If the 'country of origin' of the threats and the 'receiver country' share an involved history of conflict and, in addition, national nerves are at present raw, even the most minor 'export' of threats can be expected to trigger a storm of protest and acquire a correspondingly high political urgency.

These cross-border conflicts exhibit predictable patterns in which the dramatization in the national space of the victims contrasts with the de-dramatization in the national space of the decision-makers. If significant risks are incurred in the risk decision-maker region, while the dangerous consequences are foisted onto the others, then the resources for threat prevention and for precautionary measures against risks are similarly unequally distributed between the nations. The managers in the export countries are subject to less pressure to 'waste' their scarce resources in controlling and minimizing risks. Since one's own national public, for the simple reason that it is a national public, attaches slight value to sensitivity to threats affecting others, one can tacitly assume that the 'unseen' and 'unintentional' hazards will be felt primarily on the other side of the national garden fence.

It becomes clear above all that the unimputability and anonymity of risk are neither a systematic feature of modernity in general nor a necessary implication of the conceptual logic of the distinction between risk and catastrophe. They are the results of power strategies whose success depends on the fact that norms of equality and accountability end at the national garden fence and to what extent a country sees itself as one of the winners or losers of risk inequality. Thus, in dealing with 'large-scale' risks, in international relations something is practised as a matter of course that appears to be analytically excluded within national domains: a clear distinction is made in risk conflicts between the causers and the victims, and the question of responsibility is raised and negotiated in a politically charged way.

A textbook historical example of this is the Chernobyl reactor catastrophe. As the anthropologist Adriana Petryna delineates in her excellent study *Life Exposed: Biological Citizens after Chernobyl* (2002), the fact that the reactor catastrophe overlapped with the collapse of the Soviet Union gave rise to conflicts over the definition of threats that both aggravated and deepened the national antagonisms between Russia and Ukraine, so that one can say that, in the post-Soviet constellation, the Chernobyl reactor catastrophe made possible, or at least favoured, Ukrainian nation-building. The scientific and political uncertainties in coping with different levels of nuclear contamination became, on the one hand, a fact of life and, on the other, 'material' for conflicts over national differentiation.

Such claims reflect new experimental fabrics in which science, nation building, and market developments are interdependent, and the biology of citizens becomes a contested part of a political process and a tool of government . . . In 1991, the year Ukraine declared independence from the Soviet Union, leaders of this once socialist republic condemned the Soviet administration for the Chernobyl aftermath and began fostering their own political legitimacy. Nationalists, Communists, and Democrats alike entered into a novel (short-lived) political alliance when they unanimously denounced the Soviet administration as an 'act of genocide.' The charge of genocide referenced a national symbol of Soviet oppression, the 1930s famine . . . Legislators claimed that not only had the Soviet state apparatus failed in its obligation to protect citizens' lives during the Chernobyl disaster but that, in its denial of the event and its effort to restart the nuclear program, it had exacerbated patterns of morbidity by delaying intervention. Legislators (many of whom had had roles in the Soviet administration or were dissidents) . . . viewed their political alliance as an opportunity to quickly do away with central power. This was especially true of well-organized

Ukrainian Communist elites who, after much of the initial symbolic power of anti-Soviet nationalist groups . . . had waned, rose to central prominence. In this moment of nation building, one could observe how bioscientific knowledge became a crucial medium in state-building processes and in the establishment of new policies guaranteeing safe living, social equity, and human rights. (Petryna 2002: 21, 23)

In order to unlock national sources of legitimation, Ukrainian politicians from different parties manipulated the relations of risk definition and changed the Soviet norms governing biological risks for the population. Thus the Soviets had defined an upper dose of 35 rems as the threshold value factored over the complete lifetime of a person (equated with a life expectancy of seventy years). This value determines whether a particular level of nuclear contamination counts as contamination or not. This definition parameter laid down guidelines according to which resettlements were ordered, welfare payments allocated, etc. Ukrainian law reduced the tolerable dose to 7 rems, taking its orientation from the average value that an American is expected to tolerate over a complete lifetime. This strategic manipulation of the relations of definition to lower the tolerable threshold value unleashed a social and political tidal wave. The boundaries of the regions which now suddenly counted as contaminated expanded enormously as if by magic. Conversely, the number of workers available to perform repairs on the reactor fell dramatically. For a large proportion of the population, this new definition represented a welcome opportunity to take advantage of the corresponding state-guaranteed welfare payments for victims. For this change in the yardstick of definition transformed 'normal citizens' into 'victims', who could count on substantial financial support provided that they managed to lay claim to the status of victim. The struggle for recognition over the status of 'nuclear handicapped person' led in turn to new solidarities and boundary lines. In this way, the post-Chernobyl disaster became the key to moral, economic and political events which made deep inroads into social existence and identity and state institutions in Ukraine and enabled it to transform itself and sharpen its political profile by demarcating itself from the 'criminal perpetrator-nation' Russia.

Here too the basic principle of reflexive modernization finds confirmation. For in the Soviet and the post-Soviet responses to Chernobyl, this 'biopolitics' (Foucault) did not achieve the intended effect of controlling the behaviour of populations through scientific and state authority. Instead the exact opposite happened: it created new spaces of non-knowledge, unpredictability and uncontrollability. Old criteria of suffering and therapeutic standards lost their meaning and validity in the face of the combination of scientific and medical uncertainties. Indeed, the interconnection and intermingling of ignorance and contamination, which also affects children and grandchildren, became a new 'condition of life'. '"Friends!" cried a survivor, "yesterday Chernobyl science reassured you: Be calm, we have everything under control.

Today, now that we are contaminated, they declare us to be psychopaths. Who knows what science will tell us next"' (Petryna 2002: 27). This reveals the existential meaning of non-knowledge: non-knowing is becoming the medium and milieu from which threats and conditions of life are emerging. In the search for lost security, the 'living side effects' are compelled to provide unknown answers to questions that they had not even been able to ask until then.

Type 3: transnational actor-networks for defining and distributing risks

Existential risk situations and spaces of action that extend, overlay and place in question the national either/or through a co-national both/and are called 'transnational'. The units of investigation are no longer national societies but 'transnational constellations', hence regional spaces. Methodologically speaking, this presupposes the interconnection of (at least) two national frames of reference of social scientific observation.

The initial premise is that general analyses and statements concerning 'global' environmental change and ecological crises (such as, for example, climate change, cumulative losses in global biodiversity, global energy consumption and non-renewable resources) tell us nothing about the destruction of the environment in particular contexts and regions. Most importantly, they overlook the *social vulnerability* which becomes apparent only on the regional outlook. I will use two examples to illustrate this: comparative regional studies and a network analysis of the risk posed by SARS.

Comparative regional studies

We need analyses that are not globally or nationally but transnationally and regionally oriented – in other words, ones that define the unit of investigation for comparative regional studies such as that of Jeanne X. Kasperson und Roger E. Kasperson (2005):

Our own regional analyses suggest that the conditions of impoverishment, endangerment and criticality, and the regional dynamics that cause them, take widely different forms and arise from different circumstances in each regional context. No simple evolutionary pattern or set of regional dynamics of change holds true across all nine regions. In particular, the relationship between growing environmental degradation and changes in the wealth and well-being of inhabitants varies markedly from region to region.

Figure 10.2 suggests some cases, although many others are possible. Case 1 represents the situation often assumed in which increasing environmental degradation causes wealth and well-being to decline – in other words, growing criticality. But in case 2, a shift from an agricultural to an industrial economy allows continuing increases in wealth and well-being in the face of continuing environmental degradation

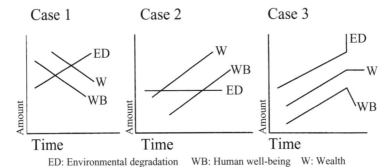

ED: Environmental degradation　WB: Human well-being　W: Wealth

Figure 10.2 Contrasting simple regional trajectories of environmental change
Source: Adapted from Kasperson and Kasperson (2005: 189).

(although, presumably, this cannot continue indefinitely). In case 3, continued exploitation of resources supports increasing accumulation of wealth, but continued deterioration of environmental quality eventually results in 'bite-back' upswings in environmentally induced disease and downwards trends in human well-being. In fact, although case 2 is counter-intuitive, it reflects a widespread pattern in our new regional studies and highlights the complexity which distinguishes the regional perspective on risk situations. (Ibid.: 188)

Thus case 2 represents a transitional phenomenon which suddenly changes into case 3 in zones of rapid industrialization (for instance in Asia).

In methodological regionalism (transnationalism), however, the questions of what influence global risks and connections between the regions and with the global economy have for particular contexts remain as insufficiently explained as corresponding causal connections and possible forms of accountability. The question of how the contexts of decision-maker regions and threat regions can and must be related to one another in the transnational space of risk distribution and of the global, international and national institutions concerned, for example, cannot really be addressed in a regionally restricted transnationality. This calls for a cosmopolitan outlook.

Network analysis of the SARS risk

'Flows' (Appadurai), 'actor-networks' (Latour), 'liquidity' (Bauman), 'scapes' (Albrow) – these metaphors are designed to render the boundary-transforming and boundary-transcending processes of 'transnational spaces' representable, understandable and susceptible to research. Viewed in this way, world risk society is a *process*, one in which the transcending and the setting of boundaries intermesh and unexpected relations and interconnections arise, are enforced or are rejected. Aihwa Ong has proposed the concept of 'global assemblage' (2004: 81) for this process. By this she understands the mobilization of significant connections between different elements whose effects on the meaning of individual and social life are open and are not easily foreseeable. She makes clear what she means by this through a network analysis of the SARS (severe acute respiratory syndrome) risk, a life-threatening virus that spreads stealthily (see also Schillmeier and Pohler 2006). The immediate responses to the SARS virus gave rise to an 'assemblage' of institutions, governments, experts and ethics across borders and great geographical distances. The health experts in Asian cities and global medical institutions in different parts of the world were included in medical measures and administrative monitoring practices. This produced a network of joint calculation efforts across national borders. The 'mobility stream' of the SARS risk gave rise to transactive, novel and unexpected connections between hospitals and doctors in Hong Kong and other Asian cities, on the one hand, and institutions such as the World Health Organization and the Center for Disease Control in Atlanta, on the other. The new diagnostic keys were developed on one side of the world and were tested and put into action on the other. In an interplay between technology, governments and monitoring agencies, 'SARS-free' and 'SARS-infected' areas were distinguished in which different norms of conduct and control were to be applied. In this way, political spaces that were otherwise sealed off from one another were transformed into overlapping, transnational zones of governance. Even the military was brought into play to an extent and drastic surveillance measures were implemented. Transnational intervention spaces arose where risk zones threatened to violate the prevailing safety norms. The primacy of safety was implemented strictly at both the local and the national level through global norms and instruments based on scientific expertise.

It all began with the outbreak of the illness in China. Initially the Chinese government succumbed to the impulse to tailor its information policy to the demands of maintaining social order by playing down and concealing the threat. However, such a non-information policy is utterly counterproductive in the case of risk networks and allocations of threats that cannot be delimited. The attempt to control risks by withholding information and covering up the spread of the threat set the emergency sirens blaring across the world. Because in the globalized world the SARS risk necessitates interventions by international organizations, in the end the Chinese authorities bowed to the requirements of transnational risk management. Only through cross-border cooperation could the necessary resources be mobilized also for local solutions, ranging from medical knowledge through strategies of containment and control up to the proclamation of global norms designed to stabilize trust and hence the markets.

Here we again encounter the law of the production of political added value in the global era: transnational cooperation is the precondition for successful national and local risk management. Not by insisting on local autonomy and national sovereignty but, on the contrary, only by expressly violating them could the sum of capabilities be mobilized that ultimately made it possible to find the shortest route to solutions to regional problems via global detours.

At the same time, these transnational actor-networks bring polarizations to light, such as the proximity of risk and exclusion and of risk and stigma (Hudson 2003). Health risks mutate into threats to the national economy (job losses, loss of wealth, etc.), which in turn jeopardize political and civil basic rights, with the result that authoritarian states in particular are able to 'overhaul' their precarious authority and legitimacy through the 'struggle against risk'. The preoccupation with security and the political exploitation of fear enable states to appeal to global institutions and their requirements to violate individual liberties without any fear of outcry or protest. This leads to an 'internal globalization' of national risk policy. Inside and outside, us and them, can no longer be clearly distinguished. This can go hand in hand with an authoritarian policy of renationalization, so that it is not completely mistaken to say that cosmopolitanization and renationalization both hinder and complement one another (Levy and Sznaider 2006).

Type 4: cosmopolitan inequalities of global risks

In recent years, the concept of cosmopolitanism has developed into one of the key concepts in social science. The newly awakened interest in this concept is fed by different sources: research on globalization in social science, research on mobility and migration in sociology, postcolonial studies, postfeminism, global culture studies, ethnography, the debate over new wars and human rights and social-psychological research on identity (diaspora), to name just a few of the most important. In sociology these analyses are crystallizing into the paradigm of a 'new cosmopolitanism' (Beck 2006; Beck and Sznaider 2006). At its centre are, on the one hand, the search for new research methods and strategies and, on the other, the question of how social ways of dealing with difference are reflected in the dynamics of inequality and conflict of world risk society.

Those who appeal to cosmopolitanism to address radical global inequalities are faced with a whole series of intractable problems. The norms which can be termed 'cosmopolitan' – namely, incorporating potentially affected non-nationals in our own decision-making – are met with complete incomprehension on the prevailing national self-understanding. The reason is the common assumption that a proud nation-state has the right to endanger not only its own environment but also that of other nation-states (and of future generations). Moreover, there is an unbridgeable chasm between the cosmopolitan conception of reciprocal, legally encoded duties across national borders and the realities of a world that makes a separation between the decision-making nations of the centre and the victim regions of the so-called Third World. One of the demoralizing paradoxes of world risk society is that the latter refuse to recognize their own victim status. With this silence born of necessity, the victim regions turn themselves into involuntary accessories to their own exploitation. By contrast, the cosmopolitan 'know-it-alls' (mostly from the centre) would have to set themselves up against all resistance as the spokespeople of global regions that reject this 'presumptuous' intercession and representation. Can one imagine anything more hopeless (assuming that this 'more hopeless' is even conceivable)?

Precisely in such a situation it is important to reflect again on the difference between *normative* and *political* cosmopolitanism, on the one hand, and *methodological* cosmopolitanism, on the other. Although both dimensions are interrelated, it is possible, indeed necessary, to reinforce the claim of the social sciences to be sciences of reality by advocating and extending empirical-analytical cosmopolitanism in the social sciences, *without* succumbing in the process to the hope that this implies the triumph of normative cosmopolitanism. For sociology would no longer be sociology if it tried to interpret the boundary-transcending anticipations of the world risk society in accordance with the inappropriate maxims of methodological nationalism. This holds even if, in light of the ever newer, more unfathomable risks that are haunting the global village, ever more people are withdrawing and barricading themselves inside their national fortresses with prophylactic trembling and gnashing of teeth. A methodological cosmopolitanism is also necessary to understand this reaction!

Notwithstanding their fuzziness – or, to be more precise, on account of their fuzziness – global environmental risks share a series of structural features. First, there is their cosmopolitan character, whereby local problems have their causes and – possibly – their solutions on the other side of the world. The premises on which the image of the world of the first modernity is founded – the either/or of internal and external, national and international – are no longer valid. With the globalization of risks, key problems have become in principle *non-linear* in their causation and their foreseeable consequences; they have become discontinuous in both space and time, which makes them inherently unpredictable, almost incomprehensible and even less 'manageable', as measured by the traditional methods of observation and control. Populations, economies, nature and culture at the beginning of the twenty-first century are interconnected at the global level in a co-evolution in which the repercussions in one or other domain influence each other in unknown ways that are difficult to predict. This places the foundations of our concepts and of the national institutions of industrial society in question.

As a result, global environmental risks combine what formerly seemed to be mutually exclusive, namely, non-knowledge and a pronounced tendency towards reflexivity and explosiveness within the global public sphere. They are widening the gap between risk experts and public perceptions. Cultural perceptions and evaluations are gaining the upper hand over factual knowledge. Accordingly, divisions are opening up between the regions in which the risks are produced and the regions in which their dangerous effects are felt – according to the accountability pattern of self-endangerment versus endangerment of others. The existing regulatory institutions are losing credibility. Thus one can say that the anticipation of global catastrophes is corroding confidence in institutional safety promises, even though this confidence is necessary if we are even to begin to develop responses to these kinds of challenges. Thus, from the perspective of sociology and political science, such global risk conflicts provide the framework and additional ammunition for political animosities between states, between social movements and states, between companies and labour unions, etc. In this sense, global environmental risks represent a *perplexing combination of lack of knowledge and ultimate importance* to which a sociology of anticipated catastrophes must become responsive (see chapter 7). Here I will present three initial steps in this direction: first, by addressing the question concerning *social* vulnerability, second, by clarifying the *global reflexivity of global risks* and, third, by explaining the connection to *global governance*.

Social vulnerability

Without the concept of *social vulnerability*, talk of global (environmental) dangers remains empty. That risk and vulnerability are two sides of the same coin is a well-worn truth for all approaches that view risk as a co-product. Yet in recent years the at once key and puzzling term 'vulnerability' has become a core element in the analysis of global social structures. Social processes and relations lead to unequal exposure to risks and the resulting inequalities must be treated as largely an expression and product of power relations at the national and global levels. Social vulnerability is a cumulative concept that includes the means and possibilities available to individuals, societies or whole populations to cope (or not) with the risks – the 'unknown unknowns' – and the (social) uncertainties that mark their lives.

A sociological conception of vulnerability has a pronounced reference to the future, yet it combines with this a profound rootedness in the past. For the 'cultural wounds' deriving from the colonial past, for instance, represent an important backdrop for understanding cosmopolitan risk conflicts. The more marginal are the available economic and political options, the more vulnerable is a particular group or population. The question which makes it possible to identify the unit of investigation is: What constitutes vulnerability in a particular context and how did this come about?

The sources of impoverishment are largely a matter of the relations linking one social unit with others, and in tracing these relations one is led beyond the boundaries of the geographical location of the impoverished population. Hence, critical approaches look for causal linkages or networks of causes whose often historical origins generally lie outside the geographical region of the social unit in question; in the process, they bring connections to light that tend to be obscured by the social construction of side effects.

For example, in south-central Mali, increased vulnerability of villages to catastrophic fires follows from state-directed fire policies that are, in turn, a response to international concerns about the deforestation and 'desertification' of the Sahelian fringe that find their way into various international accords and, ultimately, the conditions for international loans to the country in question. For much of the economically 'have-not' world, these relations are traceable to colonialism and are redirected and amplified under 'globalization'. (Kasperson and Kasperson 2005: 261)

Thus 'social vulnerability' cannot be precisely delimited either in space or in time but is a methodological implication of the cosmopolitan outlook.

At the start there is the choice of the threatened unit, the unit of analysis of social vulnerability: Who or what is exposed to what danger? The point is to examine how this context of threats can be traced back, possibly across borders, to the context of the decision-makers. In other words, the analysis of vulnerability must be geared to bringing the dynamic of 'cross-scale interactions' (Kasperson and Kasperson) into our field of vision. This means that events or phenomena on one scale influence phenomena on another scale. The erosion of the boundaries of environmental harms, legal institutions and political authorities in this sense constitutes a key standpoint for analysing vulnerability.

Driving forces often emanate from macro-forces, institutions or policies set at higher-level scales – land tenure regimes, technological change, international financial institutions and government policy – and are articulated through a finer pattern of local scales with highly variable local resource and ecological settings. Political jurisdiction links to management by way of projects and 'hot spots', not via ecosystems or populations. Similarly, the timescale of political institutions stresses business cycles, electoral terms of office and budget processes, rather than spans of biological generation or ecosystem change. As a result, many environmental problems become exports to distant places (e.g. deforestation in Indonesia and the international timber trade) or to distant generations (e.g. the disposal of hazardous chemical or radioactive materials). Moreover, the scope of political authority often matches poorly the scope of impacts and vulnerabilities, so that 'transboundary' effects on vulnerable people and places are increasingly common. (Ibid.: 271)

It has become extremely difficult for states and globally operating companies to avoid, and especially to refute, public allegations that their decisions are leading to damage to or the destruction of the natural foundations of life of particular regions or population groups. The increase in ecological discourses and regimes at the national and international levels (Meyer 2005) provides important confirmation of the fact that cross-border violations have become a potential or actual political issue that provides ample ammunition for subpolitical dramatizations, especially for globally operating civic groups of all kinds (see chapter 5).

The recognition that the issue of the environment enjoys in principle (since the 1992 conference in Rio) is one thing; the other is that it is now generally accepted that at the same time (or maybe even as a result) there is a deficit of responsibility and accountability because, notwithstanding a range of agreements and treaties in environmental law, we still lack authorities capable of translating lip service into actions. The activities and strategies of the interconnected groups and groupuscules proliferate in this legitimation vacuum together with the definition and staging power of the principal flag bearers of global civil society. This is in large part a function of the *cosmopolitan* claim of these organizations. It is they who claim to lend their voice to the violated and damaged regions of world risk society. It is they who speak for the collective interest of the world against the globally powerful interests of the Western decision-maker regions (Mason 2005).

However, this cosmopolitanism, which comes both *from below* and *from above*, is also open to criticism: from below, because it claims to be a grassroots movement, from above, because it employs the economic and military definitional power of the centre even in the victim regions. In accordance with their cross-border radius of action, these groups advocate the implementation of precautionary norms and treaties against the arbitrary freedom of the latent politics of side effects. Their activities are aimed at making states and companies really responsible for the consequences of their actions and at assigning responsibility for actual or potential violations of law, at stimulating public discussion of these kinds of injuries or threats to others, and at raising claims for corresponding forms of compensation.

Critical voices have been raised within the NGO community that charge this cosmopolitanism with a Eurocentric bias. Kellow (2000), for example, is sceptical concerning the moral cosmopolitanism claimed by Greenpeace. Both the flow of donations and the executive cooperation in four countries he investigated (Germany, the Netherlands, Switzerland and Great Britain) reflected how Western European priorities shape the topics and agenda. This is shown, according to Kellow, by how 'global' climate change is taken up in campaigns and in the process both energy efficiency and a stronger environmental services sector are promoted. Precisely this agreement between the policy of Greenpeace and the public policies of the major Western European, ecologically friendly governments reveals the 'Eurocentric cosmopolitanism'. The states, Kellow argues, anticipate the policies adopted by Greenpeace and vice versa, thereby giving rise to a new kind of transnational cooperationism under the banner of cosmopolitanism. Correspondingly, an *asymmetry of participation* is discernible in various forms between those who have appropriated the dramaturgy of climate change and those whose natural and social conditions of life are most enduringly harmed by climate change. A 'topdown' politics is also taking shape within the so-called cosmopolitanism 'from below': it is the cosmopolitan movements which emerged 'from below' in particular which are setting the tone at every level of global environmental politics.[6]

Taking our orientation from cosmopolitan analyses that transcend boundaries, dimensions and spheres of influence, therefore, we can bring to light *cosmopolitan pathologies* that have the potential to trigger the major conflicts of the twenty-first century in the overlap between natural and social conditions and threats.

In this sense, methodological cosmopolitanism must be understood as an incipient research agenda that makes it possible to lead sociology back to its original topic, namely, a reality that is no longer national or international but has become cosmopolitan. It opens up the horizon for the 'cosmopolitan realism' of a new critical theory of world risk society which is in a strong position vis-à-vis the backward-looking idealism of the national outlooks in politics, research and theory (chapter 9).

Reflexive globality: global risks and effects publics[7]

The regional inequalities in social vulnerability as a result of modernization must be seen in terms of the tension-latent relation to the totality of the global problem situations. The collapse of global financial markets or changes in climate zones affect individual regions in very different ways; nevertheless *anyone* can be affected in principle – hence coming to terms with the problems necessitates *global efforts*. One can interpret this, following Martin Albrow (1996), in such a way that the principle of 'globality' – in the sense of an increasing awareness of global interconnections – is becoming increasingly valid (see also Robertson 1992).

Thus, for example, global environmental threats could foster an awareness that the earth's population (comprising present and future generations) constitutes a 'community of fate'. The latter is by no means conflict-free. For instance, contradictions become apparent when the industrial countries call for the protection of important global resources, such as rainforests, while simultaneously reserving the lion's share of energy resources for themselves.[8] Yet these conflicts already perform an integrative function by making clear that global solutions must be found not through war but through negotiations. Solutions are difficult to imagine without new global institutions and sets of rules, and hence without a certain degree of convergence. Thus transnational risk communities and effects publics leading to an 'involuntary cosmopolitanization' of world risk society are fostered by the long-term cross-border impacts and expectations of the unexpected (see chapters 3 and 9).

However, this is just *one* possible consequence of globalized threat constellations. We can conceive of positions that draw exactly the opposite conclusion from the dilemmas posed by global threats, namely, that we should not strive for an adequate global, but instead for a better 'alternative', modernity. This alternative modernity is shaped, interestingly enough, by the problems generated by Western modernity; and thus Western modernization, with all of its 'defects', becomes the indispensable contrasting foil and point of reference for new models of development (cf. Holzer 1999: chapter 4). Politicians such as Malaysia's Muhammad Mahathir or Singapore's Lee Kuan Yew do not advocate rejecting modernity as such because they enthusiastically promote modern production methods, mass media and business. However, they play with the idea of drawing selectively from the package offered by Western modernity.

Global risks are also ambivalent in this respect. On the one hand, they are an essential medium of globality and, on the other, an occasion and reason for demarcating other modernities from the Western one. This is the necessary implication of a historical situation in which the uncertainties of a globalized second modernity merge with the regionally different points of departure of a first modernity that is still in part an aspiration, though already in part abandoned. The very disagreement over the unforeseeable consequences of modernity, therefore, gives rise to a cosmopolitan discourse across all national borders in the new 'overlapping communities of fate' (Held 2000a: 400), a cosmopolitan discourse with an associated claim to networked action.

It would be too easy to assume that globality could spontaneously generate a shared global or planetary consciousness. The everyday experience of globality does not take the form of a love affair of everyone with everyone else. It develops in the perceived emergency of global threats to civilized action – in the networks, financial flows or natural crises mediated by information technology. These consequences are creating a pressure to cooperate which is 'forcing the world to unite in the face of joint risks and transnational threats to an autoaggressive commune' (Sloterdijk 1999: 984). In other words, it is the *reflexivity of world risk society* that founds the reciprocal relation between publicity and globality. With the constructed and accepted planetary definition of threats, a joint space of responsibility and action is being created across all national boundaries and divisions, a space that *potentially* (though not necessarily) founds political action between strangers in an analogous way to the national space. This is the case when the accepted definition of threats leads to global norms, agreements and joint action. The comprehensive studies of the emergence of corresponding international and transnational regimes, however, have shown how difficult it often is to get from defining threats to defining action.[9]

However, the emergence of a globalized discursive horizon and the consequent pressure for legitimation are already discernible. Conflicts, negotiations and regime formations are increasingly concerned with externalities, the systematic costs and dangers of modernization. This can be understood as the emergence of an increasingly transnational *effects public* in Dewey's sense (see p. 59).[10] Permanent communication concerning threats is an important component of informal planetary norm-formation. Thus the process of norm-formation in the world risk society is understood too narrowly if one confines its potential to global coordinating institutions yet to be created, as for example in Held (2000a). Global norms emerge from the outrage over situations that are felt to be intolerable already *prior to* institutionalization. Norms sometimes follow as a 'by-product of their own violation, hence retrospectively' (Luhmann 1999: 250). In other words, the emergence of global norms does not necessary depend on conscious efforts of 'positive' norm-creation but can be sustained – negatively, as it were – by crisis and threat assessments.[11]

The need to accord central importance to regional vulnerability says little about what new rules and institutions follow from the political and cultural confrontation of (Western) risk and (non-Western) threat perceptions and assignments of responsibility in the global domain. It is unlikely that the new complex risks can be consistently portrayed in regional terms. In that case a methodological regionalism would also be sufficient. A methodological cosmopolitanism, by contrast, can reveal the extent to which the new lines of conflict sidestep geographical differentiations.

From civilizational self-endangerment to global governance

The finding that new geographically blurred lines of conflict are arising in the world risk society casts a new light on current discussions concerning 'plural', 'hybrid' and alternative modernities. As Jan Nederveen Pieterse (2000: 135) points out, for example, this debate suffers from the arbitrariness with which variations and differences are affirmed without specifying the underlying *issue*. In the debates over the 'cultures of capitalism' (Clegg et al. 1990; Hampden-Turner and Trompenaars 1993) and 'multiple modernities' (Eisenstadt 2000a), the unity in diversity of different forms of capitalism and modernity is often no longer even thematized.

The concept of world risk society has strategic advantages for research in this regard. It offers a clear pointer to the crucial 'interface' between inequality and integration in world society, namely, the Janus-faced character of global risks. On the one hand, global risks, crises and threats are cited as motors of a growing awareness of globality. New 'communities of fate' and a new transnational pressure for political action arise with the worldwide visibility and communicability of specific threats (Albrow 1996; Robertson 1992; Shaw 1996). On the other hand, unequal social impacts and vulnerabilities spark *risk conflicts* that stubbornly resist any global standardization.

In view of the basic antagonism over risk, it would be completely mistaken to interpret the role of such risk conflicts as merely an interesting prelude to a unified, global political solution. And yet the dichotomy of self-endangerment and endangerment of others loses its plausibility as a leitmotif of world risk society where the distinction between self-chosen risks and imposed threats collapses under the increasing pressure of global dangers. The greater the threat, the lower the likelihood of distributing it unequally. In the limit case, there is a boomerang effect in world risk society that also affects the decision-makers and those who benefit from risks (Beck 1992).

As a future-oriented (and almost inevitably negative) vision, world risk society replaces the model of imputing responsibility in terms of the dichotomy of self-endangerment and endangerment of others with the *anticipation* of the endangerment of everyone. This does not presuppose a situation in which risks are not imputable. It may very well be possible to identify the source of threats through corresponding research. We must even assume that such imputations follow in cases of catastrophic crisis. With the expansion of the authoritative horizon for assessing the consequences of decisions, however, the pragmatic utility of the future diminishes dramatically as its shadow grows longer. As an *ex post facto* matter, the attribution of causal agency in cases of irreversible harms contributes neither to prevention nor to remedying the damage.

Here new opportunities for cooperation arise in transnational politics. The cognitive uncertainty of global risks forces the political actors to rely on containing dangers through 'epistemic authorities'. However, their role should not be defined too narrowly. The interpretation of Haas, among others, which assesses the role of epistemic communities in an excessively monocausal manner, is not confirmed by the history of the evolution of the ozone regime (Litfin 1994). It transpired that, although scientific knowledge entered into the political process, it did not provide a clear-cut guide to action. The ultimate decision to take the threat of the thinning out of the ozone layer seriously was made not by the scientists but by the politicians responding to a change in the public perception of risk. The key role was played by the credible threat scenario portrayed by the first images of the hole in the ozone layer over Antarctica. To sum up the relevance of this example for our problem, the hole in the ozone layer drove the questions of costs and benefits and winners and losers of the political process into the background, and hence also the search for a possible solution in terms of the schematic opposition between self-endangerment and endangerment of others. In this case, we are all sitting in the proverbial 'same boat' and as a result are condemned to a joint effort (which was of course limited in any case by the easy availability of alternatives to harmful CFCs).

What is interesting about this form of international politics in the present context is that it in part circumvents a 'classical' politics centred on power and interests. Anyone who wants to promote their own interests in a knowledge-based regime, such as the ozone or climate change regimes, cannot fall back on a purely political basis of power but must also influence the underlying knowledge.[12] Although this is indeed possible (and is also observable), it is a very difficult process to control because of the associated additional factors of uncertainty. One-sided political lines of conflict do not thereby necessarily become less important but they do become increasingly unclear in their effects. This is exactly what is meant when we speak of dissolving old lines of conflict and opening up new ones. At stake is the fact that national or regional – hence, ultimately, politically determined – factors no longer exclusively define possible lines of conflicts and opportunities for consensus (Voss et al. 2006; Grande et al. 2006).

It is important to recognize that the orientation to knowledge binds not only scientists more strongly into transnational political processes but also other actors. For the knowledge in question is not exclusively scientific. This is why private actors are becoming increasingly important in the formation of transnational regimes (Cutler et al. 1999). In the environmental domain, a corresponding development is associated with the incorporation of NGOs into the political process (Ford 1999; Mol 2000). But private actors are involved in the formulation *and* implementation of regulatory systems as a resource of knowledge in completely different fields as well. This holds especially, for example, for the international regulation of banking, which has increasingly depended since the 1970s on 'private knowledge' to determine risks and implement regulations (Kapstein 1994; Strulik 2000).

In an attempt to take account of this development, the concept of an international regime was extended to that of *trans*national forms of regime that also include the 'subpolitics' of non-state actors (see Lucatelli 1997). Transnational regimes cannot be reduced to more or less formalized agreements between sovereign states but presuppose horizontal and vertical institutional interconnections between state and non-state actors. By contrast, only a limited number of participants and perspectives were envisaged within the straightforward 'Club Model' which long marked the WTO and other international organizations.[13] This clear-cut character has diminished markedly with the extension of membership rights, the spread of democratic ideas and the increase in the number of non-state actors (Keohane and Nye 2001: 6ff.). The increasing importance and complexity of such transnational arrangements is reflected by more recent theories which propose concepts such as 'complex multilateralism' (O'Brien et al. 2000) or 'complex global governance' (Zürn 1998, 2001) to designate them.

Binding private actors and expertise into systems of global governance also leads to a diversification of the steering mechanisms. The main lever here is not the imposition of positive law backed up by power but the diversified instruments of a 'soft law' resting on legally non-binding recommendations, rules and standards (Brunsson and Jacobsson 2000).

It is becoming apparent here that, in the confrontation with global risks, a relatively clear-cut system of international politics oriented to national interests and relative weights is being replaced by a non-clear-cut (dis)order called global governance (Hewson and Sinclair 1999). In this non-system of global self-regulation, states are just one factor alongside transnational NGOs and epistemic communities. Thus they are not the sole decisive factor in formulating and resolving conflicts. It should already be clear from this that one cannot place any hopes of an increase in cooperation and harmony *per se* in the amorphous concept of global governance. However, we have already identified the elements that could contribute to the voices of coordinated problem-solving gaining a hearing in the new polyphony. Innovative forms of cooperation cannot be excluded either, insofar as the negative future vision of global risks gains acceptance in transnational fora beyond the ascription of responsibility in terms of self-endangerment and endangerment of others.

The conclusion of this chapter is that the world risk society is not a society of global insight into threats. The globality of world risk society does not follow automatically from the geographical or social expansion of threat constellations. Globality must be construed instead as a conflict over the *definition* (and the definition-*relations*!) of globality. Three conclusions can be drawn from this. First, globality cannot be *presupposed* as a global 'community of fate'. Second, globality must be understood as a laboratory of global conflicts and problems and hence as a *crucible of global reflexivity*. This implies, third, that the theory of the world risk society does not claim to determine the direction, and especially not the result, of global change, and it certainly does not assume the existence of a world-historical subject of cosmopolitanization. Rather, it opens up a whole range of conflicting answers to global problems and conflicts at the theoretical level and makes them the centre of investigation.

In future, the concern with global risks should not remain hidebound by the perspective of the Western world of states. The challenges of depicting the environmental, financial and military risks for other regions are often of a different kind – and in some cases much greater. These marginalized regions are already confronted with the *side effects* of global industrialization while still awaiting the arrival of modernization. Thus their perspective on the associated conflicts and negotiations is a different one. The Western social sciences are guilty of shameful neglect of this fact. Research on transnational risk conflicts will have to pay a lot more attention to the role of state and non-state actors from non-Western regions.

Inequality and domination in the world risk society do not merely follow the old patterns of conflicts between rich and poor, North and South, centre and periphery, etc., in the constellations of threats and conflicts described. Not only new lines of conflict but also new proposals for solutions are emerging. The potential thus created must not be overlooked in spite of the enormous difficulties associated with all forms of global coordination. One of the tasks of a critical sociology in and of world risk society should be to draw attention – if only counterfactually – to these possibilities (on cosmopolitan political realism, see pp. 207ff.).

11

Critical Theory of World Risk Society

A critical theory of world risk society must address at least three questions: (1) What is the basis of the critique? What is 'critical' about this critical theory? (The question of the *normative horizon* of the world risk society) (2) What are the key theses and core arguments of this theory? Is it an empirical theory of society with critical intent? (3) To what extent does this theory break with the automatisms of modernization which have taken on a life of their own and rediscover the openness of human action to the future? (Political perspectives and alternatives)

1 The normative horizon of world risk society: normative and descriptive cosmopolitanism

The category of risk and its ambivalences

It is easy to underestimate the subtlety of the sociological category of risk.

- First there is its *boundless thirst for reality*: the category of risk consumes and transforms everything. It obeys the law of all or nothing. If a group represents a risk, its other features disappear and it becomes defined by this 'risk'. It is marginalized and threatened with exclusion.
- *Classical distinctions merge into greater or lesser degrees of risk*: Risk functions like an acid bath in which venerable classical distinctions are dissolved. Within the horizon of risk, the 'binary coding' – permitted or forbidden, legal or illegal, right or wrong, us and them – does not exist. Within the horizon of risk, people are not either good or evil but only more or less risky. Everyone poses more or less of a risk for everyone else. The qualitative distinction either/or is replaced by the quantitative difference between more or less. Nobody is not a risk – to repeat, everyone poses more or less of a risk for everyone else.

- *Existent and non-existent*: Risk is not the same as catastrophe, but the anticipation of the catastrophe – that is the message of this book. As a result, risk leads a dubious, insidious, would-be, allusive existence: it is existent *and* non-existent, present *and* absent, doubtful *and* suspect. In the end it can be assumed to be ubiquitous and thus grounds a politics of prevention. Anticipation necessitates precaution, and this obeys, for example, the calculation 'Spend a cent today, save a Euro tomorrow' – assuming that the threat which does not (yet) exist really exists.
- *Individual and social responsibility*: Even in the smallest conceivable microcosm, risk defines a social relation, a relation between at least two people: the decision-maker who takes the risk and who thereby triggers consequences for others, who cannot, or can only with difficulty, defend themselves. Accordingly, two concepts of responsibility can be distinguished: an *individual* responsibility that the decision-maker accepts for the consequences of his or her decision, which must be distinguished from responsibility for others, *social* responsibility. Risks pose in principle the question (which combines defence and devaluation) of what 'side effects' a risk has for others and who these others are and to what extent they are or are not involved in the decision.
- *Global space of responsibility*: In this sense global risks open up a complex moral and political space of responsibility in which the others are present and absent, near and far, and in which actions are neither good nor evil, just more or less risky. The meanings of proximity, reciprocity, dignity, justice and trust are transformed within this horizon of expectation of global risks.
- *Risk communities – a kind of 'glue' for diversity*: Global risks contain *in nuce* an answer to the question of how new kinds of 'risk communities', based neither on descent nor on spatial presence, can evolve and establish themselves in the cacophony of a globalized world. One of the most striking and heretofore least recognized key features of global risks is how they generate a kind of 'compulsory cosmopolitanism', a 'glue' for diversity and plurality in a world whose boundaries are as porous as a Swiss cheese, at least as regards communication and economics.

However, it is one thing whether this unity in diversity created (at least momentarily) by the experience of threat is described or whether a politics of recognition of diversity is affirmed in the sense of normative principles – for example, against universalism, which denies the importance of diversity, or against nationalism, which produces equality in difference only in the national context, or against multiculturalism, which affirms diversity, often understood in essentialistic terms, in the national context (see p. 56). In chapter 3, I alluded to the fact that the 'cosmopolitan moment' of the world risk society can be understood in descriptive and normative senses and that

I distinguish between two concepts of cosmopolitanism, a broader one in which I underline the *normativity* involved in the cosmopolitan moment and a narrower one in which empirical cosmopolitanization is initially explored in a *descriptive* manner.

I hardly need to underline that I am always concerned with just one, not 'the', critical theory, namely, that based on the theory of the world risk society. This already alludes to the limits of this critical theory.[1] Here the perspective shifts from a descriptive to a normative outlook (cf. Silverstone 2006).

The way in which the other is presented and represented within the framework of global risk publics is essential for establishing morality in the world. The staged experience of current and possible catastrophes and wars has become a key experience in which both the interdependence of and threat to human existence, its precarious future, impinge on everyday life. Yet, normatively speaking, the presentation and representation of the other calls not only for sound and image, but also for meaning. It presupposes *cosmopolitan understanding* – or, in the humanities and social sciences, *cosmopolitan hermeneutics*.[2]

Charles Husband (2000) complements Jürgen Habermas in this respect. Opening up the horizon of meaning of a plurality of voices for one another calls not only for a right of communication but also for the right to be understood. The presence of a plurality of voices remains substantially meaningless, Husband argues, if these voices are not equipped with the right to be heard and understood.

Cosmopolitan understanding rests, on the one hand, on a specific, but also limited, cosmopolitan competence; for the failure to hear and understand is the reverse side of an education system geared to national integration and homogeneity. On the other hand, it is impossible for everyone to listen to everyone at the same time. This means that the cosmopolitanism of listening and hearing presupposes consciously drawing the boundaries to what is not heard and not understood. Cosmopolitan understanding is first made possible by this reflected selectivity because only then does the shift in perspectives, the inclusion of the other in one's own life, become possible in a more profound way. Yet this exemplary understanding broadens the horizon in a cosmopolitan manner.

The global threat gives rise to a kind of *moral import*: among other things, in cosmopolitan risk conflicts conducted in the media,

- resources are provided for forming a judgement, however selective and sweeping;
- sensational stories are presented that jolt us out of our apathy and present new standpoints and perspectives; the result is
- an invitation to cross-border commitment;
- institutionalized claims to objectivity and truth are undermined;

- global risks enlarge our existential horizons by integrating (at least for a moment) other things and other people and the reality of suffering and destruction across borders and divides into our lives.

As Kevin Robins observed in his analysis of the representation of the Gulf War in the mass media, this form of moral import also has its limits:

The screen exposes the ordinary viewer to harsh realities, but it screens out the harshness of those realities. It has a certain moral weightlessness: It grants sensation without demanding responsibility, and it involves us in a spectacle without engaging us in the complexity of its reality. (Robins 1996: 80)

This observation is correct and incorrect at the same time. It is familiar insofar as the mediatization of catastrophes stages a kind of totalitarian occupation of everyday space. But it fails to recognize that, in the very staging of the shock, its uniqueness and authenticity, distances shrink and a closeness is generated that challenges us to adopt an ethical position that transcends borders.

The category of *hospitality* has featured centrally in normative cosmopolitanism since Immanuel Kant. The meaning of the ethical principle of hospitality is the duty to welcome strangers. Hospitality not only includes the freedom of speech but also involves the duty to listen and to understand. Kant was thinking of the right to visit to which all human beings have a claim, based on their share in the common possession of the surface of the earth. Because the earth is a sphere, human beings cannot spread out indefinitely but must come together and put up with the fact that they live in close proximity to one another; for in the beginning no one had any more right to any portion of the surface of the earth than anyone else.

What does this right to hospitality mean as regards global risks? The essential differentiation here is between the degree to which hospitality rests on an invitation and the degree to which this right means that those who have not been invited – for example, people in need – can claim the right to hospitality. Is there such a thing as 'enforced hospitality'? Derrida argues that there can be no hospitality without a home, a place of welcome and one in which someone is made welcome.

This does *not* hold for global risks. The difference resides already in the fact that, in the global space of responsibility of global risks, nobody can be excluded from 'hospitality'. In the light of the exhaustive coverage of global threats in the media, others and strangers are as much a presence for us as we are for them, whether we or they like it, realize it or want to acknowledge it, or not. And simply because of our own precarious situation as subjects in the world and because of the equal status of strangers as subjects in the threatened world, neither we nor they are in a position to reject claims to help and to pity, to listen and to understand. This actually occurs quite naturally. And one must immediately add that it occurs all the more emphatically and emotionally the more irrefutable such claims become. Eruptions of amorality and indifference, indeed of hatred, can also be understood in this way because nobody can escape this 'collective consciousness' (Durkheim) of global threats.

Perhaps the category of 'hospitality' or 'friendship towards guests' [*Gastfreundschaft*], which can easily become inverted into 'hostility towards guests' [*Gastfeindschaft*], is not appropriate to expressing the inescapability of moral proximity over geographical distance. Perhaps it makes more sense to speak of all people being transformed into neighbours? Perhaps different ways of coping with this 'globalized neighbourhood' remain open, where hospitality in the Kantian sense remains the exception (as easily occurs with the condition of global neighbours).

In legal terms, the ethical principle of recognition of others involves a kind of *risk cosmopolitan law*. This is a matter no longer merely of hospitality but of the right of the 'living side effects' of the risk decisions of others to have a say in these decisions. This may sound innocuous but it presupposes a radical reconstruction of existing national and international law. Even if it is only a matter of formulating and imposing minimum standards of this risk cosmopolitan law, this includes that 'we' and 'others' are placed on the same moral and legal footing as regards strategic risk decisions, which presupposes, in turn, that the interests of vulnerable members of other societies are placed on a higher footing than the interests of co-nationals on the basis of a universal human right of inviolability. Global risks produce harms that transcend national borders. Thus risk cosmopolitan law is possible only if the boundaries of moral and political communities can be redefined so that the others, strangers and outsiders are included in the key decisions which jeopardize and violate their existence and dignity.

Theory of world risk society

Incalculable risks and manufactured insecurities resulting from the triumphs of modernity mark the *conditio humana* at the beginning of the twenty-first century. Existing and orienting oneself in this world, therefore, increasingly involves an understanding of the confrontation with catastrophic risks ('The new historical character of the world risk society'). This confrontation is a self-confrontation with the institutional arrangements from which the threats proceed ('Theory of institutional contradictions') and with the logic peculiar to the associated conflicts. Those who enjoy the benefits of risks are not the ones who have to bear the costs ('Risk antagonism').

The cosmopolitan communicative logic evolves through the contradictions and conflicts. Global risks have the ability to press-gang, so to speak, an unlimited number of actors who want nothing to do with one another, who pursue different political goals and who may even live in incommensurable worlds ('Theory of the reflexivity and the real cosmopolitanism of global risks'). This communicative logic must be differentiated according to ecological, economic and terrorist risks. We must ask how this social theory proves its worth ('The real scientific basis of social theory with critical intent').

Then there is the related question concerning *political perspectives*. In political terms, the logic of global risks can lead to the breakthrough of a *cosmopolitan political realism*. With its combination of normative and ascriptive cosmopolitanism, it enables us to make the reflexivity of risk, the multifarious voices of criticism and conflict that find expression in society itself, into the basis of social criticism in sociology ('Critical theory of world risk society as social self-criticism').

The new historical character of the world risk society

A critique of the social sciences, and in particular of sociology, is a necessary precondition of a social theory for the twenty-first century. An overspecialized, highly abstract sociology, infatuated with its methods and techniques, has lost its sense of the historical dimension of society. As a result, it is neither equipped nor inclined to fulfil its proper task of situating the current transformation of its research object in the social-historical process and thus to offer a diagnostic perspective on the epochal signature of the new era of modernity. This abstinence regarding social history has led to a stunting of sociology's historical imagination, rendering it incapable of recognizing and overcoming the Apocalypse-blindness [*Apokalypse-Blindheit*] of its categories and theories (which constituted its strength at its birth at the beginning of the catastrophic twentieth century). Instead it perpetuates sociological platitudes saturated with masses of data and obscures the processes and empirical indicators of the deep, self-generated unease of modernity which span the spectrum from self-destruction to self-contemplation, as well as the sociocultural critiques and processes of reflection which they trigger.

The new historical character of world risk society can be rendered visible only through detailed empirical-analytical criticisms of this self-induced narrow-mindedness and historical immaturity of sociology. For the threats and uncertainties in question, in contrast to earlier eras, are not the result of the errors of modernization but of its *successes*, and hence are contingent on human decisions through which science and technology are perfected, which are immanent in society and therefore cannot be externalized. They are collectively imposed and hence are individually unavoidable, objectively uncontrollable and for that reason no longer insurable in their ultimate effects. The historical uniqueness of the world risk society, which differentiates this era as much from national industrial society as from earlier civilizations, resides in the decision-dependent possibility of control over life on earth, including the historically unprecedented possibility of self-destruction and the possibility of the anthropological self-transformation of human beings which was heralded by the discovery of the blueprint of the human genome in the summer of 2000. Thirty or forty years hence, this will probably appear in retrospect as a further founding act and driving motor, this time of the bio-world risk society (Rose 2003; May 2004).

However, the novelty of the emerging social formation comes into view in its entirety only when we relate the consequences of radicalized modernization to the social institutions which they have made possible and which, coupled with their cultural basic principles and political practices, lend the emerging risks and uncertainties their culturally, socially and politically explosive character.

Theory of institutional contradictions

As Piet Strydom (2002: 59) correctly observes, I developed this partial theory of institutional contradictions in *Ecological Politics in an Age of Risk* (2002) [German: *Gegengifte* (1988)] through a controversy with – i.e. an appropriation and critique of – Niklas Luhmann's study *Ecological Communication*, which was published in 1986, in the same year as my *Risk Society*. Luhmann bases his argument on the slogan that what cannot be controlled is not real. Because modern society consists of functionally differentiated systems that can cope with self-generated risks only in the terms of their own specific systemic logics – the economy in terms of prices, politics in terms of majorities, law in terms of guilt, science in terms of truth, etc. – modern society cannot cope with environmental and other global risks; furthermore these problems do not even exist. Those who give them expression, such as social movements and counter-experts, are the real source of danger because the 'noise' that they generate 'disturbs' the smooth functioning of the systems. I reduced this to the ironical-critical formula 'Silence detoxifies!' (1988: 171).

Hence, I turned this diagnosis from its head onto its feet. Instead of making the reality of global risks cleverly disappear in the metaphysics of systems rationality (thereby avoiding the historical falsification of one's own systems theory), I draw the opposite conclusion from a similar diagnosis, namely, that contemporary society and its subsystems are incapable of coping with their most urgent, self-generated problems. The counterpart of the non-responsibility of science is an implicit responsibility of businesses and the mere responsibility of politics for legitimacy. Responsibilities can indeed be assigned but they are spread out over several social subsystems. The global threats posed by modernization should not be assigned to science or the economy or politics but are a 'co-production' of these subsystems. Thus we are dealing with an extensive labyrinth whose construction plan is not non-responsibility or irresponsibility but, rather, the coexistence of responsibility

[*Zuständigkeit*] and impunity [*Unzurechenbarkeit*] – to be more precise, responsibility *as* impunity or: organized irresponsibility.

The contradictory nature of the basic institutions of modern society, which lay claim to both competence and impunity, is grounded in increasing social differentiation, in the factor in which Luhmann thought he had discovered the meta-solution to all problems. Thus the contradictions within and between the institutions of modern society become clearly visible at the latest in contemporary experiences of catastrophes, as magnified by the alarmism of the mass media. A core contradiction in contemporary society is the fact that advanced modernity, with the aid of its scientific instruments and its mass mediated communication, is forced to accord highest priority to the mega-threats it itself has generated, although it is clear that it lacks the necessary concepts to observe or impute, let alone 'manage', them adequately – at any rate, not as long as the institutional status quo is absolutized and held constant in an ahistorical manner.

The self-criticism of society becomes more radical to the extent that these contradictions are overcome through recurring catastrophic crises and their anticipation in the experience and memory of modernity. This self-criticism initially unfolds as *immanent* critique of the institutionalized and continually newly proclaimed promises of security and their failure in the concrete experiences of catastrophes. This includes an involuntary self-criticism of science in the conflict between experts and counter-experts as well as the inability to redeem in an anticipatory way promises of security in the face of the 'unknown unknowns', hence of the inability-to-know. Here the (unreflected) self-confrontation of modernity turns into 'reflexive' modernization in the narrower sense: conflict awakens and impresses upon consciousness that a 'misconception of the century' has crept into the relation between global risks and the institutional arrangements from which they have arisen and which are supposed to control them.

Risks can no longer be dismissed as side effects. Instead they are becoming an internal problem of apparently self-enclosed social systems. At the same time, every attempt to manage the complexity of risk creates the need to fall back on abstractions and models which give rise to new uncertainties. This is the basis of a further institutionalized contradiction. Risk and non-knowledge prompt the call for security and lead to new insecurities and uncertainties in the general groping about in the fog of insecurity and uncertainties. Moreover, the undecidability of problems, which nevertheless have to be decided, is growing along with the pressure to make decisions (Adam et al. 2000; Beck and Lau 2004).

Yet threats are not 'things'. Hence conflicts and struggles over definitions arise in the interplay of constructivism and institutionalism. These do not occur in an institutional vacuum, however. A key component of this social construction and its 'plausibility-resources' and 'truth-resources', hence its collectively binding force, resides in the relations of definition. Here, too, it is the case that the more the communicative logic of risk permeates society in all of its institutions and lifeworlds, and to the extent that every new catastrophic experience awakens memories of previous catastrophes, the more these relations of definitional power become publicly visible and themselves a political issue. This prompts the question concerning a new ethics and system of responsibility, concerning a democratization of the relations of definitional power in the world risk society – in other words, the question concerning a *responsible* modernity.

However, the brutal fact of ontological insecurity always has an ultimate addressee: the recipient of the residual risk of the world risk society is the *individual*. Whatever propels risk and makes it incalculable, whatever provokes the institutional crisis at the level of the governing regime and the markets, shifts the ultimate decision-making responsibility onto the individuals, who are ultimately left to their own devices with their partial and biased knowledge, with undecidability and multiple layers of uncertainty. This is undoubtedly a powerful source of right-wing radicalism and fundamentalism in the second modernity that is not easy to stem.

Risk antagonism

In questions of social inequality in the world risk society, the issue is not how the risks are allocated but, rather, what risks actually are or, more precisely, what they are for whom – opportunities to be seized or threats imposed by others – but, above all, who has the power to divert the hazardousness of the risks they incur onto others. This is the structural conflict built into the communicative logic of risk. There is no ontology of risk. Risks do not exist independently, like things. Risks are risk conflicts in which there is a world of difference between the decision-makers, who could ultimately avoid the risks, and the involuntary consumers of dangers, who do not have a say in these decisions and onto whom the dangers are shifted as 'unintentional, unseen side effects'. Risks disintegrate systematically into these antagonistic, perhaps even incommensurable worlds: those who run risks and define them versus those to whom they are allocated.

This is especially flagrant in the case of the new risk wars, in which the military means of violence are deployed in such a way that the war-making nations seek to maintain the illusion of peace for themselves, hence to render the horror of war latent by shifting it onto the other side. 'Collateral damage' is the scare word intended to render victims anonymous. It is supposed both to reveal and to conceal the nature of the killing of others as an 'unintended side effect'; but in fact it points to this division of worlds into peace for us who are waging war and war for those for whom the danger of destruction and death is becoming an everyday reality.

The concept of the enemy derived from the old wars between states is too undifferentiated to capture this way of shifting the risk of violence of war from the decision-makers onto 'those affected'. In the Iraq War, for example, the US government did not intend to wage war against the Iraqi people. On the contrary, the goal was to liberate the Iraqi people, hence to crush the dictatorship of Saddam Hussein and his military and power apparatus. The US may even have hoped for a *post hoc* internal revolution *after* the goal of the military intervention, the overthrow of Saddam's regime as a 'military operation' on the living body of the Iraqi people, had been successfully completed. However, such a limited aim (assuming, for the sake of argument, that one wants to lend it plausibility out of the numerous alternative public attempts by the Bush administration to legitimize its self-authorized Iraq War) entangles this form of risk-redistribution war in serious contradictions. For precisely the faceless term 'collateral damage' designates the toll of lives which the Iraqi civilians, who were supposed to be 'liberated', have to pay for the war which was forced upon them. At this point, the basis of legitimation breaks down, however, quite apart from the fact that a more instructive example of the institutionalized contradictions of the management of the risk of war by the state is hard to imagine. The war gave rise to what was supposed to be prevented, namely, the spread of terrorist violence – Iraq has become the playground and recruitment centre of global terrorism.

This antagonism of risk takes many forms. Interestingly, it becomes both more and less acute under conditions that are often rather carelessly described in terms of the 'globalization of risk'. It becomes less acute because the equality and relevance horizon of the national outlook becomes inapplicable and is replaced by the reciprocal irrelevance and inattentiveness institutionalized by the national boundary. The incommensurability which is the reverse side of the internal orientation of national politics reinforces the complex relations between risk-giver and risk-receiver countries, which are in any case difficult to disentangle. At the same time, however, it aggravates the potential for conflict because the vagueness and indeterminability of the risks throws open the door to cultural perceptions and neuroses. The more overtly global risks elude the scientific methods for calculating them, the more influential becomes the perception of risk. The distinction between real risks and the perception of risk becomes blurred (Douglas and Wildavsky 1982). Who *believes* in a risk and why becomes more important than the sophisticated probability scenarios of the experts.

The principal lines of conflict during the Cold War were clearly political and derived their explosiveness from questions of national and international security. The geopolitical lines of conflict in the world risk society run between different risk perception cultures. We are witnessing an invasion of politics by culture. An outstanding example of this is the contrasting urgency, indeed reality, attributed to the dangers of climate change and transnational terrorism, respectively, in Europe and the United States. We should not overlook one phenomenon here, however, namely, the possibility of a sudden change in perception – the *conversion effect*. Before 11 September 2001, conflicting perceptions and evaluations of the climate risk, but *not* of the terrorist risk, prevailed on the two sides of the Atlantic. Only as a result of September 11 did North America (if one can speak in such blanket terms) abandon its general risk agnosticism concerning the prophesies of the 'collapse of civilization' coming mainly from Europe and abandon the role of exporter of optimism for that of exporter of pessimism in the special domain of transnational terrorism. Not only are the cultural perceptions and definitions of risk and threat in Europe and America drifting far apart; because they are drifting far apart, Europeans and Americans are effectively living in different worlds.

Thus the globality of the world risk society finds expression in a contradictory dynamic: unity and disintegration are simultaneous occurrences. The politically extremely important 'risk community of fate' is cleaving over the questions of who shares which definitions of risk and how the threats should be dealt with. Of decisive importance here is, for example, how much the terrorist risk permeates the perception of international politics and whether it favours the breakthrough of a preventive-military or a preventive-political view of the world. A shift in perception in a primarily military direction would force Europe into the role of the outsider who cultivates and champions luxury problems. Thus new lines of conflict and alternatives are emerging not least between different constructions, dimensions and potential sources of global risks.

In contemporary society, where we are witnesses of a profound transformation of the cognitive organization of social life, this competition and conflict have taken on a graphic profile in the context of the risk discourse. Here it manifests itself as a new form of class conflict, possessing also a gender dimension . . . The culturally constituted cognitive structures which guided science, technology, industry, capitalism and the state, and which culminate in the experimenting society, are confronted by another set. The latter was introduced into the public sphere by a mobilized public and the new social movements and is currently pursued by citizens in many capacities in the direction of participatory or deliberative democracy and a cosmopolitan democratic form of governance. . . . Collective responsibility, or co-responsibility, stands for this set of cognitive structures. Responsibility in this sense, as the constructivist approach suggests, does not imply an absolute prohibition against potentially harmful research and experimentation, but rather a reasonable and balanced arrangement based on new cognitive structures arising from the latest evolutionary spurt. (Strydom 2002: 152f.)

Joost van Loon poses a key question in this context when he asks whether the multiplication of risks is a dead end, or whether there is an escape from the negative dialectic of risk and risk aversion and the entropy of ambivalence (2002: 41).[3]

Theory of the reflexivity and the real cosmopolitanism of global risks

Let us recapitulate the steps of the argument thus far. The specific ontology of risk finds expression in the overcoming of the difference between reality and representation, where the key factor is the anticipation of the becoming-real. An increasing number of such risks is undermining the operative logic of the institutions of the nation-state and of industrial society, because these anticipated, staged risks can no longer be confined to specific geographical or temporal spaces but are exerting global and simultaneous effects. What then does the reflexivity of risk mean?

Enforced cross-border communication: As regards the horizon of global risks, everyone is living in an at once direct and universal proximity with everyone else. Cosmopolitanism in this new sense of a unification enforced by threats is a *condition*, not a *choice*. The conjecture that what is common to all human beings today is the longing for a world that is a little less unified is not unfounded. This negative solidarity based on the fear of global destruction once again exhibits the communicative logic of the world risk society. I stated earlier that what lends the production and distribution of risks in the contemporary world their political potency is that it is impossible to externalize the resulting problems. In other words, systemic closures are no longer an option because we are all bound into this World Wide Web of the production and definition of risk.

> That is to say, reflexivity disassembles autopoiesis and reassembles communication flows into hybrid systems. Closures offered by expertise, legislation and moral panics are not met with trust in the systems that produced them. The technical fix can no longer be formed. The reinvention of politics . . . necessitates a reversal of autopoiesis, an opening of intrasystemic closures. (Loon 2002: 40, 43)

This is precisely what is accomplished by the reflexivity of risk: it dissolves the identity of subject and reflection; this is the reverse side of the enforced communication which remains bound to different media, technologies, actions, meanings, networks, 'actants', values (Latour).

> The political challenge of the risk society lies in the systems being able to act upon each other without complete conversion. That is to say, politics that enable communications between different information flows without reducing them to the logic of one system only. For Luhmann, this is impossible, hence his political quietism. For Beck and Habermas, there is no alternative. (Loon 2002: 43)

Many will dismiss this as wishful thinking. But that fails to recognize the turn towards a 'cosmopolitan political realism' which is already discernible today under the cultural and political contradictions of world risk society (see below).

Finally, risk rationality develops an existential 'logic' of shock, suffering and pity on a global scale in opposition to the 'instrumental rationality' which Max Weber places at the centre of his sociology and Horkheimer and Adorno and, most recently, also Jürgen Habermas have criticized (albeit in completely different ways). One could say that risk reflexivity – or, more generally, reflexive modernization – is an ambivalent, *realist* critique of instrumentally stunted reason. Here in key domains of social rationalization it can be empirically and theoretically demonstrated how the radicalization of modernity leads to a self-confrontation, self-delegitimation and self-transformation of instrumental rationality. This is motivated exclusively by the maximization of effectiveness and efficiency. Emotions, by contrast, are as little their concern as is the 'concern with being', one's own or that of others, which is among the central existential, boundary-transcending experiences of the world risk society (Ritter 2004). Global experiences of risk bring to light a traumatic-existential deep dimension of sympathy (tsunami) and an abyss of ontological insecurity (failure of science, law, police, the military) and hatred (suicide terrorism). Admittedly, instrumental rationality involves a certain degree of reflection – means and ends must be brought into relation to, and balanced off against, one another. The reflexivity of global risks has an entirely different character, however; it includes both the voyeurism of the global mass media and the anthropological shock, the selfless concern and fear, though also the panic-stricken anxiety and its instrumentalization by a whole range of political players.

Divergent logics of global risks: on the distinction between economic, environmental and terrorist risks

At least three axes of conflict in world risk society must be distinguished in the communicative logic of global risks: first, *environmental risk conflicts*, which spontaneously generate a global dynamic; second, *global financial risks*, which are at first individualized and nationalized; and, third, the *threat posed by terrorist networks*, which are both empowered and disempowered by the states. In the case of environmental risks that pose physical threats, there is on the one side *affluence-induced* environmental destruction, as in the case of the hole in the ozone layer and the greenhouse effect, which may justifiably be laid primarily at the door of the Western industrial world, though their impact is, of course, global. From this we must distinguish *poverty-induced environmental* destruction, such as the clearing of the rainforest, which is mainly confined to particular regions though its scale is no less alarming.

Then there are the global *economic* risks, the imponderabilities of globalized currency and financial markets which have commanded increasing public attention in recent times (LiPuma and Lee 2004: 141-60; Holzer and Millo 2005). This global market risk is also a new form of 'organized irresponsibility'. Facilitated by the information revolution, the financial flows determine the winners and the losers. Because of the structural dominance of competition in this sector, no player is sufficiently powerful to change the direction of the flows. Nobody controls the global market risks. Because there is no world government, the market risk cannot be curbed on national markets. On the other side, no national market can seal itself off completely from the globalized markets.

However, this neoliberal economic policy faces a central problem. Too few leading minds in the international economy have noticed that the world has become increasingly democratic. Voters have a tendency to vote against decisions that place painful restrictions upon them. They are generally too short-sighted to wait for the improvement in their situation consistently invoked by the economists which, as Keynes put it, arrives in the long run when we are all dead. As the 'Asian crisis', the 'Russian crisis' and finally the 'Argentinian crisis' demonstrated, the middle classes are the worst hit by financial crises. Waves of bankruptcies and job losses shook the respective regions. Western investors and commentators viewed the 'financial crises' exclusively from the perspective of the possible threat they posed for the financial markets. However, global financial risks, like global ecological crises, cannot be confined to the economic subsystem but mutate into social upheavals and thus into political threats. In the case of the 'Asian crisis', such a chain reaction destabilized whole states and led simultaneously to outbreaks of violence against minorities, who were painted as scapegoats.

And what was unimaginable just a few years ago is now becoming a real possibility, i.e. the iron law of the globalization of the free market is in danger of collapsing and with it the associated ideology. All over the world – not just in South America, but in the Arab world and in Europe – politicians are taking measures against globalization. Protectionism is experiencing a revival; some call for new transnational institutions to control global financial flows, whereas others plead for transnational insurance systems or a renewal of international institutions and regimes. The result is that the era of free-market ideology is becoming a distant memory and is being overshadowed by its opposite, namely, the *politicization* of the global market economy. Even advocates of a global free market are increasingly expressing openly the suspicion that, after the collapse of communism, only *one* opponent of the free market remains, namely, the unbridled free market which has shrugged off its responsibility for democracy and society and operates exclusively on the maxim of short-term profit-maximization.

There are surprising parallels between the Chernobyl reactor catastrophe and the Asian financial crisis. The traditional methods of steering and control are proving to be inoperable and ineffectual in the face of global risks. The millions of unemployed and poor cannot be financially compensated; it makes no sense to insure against the impacts of a global recession. At the same time, the social and political explosiveness of global market risks is becoming palpable. Governments are being overthrown and civil wars are threatening to break out. As risks come to public awareness, the question concerning responsibility becomes loud. This dynamic leads to an inversion of neoliberal policy – not the economization of politics, but the politicization of the economy.

Serious consideration should be given to establishing an Economic Security Council within the United Nations ... There are many issues, including governance of currency markets and responding to ecological risks, that cannot be resolved without collective action involving many countries and groups. Not even the most liberalized national economy works without macroeconomic coordination; it makes no sense to suppose that the world economy is different. (Giddens 1998: 176)

To be sure, economic crises are as old as the markets themselves. And, since the global economic crisis of 1929 at the latest, it has been clear to everyone that financial crashes can have catastrophic effects – especially for politics. The Bretton Woods institutions established following World War II were conceived as global political answers to global economic risks, and the fact that they functioned was a key factor in the emergence of the European welfare state. Since the 1970s, however, those institutions have been largely dismantled and replaced by a succession of *ad hoc* solutions. Thus we face the paradoxical situation that, whereas markets have never been more liberal and more global, the powers of the global institutions that monitor their effects have been drastically curtailed. Under these conditions, we cannot rule out the possibility of a worldwide financial disaster on the scale of 1929.

During the financial crises in 2008 the memories of the world economic crises of the last century were reawakened in order to save the banks from disaster. The market failed because the incalculable risks of mortgages and other loans were deliberately concealed in the expectation that the risks would be minimized by distributing and concealing them. However, it is now evident that this minimization strategy has turned into its opposite, namely a strategy of maximizing and disseminating incalculable risks. Suddenly the risk virus is spreading everywhere, at least as an anticipation.

Faced with this danger, hardcore neoliberals have converted from faith in the market to faith in the state. Now they are praying, begging and pleading for the mercy of state intervention and for the multibillion pound hand-outs of taxpayers' money which they condemned as long as the profits were pouring in. What a priceless comedy of conversion is unfolding on the world stage at present! It is not the workers, or New or Old Labour or the communists, not the poor or those on benefits, but the heads of banks and the managers of the world's top companies who are demanding that the state must intervene to save business from itself.

At the same time, the epochal changes in the global financial systems can be characterized as a textbook example of reflexive modernization. The World Bank and the International Monetary Fund are in danger of being overwhelmed by the tidal wave of globalization which they initiated. As a side effect of their success, the once most powerful financial institutions in the world have lost their moorings and thus their understanding of themselves and their role in global economic politics. The whole international financial architecture established in the post-war period is beginning to totter, in large part because the power relations between the centre and the periphery, between the highly developed and the developing countries, have shifted dramatically. The IMF and the World Bank, which for a long time were the sole fundraisers for the so-called Third World, are in danger of losing their customers, and hence their *raison d'être*. Driven by global trade and newly channelled financial flows, the poor countries can now also raise money with ease on the capital markets. Thanks to the recent rapid increase in the price of raw materials, many once crisis-plagued countries, such as Brazil, have paid back their debts and are not drawing on any new credits. And the old pecking order in the world economy has been turned on its head: the one-time borrower states have become major economic powers and are themselves generously distributing loans as a means of securing loyalty and raw materials. China, for example, allocated more than $20 billion to African countries in recent years. India, too, is announcing massive investments in so-called developing countries, for example a doubling of loans to African countries to over $5 billion. The loss of power of the once dominant financial powers is shown not least by the fact that summits which serve the World Bank and the IMF to thematize their new role have lost much of their political volatility. In Washington, for example, there were no protesters to be seen.

The IMF in particular is running out of time to find a new role for itself. Its earnings are dropping. As the number of loans decreases, the fund receives less of the interest income through which it finances itself. Moreover, in the global debate over anticipated catastrophic financial risks in early 2008, the World Bank and the IMF made a strangely awkward and old-fashioned impression. The rising prices for raw materials have led to much greater improvements in the economic position even of countries with small reserves of oil, iron ore or copper than the reform measures and aid programmes of the World Bank and the IMF over the previous decades.

An additional factor are new players who are entering the stage as powerful and effective competitors. China, in particular, which is sitting on currency reserves of $1.5 trillion, is making vigorous efforts to secure raw materials to satisfy the growing hunger of its industries and readily accords generous loans to ensure access to oil in Nigeria or copper in Zambia, for example. But this means that the old global financial political order is out of joint with empowerment and disempowerment going hand in hand. And it is not far from the truth to see the emergence of a new kind of 'competition among systems', neither an East–West conflict nor a North–South conflict but a different, hybrid form of conflict in which authoritarian, state-controlled models of capitalism are enhancing their global economic position and power and are challenging the pre-eminence – or at any rate the claim to a monopoly on modernity – of the American combination of market liberalism and democracy.

In contrast to environmental and technological risks, whose physical effects first win social relevance 'from outside', financial risks also affect an immediately social structure, namely, the economy or, more precisely, the guarantee of solvency, which is indispensable to its normal functioning. This means, first, that the impact of financial risks is also much more strongly mediated by other social structures than the impact of global environmental risks. Hence, financial risks can be more easily 'individualized' and 'national-ized', and they give rise to major differences in perceptions of risk. Finally, global financial risks – not least in their worldwide (statistical) perception – are attributed as *national* risks to particular countries or regions. Of course, this by no means implies that economic interdependence risks are any less risky. Since all of the subsystems of modern society rely on the other sub-systems, a failure of the financial system would be catastrophic. No other functional system plays such a prominent role in the modern world as the economy. Thus, the world economy is without doubt a central source of risk in the world risk society.

The threat posed by global terrorist networks, by contrast, is a completely different matter. As we have seen, environmental and economic conflicts can be understood as side effects of radicalized modernization. Terrorist activi-ties, by contrast, must be understood as *intentional* catastrophes. More precisely, they conform to the principle of the intentional triggering of unin-tentional side effects. Hence, the principle of deliberately exploiting the mani-fest vulnerability of modern civil society replaces the principle of chance and accident. The concept of an accident, which is based on the calculation of the probability of cases of loss, is no longer applicable. Terrorists need only target so-called residual risks and the civil consciousness of a highly complex and interdependent world to globalize the 'felt violence' which paralyses modern society and causes it literally to freeze with panic. Correspondingly, the ter-rorist risk leads to an extreme expansion of the domain of 'dual use goods' that serve both civil and military purposes (Bauer 2006). Transnational ter-rorism differs from national terror in that it neither pursues national goals nor depends primarily or exclusively on national actors within nation-states. Thus 'transnational' means multinational terrorist networks with the poten-tial to attack 'the West' and 'modern society' anywhere. What is striking is that, and how, the global anticipation of terrorist attacks is ultimately 'manu-factured' in involuntary interaction with the power of the Western mass media, Western politics and Western military. To put it pointedly, the belief in 'global terrorism' springs from an unintended self-endangerment of modern Western society.

For all their differences, environmental, economic and terrorist global risks have two key features in common. First, they all promote or dictate a policy of proactive countermeasures that annuls the basis of the existing forms and alliances of international politics, necessitates corresponding redef-initions and reforms, and calls forth new political philosophies. This means that the premises of what counts as 'national' and 'international' and of how these dimensions should be related to and demarcated from each other are collapsing and must now be renegotiated under the banner of risk prevention in the meta-power game of global and national security policies (Beck 2005). This invites, among other things, the question: Does a Europe enamoured of its pacifist worldview (of environmental risks) recognize that Islamic terrorists are not anti-American (as many Europeans believe) but anti-Western, anti-European and anti-cosmopolitan? Will a clandestine coalition develop between Islamic terrorist anti-Americanism and European anti-Americanism based on the maxim 'the enemy of my enemy is my friend'? Or will Europe stand alongside America because it recognizes that Islamic terrorist fundamentalism hates and wants to destroy everything that Europe stands for, namely, non-religious liberal-mindedness, loss of binding traditions, an agnostic ethos of respect among those who accept uncertainty as part of the human condition?

Second, it holds true for environmental, economic and terrorist risks alike that they cannot be shunted into the environment as *external* threats but must be understood as consequences, acts and uncertainties that are produced by civilization. Accordingly, the risks of civilization may give rise to a more acute global normative awareness, and found a public space and perhaps even a cosmopolitan outlook.

2   The real scientific basis of social theory with critical intent

Social theory, whatever its provenance, must make explicit its empirical basis if it is not to remain historically and empirically empty and immune to refutation. If social theory no longer wants to be a science of unreality that is oblivious to its own historical origins, and has absolved itself apodictically of any historical-empirical danger of falsification (and hence is 'worse than false' because it can neither be confirmed nor disconfirmed) and again become a curious, normatively and historically sensitive 'science of reality' (Max Weber) inspired by the intellectual pioneering spirit of the classics, then it must prove itself in the present. An account of the transition to the world risk society 'is based in reality, socially constructed, to be sure, but the collective outcome of innumerable social transactions is no more unreal or wishable away than the bodies in Hiroshima in 1945' (Albrow 1996: 106). Thus the foundation for such a renewed social historiography resides in the *social facticity of global risks*.

Two conditions must be fulfilled in order to grasp this 'meta-change' (i.e. change in the system of reference of social change). First, a lifeworld phenomenology of the world risk society must be worked out, that is, a precise empirical record of everything which changes in the lives of human beings as the influence of the globality of risk increases. Hence, we must develop new categories and methods that enable us to observe and describe how the practical experiences of human beings are reflected in the globalized world in recognizable 'cosmopolitan' social forms (i.e. ones which blur the existing basic differentiations and national boundaries) and how this affects the self-images of human beings, groups and populations and is expressed in action.[4]

The second condition is that we need a theory of the world risk society. This must include the institutional consequences and contradictions and the resulting dynamic of the new era, define the meaning of new practical experiences, and throw light upon the interrelation between historical change and lifeworld experiences and practices.

Edmund Husserl also describes these two conditions in very general terms. He assumed that 'the total phenomenological attitude and the epoché belonging to it are destined in essence to effect, at first, a complete personal transformation, comparable in the beginning to a religious conversion' (1970: 137). Thus the basis of a theory of world risk society in a science of the real resides in the fact that it succeeds in tracing how global risks permeate and revolutionize everyday lifeworlds – not unlike a 'religious conversion'.

An outstanding example of this is undoubtedly climate change. Here the globalization of risk has actually altered the framework of human experience and social action (though many think not extensively enough). The worldwide linkage of side effects of industrial triumphs promotes a global consciousness and makes it possible to conceptualize global risks. Once the endangered earth itself becomes the reference point of human action, the globality of risks will become an indispensable feature of thought and action. Even the negation – an appropriate answer to climate change must make the impossible possible, namely, that humanity constitutes itself as a political actor, renounces reckless industrialism and successfully orchestrates a transformation of lifestyles – reflects this quasi-religious conversion. Thus the dynamic of world risk society releases an actual or potential avalanche of lifeworld changes that are triggered when risk ceases to be a limited individual problem and becomes a global phenomenon of far-reaching political significance.[5] As I have argued, however, the contours of world risk society essentially take shape outside the field of vision of 'unseen and unwanted side effects'. But this means that the social facts do not appear as such. They first have to be sifted out of the understanding of linear theories of modernization that specifically maintain the latency of risks and their side effects character. This is why it is indispensable to make a specific, perhaps even a methodologically informed, connection between theory and experience in order to work out the phenomenology of global risks, as was demonstrated in an exemplary way in chapter 10 with reference to 'methodological cosmopolitanism'. Only in this combination is it possible to reconstruct empirically how the new practical experiences transform our understanding of old concepts and what prompts the development of new ones.

Underlying this is a 'contextual universalism' (Beck 2000a: 81–6) that takes a sceptical view of the possibility of ever discovering eternal truths in human, social and natural processes. At the same time, it insists on the necessity of uncovering and designating to the best of our knowledge the 'contextual universalisms' in present-day experience.

This leads to a competition among interpretations. Theories of linear modernization and rationalization confront theories of the world risk society, and both focus on the lifeworld phenomenology of global risks. Realistically speaking, the competing interpretive approaches can lead to a kind of 'stalemate of explanations'. For, even where a watershed between eras is asserted and demonstrated, there arise overlaps and hybrid forms of old and new phenomena, and hence a both/and in which *all* of the competing social theories can find confirmation for their assumptions. Thus, it is certainly possible to make the new era into an appendage of the old and to project the features of the old order into the future. This procedure is not fruitless either, because the social structures and institutions of the first modernity by no means collapse as a whole at a particular historical juncture. Thus, methodologically speaking, one must indeed practise what Max Weber called 'double-entry bookkeeping'. He assigned it a major role in the rise of capitalism. 'Double-entry bookkeeping' is also needed in this sense in order to record the rise of the world risk society.

Nevertheless, there are decisive moments that, in the sense of Thomas Kuhn's (1962) concept of a paradigm shift, first render the novelty of social facts describable and knowable. For uncovering the empirical facts of the world risk society presupposes the availability not only of a corresponding theory but also of *practical* changes in the social and methodological organization of the social sciences. A key issue here is undoubtedly overcoming 'methodological nationalism'. If one defines 'culture' (or 'society') as the development of universally shared meanings based on collective practical experience, then the world risk society breaks with the conception of separate and closed cultures and introduces the practical experiences that transcend cultural differences into everyday life. In this respect, the world risk society represents a threat to the traditional concept of culture and society. Cultural boundaries and oppositions are broken down in staged global experiences of threats, and it becomes apparent that their alleged inherent incommensurability rests on decisions concerning national demarcations backed up by power. It likewise becomes apparent that forms of social organization – for example, a nation-state that erects barriers against the outside world – in reality erect barriers to mutual understanding. Other cultures cannot be understood on the basis of universal classifications and surveys that the social sciences have borrowed from the natural sciences. A *cosmopolitan hermeneutics* is both normatively and empirically necessary in order to understand this conflict dynamic of world risk society.

Only the *summation* of the phenomenology of internally globalized lifeworlds based on combining theory and description yields 'historical falsification criteria'. The latter proceed from the epochal shift, yet they can form the point of departure and guideline for innovations in social theory. In the early modern period, the collapse of the transcendently legitimated social order was just such a 'historical falsification criterion'; at the beginning of the nineteenth century, i.e. of industrial modernity, it was the key experience of the internal dynamic and self-empowerment produced by human decisions and of the political explosiveness of the associated class conflict; then later it was also the integrating effect based on the connection between national society and nation-state which opened up the horizons of sovereignty, democracy and the welfare state (also as a national answer to the class conflict, which Marx understood in transnational terms). These are historical criteria of falsification dealt with by the founding classics and over which they struggled for answers in their conceptual and empirical studies.

Since the 1980s at the latest ('environmental crises, individualization'), but especially at the beginning of the twenty-first century, it is the many faces of uncontrollable, manufactured uncertainties and risks which are experienced and given expression in the most prominent public debates, controversies and conflicts by social movements, scientists, experts, politicians and – not least – terrorists. Here, as I said, working out the new epochal quality of this planetary uncertainty, which is the result of all striving to overcome it, is of major importance. The key issue in many areas of everyday life is not just the concrete experience of uncontrollability but the loss of credibility and disintegration of the guiding ideal of rationality and control, and this is shown in people's practical experiences.

Thus the concept of 'practical experience' (similar to Pierre Bourdieu's (1984) concept of 'habitus') seeks to provide an answer to the problem of how to find a sociological concept for the preconceptual, non-ideational foundation of discourse (Poferl 2004). Just this constitutes the extra-theoretical, extra-sociological point of departure for an empirical social theory of world risk society: on a large and a small scale, in everyday life and in global politics, human beings are searching for the security they have lost.

With this we have also identified the limits grounded in the *theory* of world risk society. What the chapters of this book attempt to show comes together to form nothing more, but also nothing less, than the theoretical framework that makes possible concrete historical-empirical analyses and case studies, a task that could only be begun in the present book. At the same time, however, the critical theory of the world risk society must also be measured by how far it overcomes the obstacles to action posed by the linear, automatized modernization and opens up the horizon for political alternatives.

3   Political perspectives: cosmopolitan political realism

Traces of a future politics can certainly be discerned in the interactions and antagonisms of risk conflicts, i.e. of the cosmopolitan political realism whose basic principles can be summed up in five points.

First: World risk society exhibits the new historical reality that no nation can master its problems alone. This is no longer an idealistic principle of utopian internationalism or a social scientific ivory tower philosophy but an insight of political realism. It is the fundamental law of cosmopolitan realism, which contradicts the unilateralism of the US government as much as the counterforce fantasies of the Europeans.

Second: Global problems give rise to transnational commonalities. Those who play the national card lose. Only those who understand and conduct national politics in a cosmopolitan way can survive. National states, regardless of whether they are weak or strong, are no longer the primary units for solving national problems. Interdependence is not a *scourge* of humanity but the precondition for its survival. Cooperation is no longer a means but the end. Individual states mostly operate both unilaterally and multilaterally, depending on the issues with which they are dealing and the areas in which they are operating. The more globality is consciously recognized, and thus the more cultures, countries, governments, regions and religions are affected, the more ineffective and unrealistic unilateral action becomes. For the likelihood of failure is greater because both effectiveness and legitimacy are products of cooperation among states. In short, the method of cosmopolitan political realism provides the detour. Progress in the interminable Middle East conflict, for example, cannot be achieved in isolation through direct interaction between Israelis and Palestinians but only via the detour of a globally arranged and moderated regional compromise in which every nation has something to gain in a major give and take: security for Israel, sovereignty for the Lebanese, a state for the Palestinians, and the Golan Heights, currently occupied by Israel, for Syria. For this it is necessary to speak and negotiate with one another in spite of divisions and hatreds in order to replace the national zero-sum game with a positive-sum game based on peaceful mutual dependence.

Third: International organizations are not merely the continuation of national politics with other means. They bundle and transform national interests, giving rise to the positive-sum game among the states concerned that can supersede the negative-sum game of national autonomy. National (neo)realism asserts that international organizations serve primarily national, not international interests. Cosmopolitan realism states that international organizations serve neither national (in the old sense) nor primarily international interests, but that they transform, maximize and extend national into transnational interests and open up new transnational spaces of power and action for a wide range of global political players, though also for individual states. Who or what sustains this cosmopolitan integration among states? Certainly the 'national' calculation of the states and governments concerned (as the realists in political science assert), though one transformed to its core by a *cosmopolitan supplement*. This is ultimately to everyone's benefit, because only thus can regional and global problems, which are also national problems, be, if not solved, then at least reined in within expanded political spaces. The creation of international organizations presupposes that the United States will limit its power of its own accord as a strategy for the legitimation and cooperative extension of power. Something different and new arises when states that stand in asymmetrical power relations cooperate in the face of global threats under conditions of law and respect for democratic values.

Fourth: The refusal of some European states and of the UN Security Council to act as a rubber stamp for US military unilateralism did not lead to a loss of power of the EU and the UN, as many commentators suspected; on the contrary, both have gained in global credibility. The legitimacy of global risk politics is founded essentially on a global division of powers between the power to employ military force and the procedural power of global public consensus. Only the autonomy of the EU and the UN vis-à-vis unipolar US military power can furnish the latter with the requisite legitimacy. The seemingly indispensable direct link between national power and its national legitimacy in the national sovereignty paradigm is counterproductive at the global level. If the United States seeks agreement with the EU, it will optimize its chances of winning the support of the UN and thus the political premium of the *unanimity* of the US, the UN and the EU.

Fifth: Unilateralism is uneconomic. Cosmopolitan realism, by contrast, is also *economic* realism. It reduces and redistributes costs, not only because military expenditures are in any case many times higher than the costs of a strategy of political prevention, but also because costs rise exponentially with the loss of legitimacy. Conversely, shared responsibility and shared sovereignty also mean shared costs. For example, it might even be possible to fund US experts from the UN budget and to deploy them with the blessing of international law. Such practical options of transnational politics are ruled out by national unilateralism. In other words, cooperation between states – an important element of cosmopolitan realism – is also good business.

Critical theory of world risk society as social self-criticism

The troublesome, though not unanswerable question 'How is critique possible?' no longer even arises for the majority of sociological theories. Apparently something like 'critical sociology' or 'critical theory' cannot be easily reconciled with positions that lean towards constructivism or relativism. Sociologists who conduct their business on the basis of such epistemological positions are not especially bothered or spurred to reflection when alerted to the fact that they are adopting certain premises of the institutional order which they are investigating and are thereby affirming (whether intentionally or not) this status quo. Normativity is in bad odour. It is generally assimilated to procedures in which a normative ideal is opposed to a deformed reality in order to deduce the predictable conclusions. Such endeavours induce a sense of embarrassment, at least among German sociologists concerned with clinical value freedom. For they cherish the belief that they have finally rid themselves of the unpleasant sweaty odour that clings to such exertions.

However, they fail to recognize that a sociology that unreflectedly succumbs to the premises of its research object, and is in this sense uncritical, fails to fulfil its most basic task. It succumbs to, rather than breaks with, the fixations of society's self-descriptions and thus remains incapable of registering either empirically or analytically what drives social and political reality and splits it apart. The most wonderful epoch-specific example of this is the 'methodological nationalism' which leads sociology to assume unreflectively that it is condemned to being a 'national sociology' in which nationals study nationals for nationals. Here the world is divided according to the distinction between us and the rest. Sociology studies 'us', whereas the study of others is a field for others – anthropologists, ethnologists, etc. It is no surprise that, committed to this division of labour, sociology systematically misses the involved contingencies and complexities of world risk society. Hence, a realistic science of the world risk society presupposes the emphatic critique of the cognitive contours of the national contexts of action, for only through a decisive break with the homogeneity between the basic premises of political and methodological nationalism can the structures, contradictions, options and constraints of national patterns of action in the world risk society be laid bare. In this way, the critical theory of world risk society becomes at once realistic and critical; indeed, it becomes realistic because it is critical, and thus capable of distancing itself in a critical way from the cognitive structures of the national outlook which dominate social and political action. This kind of *realistic* critical theory does not hamper a realistic scientific sociology but first makes it possible.

Because risk is synonymous with risk conflict, the antagonism among social actors within and between institutions, political and subpolitical fields of action, and social movements becomes a fruitful source of possible alternatives. On the other hand, it is the sense of reality, rather than normative exuberance, that forces us to develop the abilities and sensibilities which first enable us to register in sociological terms the full spectrum of culturally defined alternatives within institutionalized practices and the constitution and organization of society. If the national sociology fixated on integration still had an unreflective awareness of the guiding norm, and of what is 'normal' and what 'deviant' by this standard, this dualistic way of thinking is becoming incapable of grasping reality under the conditions of the world risk society. The paradoxes and contradictions built into the dynamic of world risk society which come to the fore along with it smash to pieces the carefully organized, one-dimensional categories of normal versus deviant behaviour, equilibrium versus disruption, subjectivism versus structuralism, etc. The distinction between possibility and reality also disintegrates in the real virtuality of risk. In other words, anyone interested in a realistic approach to risks must open him or herself up for alternatives. Here, too, the sense for possibility becomes a sense of reality (to borrow a formulation of Robert Musil).

Thus critical theory of world risk society also means that we must become alert to the manifold, real self-critical voices of the developing world risk society. Insurance experts criticize the zero-risk thesis of the engineers and managers who want to reduce insurance costs. Of course, they do not do this because they want to become involved in or switch over to the national or global power game as ersatz critics but out of pure economic self-interest: high risks are good for business. Postcolonial social movements blame the 'outside threats' to which they once again find themselves exposed, this time due not to a lack of modernization but to the export of the problems created by radicalized modernization under the false banner of 'unseen side effects'. Even in the seemingly most homogeneous, hierarchical and closed organizations, such as the armed forces, critical voices are raised internally, though often also publicly, when it comes to the risks of a planned deployment. There is no shortage of 'whistle blowers', as the counter-experts to the zero-risk pronouncements are judiciously termed. And the law also holds universally that after the catastrophe the warning counter-experts are proved right. Moreover, the end of one catastrophe is merely the prelude to another.

The polarization of risk expands the spectrum of self-criticism from within society. Not to suppress and fail to understand this out of a false evaluative horizon of homogenizing norms – again inspired by the aim of producing a science of the real – constitutes the critical realism of a critical theory of the world risk society. That this is not sufficient of itself will be shown in the next, concluding chapter, 'Dialectics of Modernity'.

12

Dialectics of Modernity: How the Crises of Modernity Follow from the Triumphs of Modernity

In 1861, during the birth pangs of modern society, Charles Baudelaire wrote in the foreword to *Les Fleurs du mal*: 'Paris is the centre and splendour of universal stupidity. Who would ever have believed that France would pursue the path of progress with such verve?'

What Baudelaire calls 'universal stupidity' is nothing other than modernity's belief in itself, in its unstoppable victory march: argument triumphs over superstition and belief, the human being becomes the measure of all things and, by continually extending the boundless plasticity of modern technology, everything accidental can be cast off. All that is fixed evaporates, the future is colonized by the present. Historically speaking, this ceaseless change appears as a transition from darkness into light, as an implicit theory of the process of moral evolution which we call 'progress'. Science, which displaces God and religion from the centre, operates with a 'mythology' of its own that captures the old distinction between the sacred and the profane as a distinction between lay opinion and expert rationality, and this becomes the source of secular and religious visions of deliverance.

Two questions arise. First, How was it even possible, in the moral and intellectual ruins of thirty years of religious wars, after the 'eternal truths' of the divinely ordained and divinely assured medieval social order had collapsed, to transform the reigning doubts, fears and premonitions into the unreflected, 'anthropological' self-confidence of modernity? And second, the counter-question: Can we imagine a power capable of shattering these idols of modern society?

The counter-actors and countervisions heralded by the self-empowerment of modernity and subsequently dethroned – the proletariat, communism, socialism, nationalism, the new intelligentsia or the mute force of public argument – have not withstood the test of history, as the twentieth century shows. Of course, this does not preclude that scattered groups of these increasingly abstract avant-gardes of hope will continue to fly their flags. If there is any countervailing force that could transform this immanent metaphysics of modernity then, I would argue, it is the self-perpetuating power of modernity itself.

Modern society's belief in linear progression contradicts the self-disenchantment of modernity. Contrary to the social theories of Comte, Marx, Durkheim and Weber, through Horkheimer, Adorno, Parsons and Gehlen, up to Foucault and Luhmann, I maintain that the apparently independent and autonomous system of industrialism has transgressed its logic and boundaries and has thereby begun a process of self-dissolution. This radical turn marks the current phase in which modernization is becoming reflexive. Instead of contenting itself with tracing various paths and potentials within industrial modernity, modernization is now impinging upon the very social, political and cultural basic principles and institutions of the industrial society of the nation-state, is breaking them down and is giving rise to new potentials in opposition to industrial modernity. In this way, the process of reflexive modernization is leading from the national industrial society to the (still indeterminate ambiguity of) world society.

Of course, the triumph of modernity was shadowed from the beginning by criticism. Literature, in particular, had already buried modernity before it was fully born. However, this self-disenchantment did not produce political effects until the latter half of the twentieth century, in a pincer movement of environmentalist criticism, philosophical postmodernism and postcolonial liberation theory. The latter measured, rejected and dethroned Europe employing its own standards, thus opening up the horizon of a plurality of past and future modernities. Even the key concepts of Europe's self-description reveal this decline. First 'modern' became 'progressive', then 'progressive' became 'innovative', and in the process the promise of salvation lost its lustre. Innovations are always good for companies, only rarely for human beings. The venerable 'Enlightenment' did not fare much better. First it was called 'modernity', then it shrank to the 'project of modernity', then to 'postmodernity', and now it turns out to be 'world risk society'. At first sight, this roll-call of the key diagnostic concepts of the times seems to confirm the diagnosis of 'universal stupidity'. For the lay prophets of the Apocalypse often have difficulty in interpreting the signs of the increasingly rapid approach of the Last Judgement, though now the theory of world risk society seems to be coming to their rescue.

Yet the concept of global risk must be clearly distinguished from that of the Apocalypse (see pp. 9ff.). The only thing they share is the anticipation of decline. Thus, to pose the question in a spirit of self-irony: aren't the 'last judgements' of the approaching Apocalypse – the proliferation of nuclear, chemical and biological weapons, 9/11, the tsunami catastrophe, Hurricane Katrina, avian flu, AIDS – beginning to unfold their terrible power in the present? And isn't the author of *World at Risk* himself a product and agent of this fashionable rhetoric of fear?

1   On the distinction between the basic principles and basic institutions of modernity

All suppositions to the contrary, opportunistic cultural criticism [*Kulturkritik*] has never been my thing. My passion and curiosity has always been devoted to the change gripping and permeating all social domains. I struggle to render this thoroughness visible and understandable, to conceptualize and explain it. Is there a guiding principle, a hidden intuition, from which I take my orientation? I would like to use this concluding chapter to introduce the distinction between *basic principles* and *basic intuitions* of modernity as such an underlying motif (on this, see Beck and Lau 2004). This distinction makes it possible – depending on the relation between continuity and discontinuity – to identify different dialectics of modernity. I would first like to present this in an abstract analytic form before going on to develop it using concrete examples (see table 12.1).

Dialectics of 'more-modernity' develop out of the (radicalized) continuity of the basic *principles* of modernity (rationalization), which annuls the foundations of the basic *institutions* (full employment society). Dialectics of *anti-modernity*, by contrast, arise out of the discontinuity of the basic principles themselves. The sacrosanct aspect of modernity, the basic principles, become decidable themselves, with unforeseeable moral consequences. In this way, I want to examine first how far the suspicion of a doubling of fear can be overcome once and for all and then how far this distinction can be used as a ladder to reach new, dangerous insights and prospects. Someone who wants to climb so high would be well advised to start at the very bottom – in other words, with an example.

Dialectics of more-modernity: is work becoming scarce?

I open the newspaper and happen upon a story on the question 'Is work becoming scarce?' The question is not new. Hannah Arendt discussed it around four decades ago. But at the beginning of the twenty-first century, I

Table 12.1 Dialectics of modernity

	Basic principles of modernity	Basic institutions of modernity
Dialectics of more-modernity	Radicalized continuity: de-limitation	Discontinuity: change in basic institutions in which the basic principles impose themselves
Dialectics of anti-modernity	Intentional discontinuity: negation	(Dis)continuity: change in basic institutions in which the basic principles are negated

learn, this heretical question appears less rhetorical than ever, 'for there are almost 30 million people out of work in the OECD countries.' And, as if that were not enough: 'Out of 370 million Europeans, 53 million are already living below the poverty line.' Faced with such facts, 'the sacred cow around which modern societies were constructed – i.e. gainful employment – is losing its lustre.' In election campaigns, by contrast, 'the commitment to full employment' remains unruffled by any doubt, from the left to the far right, including all political shades in between. Reading further, I pass from politicians via retirees and young people to women. The 'mega-issue "globalization"' is introduced as a connecting link. I see that it has repercussions 'not only for the phenomenon of work but also for the state which lays down the social framework conditions of work.' Globalization 'attacks' the economic basis of the welfare state. Reflecting on the future of work is 'in large part also synonymous with reflection on the future roles of the sexes and on the future relation between young and old.' The European societies are becoming older, something which need not be interpreted automatically as a catastrophe. That changes 'once the financing of retirement benefits becomes a central issue': 'Fewer and fewer young people are financing the retirement benefits of ever more old people', a development associated with rampant 'unemployment among the young'. The problem areas are becoming intertwined, and I must ask how the scarcity of gainful employment is threatening to cause 'tectonic shifts in relations between the sexes'. I read that the assumption that 'this is merely a sociological consequence of feminism and women's emancipation' cannot withstand closer scrutiny. For, in reality, 'an epochal turning point in the history of the Western (working) world' is imminent. 'The death knell of patriarchy is tolling like thunder from the Valhalla of the West. And as always it is the women who are complaining the loudest. And rightly so. For until now the transformation of masculinity and femininity has been a question of women adapting to the work ethos of men.'

One and the same article jumbles together the negative work ethos of the ancient Greeks with the increase in productivity, the problem of retirement benefits, relations between generations and gender issues. The reader is continually alerted to the importance of 'modernization', which sometimes points in one direction, sometimes in another and then again in the opposite direction. A guiding thread unites countless millions of unemployed people throughout the world with the exploitation of the peripheral countries by those at the centre. I read that 'the resources of the periphery can be had as cheaply as in colonial times, only that we are spared the expense of a colonial administration.' The connection with the issue of retirement benefits is no less clear than with that of justice between the sexes or of justice between generations.

The key question is: How far can the distinction between the basic principles and basic institutions of modernity throw light on this completely normal chaos of real social relations?

Let me begin with two marginal zones in this typography of issues, i.e. retirement benefits and the increase in the numbers of the elderly. Both are rooted in the *triumphs* rather than the crises of modernity. People are living longer because medical progress, better nutrition, etc., have drastically reduced child mortality and in less than a century have almost doubled the average life expectancy in the wealthy countries of the West. These shifts in the age structure can be observed, albeit in less dramatic forms, in almost all countries in the world. More precisely, the greater the successes of modernization, the more threateningly looms the 'catastrophe' of greying societies.

If we apply the distinction mentioned to these conditions, this idea can be expressed even more clearly: it is the application of certain 'basic principles' of modernity – here, that of (medical) progress – that undermines the histori- cal foundations of the institutions of industrial society – in this case, the welfare state system of retirement benefits. Thus the issue of retirement benefits, the fall in birth rates and the greying of society cannot be easily forced into the pigeonhole of cultural criticism. The 'shock' which grips society here is the result of the confrontation with an unforeseen, uninten- tional side effect of its successes, and the obstacles to the reform of social assistance for the elderly is the reverse side of the 'artificial naturalness' of basic institutions.

Mass unemployment need not be experienced as a catastrophe either but can also mark the beginning of a liberation from the yoke of the requirement to work. The central status of work in modern society first had to be manu- factured as 'natural' through a process of revaluation without historical parallel. The present-day 'certainty' that gainful employment is the centre of modern society had to be painfully achieved step by step and setback by setback out of the earlier idea that work was beneath the dignity of a man and citizen. To put it pointedly, for the ancient Greeks, work counted as a criterion for excluding individuals from the community of citizens, whereas in modern society it is venerated as an indispensable mode of integration. The thesis that human beings can find fulfilment only in work, this anthropolo- gization of the claim to meaning of work, is a product of modernity, which culminates in the orthodoxy of the full employment society.

However, the basic principle of scientific-technological rationality also undermines the basic institutions of the full employment society. Mass unem- ployment is not the result of a failure but of the successes of rationalization: many times more can be achieved with less and less human labour power. Mass unemployment becomes a 'catastrophe' only when the no-longer-full employment society clings tenaciously to the guiding principle of full employ- ment and the individuals for whom wage labour has become second nature see no alternative way of securing their existence and constructing a social identity. To assume that these issues can be dealt with through reforms of the retirement and tax systems within the nation-state is to ignore completely people's premonitions, fears and hopes. And the key question remains hidden:

How can one have a meaningful life in modern society even if one cannot find a job?

How does the conversation with the future become possible?

A couple of years ago the US Congress established a scientific commission to develop a language or symbolism capable of warning against the threats posed by American nuclear waste dumps ten thousand years from now.[1] The problem to be solved was: How must concepts and symbols be designed in order to convey a message to future generations millennia from now? The commission was composed of physicists, anthropologists, linguists, neuroscientists, psychologists, molecular biologists, classical scholars, artists, etc. The first question it had to address was: Will the United States even exist ten thousand years from now? Of course, the commission had no trouble answering that question: *USA forever!* However, the central problem of how to begin a conversation with a future proved to be insoluble. The experts looked for models in the oldest symbols of humanity; they studied the construction of Stonehenge (*c.* 1500 bc) and the pyramids, they researched the history of the reception of Homer and the Bible, and they sought explanations of the life-cycle of documents. But these reached back at most a couple of thousand years, not ten thousand. The anthropologists recommended the symbol of the skull and crossbones. A historian reminded the commission, however, that the skull and crossbones symbolized resurrection for the alchemists, and a psychologist conducted an experiment with three-year-olds: if the symbol was affixed to a bottle they anxiously shouted 'poison!', if it was placed on a wall they yelled excitedly 'pirates!'.

Other scholars proposed paving the ground around the waste sites with ceramic, metal and stone plaques with characters expressing all kinds of warnings. But the linguists were unanimous that they would only be understood for two thousand years at most. The very scientific meticulousness of the commission showed how the crises of modernity follow from its triumphs. Even language fails when faced with the task of warning future generations against the dangers we have introduced into the world by using certain technologies. Once we have finally managed to identify the hazards also produced by modernity, they become incommunicable over the course of ten millennia because of the inadequacy of words.

The world has often come to an end

The distinction between fundamental principles and fundamental institutions makes it possible to specify what the rhetoric of decline fails to recognize. First, modernity is a *workshop of certainty* without historical precedent. To represent it, following Max Weber, as a disenchanting power does not go nearly far enough. Modernity dissolves certainties, but it also cements and celebrates new certainties. It is the idealist–philosophical outlook that obscures the fact that true certainties do not descend *from above* (as from some kind of tree of knowledge) but are produced, achieved and practised *from below*. Solutions and redemption were always fashioned out of the discarded certainties of the previous age. Behind every sociological axiom lies a deep wound. To simplify somewhat, the intellectual world of modernity is composed of 'machines of reason' into which doubts were fed and necessities came out the other end. Modernity is inconceivable without the ability to transform uncertainty and chaos into anthropological certainty and self-justification. Classics are classics because they completely master the art of producing evidence.

We have inquired long enough into the disenchantment engendered by modernity. Yet how should we decipher this architecture of an 'imminent' metaphysics? Take science, for example. Redemption through science presupposed a deity so constituted that science could discover it as its equal. 'In the scientific redeemer, the rationally aware human being created God in his own image. . . . The rational human being sought redemption only from a rational God . . . The more use human beings made of their reason, the more God became reason, and the more the path of science became the path to salvation' (Marcuse 1981: 50f.).

How could human beings be brought to believe the strangest things, for example that problems produced by technology could be solved by ever newer technologies? Why should more market be the solution to the problems produced by less market? Paradoxically enough, cultural criticism is deeply implicated in this transformation of dust into gold, of doubt into truth. Max Weber warned about the iron cage of bondage to rationality. Doesn't this cultural critical prophecy exude an uncontrolled optimism concerning control? And doesn't precisely this negative portent make possible an especially subtle affirmation of the imperturbable march of modernity?

The veneration of unfinishedness is the principal religion of the first modernity. For the dialectic of basic principles and basic institutions also dissolves this self-generated certainty of a stunted modernity, not because it marks the beginning of postmodernity, but because the principles of modernity are no longer content with the unfinishedness of its basic institutions. To speak with and against Marx: all the certainties of modernity become antiquated before they can ossify. All that is solid, all that modernity has created, melts into air. It is a kind of involuntary release from the forms of self-incurred tutelage characteristic of industrial society. It is the end not of the world, but of the world certainties of the first modernity.

Looking back, we can state with a certain degree of satisfaction that the world has already come to an end many times! – at any rate if we take seriously the fears expressed by contemporaries during the depressive phases of the various epochs. Historical research teaches us that in the early modern period, i.e. in sixteenth-century Europe, the world which then dominated people's minds came to an end. A similar decline occurred in the middle of the nineteenth century, when what held the world together at its core once again fell apart. And, unless I'm completely mistaken, take-for-granted certainties have once again undergone a systematic transformation since the 1970s. Even the most elementary logical principles suggest that so many endings imply a couple of new beginnings.

Thus it is easier to point to past world declines to stress what *arose* at the time before the unseeing eyes of the time. At the beginning of the twenty-first century, however, this is difficult. For, although we are witnessing the destruction of the certainties of the national phase of industrial modernity at many levels, a new order has not (yet) emerged. That 'the' end of the world has become many ends should alert us to how dangerous and self-referential talk of the 'end of the world' is. For it implies glossing over our own inability to recognize the signs of new world beginnings and to render them understandable, controllable and thus liveable for contemporaries and future generations – something which today is also possible and desirable.

Thus the customary cultural criticism fails because it does not make the necessary distinction between one end of the world and another. For, in lamenting the end of *the* world, it remains silent concerning the decline of its own unreflected certainties about the world. Big talk and obstinate secrecy are intimately interrelated. We dramatize the decline of values, freedom, democracy, etc., so as to avoid having to acknowledge the catastrophic collapse of our own certainties about the world (though only for ourselves). Thus the posture of cultural criticism does not only involve avoidance of the conceptual work necessary for understanding the new. The cultural critical outlook is blind and naïve concerning political realities. It fails to realize that where it sees a world coming to an end the world order is in fact being transformed, that the rules and structures of power and domination are being renegotiated in the global age (Beck 2005). Precisely the apocalyptic rhetoric – the conflict of ideas over global risk – opens up new, transnationally networked arenas for publics, social movements, sciences, terrorist networks, failing states and new and old wars. This is the scene of the rhetorical-legitimatory and military battles over who must bear the risks of global risks and how in the process norms and resources of the future global order are being negotiated and assigned in the present.

Ambivalences of individualization

How much conventional cultural criticism becomes trapped in its own linearity can also be shown by elucidating the distinction between basic principles and basic institutions in terms of *individual autonomy* and *institutionalized individualism*. Scarcely any desire is more widespread within the Western world and beyond than to 'live one's own life'. Anyone who today travels in Europe and, needless to say, the United States, though also in South America, Singapore, Tokyo or South Korea, and asks what motivates people, what they strive for, what they struggle for, what is really important for them, receives the answers: money, jobs, power, love, God, etc., but also increasingly the promises of individualism. Money means one's own money, space means one's own space, as elementary preconditions for a 'life of one's own'. Even love, marriage and parenthood, which are longed for more than ever as the future becomes uncertain, are subject to the proviso of uniting and holding together individual biographies that are drifting apart. It is only a mild exaggeration to say that the daily struggle for the autonomy of one's own life has become the collective experience of the world as a whole which expresses a new kind of residual community of all.

Of course, there is no authority that could lay down 'the' basic principles of modernity for all, no matter what insights and procedures it appeals to. Clearly it would be no less mistaken to derive the basic principle from the heaven of reason, as the cause of its own realization as it were, and to transplant it into people's hearts. A causal interpretation according to which the radicalization of a basic principle in each case leads to the dissolution of a basic institution would be patent nonsense and would be at odds with both sociological and historical realism. At the same time, however, the basic principle comprises a high social regard – and its validity can be reconstructed among the fluctuating interpretations only through historical examination and painstaking research. To think that it is possible to derive the basic principle of individual autonomy *post hoc* from the observed processes of social individualization would be to fall prey to a 'retrospective teleology' (Mulsow).

Talk of the 'basic' principle – in this case of individual autonomy – assumes that the principle is deeply rooted in human consciousness. In fact, 'one's own life' in this sense is a modern invention. It had to be detached from the opposite notion and be realized one small step at a time over history. For the individual remained a generic term in the spaces of closed society, namely, the smallest unit of an imagined whole. Only the opening of society, the multiplication of its contradictory functional logics, lends the high esteem accorded the individual social space and meaning. Throughout history, individual behaviour was long equated with deviant or even 'idiotic' behaviour.

When individuality makes its appearance in the consciousness of a worldview, it appears as tainted with a stigma or defect . . . In Greek, in the *kainón* of what is shared in common, individual behaviour seems to have meant something deviant, idiographic, indeed ultimately 'idiotic' . . . Similarly . . . for large parts of the early Middle Ages individuality was interpreted primarily as a deviant and sinful form of conduct or existence to be shunned. This derogatory meaning of individuality extends far beyond antiquity and the Middle Ages into the scientific and bourgeois world and into the motto above Sartre's famous formula: 'merely an individual' – that is the most succinct expression of the contrary position to the early romantic rehabilitation and redefinition of the essence of individuality . . . Presumably this devaluation is connected with the necessary privileging of the universal over the particular and the individual within the horizon of Occidental rationality. (Koenen 1993: 101)

In fact, it was only with the early Romantics – Friedrich Schleiermacher, Wilhelm von Humboldt and especially Friedrich Schlegel – that the hierarchy of values of the universal and the individual was inverted. The guiding idea was that 'the "individual" signifies a part or element that can never be arrived at through a series of logical deductions from the concept of the whole. The universal is interpreted in individual terms as universal, its claim to universal validity is refracted through the originality of individual meaning' (Frank and Haverkamp 1988: ix).

Interestingly enough, this overthrow, this revaluation, was a consequence of the fact that what had legitimized the devaluation of the individual for centuries now justified its positive revaluation: the individual cannot be derived from the universal. The henceforth merely presumptively universal runs up against the *originality* of the individual. The 'essence of individuality' can thus be grasped and defined by radical non-identity. Then, at the beginning of the twentieth century, Émile Durkheim speaks of the 'religion of individualism', emphasizing the worldly sanctity acquired in the interim by individual autonomy as the basic principle of modern society, even though this positive valuation of the individual remains to be accepted without qualification even to this very day, as is shown by the talk of the 'egoistic' or 'me first' society. Viewed in this way, we are currently witnessing not a decline but a shift in values in accordance with the demands of the second modernity.

Contemporary historical studies – such as that of Ulrich Herbert (2007) – are instructive because they throw additional light on the relationships between basic principles and basic institutions in contemporary Western societies. These kinds of historical analyses demonstrate in detail that the guiding ethical models have changed dramatically, not only in Germany, but also in other European countries since the 1980s at the latest. Attitudes towards homosexuality can serve as an example here. In the 1960s, the penal code still marked and excluded it as a criminal offence. Then, from the late 1960s to the mid-1990s, the same activity was progressively decriminalized (similar developments can be observed in Austria, France, the Netherlands, Great Britain, etc.). What is astonishing about this is that what had previously been enshrined in law as a 'natural', 'anthropological' core of morality is now regarded as a matter of individual choice. Within the space of approximately fifteen years, a similar shift in mentality occurred more or less simultaneously in virtually all Western European societies. Here – as the example of homosexuality shows, but also similar changes in civil law, family law and divorce law – the basic principle of individual autonomy, which originally applied exclusively to men, gradually gained universal acceptance through a progressive transformation of the principles underlying penal law, family law, etc. (see table 12.2). And this holds not only for some groups, but for all groups within the space of a single generation. There is no historical precedent for such a profound transformation of a basic institution in such a short time.

This apparently explosive change should be seen against the background of an 'incubation phase' at the beginning of the twentieth century when modernity reached a new climax with the sudden breakthrough of experimental forms of life and art that inspired fear and enthusiasm in equal measure. In Gottfried Benn's description of this intellectual expressionism: 'The feeling for form will be the major transcendence of the new age, the link uniting the second era; the first God created in His image, the second Man in accordance with his forms, the twilight world of nihilism is no more. In the former reigned causality, original sin, the pathos of ancestry, psychoanalysis, ressentiment and reaction, in the new, flexible principles, constructions within defined horizons' (Benn). The political developments of the 1920s should be seen in this context. Nationalism and socialism can be viewed as reactions to the eruption of these 'critical experiments' of modernity in the interwar years.

After World War II, there was at first a rollback, the moral certainties of the turn of the century were reactivated and 'perfect-world' interpretations prevailed. Only with the experience of social stability and the Cold War 'peace' of the 1960s 'economic miracle' was there again room for new advances in individualization, which were then able to exercise social effects with the expansion of education and its consequences. The new social movements which are now emerging – from the peace movement and the women's movement to the environmental movement, the gay rights movement and multiculturalism – are an expression of *political individualism* because they break

Table 12.2 Transformation of family law in Germany

	Original version of the German Civil Code, in effect since 1 January 1900	*Marriage Law Reform Act, in effect since 1 July 1977*
§1354	The husband has the right to decide in all matters regarding married life; in particular, he determines the place of residence and the home	Annulled
§1355	The wife assumes her husband's family name	The couple can adopt the birth name of the husband or the maiden name of the wife . . . as their married name
§1356	The wife is . . . entitled and obliged to manage the common household	Both husband and wife have a say in how the household is managed

with pre-given, seemingly anthropologically rooted laws, group member-
ships and shared destinies, and hence also with the associated normative
expectations – and set self-generated social ties and obligations against
them.

If this interpretation is correct it means that *cultural pessimism has been
refuted by history. Kinder der Freiheit* (Beck 1997b) reveals a form of individualization that does not threaten democracy, as is commonly assumed, but
on the contrary first makes democracy possible – indeed fills it with life –
because it reflects an altruistic, socially aware individuality.

2   Dialectics of anti-modernity

This dialectic of the continuity of basic principles and discontinuity of basic
institutions highlights the fact that, historically speaking, the basic principles,
notwithstanding all cultural criticism, were not open to challenge until now.
The talk of 'postmodernity' is misleading, even false, because the catastrophes
and crises which confront us at the beginning of the twenty-first century are
almost exclusively products of the triumphs of a modernization that has
become self-perpetuating. It is precisely these 'victorious results' that make
it imperative to rewrite and rethink the theories of the conventional,
'un-dialectical' sociology of modernization if we are to be able to grasp
the dialectics of modernity with their intrinsic potential for change and
destruction.

The distinction between basic principles and basic institutions of modernity raises the further question of the discontinuity of the basic principles
themselves. To what extent and under which conditions are the moral
and functional basic principles of modernity defined as changeable and decidable – like everything affected by modernity? To put it more radically: How
does unrestricted modernization, which cancels its own foundations, make
anti-modernity possible? The fear which spreads with the awareness that the
basic institutions are becoming fragile may be a reflection of the premonition
that radicalized modernity has set something unimaginable in train. Its own
victories mean that its constitution, its basic principles (e.g. the universal
human right of the sanctity and dignity of life; individual autonomy; the
obligation to provide rational justifications in public discourse; the legal
restriction and democratic legitimation of political power)[2] are drawn into
the space of possible decisions and interventions. This creates the possibility
that inviolable basic principles could be qualified or even done away with
altogether.

This radical discontinuity, this possibility of a constitutional breach within
modernity, leads to a second figure of the dialectic of modernization: *dialectics of anti-modernity.* That this is again a variant of the unity of the triumphs
and the self-endangerments of modernity will be outlined in what follows

with reference to the major world-political upheavals and traumas of our era.

The atomic bomb

Hiroshima: this word forever stands for the first time the atomic bomb was dropped. This event, which was a result of the successes of the natural sciences (in this case, nuclear physics), revealed the radical ambivalences of 'progress' and inspired universal horror. It became apparent that the apocalyptic proclamations of a new 'wonder weapon' were not an exaggeration but, on the contrary, fell far short of the reality. Only the inconceivable, unimaginable scale of the destruction showed what lay hidden in the everyday normality of science, research and theory. The triumph of modernity had given birth to a demonic weapon which left the fate of humanity in the hands of those who controlled – or managed to get their hands on – the levers of power.

The decline of the human race was no longer merely an apocalyptic vision of fundamentalist religious splinter groups. The march of progress turned it into a real possibility, indeed a global risk, which, because it can no longer be banished from the world, creates a new situation and transforms the foundations of all futures for all time. However, this triumph of modernity leads to the collapse of a conviction that had been regarded as obvious until then, namely, that there are *technical* limits to the cruelty of which human beings are capable. The commandment 'Thou shalt not kill!' is heightened into 'Thou shalt not kill humanity!'. This 'Thou shalt not kill humanity!' made no sense before the atomic bomb was dropped; but after it was dropped the worldwide search began for answers to the question of the moral and intellectual content of the principle and how it could be made politically and militarily binding.

The logic of war and peace valid until that moment lost its meaning. Where victory is no longer victory and defeat no longer defeat, the warring parties had to create new institutions that make it possible to go on living, thinking and debating under the Damocles sword of nuclear self-annihilation. Günther Anders speaks in this context of the 'antiquatedness of humanity' and the 'blindness to Apocalypse' of our thought and institutions; the Cold War 'nuclear stalemate' led to new forms of cooperation between the hostile military blocs; indeed this 'nuclear threat' ultimately made possible the Ostpolitik geared to 'humanitarian relief' of German Chancellor Willy Brandt and his strategic advisor Egon Bahr. In this case politicians realized that security could no longer be achieved through national unilateralism but only through transnational corporation.

This peace order of terror erected on the basis of arms control agreements broke down, however, with the end of the Cold War bipolar order. The global space of power was now opened up once again. The temptation on the part of the atomic powers and of the atomic have-nots to achieve national invulnerability through the atomic bomb is growing. India and Pakistan have long since acquired nuclear weapons, Iraq was ready to, Libya too, North Korea without a doubt, and Iran is on the way to acquiring them. Egypt is eyeing the prospect, Saudi Arabia also, and Israel has them already. Twenty further states are poised on the nuclear threshold, most of them in the war zones stretching from North Africa to the Middle East.

The secret maxim of the bomb is identical with that of nihilism: the bomb behaves like a nihilist. It treats everything, regardless of whether it is man or machine, bread or book, house or forest, plant or animal, *in the same way*, namely, as nature – which in this case means, as something accessible to radioactive contamination. Nothing else exists for it. And if it could speak, its words would be identical with those of the nihilist: 'It's all the same. It's all the same whether the world exists or not. What difference does it make if it does not exist?' (Anders 1983: 301)

It is the enormous successes of modernity, its achievements, its dynamism, which have created the possibility of the self-destruction of mankind. Global risk means that the basic principles of modernity are open to challenge and that the power of modernity can be used to decide against the basic principles of modernity. The atomic bomb does not merely potentially destroy modernity; the anticipation of self-annihilation also immediately destroys the self-confidence and the basic concepts and theories of modernity. For example, the principle of precaution now says: when in doubt, *against* the accused. For as long as the potential perpetrator has not abolished the atomic bomb, as long as it poses a threat for the simple reason that he has it (or tries to get it), all that time he must also be viewed as guilty – 'as guilty of nihilism, of nihilism on a global scale' (Anders 1983: 294). Hence, anticipatory conflicts are breaking out on the stages of world politics.

In the interplay between suicidal terrorism, new and old wars and the nuclear temptation, new and extremely dangerous dialectics of modernity are unfolding. This also means that the global power order is being rewritten under conditions of perceived global threats – though new structures, norms, institutions, winners and losers are not yet clearly discernible.

Holocaust

In his book *Survival in Auschwitz* (1993), Primo Levi recounts an apparently minor incident that occurred during his first days in the concentration camp. Terribly thirsty, he reached out of a window to break off an icicle. The guard drove him back with a stick. 'Why?', asked Levi. The answer was clear: 'There is no why here' (quoted from Levy and Sznaider 2004). Modernity lives from the 'why' and dies with it. The destruction of the 'why' prepares the way for totalitarian nihilism, for the Holocaust. Beyond the 'why' 'everything is possible'.

By contrast, Zygmunt Bauman argues: 'It was the rational world of modern civilization that made the Holocaust possible' (1989: 13). On this view, everything that occurred in Nazi Germany – the organized, technologically perfected destruction of the Jews – was a consequence of radicalized modernization, for the specific reason that modernity has uncoupled goal-oriented, technologically refined action from any moral constraint. This is why the Holocaust also went beyond the genocides which took place before and afterwards in many parts of the world.

Genocide is not a modern invention . . . The Holocaust, by contrast, is a modern invention: as a genocide with an explicit, legally recognized goal, as a carefully planned crime committed over a considerable period, and as a mass murder that was committed with the aid of the most advanced technology (in fact, only made possible by it), to which the scientific, rational organization of work, this by far the most cherished achievement of the modern period, also belonged. (Bauman 1994: 2)

In *Dialectic of Enlightenment* (1947), Horkheimer and Adorno interpret the Nazi terror in a similar way as a form of barbarity, as an event implicit in the logic of modernity itself and not as a result of political decisions that corrupt the basic principles of modernity. In their view, the break with the norms of civilization is implicit in the process of rationalization and bureaucratization which goes hand in hand with modernization. It is precisely the collapse of reflexivity within modernity that set free the self-destructive possibilities of modernity.

Hannah Arendt offers a different argument.[3] Concentration camps remain utterly incomprehensible as long as we cling to the basic assumptions of the rationalization process. Whereas Horkheimer and Adorno and Bauman interpret Auschwitz as the ultimate, 'logical' consequence of the technologically stunted process of rationalization, Arendt by contrast sees it as a decisive break with the modern principle of rationality. Why? The capitalist spirit of scientific-technological rationality is essentially conditioned by utilitarian principles. It is concerned with utility. The bureaucratically organized destruction of the Jews, however, did not spring from any utilitarian motive. According to Hannah Arendt, the German fascists were more fixated on operating the factories of destruction 'efficiently' than on winning the war.

For it belongs to the essence of the totalitarian fiction that it not only makes the impossible possible, but above all also that it already treats everything as real . . . that it 'foresees' as possible according to its ideological scheme. Since history is foreseeable and calculable in the totalitarian fiction, something real must also correspond to each of its possibilities. This 'reality' is then manufactured no less than other 'facts' in this purely fictional world. (Arendt 1968)

Anti-modernity, the active negation of the basic principles of modernity, springs from the totalitarian anticipation: beyond the 'why' everything is possible! For Hannah Arendt, in the end this 'politics' leads to the 'manu-facture of corpses' (ibid.). The 'possibility' anticipated here must accordingly be 'manufacturable' – with the instruments of power of advanced modernity. At the same time, this break with the basic principles of human social exis-tence must be conceived as a 'totalitarian project' that destroys human plural-ity and turns human beings into 'things' whose destruction can then become an 'organizational problem'.

The phenomenon of anti-modernity, hence of hostility towards moder-nity, when interpreted within the horizon of the distinction between basic principles and basic institutions of modernity, is fundamentally ambiguous: enemies of modernity can ally themselves with the basic *institutions* of moder-nity in order to wage war even more effectively against the basic *principles* of modernity. Indeed, one can even say that the enemies of modernity who were lurking from the beginning can realize their potential for power and violence only with the radicalization of modernity, that is, with the perfected instruments of modernity (bureaucratic organization, weapons systems, law, democratic legitimation). At the same time, it is unrestricted modernity that creates the preconditions by consuming and transforming its own principles. The enemies of modernity are ultimately empowered by the development of modernity itself. That is an old dialectical game. In the second half of the nineteenth century Richard Wagner launched vigorous attacks on the modern age, which was then on the rise in Germany – but in doing so he employed the reviled machinery of modernity in the service of his theatrical revolt against modernity. At the beginning of the twenty-first century, however, this dialectic liberates 'glocal' power potentials with the untethered world risk society.

Suicidal terrorism

Perhaps at some point in human history 11 September 2001 will also stand for the failure of language in the face of this cosmopolitan trauma: 'war', 'crime', 'enemy', 'victory' and 'terror' – 'the concepts fall apart in the mouth like putrid mushrooms' (Hugo von Hofmannsthal).

The collapse of the Twin Towers in New York was followed by an explo-sion of eloquent silence and meaningless action. To quote from Hugo von Hofmannsthal again: 'I was no longer able to grasp reality with the simplify-ing gaze of habit. Everything disintegrated into parts, and the parts in turn into parts, and nothing could be compassed with a concept. The individuals' words swam around me; they congealed into eyes that stared at me and into which I had to stare again' (Hofmannsthal 2005).

The circle of evil

Aren't we forced to reintroduce the concept of 'evil' by the possibility and reality of negating the basic principles of modernity announced by its radicalization? 'Evil' would then designate actions and thoughts that can neither be conceptualized nor imagined, beyond any justification, beyond defence and crime, for crimes take place within the framework of the law and there are procedures for condemning and punishing them.

Since Kant we know that evil is the reverse side of freedom, not as a deficit but as a fundamental component of freedom, something which human existence at once presupposes and negates.

Nothing about evil is without contradiction. Nothing about evil is certain. Yet no aspect of the human condition needs to be more certain. And no thing, consequently, is more pressing . . .

This is most famously visible in Holbein's painting of *The French Ambassadors* (1533), in which two grand figures who embody power, wealth, glory and not a little smugness stand on either side of a series of objects symbolic of early Enlightenment knowledge, learning and art. At their feet, as if projected from another place, is a distorted image that can only be deciphered by looking at the picture from an angle, from the side. Doing so reveals the image of a skull, an indication, for those who know how to read Christian symbolism, of a hidden reality, a message of the instability of the world, the necessity of abandoning vainglory and of human mortality. For those who know how to read the images of naked prisoners, taunted and tortured, and perhaps that is most of us, the message will be similarly familiar. Suddenly we (at least in the West, at least those in the US) are being asked to see ourselves both as other and as vulnerable. (Silverstone 2006: 57, 58)

Evil is a shifting, unstable concept. It is, of course, not unproblematic to introduce the categories of evil into thought. I see at least two dangers. First, there is a connection, a proximity between the concept of evil and the concept of the stranger [*des Fremden*]. The evil person is a stranger, not a neighbour or one of us. Second, to say that something is the work of evil is to stop thinking. The rhetoric of evil also dismisses the 'why'. The easiest response to the hyper-complexity and contingency of world risk society is to say that it is the work of evil. The consequences have become causes and the causes agents.

Those who make the evil of strangers the cause of the catastrophe exonerate themselves – and at the same time empower themselves. The category of evil tacitly becomes carte blanche for self-empowerment. For evil must be eliminated, not only from society, but ultimately from the human race.

A satanic logic is at work here: the more sacrosanct the value – for example, the inviolability of children – the greater the potential for transforming this concern into strategic goals to exploit traumas to the maximum through the mass media. The negation of the basic principles creates a new kind of difference, not just between victims and aggressors, but also between those who live and act in accordance with the rules of modernity – i.e. enlightenment, the state's monopoly on violence, etc. – and those who do not recognize these rules and consequently have no inhibitions in exploiting the associated inhibitions. The power of those who negate the basic principles of modernity is increasing in a radically inverse relation to the powerlessness of those who observe these basic principles. Not: 'Hell is us', but: human beings can erect hell upon earth on the basis of the freedom and triumphs of modernity.

Critique of cultural criticism

Even the most radical cultural critiques look like caricatures compared to the catastrophic potentials of full-blown modernity. Indeed, one must even go an essential step further: in comparison to the horizon opened up by the negation of the basic principles of modernity, most cultural criticism looks outdated and 'idyllic', i.e. blind to its own presuppositions or even downright affirmative. Underlying it is a concealed optimism. For cultural criticism generally engages in immanent critique ('anomie', 'alienation') which presupposes and reinforces the basic principles of modernity as a measure of value without questioning them. This kind of affirmation is the one objection; the other is that cultural criticism *fails to recognize the dialectics of anti-modernity*. Insofar as the events which are currently perceived across the world as catastrophes are the result of violations of the basic principles of modernity, they reaffirm the explosive character of these principles and their social importance. Public outrage first creates and sharpens normative consciousness and only *afterwards*, thus retroactively, founds the public political character of action, as Niklas Luhmann argues:

Legal experts typically think that a norm violation can only be established if the norm already exists. Sociologists of law and above all anthropologists of law, however, also recognize the converse case, namely, that norms take shape when expectations are disappointed and spectacular occurrences make clear that this cannot be tolerated. This holds, for example, for torture in prisons, for political murders, perhaps before long also for serious violations of nuclear security or of minimum standards of environmental consideration. Today it holds for so-called ethnic cleansing, for the expulsion of large populations from their ancestral territories, something practised on a massive scale in 1945 without any legal scruples being expressed. It holds for the criminal legal condemnation of war crimes, independently of whether the positive law of the state in question contained a corresponding criminal legal statute at the time of the transgression (and thus represents a spectacular violation of the equally valid rule that criminal statutes should not be applied retrospectively). One can observe clearly processes of the worldwide emergence of norms; perhaps ethics is merely an incorrect designation for them, for they do not merely concern problems of conscience or of moral respect, but actually constitute a kind of law for which possibilities of sanction must be sought. (Luhmann 1999: 250)

In other words, it is the *violation* of the basic principles of modernity which first makes visible their enormous significance, their sanctity, their immanent metaphysics, and thereby opens up a new cosmopolitan horizon of responsibility that is taking concrete shape, possibly through corresponding positings of norms and foundings of organizations (UN Security Council, International Criminal Court in The Hague, etc.). Global risk, as felt and anticipated endangerment of humanity, thereby prepares the way for involuntary enlightenment (see also chapter 3).

For it is astounding that a Max Weber, an Adorno or a Foucault assume without the slightest reflection that the basic principles of modernity are human creations, that they fundamentally determined social thought and action, yet at the same time are fundamentally immune to intervention and change. How is that possible? To answer this question would require a chapter of its own; thus here I would merely cite the following points by way of example. 'In the scientific redeemer, the rationally aware human being created God in his own image' (Marcuse 1981). The more use human beings made of science, the more God became science – and the more the path of science became the route to redemption. Thus Hegel saw the most important task of philosophy as residing in the fact that 'in the end the necessity of what happens to the individual can appear as absolute rationality and the mind finds true ethical peace.'

The scholastics were not limited to the Middle Ages; there were also the scholastics of the (first) modernity. Systems theory is the opium of the uncertain and disoriented. In an attempt to found order in the topsy-turvy world, the systems theorist becomes infatuated with his systems-theoretical tools and discovers in the dense network of concepts the sought-for protection which he then proclaims to his followers.

A new credo arises out of the very shock that the basic norms of modernity can be destroyed: *never again!* As an anticipation of future violations, this becomes a new kind of mobilizing force. The twentieth century ended with a capitulation before the future. The age of ideologies, of radical utopias of modernity, of revolutionary metaphors aimed at the intentional transformation of the basic structure of society, has exhausted itself. The utopian energies have been used up ('the end of history'). The residual utopias are determined by technology and economics.

However, that is just one side of the development. Modern futures as *opportunities* for action are being replaced by the theoretically and politically still completely unexplored meaning horizon of risky futures as the *compulsion to preventive (counter-)action*. The 'disillusionment' [*Abklärung*] over 'too much future' is being joined by the sceptically rejuvenated enlightenment [*Aufklärung*] concerning the necessity of preventively shaping the future: the future is being given a negative meaning and is *thereby* being opened up to action. We are condemned to shape the future in order to survive. The key point here is that the transformation of negatively antici-pated futures is itself giving rise to cross-border obligations, while vague universalistic appeals remain largely ineffectual. Thus the global knowledge concerning the moral and physical catastrophic potential of modernity, which is made accessible by the negation of the basic principles, contains a present power mediated by the future that – at the extreme – makes the impossible possible. It makes it possible to cancel distinctions between the national and the international and to open up new, transnational spaces of responsibility with multiple agencies of intervention.

3 Dilemmas

A basic theme of the theory of reflexive modernization – namely, the distinc-tion between basic principles and basic institutions of modernity – opens our eyes to a variety of dialectics of modernity: *ambivalences of more-modernity* (not post-modernity) and *ambivalences of anti-modernity.*

Ambivalences of more-modernity: The triumphs of basic principles give rise to 'crises' of basic institutions. Here 'crisis' is both the correct and the incorrect term: it is correct because it accords central importance to the dis-solution of the naturalized certainties of the national first modernity and the associated experience of uncertainty; 'crisis' is correct because it threatens new inequalities, and the rampant disorientation and uncertainty empower anti-modernity. The talk of crisis is incorrect because it is more-modernity and not postmodernity that has annulled, or at any rate dramatically altered, the institutional foundations of the modernity of the nation-state. All the 'crisis phenomena' with which the countries of the West are struggling – reforms of the welfare state, falling birth rates, ageing societies, loss of defini-tion of national societies, mass unemployment, not to mention the self-doubts of science and expert rationality, economic globalization and advances in individualization that undermine the foundations of marriage, the family and politics, and, finally, the environmental crisis, which calls for a revision of industrial society's exploitative conception of nature – can be understood in terms of the distinction as transformations of basic institutions in which the basic principles of modernity retain their validity. Thus the dialectic of more-modernity both is and is not a crisis. In a nutshell: the *continuity* of the basic principles (their loss of definition and their increasing reflexivity) leads to *dis*-continuity in the basic institutions.

This cultural earthquake has been expressed loudly in the melancholy of poets and musicians, in the eternal lament over self-centredness and the ego-centric society, in a hundred frantic attempts to identify some deity who can still provide reassurance; importantly also in the 'suffering from modernity' which revels in the cultural-critical diagnoses of the 'decline' of the family, the nation, democracy, etc. All these Strindbergs, Kierkegaards, Nietzsches, Ibsens and Benns merely anticipated in literature what is everywhere unfolding today as a profane and democratized mass phenomenon behind the hollowed-out façades of normality. The realistic core of the diagnosis of crisis, however, is that greater security is not compatible with greater freedom in the era of world risk society. This posture of cultural criticism appears antiquated and ossified because it blinds us to the increase in reason and in the scope for individual action, but above all because it blinds us to the real threat.

Ambivalences of anti-modernity: What causes the inhabitants of the world risk society an anthropological shock is no longer the metaphysical homelessness of a Beckett, the absent Godot, or the nightmare visions of a Foucault, nor the mute despotism of rationality which frightened Max Weber. Like good old communism, the spectre of good old postmodernism no longer keeps Europeans awake at night. What worries people nowadays is the premonition that the anthropological certainty of modernity is founded on quicksand. It is the temptation and the horror of anti-modernity, the panic-stricken fear that the fabric of our material dependencies and moral obligations could rend and the delicate functional system of world risk society collapse.

Thus everything is turned on its head: what for Weber, Adorno and Foucault was a terrifying vision – the perfected surveillance rationality of the administered world – is a promise for those living in the present. It would be a fine thing if surveillance rationality really worked, or if we were terrorized only by consumption and humanism, or if the smooth operation of systems could be re-established by appeal to 'autopoiesis' or through 'national federalism reforms' and 'technological innovation offensives'. It would be a fine thing if the liturgical chants of more market, more technologies, more growth and more flexibility could still provide reassurance in troubled times.

As I have said, the fact that the world of the reigning certainties is in decline is nothing new. However, throughout history it has always been possible to transform the unbearableness of an alien world into a comfortable home. Most recently (something unknown to earlier eras) 'national homes' were created out of national flags, national hymns, national holidays and national heroes and places as cultural reassurance against the lost security of the premodern world. Whether something analogous can succeed again in the era of the world risk society is doubtful: *dis-embedding without re-embedding* – that is a better description of the situation. Or could the fear of descending into a world of self-produced threats nevertheless be successfully transformed into a locally rooted openness to, and love of, the world, into 'cosmopolitan homes'?

What is historically new about the world risk society? 'The separation of the Germans from the other European nations is justified by Nature' (hence

God), argued Johann Gottlieb Fichte with transcendental skill. And to this day, the Germans still feel this in their bones. Many philosophers and most theorists of modern society have operated as 'necessity machines' in this sense. Doubts were fed in at the top and necessary concepts were spat out at the bottom that elevated the stunted modernity of the nation-state to modernity as such. Most of the thinkers of the nineteenth and twentieth century directly or indirectly advocated the immortalization of self-enclosed national sovereignties in this sense. Only a few thinkers raised serious doubts about this notion that the human race is made up of national islands and underlined the realities that prove the contrary: border-transcending interrelations, interdependencies, causalities, responsibility, solidarity and communities of fate. First, Kant identified the ability of everyone always to think for him- or herself as the maxim of enlightenment. It is this rebellious question and power of the 'why?' that poses a threat – in principle – to everything existing across all barriers and boundaries. Second, Marx showed how the boundless dynamic of capital interconnects the apparently isolated destinies of the nations and individuals in conflictual ways – for the most part against their will! Third, Nietzsche destroyed the anthropology which held that humanity divides up into fixed kinds of groups whose cultures assemble them into religious and territorial units. His rebellion focused on the practitioners of the self-immortalization of bourgeois society and of 'bourgeois reason' who tried to render the truth of the bourgeois theory of humanity and the goodness of bourgeois reality invulnerable.

However, the developing world risk society delivers the hardest blow to insular national thought, to political and methodological nationalism. For here the seemingly natural, hence divinely ordained, connection between sovereignty, the right of self-determination, the nation and isolationism is dissolved with the dialectic of modernity itself and the mobilizing power of the anticipated self-destruction of all – in other words: the cosmopolitan moment is set free (chapters 3 and 11). Unilateral national policies are now backward-looking idealisms; cosmopolitan cooperation is the heart of the new political realism. National isolationism is an illusion, a fiction, a relic – it is counterproductive and condemned to failure. Even the superpower, the United States, was forced to recognize this recently. The autonomy of the state has ceased to exist among the threats to self and others of world risk society; it first arises out of the cooperative added value generated by the merging of national sovereignties. This added value of cooperation first enables and empowers national sovereignty to solve national problems as well. The world risk society could turn the national global order from its head onto its feet. National sovereignty does not make cooperation possible; rather, it is transnational cooperation that makes national sovereignty possible.

To conclude, let me at least pose this question on my own account: What follows from the dialectics of anti-modernity for sociology? What does critical theory of the world risk society then mean? On which side do we stand? Can one theorize and conduct research in a 'neutral' and 'value-free' manner if the unreflected human foundations of the social sciences are also negated and if this final 'no' becomes an object of sociological theory and research?

It is not possible to theorize and research the rupture of the basic principles of modernity without condemning. Value freedom presupposes the validity of and consensus over values. One can conduct research on intentional and organized catastrophes, concentration camps, genocide and terrorist attacks only with revulsion – but is it then still possible to do research?

It is not only language in general but also the sociological concept of risk that fails. Sociology as conceptual schema is blind to Apocalypse. Hence it is also blind concerning its situation and the dilemmas inherent in its situation. Talking about the 'terrorist risk' means that a future attack can occur – or not. Expectation and action may diverge even more dramatically than in the case of the probability of suffering a fatal road accident. But this probability of catastrophe is not counterbalanced by any compensatory utility – quite the contrary: the sociologist who accords central importance to the *anticipation* of intentional terrorist attacks devotes himself to weakening the inhibitions of the dark imagination which feeds the activity of the terrorists. Or not?

The dilemma of a critical social theory of world risk is concealed in both questions: Isn't enlightenment concerning anti-modernity naïve because it prepares the way for the anti-moderns?

Isn't non-enlightenment concerning the apocalyptic visions of anti-modernity naïve because it prepares the way for the anti-moderns? Isn't it this second banishment from Paradise – this time from the secular paradise of belief in the pre-established functionality and morality of modern society – that undermines all previous sociology, and provides the inspiration for a new beginning?

Notes

Chapter 1   Introduction

1   A prime example of this Kafkaesque, tragic individualization in world risk society can be seen at present in Ukraine in the banalization of catastrophe which began after the Chernobyl nuclear reactor accident; on this, see ch. 7, pp. 116ff.

2   Thus 'risk society' does *not* mean a modern society in which – at least in principle – decision-dependent, industrially generated insecurities and dangers have been successfully made controllable by means of the risk logic (as Max Weber, for example, assumes). Hence this category does not refer to the first, national modernity of nineteenth- and early twentieth-century industrial society, but to the emergence of new risks which began in the latter half of the twentieth century, and hence to the historical experiences of environmental crises and the retrenchment of welfare state guarantees, etc.

3   In sociology, what I here call the 'staging' of world risk is also discussed under the heading of the 'social construction' or 'social definition' of risk; on this, see ch. 5.

4   As it happens, this provides a clue to linking the global character of the terrorist risk to the theory of reflexive modernization; for the latter works with the model of 'self-endangerment'. According to this, it is Western society itself which places its own foundations in question through unintended side effects. Assuming that transnational terrorism challenges the foundations of national security such as freedom and democracy, then the role played by the *staging* of the terrorist threat should not be underestimated. The problematization of the controlling institutions of the nation-state is (also) the *unintended side effect* of the staging of terrorism in the mass media and politics as a *global* threat which grips people's minds. Of course, the transnational terrorist networks are very clever in playing along with this. It is they, after all, who provoke the sensationalism of the mass media.

5   The distinction between risk and catastrophe and the diminishing possibility of differentiating risk from the perception of risk are at odds with the difference, which Niklas Luhmann, for example, underlined, between *risks*, which are the results of decisions, and *dangers*, which relate to a large number of people or

groups who are affected or plagued by risks that others take (and could avoid). I will return to this important distinction when I discuss issues of global inequality (chs 9 and 10). In fact, the 'second-order threats' – i.e. the return of insecurity in the course of radicalized modernization – to which Wolfgang Bonss (1995) draws attention in opposition to Luhmann, lose their sharp contours when they are no longer merely historically introduced but themselves become objects of study. However, the result is that my concept of risk – which shifts the focus onto the distinction between risk and catastrophe, or the indistinguishability of risk and the perception of risk, in order to uncover the dynamics of the staging of world risk society – is ambiguous with respect to the aforementioned distinction which is now established in risk studies. We will return to this problematic repeatedly in the following chapters.

6 What is the relation between the theory of world risk society and the theory of reflexive modernization (Beck and Bonss 2001; Beck and Lau 2004)? Speaking very generally, the theory of reflexive modernization can be divided into three complexes: the theorem of risk society, the theorem of forced individualization and the theorem of multidimensional globalization or cosmopolitanization. All three theorems develop and interpret the same figure of argumentation and are mutually reinforcing: 'risk society', 'individualization' and 'cosmopolitanization' are conceived as radicalized forms of the dynamic of modernization which, when applied to itself at the beginning of the twenty-first century, is superseding the formula of simple modernity. This modernity formula follows a logic of order and action that drew sharp boundaries between categories of people, things and activities and made sharp distinctions between spheres of action and forms of life, which in turn made possible institutional ascriptions of authorities, competences and responsibilities. This *logic of unequivocalness* – one could speak metaphorically of a *Newtonian* social and political theory of the first modernity – is being superseded by a *logic of ambiguity* – as it were, a *Heisenbergian* uncertainty principle of social and political reality. In this book, the intermeshing of 'risk society' and 'cosmopolitanization' features centrally, whereas the dynamics of individualization are touched upon only occasionally. Deciphering the intermeshing (and opposition) of 'individualization' and 'cosmopolitanization' (for example) is reserved for a later study.

7 Access both to the theory of risk society and to the theory of reflexive modernization stands and falls with the correct understanding of this key idea. It is not the fact that new insecurities and dangers arise that constitutes the peculiar character of world risk society; rather, the guiding assumption that these can be controlled at the national level, and not through omissions but through more and better knowledge, is collapsing. It is an open question how this basic idea can be encapsulated in a suggestive yet rigorous terminology. In English, Anthony Giddens and I speak of 'manufactured uncertainties (insecurities)'. In the literature, one also finds, among other things, the hackneyed and not altogether accurate sociological expression 'structural uncertainty'.

8 *World at Risk* is thus conceived as a further study – following on *Power in the Global Age* (Beck 2005) and the study on 'Europeanization' co-authored with Edgar Grande (Beck and Grande 2007) – which aims to uncover the real dynamics of the new cosmopolitanism in its contradictions and ambivalences and to analyse it through examples.

Chapter 2 Relations of Definition as Relations of Domination

1 This occurs under the historical conditions of a fusion of nature and society in which even apparently externally determined natural catastrophes, such as flooding, landslides, etc., seem to have human causes (Beck 2002, ch. 2).

2 This does not mean, of course, that there are not still risks that can and must be regulated at the national level (for instance, traffic and workplace accidents).

3 The controversies over so-called catastrophic medicine are exemplary in this respect. The key issue is to what extent the principle of compensation, which allows for accidents, holds, or whether the principle of prevention is employed which precludes learning from accidents (see Ewald 2002 and ch. 6 below).

4 Hence, at issue are not only questions of a new ethics of civilized action but the fact that the established categories and criteria of action stem from institutions belonging to a different world.

5 This insurance principle is controversial; see ch. 6.

6 With the concept of 'forces of production' (which is still captivated by faith in progress), Marx had in mind this contradictory interdependence of the two dynamics.

7 The conflicts of classical industrial society have not ended, so that overlaps can be expected to occur between the social structure and conflict dynamics of industrial and risk society. I cannot deal with this issue here.

8 'That there are symptoms of such a block formation can be seen in the West German nuclear industry following Chernobyl: works councils and employers' representatives jointly defended existing West German energy policy against any change of course' (Schumann 1987: 18ff.). Contrary to what is generally assumed, Heine and Mautz concluded in the corresponding study: 'With the trend to professionalization of production work in the chemicals industry, chemical workers could in future constitute a growing potential of ecologically vigilant production workers who are capable of reflecting critically on the ecological conditions and consequences of their own labour and provide support for ecologically motivated political interventions' (1989: 187).

9 This view is based on the general distinction in social theory between simple and reflexive modernization. Whereas simple modernization, roughly speaking, runs within the framework of categories and organizing principles of industrial society, the second case involves a phase of global social transformation in which modernization changes the face of industrial society by dint of its internal dynamics. Class, social strata, occupation, gender roles, enterprise, sectoral structure and, in general, the presuppositions and the courses taken by 'natural' technological-economic progress are being placed in question. The world of classical industrial society is becoming just as much a tradition to be steamrollered and demystified as, during the nineteenth century, industrial modernization steamrollered and demystified corporative feudal society. Modernization is undercutting modernization unawares and in contradiction with its own plans. In that way, however, restratifications in social structures and power shifts are arising, new cleavages, possibilities for and restrictions on coalitions. Social movements, the public arena, ethics, the moral courage of individuals and the networks of differential

politics are gaining opportunities to exercise historical influence (Beck, Giddens and Lash 1994; Beck, Bonss and Lau 2001; Beck and Lau 2004).

10   Figuratively speaking, making radioactivity itch is a central task of political education in risk society (see Claussen 1989).

Chapter 3   The 'Cosmopolitan Moment' of World Risk Society or: Enforced Enlightenment

1   Max Weber captures these two dimensions of the meaning of normativity in the concept of 'value relation'. In what follows, therefore, I will introduce the cosmopolitan moment of world risk society as a cultural and social scientific value relation.

2   In what follows I employ two concepts of cosmopolitanism, a narrower and a broader one. In the broader sense, I speak of the 'cosmopolitan moment' of world risk society, in the narrower of 'enforced cosmopolitanization'. The innovation of the present book over my earlier books resides in this extension, in the question concerning the actually effective normative horizon and moment of world risk society.

3   Hence, 'no longer only natural decision-based catastrophes' could and should be accepted into the canon of global risks as an additional type of risk with its own social and political logic. However, this is not possible within the scope of the present book.

4   In the broader sense, as I indicated, it means the 'cosmopolitan moment' of world risk society.

5   The ideological ambivalence inherent in the idea of cosmopolitanism from the beginning is the reason why, in the closing chapter of *Power in the Global Age* (2005), I warn against the abuse of cosmopolitanism in an (ironic) self-critique, 'A Brief Funeral Oration at the Cradle of the Cosmopolitan Age'.

Chapter 4   Clash of Risk Cultures

1   On this see also ch. 9, §2, *Risk wars or: Staging organized violence in the world risk society.*

Chapter 5   Global Public Sphere and Global Subpolitics

1   On 'reflexive modernization', see the contrasting positions of Beck, Lash and Giddens (1994) and the results of the continuing Munich Collaborative Research Centre on Reflexive Modernization collected in Beck and Bonss (2001) and Beck and Lau (2004).

2   See the historical analysis of basic concepts and theories of nature and the concept of 'nature after the end of nature' in Böhme (1991); for an account of the both universal and subculturally specific images of nature among environmental activists, industrial managers, and so on, from the perspective of cultural theory, see Schwarz and Thompson (1990); and on the general images of nature in modern society, see Hitzler (1991), Daele (1992) and Gill (2003).

3   This is bringing to a close a long period in the history of sociology in which – in strict accordance with its original division of labour with the natural sciences – it could abstract from 'nature' as the other, the environment, what is already given.

This disregarding of nature corresponded to a certain relation to it. Comte stated this explicitly. He expressly wanted the relationship of national conquest to be replaced with one of natural conquest by the rising bourgeois-industrial society, so as to defuse conflicts within society. Right up to the present day this theme has lost none of its importance. Abstraction from nature thus presupposes domination over nature. In this way, the 'process of consuming nature' – which is how Marx understood the labour production process – could be driven onward. When people speak today of 'ecological citizenship', arguing that basic rights must be extended to animals, plants, and so on, they are expressing the transposition of this subordination–abstraction relationship into its polar opposite.

4   Moreover, it is difficult to square the claims of cultural theory to transhistorical, context-independent validity with its interest in precision, relativity and cultural construction. In which context-culture does this almost unconsidered universalism originate? It is hard to give an answer without pointing to Eurocentrism.

5   'In the 1970s local claims were made by ordinary people living near the Sellafield nuclear reprocessing complex, that excess childhood leukemias were occurring in the area . . . This issue came to the attention of TV researchers, and a national documentary programme was eventually broadcast in 1983.' In the end, however, the excess cancers around Sellafield 'were almost routinely referred to as having been *discovered* by the Black Committee' (Wynne 1996a: 49).

6   Latour's *We Have Never Been Modern* (1995) is, however, one of the most outstanding and challenging works to have appeared for years on the sociology of technology. Perhaps even more important is his book *Politics of Nature* (2004), which has revolutionized political ecology.

7   On the framework conditions for creating international regimes, see Zürn (1995); Voss et al. (2006).

8   For example, Martin Rees, the president of the Royal Society, stated: 'This should be a turning point in a debate which has pitted short-term economic interests against long-term costs to the environment, society and the economy' (*The Guardian*, 31 October 2006, p. 7).

Chapter 6   The Provident State

1   In the meantime there is a consensus on this aspect: see Perrow (1984); Ewald (1993); Evers and Nowotny (1987); Lagadec (1981); Halfmann (1990) as well as the other essays in Halfmann and Japp (1990); Prittwitz (1990); Bonss (1991); Brock (1991); Lau (1991); Beck (1992, 2002); Hahn et al. (1992); Japp (1992); and Luhmann (2003).

Chapter 7   Knowledge or Non-Knowledge?

1   Here I follow the excellent anthropological study by Adriana Petryna, conducted in 1996 and published in 2002, *Life Exposed: Biological Citizens after Chernobyl*.

2   This has been developed further in particular by Brian Wynne (1991, 1996a) in numerous publications; see also Hajer (1995).

3   That side effects are also a social power(-construct) that plays a central role in the distribution and allocation of global risks will be explored in ch. 10.

Chapter 8   The Insurance Principle

1   On this, see pp. 204ff, and, on Dürrenmatt, also Matthias Haller (2004).

Chapter 9   Felt War, Felt Peace

1   This chapter is not concerned to develop a general theory of war or of organized violence but to introduce a key idea, namely, that of 'risk war'.

2   I owe this idea to a conversation with Edgar Grande.

Chapter 10   Global Inequality, Local Vulnerability

1   This dimension of global social inequality built into the talk of 'side effects' is not yet taken into account in the otherwise very precise and stimulating volume of Böschen et al. (2006).

2   Cf. also Habermas's concept of cross-border communities of dialogue. Luhmann's pluralization and depoliticization scenario makes clear that reflection moves along the tracks of existing, organized impunity. However, this presupposes a constant apparatus of norms and law. It is interesting that the latter, in turn, presupposes a national outlook. Luhmann's construction of the unimputability and anonymization of risks succeeds more in national than in international, global relations. An important role is played here by the fact that the causal assignment of risks to decision-makers in any case succeeds only in exceptional cases, and even in cases in which it is firmly institutionalized – for example, traffic accidents – it is legally sanctioned modes of perception, rather than the causal relations, however constituted, that lend this mode of ascribing responsibility its plausibility and practicality. Faced with the alternative between trusting the reality of global risks or the institutionalized national-legal outlook, Luhmann sees no need to make a decision: the legally institutionalized national outlook renders the reality of global threats unreal.

3   On this, see OECD 1972.

4   This distinction, which Daniel Chernilo introduced, is helpful. At the same time, the author commits an error. In his view, my thesis concerning methodological nationalism is exaggerated (also because he takes the word 'methodological' literally instead of metaphorically). He concludes on this basis that the turn to methodological cosmopolitanism is superfluous, even dogmatic. This involves a striking fallacy: in this case a research programme for renewing sociology is supposed to be written off without any opportunity for empirical testing, without the 'positive problem shift' (Imre Lakatos) – i.e. opening up new empirical facts and fields of research – which this book seeks to provide, even being considered.

5   Something similar also holds for methodological contextualism and localism; in opposition to the armchair universalism of sociological theory, many anthropologists, ethnologists and cultural sociologists (e.g. Mary Douglas and Aihwa Ong) organize their research in accordance with the principle that the reality of risks can ultimately be deciphered only in a contextual way. But this also fails to understand the 'transnational', 'transcontextual', 'transdimensional' character of risk deciders, risk recipients, strategies for shifting responsibility, accountability,

side effects of side effects and the problems of rendering the unexpectable expectable.

6   On this and the whole literature on civil society cosmopolitanism and its consequences, controversies and normative and legal presuppositions, see Mason (2005).

7   I published the following two sections of this chapter in collaboration with Boris Holzer under the title 'Wie global ist die Weltrisikogesellschaft?' (2004); I am sincerely grateful to Boris Holzer for permission to include our co-authored text (in a lightly revised form) in this context.

8   On this question, see the detailed discussion in Agarwal and Narain (1991).

9   From the research on regime formation in the environmental domain, see, for example, Vogler (1992), Haas et al. (1993), Litfin (1993, 1994), Young et al. (1996) and Zürn (1997); for a good overview, see Little (1997).

10   Here I am drawing on Dewey's proposal that publics should be understood primarily as mechanisms for regulating the indirect consequences of social action: 'publics are constituted by recognition of extensive and enduring indirect consequences of acts' (1946: 47). Keohane and Nye now make a similar argument concerning the possibility of 'global public space': 'The public is the group of people who communicate and agitate over their shared externalities in that space' (Keohane and Nye 2001: 13).

11   Especially also, as Levy and Sznaider (2004) show in the case of the Holocaust, on the basis of collective memory of genocide and human rights violations (see ch. 12).

12   When power is openly used in the formation of regimes, as for example by the United States in the climate change regime, this is not necessarily a counter-argument. The example of climate change in particular shows instead that one may be able to prevent, but can scarcely influence, a regime through the open use of power. Thus the long-term strategy of the United States (and of affected American companies) is also geared much more to influencing the definition and articulation of the relevant knowledge.

13   Keohane and Nye (2001) use the term 'Club Model' to describe the negotiation and definition of global norms in closed regulatory bodies controlled by a few major powers. Examples, in addition to the GATT–WTO negotiations, are a number of established private–public institutions in the financial field, for example, the London Club and the Paris Club. On the latter, see Lucatelli (1997).

Chapter 11   Critical Theory of World Risk Society

1   These could even be extended further by the other dimensions of the theory of reflexive modernization, namely, individualization and globalization.

2   Although there is much talk of 'the Other' in classical sociology, by this is meant the universalized Other, not the concrete others who speak different languages and who live in partially overlapping, partially incommensurable pasts and futures.

3   I take up this question in chapter 12.

4   On this, see, by way of example, the section 'The anticipation of catastrophe is changing the world' in chapter 1 of this book; see also chapters 3 and 10.

5   The empirical studies of the Collaborative Research Centre on Reflexive Modernization in Munich, which has been working on these questions in a broad thematic spectrum of research projects since 1999 in collaboration with several universities, have in fact succeeded in establishing that such phenomena of a meta-change occurred in the period between 1960 and 1990. To this extent an empirical phenomenology of reflexive modernization has in fact been systematically worked out (though one which does not deal with the example of the life-world experience of global risks) (Beck and Lau 2004).

Chapter 12   Dialectics of Modernity: How the Crises of Modernity Follow from the Triumphs of Modernity

1   On this, see Benford (1999); also Schirrmacher (2000), to whom I owe this example.
2   This is merely a list of examples and is not intended to be systematic or complete. Whether such claims are even meaningful and possible is an open question.
3   On this, see also Levy and Sznaider (2004).

References and Bibliography

Adam, Barbara (1995) *Timewatch: The Social Analysis of Time.* Cambridge: Polity.

Adam, Barbara (1998) *Timescapes of Modernity: The Environment and Invisible Hazards.* London: Routledge.

Adam, Barbara, Beck, Ulrich, und Loon, Joost van (eds) (2000) *The Risk Society and Beyond: Critical Issues for Social Theory.* London: Sage.

Adams, John (1995) *Risk.* London: UCL Press.

Adorno, Theodor W. (1974) *Minima Moralia*, trans. Edmund Jephcott, London: NLB.

Agamben, Giorgio (2005) *State of Exception.* Chicago: University of Chicago Press.

Agarwal, Anil, and Narain, Sunita (1991) *Global Warming in an Unequal World.* New Delhi: Centre for Science and Environment.

Aggleton, Peter, Davies, Peter, and Hart, Graham (eds) (1995) *Aids: Safety, Sexuality and Risk.* London: Taylor & Francis.

Albrow, Martin (1996) *The Global Age: The State and Society beyond Modernity.* Cambridge: Polity.

Alexander, Jeffrey C. (1996) Critical reflections on 'Reflexive Modernization'. *Theory, Culture and Society* 13/4: 133–8.

Alexander, Jeffrey C., and Smith, Philip (1996) Social science and salvation. *Zeitschrift für Soziologie* 25/4: 251–62.

Allan, Stuart, Adam, Barbara, and Carter, Cynthia (eds) (2000) *Environmental Risks and the Media.* London: Routledge.

Anders, Günther (1983) *Die Antiquiertheit des Menschen*, Vol. 1. Munich: Beck.

Apel, Karl-Otto (1987) The problem of a macroethic of responsibility to the future in the crisis of technological civilization. *Man and World* 20: 3–40.

Apel, Karl-Otto (1988) *Diskurs und Verantwortung.* Frankfurt am Main: Suhrkamp.

Apter, David E. (1968) *Some Conceptual Approaches to the Study of Modernization.* Englewood Cliffs, NJ: Prentice Hall.

Archibugi, Daniele, and Held, David (eds) (1995) *Cosmopolitan Democracy.* Cambridge: Polity.

Archibugi, Daniele, Held, David, and Köhler, Martin (eds) (1992) *Zur Anwendung der Diskursethik in Politik, Recht und Wissenschaft.* Frankfurt am Main: Suhrkamp.

Arendt, Hannah (1968) *Totalitarianism: Part Three of The Origins of Totalitarianism.* San Diego: Harcourt Brace Jovanovich.

Arendt, Hannah (1993) *Was ist Politik?* Munich: Piper.

Arnoldi, Jakob (2003) Making sense of causation. *Soziale Welt* 54/4: 405–27.

Arnoldi, Jakob (2004) Derivatives – virtual values and real risks. *Theory, Culture & Society* 21/6: 23–42.

Arrighi, Giovanni (1990) The developmentalist illusion: a reconceptualization of the semiperiphery. In William G. Martin (ed.), *Semiperipheral States in the World-Economy*. Westport, CT: Greenwood Press, pp. 11–42.

Axelrod, Robert (1984) *Evolution of Cooperation*. New York: Basic Books.

Bankoff, Greg, Frerks, Georg, and Hilhorst, Dorothea (eds) (2004) *Mapping Vulnerability*. London: Earthscan.

Bauer, Michael (2006) Reflexive Modernisierung und Terrorismus. Unpublished MS, Munich.

Bauman, Zygmunt (1989) *Modernity and the Holocaust.* Ithaca, NY: Cornell University Press.

Bauman, Zygmunt (1992a) *Modernity and Ambivalence.* Cambridge: Polity.

Bauman, Zygmunt (1992b) The solution as problem. *Times Higher Education Supplement* 13 (November): 25.

Bauman, Zygmunt (1994) Ist der Holocaust wiederholbar? *Polis: Analysen-Meinungen-Debatten* 8. Wiesbaden: Hessische Landeszentrale für politische Bildung.

Bauman, Zygmunt (1999) *In Search of Public Space.* Cambridge: Polity.

Bechmann, Gotthard (ed.) (1993) *Risiko und Gesellschaft.* Opladen: Westdeutscher Verlag.

Beck, Ulrich (1983) Soziale Wirklichkeit und Modernität: Versuch einer gegenwarts-historischen Bestimmung der Soziologie. Unpublished MS, Ambach.

Beck, Ulrich (1988) *Gegengifte: Die organisierte Unverantwortlichkeit.* Frankfurt am Main: Suhrkamp.

Beck, Ulrich (1991) *Politik in der Risikogesellschaft.* Frankfurt am Main: Suhrkamp.

Beck, Ulrich (1992) *Risk Society: Towards a New Modernity.* London: Sage.

Beck, Ulrich (1995) *Die feindlose Demokratie.* Stuttgart: Reclam.

Beck, Ulrich (1996) World risk society as cosmopolitan society? Ecological questions in a framework of manufactured uncertainties. *Theory, Culture & Society* 13/4: 1–32.

Beck, Ulrich (1997a) *The Reinvention of Politics: Rethinking Modernity in the Global Order.* Cambridge: Polity.

Beck, Ulrich (ed.) (1997b) *Kinder der Freiheit.* Frankfurt am Main: Suhrkamp.

Beck, Ulrich (1999a) *Schöne neue Arbeitswelt.* Frankfurt am Main: Campus.

Beck, Ulrich (1999b) *World Risk Society.* Cambridge: Polity.

Beck, Ulrich (2000a) *What is Globalization?* Cambridge: Polity.

Beck, Ulrich (2000b) *The Brave New World of Work.* Cambridge: Polity.

Beck, Ulrich (2001) Risk and power: the loss of confidence and the fragility of markets in global risk society. Lecture delivered at Harvard University, Cambridge, MA.

Beck, Ulrich (2002) *Ecological Politics in an Age of Risk.* Cambridge: Polity.

Beck, Ulrich (2003) *Das Schweigen der Wörter – über Terror und Krieg.* Frankfurt am Main: Suhrkamp.

Beck, Ulrich (2005) *Power in the Global Age.* Cambridge: Polity.

Beck, Ulrich (2006) *The Cosmopolitan Vision.* Cambridge: Polity.

Beck, Ulrich (ed.) (2007) *Generation Global.* Frankfurt am Main: Suhrkamp.

Beck, Ulrich, and Beck-Gernsheim, Elisabeth (1990) *Das ganz normale Chaos der Liebe.* Frankfurt am Main: Suhrkamp.

Beck, Ulrich, and Beck-Gernsheim, Elisabeth (eds) (1994) *Riskante Freiheiten – Individualisierung in der modernen Gesellschaft.* Frankfurt am Main: Suhrkamp.

Beck, Ulrich, and Bonss, Wolfgang (eds) (2001) *Die Modernisierung der Moderne.* Frankfurt am Main: Suhrkamp.

Beck, Ulrich, and Grande, Edgar (2007) *Cosmopolitan Europe.* Cambridge: Polity.

Beck, Ulrich, and Holzer, Boris (2004) Wie global ist die Weltrisikogesellschaft? In Ulrich Beck and Christoph Lau (eds), *Entgrenzung und Entscheidung: Was ist neu an der Theorie reflexiver Modernisierung?.* Frankfurt am Main: Suhrkamp, pp. 421–39.

Beck, Ulrich, and Lau, Christoph (2004) Entgrenzung und Entscheidung: Was ist neu an der Theorie reflexiver Modernisierung? In Ulrich Beck and Christoph Lau (eds), *Entgrenzung und Entscheidung: Was ist neu an der Theorie reflexiver Modernisierung?.* Frankfurt am Main: Suhrkamp.

Beck, Ulrich, and Sznaider, Natan (eds) (2006) Cosmopolitan sociology. *British Journal of Sociology* 57/1 [special issue].

Beck, Ulrich, Bonss, Wolfgang, and Lau, Christoph (2001) Theorie reflexiver Modernisierung – Fragestellungen, Hypothesen, Forschungsprogramme. In Ulrich Beck and Wolfgang Bonss (eds), *Die Modernisierung der Moderne.* Frankfurt am Main: Suhrkamp, pp. 11–59.

Beck, Ulrich, Giddens, Anthony, and Lash, Scott (1994) *Reflexive Modernisation.* Cambridge: Polity.

Becker, Egon (1990) Transformation und kulturelle Hülle. *Prokla* 79: 12–27.

Beck-Gernsheim, Elisabeth (ed.) (1993) *Welche Gesundheit wollen wir?* Frankfurt am Main: Suhrkamp.

Bellah, Robert N. (1964) Religious evolution. *American Sociological Review* 29: 358–74.

Benford, Gregory (1999) *Deep Time: How Humanity Communicates across Millennia.* New York: Avon.

Benhabib, Seyla (2007) Das Ende staatlicher Souveränität oder die Entstehung kosmopolitischer Normen? In Ulrich Beck (ed.), *Generation Global.* Frankfurt am Main: Suhrkamp.

Benn, Gottfried (1986) *Das Gottfried Benn Brevier.* Munich: Fischer.

Berger, Peter L., and Luckmann, Thomas (1971) *The Social Construction of Reality: A Treatise on the Sociology of Knowledge.* London: Penguin.

Bernstein, Peter L. (1997) *Wider die Götter.* Munich: Gerling Akademie Verlag.

Blühdorn, Ingolfur (1997) A theory of post-ecological politics. *Environmental Politics* 6/3: 125–47.

Bogard, William C. (1989) *Bhopal Tragedy: Language, Logic, and Politics in the Production of a Hazard.* Boulder, CO: Westview Press.

Bogun, Roland, Osterland, Martin, and Warsewa, Günter (1992) Arbeit und Umwelt im Risikobewußtsein. *Soziale Welt* 43/2: 237–45.

Böhle, Fritz, Bolte, Annegret, Dunkel, Wolfgang, Pfeiffer, Sabine, Porsche, Stephanie, and Sevsay-Tegethoff, Nese (2004) Der gesellschaftliche Umgang mit Erfahrungswissen – Von der Ausgrenzung zu neuen Grenzziehungen. In Ulrich Beck and Christoph Lau (eds), *Entgrenzung und Entscheidung.* Frankfurt am Main: Suhrkamp.

Böhme, Gernot (1991) *Die Natur im Zeitalter ihrer technischen Reproduzierbarkeit.* Frankfurt am Main: Suhrkamp.

Böhme, Gernot, and Stehr, Nico (1986) *The Knowledge Society.* Dordrecht: Reidel.

Bonss, Wolfgang (1991) Unsicherheit und Gesellschaft – Argumente für eine soziologische Risikoforschung. *Soziale Welt* 42: 258–77.

Bonss, Wolfgang (1995) *Vom Risiko: Unsicherheit und Ungewißheit in der Moderne.* Hamburg: Bund.

Bonss, Wolfgang (2003) *Modelle kritischer Gesellschaftstheorie: Traditionen und Perspektiven der Kritischen Theorie.* Stuttgart: Metzler.

Böschen, Stefan, and Wehling, Peter (2004) *Wissenschaft zwischen Folgenverantwortung und Nichtwissen.* Wiesbaden: GWX.

Böschen, Stefan, Kratzer, Nick, and May, Stefan (eds) (2006) *Nebenfolgen: Analysen zur Konstruktion und Transformation moderner Gesellschaften.* Weilerswist: Velbrück-Wissenschaft.

Böschen, Stefan, Lau, Christoph, Obermaier, Hans, and Wehling, Peter (2004) Die Erwartung des Unerwarteten. In Ulrich Beck and Christoph Lau (eds), *Entgrenzung und Entscheidung.* Frankfurt am Main: Suhrkamp, pp. 123–48.

Bougen, Peter (2003) Catastrophe risk. *Economy and Society* 32: 253–74.

Bourdieu, Pierre (1984) *Distinction: A Social Critique of the Judgement of Taste.* Cambridge, MA: Harvard University Press.

Boyne, Roy (2003) *Risk.* Buckingham: Open University Press.

Breen, Richard (1997) Risk, recommodification and stratification. *Sociology* 31/3: 473–89.

Brock, Dietmar (1991) Die Risikogesellschaft und das Risiko soziologischer Zuspitzung. *Zeitschrift für Soziologie* 20/1: 12–24.

Bronner, Stephen E. (ed.) (2005) *Planetary Politics.* Oxford: Rowman & Littlefield.

Brown, Jennifer (1989) *Environmental Threats.* London: Belhaven.

Bruggemeier, Gert (1988) Umwelthaftrecht: Ein Beitrag zum Recht in der 'Risikogesellschaft'. *Kritische Justiz* 2: 209–30.

Brunsson, Nils, and Jacobsson, Bengt (2000) *A World of Standards.* Oxford: Oxford University Press.

Bryant, Bunyan (ed.) (1995) *Environmental Justice.* Washington, DC: Island.

Butler, Judith (1993) Endangered/endangering: schematic racism and white paranoia. In Robert Gooding-Williams (ed.), *Reading Rodney King: Reading Urban Uprising.* London: Routledge.

Butler, Judith (2004) *Precarious Life.* London: Verso.

Buttel, Frederik H., and Taylor, Paul J. (1994) Environmental sociology and global environmental change. In Michael Redclift and Ted Benton (eds), *Social Theory and the Global Environment.* London: Routledge.

Byk, Christian (1992) The human genome project and the social contract. *Journal of Medicine and Philosophy* 17/4: 371–80.

Byk, Christian (1999) Law and the cultural construction of nature. In Patrick O'Mahony (ed.), *Nature, Risk and Responsibility.* London: Macmillan.

Campbell, Scott, and Currie, Greg (2006) Against Beck: in defence of risk analysis. *Philosophy of the Social Sciences* 36: 149–72.

Cannon, Geoffrey (1995) *Superbug: Nature's Revenge: Why Antibiotics Can Breed Disease.* London: Virgin.

Castells, Manuel (1996) *The Information Age*, Vol. 1. Oxford: Blackwell.

Chakrabarty, Dipesh (2000) *Provincializing Europe.* Princeton, NJ: Princeton University Press.

Chapman, Graham, Kumar, Keval J., Fraser, Caroline, and Gaber, Ivor (1997) *Environmentalism and the Mass Media: The North–South Divide.* London: Routledge.

Chernilo, Daniel (2006) Social theory's methodological nationalism. *European Journal of Social Theory* 9/1: 4–22.

Christoff, Peter (1996) Ecological modernization, ecological modernities. *Environmental Politics* 5/3: 476–500.

Clark, Nigel (1998) Nanoplanet: molecular engineering in the time of ecological crisis. *Time & Society* 7/2: 353–68.

Clark, Simon (2006) *From Enlightenment to Risk.* New York: Palgrave.

Claussen, Bernhard (1989) Politische Bildung in der Risikogesellschaft. *Aus Politik und Zeitgeschichte* 36: 231–7.

Clegg, Stewart R., Redding, S. Gordon, and Cartner, Monica (eds) (1990) *Capitalism in Contrasting Cultures.* Berlin and New York: de Gruyter.

Cohen, Stanley (2001) *States of Denial: Knowing about Atrocities and Suffering of Others.* Cambridge: Polity.

Cottle, Simon (1997) Ulrich Beck, 'risk society' and the media: a catastrophic view? *European Journal of Communication* 12: 429–56.

Cutler, A. Claire, Haufler, Virginia, and Porter, Tony (eds) (1999) *Private Authority and International Affairs.* Albany: State University of New York Press.

Cutter, Susan L. (1993) *Living with Risk: The Geography of Ecological Hazards.* New York: Edward Arnold.

Czada, Roland, and Drexler, Alexander (1988) Konturen einer politischen Risikoverwaltung. *Österreichische Zeitschrift für Politikwissenschaft* 1: 52–67.

Daase, Christopher (2002) Internationale Risikopolitik: ein Forschungsprogramm für den sicherheitspolitischen Paradigmenwechsel. In Christopher Daase, Susanne Feske and Ingo Peters (eds), *Internationale Risikopolitik.* Baden-Baden: Nomos.

Daase, Christopher, Feske, Susanne, and Peters, Ingo (2002) (eds) *Internationale Risikopolitik.* Baden-Baden: Nomos.

Daele, Wolfgang van den (1992) Concepts of nature in modern societies. In Meinolf Dierkes and Bernd Biervert (eds), *European Social Science in Transition.* Frankfurt am Main: Campus, pp. 526–60.

Daele, Wolfgang van den (1995) Politik in der ökologischen Krise. *Soziologische Revue* 18/4: 501–8.

Darier, Eric (1996) Environmental governmentality. *Environmental Politics* 5/4: 585–606.

Delanty, Gerard (1999) Biopolitics in the risk society. In Patrick O'Mahony (ed.), *Nature, Risk and Responsibility.* London: Macmillan.

Delanty, Gerard (2006) The cosmopolitan imagination. *British Journal of Sociology* 1: 25–48.

Deleuze, Gilles, and Guattari, Félix (1994) *What is Philosophy?* London: Verso.

Derrida, Jacques (2002) *On Cosmopolitanism and Forgiveness.* London: Routledge.

Dewey, John (1946) *The Public and its Problems.* Chicago: Gateway Books.

Dobson, Andrew (2006) Thick cosmopolitanism. *Political Studies* 54: 165–84.

Doherty, Brian, and Geus, Marius de (eds) *Democracy and Green Political Thought.* London: Routledge.

Doubiago, Sharon (1989) Mama Coyote talks to the boys. In Judith Plant (ed.), *Healing the Wounds: The Promise of Ecofeminism*. Philadelphia: Green Print.

Douglas, Mary (1966) *Purity and Danger: An Analysis of the Concepts of Pollution and Taboo*. London: Routledge.

Douglas, Mary (1986) *Risk Acceptability in the Social Sciences*. London: Routledge.

Douglas, Mary (1987) *How Institutions Think*. London: Routledge.

Douglas, Mary (1994) *Risk and Blame*. London: Routledge.

Douglas, Mary, and Wildavsky, Aaron (1982) *Risk and Culture: An Essay on the Selection of Technological and Environmental Dangers*. Berkeley: University of California Press.

Dressel, Kerstin, and Wynne, Brian (1998) Anglo-German comparison of modern risk political cultures: the BSE case. Unpublished MS, Centre for the Study of Environmental Change, Lancaster University.

Dürrenmatt, Friedrich (1982) *Plays and Essays*. New York: Continuum.

Eade, John (ed.) (1997) *Living the Global City*. London and New York: Routledge.

Eder, Klaus (1998) Taming risks through dialogues. In Maurie J. Cohen (ed.), *Risk in the Modern Age*. Basingstoke: Macmillan.

Eichler, Margrit (1993) 'Umwelt' als soziologisches Problem. *Das Argument* 205: 359–76.

Eisenstadt, Shmuel N. (2000a) *Die Vielfalt der Moderne*. Weilerswist: Velbrück.

Eisenstadt, Shmuel N. (2000b) Multiple modernities. *Daedalus* 129/1: 1–29.

Elkins, David J. (1995) *Beyond Sovereignty*. Toronto: University of Toronto Press.

Emmanuel, Arghiri (1972) *Unequal Exchange: A Study of the Imperialism of Trade*. New York: New Left Books.

Eppler, Erhard (2002) *Vom Gewaltmonopol zum Gewaltmarkt?* Frankfurt am Main: Suhrkamp.

Ericson, Richard V., and Doyle, Aaron (2004) Catastrophe risk, insurance and terrorism. *Economy and Society* 33/2: 135–73.

Ericson, Richard V., and Haggerty, Kevin D. (1997) *Policing the Risk Society*. Oxford: Clarendon Press.

Escobar, Arturo (1995) *Encountering Development: The Making and Unmaking of the Third World*. Princeton, NJ: Princeton University Press.

Evers, Adalbert, and Nowotny, Helga (1987) *Über den Umgang mit Unsicherheit*. Frankfurt am Main: Suhrkamp.

Ewald, François (1986) *L'État-Providence*. Paris: Grasset.

Ewald, François (1991) Insurance and risk. In Graham Burchell, Colin Gordon and Peter Miller (eds), *The Foucault Effect: Studies in Governmentality*. Chicago: University of Chicago Press, pp. 197–210.

Ewald, François (1993) *Two Infinities of Risk*. In Brian Massuni (ed.), *The Politics of Everyday Fear*. London: University of Minnesota Press.

Ewald, François (2002) The return of Descartes' malicious demon: an outline of a philosophy of precaution. In Tom Baker and Jonathan Simon (eds), *Embracing Risk: The Changing Culture of Insurance and Responsibility*. Chicago: University of Chicago Press, pp. 273–301.

Falk, Richard (1994) The making of global citizenship. In Bart van Steenbergen (ed.), *The Conditions of Citizenship*. London: Sage.

Fetscher, Iring (2006) Sollte diese Qual uns quälen'/da sie unsere Lust vermehrt? *Fortschritt und Katastrophe von Goethe bis Benjamin: Jahrbuch für Romantik.* Frankfurt am Main: Athenäum.

Fischer, Joschka (1989) Der Umbau der Industriegesellschaft. Frankfurt am Main: Eichborn.

Ford, Lucy H. (1999) Social movements and the globalisation of environmental governance. *IDS Bulletin* 30/3: 68–74.

Foucault, Michel (1991) Governmentality. In Graham Burchell, Colin Gordon and Peter Miller (eds), *The Foucault Effect.* Chicago: University of Chicago Press.

Frank, Andre Gunder (1969) *Latin America: Underdevelopment or Revolution.* New York: Monthly Review Press.

Frank, Manfred, and Haverkamp, Anselm (1988) *Poetik und Hermeneutik*, Vol. 13: *Individualität.* Munich: Fink.

Frankenfeld, Philip (1992) Technological citizenship: a normative framework for risk studies. *Science, Technology and Human Values* 17/4: 459–84.

Franklin, Jane (ed.) (1998) *The Politics of Risk Society.* Cambridge: Polity.

Franklin, Sarah (1997) *Embodied Progress: A Cultural Account of Assisted Conception.* London: Routledge.

Franklin, Sarah (2005) Stem cells RUS: emergent life forms and the global biological. In Aihwa Ong and Stephen J. Collier (eds), *Global Assemblages.* Oxford: Blackwell.

Friedman, Thomas L. (2006) Allies dressed in green. *New York Times*, 27 October.

Froot, Kenneth A. (1999) *The Financing of Catastrophe Risk.* Chicago: University of Chicago Press.

Fuller, Steve (1999) *The Governance of Science.* Buckingham: Open University Press.

Giddens, Anthony (1990) *The Consequences of Modernity.* Cambridge: Polity.

Giddens, Anthony (1994a) Living in a post-traditional society. In Ulrich Beck, Anthony Giddens and Scott Lash, *Reflexive Modernization: Politics, Tradition and Aesthetics in the Modern Social Order.* Cambridge: Polity.

Giddens, Anthony (1994b) *Beyond Left and Right.* Cambridge: Polity.

Giddens, Anthony (1998) *The Third Way: The Renewal of Social Democracy.* Cambridge: Polity.

Giddens, Anthony (1999) *Runaway World.* London: Profile Books.

Giddens, Anthony, and Pierson, Christopher (1998) *Conversations with Anthony Giddens: Making Sense of Modernity.* Cambridge: Polity.

Gill, Bernhard (2003) *Streitfall Natur.* Opladen: Westdeutscher Verlag.

Gilroy, Paul (2000) *Against Race: Imagining Political Culture beyond the Color Line.* Cambridge, MA: Harvard University Press.

Goldblatt, David (1996) *Social Theory and the Environment.* Cambridge: Polity.

Gottweis, Herbert (1988) Politik in der Risikogesellschaft. *Österreichische Zeitschrift für Politikwissenschaft* 1: 3–18.

Grande, Edgar (2004) Politik gegen Institutionen? Die neuen Souveräne der Risikogesellschaft. In Angelika Poferl and Natan Sznaider (eds), *Becks kosmopolitisches Projekt: Auf dem Weg in eine andere Soziologie.* Baden-Baden: Nomos.

Grande, Edgar, and Pauly, Louis W. (eds) (2005) *Complex Sovereignty: Reconstituting Political Authority in the Twenty-First Century.* Toronto: University of Toronto Press.

Grande, Edgar, and Risse, Thomas (2000) Bridging the gap: Konzeptionelle Anforderungen an die politikwissenschaftliche Analyse von Globalisierungsprozessen. *Zeitschrift für Internationale Beziehungen* 7: 235–66.

Grande, Edgar et al. (2006) Politische Transnationalisierung. In Stefan A. Schirm (ed.), *Globalisierung*. Baden-Baden: Nomos, pp. 119–46.

Gray, John (1998) *False Dawn*. London: Granta.

Haas, Ernst Bernhard (1990) *When Knowledge is Power: Three Models of Change in International Organizations*. Berkeley: University of California Press.

Haas, Peter M. (1989) Do regimes matter? Epistemic communities and Mediterranean pollution control. *International Organization* 43/3: 377–403.

Haas, Peter M. (1992) Epistemic communities and international policy coordination: introduction. *International Organization* 46/1: 1–35.

Haas, Peter M., Keohane, Robert O., and Levy, Marc A. (eds) (1993) *Institutions for the Earth: Sources of Effective International Protection*. Cambridge, MA, and London: MIT Press.

Habermas, Jürgen (1999) *The Inclusion of the Other*. Cambridge: Polity.

Habermas, Jürgen (2001) *The Postnational Constellation: Political Essays*. Cambridge: Polity.

Häfele, Wolf (1974) Hypotheticality and the new challenges: the pathfinder role of nuclear energy. *Minerva* 12/1: 313–21.

Haggard, Stephan, and Simmons, Beth A. (1987) Theories of international regimes. *International Organization* 41/3: 491–517.

Hahn, Alois, Eirmbter, Willy H., and Jacob, Rüdiger (1992) Aids: Risiko oder Gefahr? *Soziale Welt* 43/4: 400–21.

Hajer, Maarten A. (1995) *The Politics of Environmental Discourse*. Oxford: Oxford University Press.

Halfmann, Jost (1990) Technik und soziale Organisation im Widerspruch. In Jost Halfmann and Klaus Peter Japp (eds), *Riskante Entscheidungen und Katastrophenpotentiale*. Opladen: Westdeutscher Verlag.

Halfmann, Jost, and Japp, Klaus P. (eds) (1990) *Riskante Entscheidungen und Katastrophenpotentiale*. Opladen: Westdeutscher Verlag.

Haller, Matthias (2004) 'Je planmässiger die Menschen vorgehen, desto wirksamer vermag sie der Zufall zu treffen' (Friedrich Dürrenmatt): Abschiedsvorlesung vom 8. Juni 2004. *Jahresbericht 2003*. St Gallen: Institut für Versicherungswirtschaft.

Hampden-Turner, Charles, and Trompenaars, Fons (1993) *The Seven Cultures of Capitalism: Value Systems for Creating Wealth in the United States, Japan, Germany, France, Britain, Sweden, and the Netherlands*. New York: Currency/Doubleday.

Haraway, Donna (1990) A manifesto for cyborgs: science, technology and socialist feminism in the 1980s. In Linda J. Nicholson (ed.), *Feminism/Postmodernism*. New York: Routledge.

Haraway, Donna (1991) *Simians, Cyborgs and Women: The Reinvention of Nature*. London: Routledge.

Haraway, Donna (1997) *Modest_Witness@Second_Millennium. FemaleMan©_Meets_OncoMouse™*. London: Routledge.

Hardin, Garrett (1968) The tragedy of the commons. *Science* 162: 1243–8.

Harvey, David (1989) *The Condition of Postmodernity*. Oxford: Blackwell.

Heine, Günter, and Meinberg, Volker (1988) Empfehlen sich Änderungen im strafrechtlichen Umweltschutz, insbes. in Verbindung mit dem Verwaltungsrecht:

Gutachten D für den 57. Juristentag. In Ständige Deputation des Deutschen Juristentages (ed.), *Verhandlungen des 57. Deutschen Juristentages*, Vol. I, Part D.

Heine, Hartwig (1992) Das Verhältnis der Naturwissenschaftler und Ingenieure in der Großchemie zur ökologischen Industriekritik. *Soziale Welt* 43/2: 246–55.

Heine, Hartwig, and Mautz, Rüdiger (1989) *Industriearbeiter contra Umweltschutz?* Frankfurt am Main: Campus.

Heine, Heinrich (1981) *Zur Geschichte der Religion und der Philosophie in Deutschland.* In Heinrich Heine, *Gesammelte Werke*, Vol. 5. Weimar: Klassiker.

Held, David (1995) Democracy and globalization. In Daniele Archibugi, David Held and Martin Köhler (eds), *Re-imagining Political Community*. Cambridge: Polity, pp. 11–27.

Held, David (2000a) Regulating globalization? The reinvention of politics. *International Sociology* 15/2: 394–408.

Held, David (ed.) (2000b) *A Globalizing World? Culture, Economics, Politics*. London: Routledge.

Heller, Agnes (1994) Zerstörung der Privatsphäre durch die Zivilgesellschaft. *Ästhetik und Kommunikation* 85/6: 23–35.

Herbert; Ulrich (ed.) (2002) *Wandlungsprozesse in Westdeutschland*. Göttingen: Wallstein Verlag.

Herbert, Ulrich (2007) Europe in High Modernity. *Journal of Modern European History* 5/1: 5–21 [special issue].

Hewson, Martin, and Sinclair, Timothy J. (1999) *Approaches to Global Governance Theory*. Albany: State University of New York Press.

Hildebrandt, Eckart, Gerhardt, Udo, Kühleis, Christoph, Schenk, Sabine, and Zimpelmann, Beate (1994) Politisierung und Entgrenzung: Am Beispiel ökologisch erweiterter Arbeitspolitik. *Soziale Welt* 9: 429–44 [special issue].

Hitzler, Roland (1991) Zur gesellschaftlichen Konstruktion von Natur. *Wechselwirkung* 50: 43–8.

Hobbes, Thomas (1968) *Leviathan*. Harmondsworth: Penguin.

Hofmannsthal, Hugo von (2005) *The Lord Chandos Letter and Other Writings*. New York: New York Review Books.

Holzer, Boris (1999) *Die Fabrikation von Wundern: Modernisierung, wirtschaftliche Entwicklung und kultureller Wandel in Ostasien*. Opladen: Leske & Budrich.

Holzer, Boris, and May, Stefan (2005) Herrschaft kraft Nichtwissen. *Soziale Welt* 56/2–3: 317–35 [special issue: 'Theorie reflexiver Modernisierung'].

Holzer, Boris, and Millo, Yuval (2005) From risks to second-order dangers in financial markets: unintended consequences of risk management systems. *New Political Economy* 10/2: 223–45.

Holzer, Boris, and Sørensen, Mads P. (2003) Rethinking subpolitics: beyond the 'iron cage' of modern politics? *Theory, Culture & Society* 20/2: 79–102.

Horkheimer, Max, and Adorno, Theodor W. (1993) *Dialectic of Enlightenment*. New York: Continuum.

Hudson, Barbara (2003) *Justice in the Risk Society: Challenging and Re-affirming Justice in Late Modernity*. London: Sage.

Husband, Charles (2000) Media and the public sphere in multi-ethnic societies. In Simon Cottle (ed.), *Ethnic Minorities and the Media*. Buckingham: Open University Press, pp. 199–214.

Husserl, Edmund (1970) *The Crisis of the European Sciences and Transcendental Phenomenology*. Evanston, IL: Northwestern University Press.

Ignatieff, Michael (2001) *Virtual War*. London: Vintage.

IPCC (2007) *Climate Change 2007: Mitigation of Climate Change: Contribution of Working Group III to the Fourth Assessment Report of the Intergovernmental Panel on Climate Change*, ed. Bernd Metz et al. Cambridge: Cambridge University Press.

Irwin, Alan (2000) Risk, technology and modernity: re-positioning the sociological analysis of nuclear power. In Barbara Adam, Ulrich Beck and Joost van Loon (eds), *The Risk Society and Beyond: Critical Issues for Social Theory*. London: Sage.

Jacobs, Michael (ed.) (1997) Greening the millennium? The new politics of the environment. *Political Quarterly* [special issue].

Japp, Klaus Peter (1992) Selbstverstärkungseffekte riskanter Entscheidungen. *Zeitschrift für Soziologie* 1: 33–50.

Jasanoff, Sheila (2003) Technologies of humility: citizen participation in governing science. *Minerva* 41: 223–44.

Jasanoff, Sheila, Markle, Gerald E., Petersen, James C., and Pinch, Trevor (eds) (1995) *Handbook of Science and Technology Studies*. London: Sage.

Joas, Hans (1992) *Die Kreativität des Handelns*. Frankfurt am Main: Suhrkamp.

Jonas, Hans (1984) *The Imperative of Responsibility*. Chicago: University of Chicago Press.

Kahn, Paul W. (1999) War and sacrifice in Kosovo. *Philosophy and Public Policy Quarterly* 19; http://www.puaf.umd.edu/IPPP/spring_summer99/kosovo.htm.

Kaldor, Mary (2007) *New and Old Wars: Organized Violence in a Global Era*. 2nd rev. edn, Cambridge: Polity.

Kapstein, Ethan B. (1994) *Governing the Global Economy: International Finance and the State*. Cambridge, MA: Harvard University Press.

Kasperson, Jeanne X., and Kasperson, Roger E. (2005) *The Social Contours of Risk*, 2 vols. London: Earthscan.

Kellow, Ansley (2000) Norms, interests and environment NGOs: the limits of cosmopolitanism. *Environmental Politics* 9/3: 1–22.

Keohane, Robert O., and Nye, Joseph S., Jr. (2001) *Between Centralization and Fragmentation: The Club Model of Multilateral Cooperation and Problems of Democratic Legitimacy*. KSE Working Paper: 01–004.

Kermani, Navid (2007) Dynamit des Geistes. In Ulrich Beck (ed.), *Generation Global*. Frankfurt am Main: Suhrkamp.

Keynes, John Maynard (1937) The general theory of employment. *Quarterly Journal of Economics*: 209–33.

King, Ynestra (1989) The ecology of feminism and the feminism of ecology. In Judith Plant (ed.), *Healing the Wounds: The Promise of Ecofeminism*. Philadelphia: Green Print.

Knight, Frank (1921) *Risk, Uncertainty and Profit*. New York: Houghton Mifflin.

Koenen, Elmar (1993) Heinrich und Ulrich: Einige poetisch-hermeneutische Hinweise zur Individualisierung in der Geschichte der Moderne. In Joachim Hohl and Günter Reisbeck (eds), *Individuum Lebenswelt Gesellschaft: Texte zur Sozialpsychologie und Soziologie. Heiner Keupp zum 50. Geburtstag*. Munich: Profil, pp. 89–106.

Koenen, Elmar (2004) Leitmotive: Thematische Kontinuitäten im Werk von Ulrich Beck. In Angelika Poferl and Natan Sznaider (eds), *Becks kosmopolitisches Projekt: Auf dem Weg in eine andere Soziologie*. Baden-Baden: Nomos, pp. 23–34.

Kommission für Zukunftsfragen (1997) *Arbeitsmarktentwicklungen: Bericht Teil II*. Bonn: Bayerische Staatsregierung.

Korea: a 'risk society' (1998) *Korean Journal of Sociology* 39/1 [special issue].

Krimsky, Sheldon, and Golding, Dominic (eds) (1992) *Social Theories of Risk*. Westport, CT: Praeger.

Krohn, Wolfgang, and Weyer, Johannes (1989) Gesellschaft als Labor. *Soziale Welt* 40/3: 349–73.

Kuei-Tien (2007) Biomedtech island project and risk governance: paradigm conflicts within a hidden and delayed high-tech risk society. *Soziale Welt* 58/2: 123–44.

Kuhn, Thomas S. (1962) *The Structure of Scientific Revolutions*. Chicago: University of Chicago Press.

Kundera, Milan (2003) *The Art of the Novel*. New York: Perennial Classics.

Lagadec, Patrick (1981) *La Civilisation du risque: catastrophes technologiques et responsabilité*. Paris: Seuil.

Lakatos, Imre (1978) *The Methodology of Scientific Research Programmes*. Cambridge: Cambridge University Press.

Laqueur, Walter (1996) Postmodern terrorism. *Foreign Affairs* 75/5: 24–36.

Lash, Scott (1994) Reflexivity and its doubles: structure, aesthetics, community. In Ulrich Beck, Anthony Giddens and Scott Lash, *Reflexive Modernization: Politics, Tradition and Aesthetics in the Modern Social Order*. Cambridge: Polity.

Lash, Scott (2000) Risk culture. In Barbara Adam, Ulrich Beck and Joost van Loon (eds), *The Risk Society and Beyond: Critical Issues for Social Theory*. London: Sage.

Lash, Scott, and Urry, John (1994) *Economy of Time and Space*. London: Sage.

Lash, Scott, Szerszynski, Bronislaw, and Wynne, Brian (eds) (1996) *Risk, Environment and Modernity: Towards a New Ecology*. London: Sage.

Latour, Bruno (1995) *We Have Never Been Modern*. Cambridge, MA: Harvard University Press.

Latour, Bruno (2003) Is remodernization occurring – and if so, how to prove it? *Theory, Culture and Society* 20/1: 35–48.

Latour, Bruno (2004) *Politics of Nature: How to Bring the Sciences into Democracy*. Cambridge, MA: Harvard University Press.

Lau, Christoph (1989) Risikodiskurse. *Soziale Welt* 40/3: 418–36.

Lau, Christoph (1991) Neue Risiken und gesellschaftliche Konflikte. In Ulrich Beck (ed.), *Politik in der Risikogesellschaft*. Frankfurt am Main: Suhrkamp.

Leiss, William (1996) Three phases in the evolution of risk communication practice. *Annals of the American Academy of Political and Social Science* 545: 85–94.

Levi, Primo (1993) *Survival in Auschwitz: The Nazi Assault on Humanity*. New York: Collier Books.

Levy, Daniel, and Sznaider, Natan (2004) *Memory in the Global Age: The Holocaust*. Philadelphia: Temple University Press.

Levy, Daniel, and Sznaider, Natan (2006) Sovereignty transformed: a sociology of human rights. *British Journal of Sociology* 57/4: 657–76.

Levy, Marion (1966) *Modernization and the Structure of Societies*. Princeton, NJ: Princeton University Press.

Linklater, Andrew (1998) *The Transformation of Political Community: Ethical Foundations of the Post-Westphalian Era.* Columbia: University of South Carolina Press.

Linklater, Andrew (2001) Citizenship, humanity, and cosmopolitan harm conventions. *International Political Science Review* 22/3: 261–77.

LiPuma, Edward, and Lee, Benjamin (2004) *Financial Derivatives and the Globalization of Risk.* Durham, NC: Duke University Press.

Litfin, Karen (1993) Eco-regimes: playing tug of war with the nation-state. In Ronnie D. Lipschutz and Ken Conca (eds), *The State and Social Power in Global Environmental Politics.* New York: Columbia University Press, pp. 94–117.

Litfin, Karen (1994) *Ozone Discourses: Science and Politics in Global Environmental Cooperation.* New York: Columbia University Press.

Little, Richard (1997) International regimes. In John Baylis and Steve Smith (eds), *The Globalization of World Politics.* Oxford: Oxford University Press, pp. 231–48.

Löfstedt, Ragnar E., and Frewer, Lynn (eds) (1998) *The Earthscan Reader in Risk and Modern Society.* London: Earthscan.

Loon, Joost van (2000) Virtual risks in an age of cybernetic reproduction. In Barbara Adam, Ulrich Beck and Joost van Loon (eds), *The Risk Society and Beyond: Critical Issues for Social Theory.* London: Sage.

Loon, Joost van (2002) *Risk and Technological Culture: Towards a Sociology of Virulence.* London: Routledge.

Lucatelli, Adriano (1997) *Finance and World Order.* Westport, CT, and London: Greenwood Press.

Luhmann, Niklas (1989) *Ecological Communication*, trans. John Bednarz, Jr. Chicago: University of Chicago Press.

Luhmann, Niklas (1990) Risiko und Gefahr. In Niklas Luhmann, *Soziologische Aufklärung 5.* Opladen: Westdeutscher Verlag, pp. 131–69.

Luhmann, Niklas (1991) Verständigung über Risiken und Gefahren. *Politische Meinung* 36: 86–95.

Luhmann, Niklas (1992) Describing the Future. In Luhmann, *Observations on Modernity*, trans. William Whobrey. Stanford, CA: Stanford University Press, pp. 63–74.

Luhmann, Niklas (1999) Ethik in internationalen Beziehungen. *Soziale Welt* 50/3: 247–54.

Luhmann, Niklas (2003) *Risk: A Sociological Theory*, trans. Rhodes Barrett. New York: de Gruyter.

Lupton, Deborah (1999a) *Risk and Sociocultural Theory.* Cambridge: Cambridge University Press.

Lupton, Deborah (1999b) *Risk.* London: Routledge.

MacKenzie, Donald (2005) Mathematizing risk: models, arbitrage and crisis. In Bridget Hutter and Michael Power (eds), *Organizational Encounters with Risk.* Cambridge: Cambridge University Press, pp. 167–89.

Mair, Stefan (2002) Die Globalisierung privater Gewalt: Kriegsherren, Rebellen, Terroristen und organisierte Kriminalität. *SWP-Studie 2002/S.*

Mäkinen, Heikki (2007) *Risk Society and Risk Network.* http://www.yhteiskunnantieto.fi/risk_society_network.pdf.

Mandelbrot, Benoit, and Taleb, Nassim (2006) A focus on the exceptions that prove the rule. *Financial Times*, 23 March: 2.

Marcuse, Herbert (1981) *Das Märchen von der Sicherheit*. Zurich: Diogenes.

Mason, Michael (2005) *The New Accountability: Environmental Responsibility across Borders*. London: Earthscan.

Mau, Steffen (2007) *Transnationale Vergesellschaftung: Zur Entgrenzung des nationalstaatlichen Raumes*. Frankfurt am Main: Campus.

May, Stefan (2004) Rechtspolitische Nebenfolgen und Entscheidungskonflikte der Biomedizin. In Ulrich Beck and Christoph Lau (eds), *Entgrenzung und Entscheidung*. Frankfurt am Main: Suhrkamp.

May, Stefan (2007) *Neue Risiken – Neue Regeln*. Frankfurt am Main: Campus.

May, Tim (2000) A future for critique? Positioning, belonging and reflexivity. *European Journal of Social Theory* 3/2: 157–73.

Merten, Roland, and Olk, Thomas (1992) Wenn Sozialarbeit sich selbst zum Problem wird: Strategien reflexiver Modernisierung. In Thomas Rauschenbach and Hans Gängler (eds), *Soziale Arbeit und Erziehung in der Risikogesellschaft*. Neuwied: Luchterhand.

Meyer, John W. (2005) *Weltkultur: Wie die westlichen Prinzipien die Welt durchdringen*. Frankfurt am Main: Suhrkamp.

Mol, Arthur (1996) Ecological modernization and institutional reflexivity. *Environmental Politics* 5/2: 302–23.

Mol, Arthur P. J. (2000) The environmental movement in an era of ecological modernization. *Geoforum* 31/1: 45–56.

Mol, Arthur, and Spaargaren, Gert (1993) Environment, modernity and the risk society. *International Sociology* 8/4: 431–59.

Müller-Jung, Joachim (2007) Ein ökologischer Neuanfang. *Frankfurter Allgemeine Zeitung*, 5 February: 1.

Münch, Richard (1996) *Risikopolitik*. Frankfurt am Main: Suhrkamp.

Münch, Richard (2001) *Offene Räume: Soziale Integration diesseits und jenseits des Nationalstaats*. Frankfurt am Main: Suhrkamp.

Münkler, Herfried (2004) *The New Wars*. Cambridge: Polity.

Münkler, Herfried (2004) Ältere und jüngere Formen des Terrorismus. In Werner Weidenfeld (ed.), *Herausforderung Terrorismus: Die Zukunft der Sicherheit*. Wiesbaden: Verlag für Sozialwissenschaften, pp. 29–43.

Musharbash, Yassin (2006) Neues Betriebssystem für Al Qaida. *Internationale Politik* 60/11: 22–7.

Mythen, Gabe (2004) *Ulrich Beck: A Critical Introduction to the Risk Society*. London: Pluto Press.

Mythen, Gabe, and Walklate, Sandra (eds) *Beyond the Risk Society*. London: Open University Press.

Nassehi, Armin (2006) *Der soziologische Diskurs der Moderne*. Frankfurt am Main: Suhrkamp.

Nederveen Pieterse, Jan (2000) Globalization North and South: representations of uneven development and the interaction of modernities. *Theory, Culture & Society* 17/1: 129–37.

Nelkin, Dorothy (ed.) (1992) *Controversy: Politics of Technical Decisions*. London: Sage.

Nielsen, Torben (2005) Beyond zombie concepts? Unpublished MS, Norway.

Nowicka, Magdalena (2006) *Transnational Professionals and their Cosmopolitan Universes*. Frankfurt am Main: Campus.

Nye, Joseph (2001) *The Paradoxes of American Power*, 2 vols. New York: Oxford University Press.

O'Brien, Robert, Goetz, Anne Marie, Scholte, Jan Aart, and Williams, Marc (2000) *Contesting Global Governance: Multilateral Economic Institutions and Global Social Movements*. Cambridge: Cambridge University Press.

Oechsle, Mechtild (1988) *Der ökologische Naturalismus*. Frankfurt am Main: Campus.

OECD (1972) *Problems of Environmental Economics*. Paris: Organization for Economic Co-operation and Development.

Offe, Claus (1986) Die Utopie der Null-Option. In Johannes Berger (ed.), *Die Moderne: Kontinuitäten and Zäsuren*. Göttingen: Schwartz.

O'Malley, Peter (2003) Governable catastrophes. *Economy and Society* 32: 275–9.

Ong, Aihwa (2004) Assembling around SARS: technology, body heat and political fever in risk society. In Angelika Poferl and Natan Sznaider (eds), *Becks kosmopolitisches Projekt*. Baden-Baden: Nomos.

Ong, Aihwa, and Collier, Stephen J. (eds) (2005) *Global Assemblages*. Oxford: Blackwell.

Otway, Harry (1987) Experts, risk communication, and democracy. *Risk Analysis* 7/2: 125–9.

Outhwaite, William (2006) *The Future of Society*. Oxford: Blackwell.

Parsons, Talcott (1964) Evolutionary universals in society. *American Sociological Review* 29/3: 339–57.

Parsons, Talcott (1966) *Societies: Evolutionary and Comparative Perspectives*. Englewood Cliffs, NJ: Prentice Hall.

Perrow, Charles (1984) *Normal Accidents: Living with High-Risk Technologies*. New York: Basic Books.

Peters, Bernhard (1993) *Die Integration moderner Gesellschaften*. Frankfurt am Main: Suhrkamp.

Petryna, Adriana (2002) *Life Exposed: Biological Citizens after Chernobyl.* Princeton, NJ: Princeton University Press.

Poferl, Angelika (2004) *Die Kosmopolitik des Alltags*. Berlin: Sigma.

Poferl, Angelika, and Sznaider, Natan (eds) (2004) *Becks kosmopolitisches Projekt: Auf dem Weg in eine andere Soziologie*. Baden-Baden: Nomos.

Pries, Ludger (1991) *Betrieblicher Wandel in der Risikogesellschaft*. Opladen: Westdeutscher Verlag.

Prittwitz, Volker von (1990) *Das Katastrophen-Paradox*. Opladen: Leske & Budrich.

Rammert, Werner (1993) Wer oder was steuert den technischen Fortschritt? In Werner Rammert, *Technik aus soziologischer Perspektive*. Opladen: Westdeutscher Verlag.

Randeria, Shalini (1999) Jenseits von Soziologie und soziokultureller Anthropologie. *Soziale Welt* 50/4: 373–82.

Rauschenbach, Thomas (1992) Soziale Arbeit und soziales Risiko. In Thomas Rauschenbach and Hans Gängler (eds), *Soziale Arbeit und Erziehung in der Risikogesellschaft*. Neuwied: Luchterhand.

Reiss, Albert J. (1992) The institutionalization of risk. In James F. Short and Lee Clarke (eds), *Organizations, Uncertainty and Risk*. Boulder, CO: Westview Press, pp. 299–308.

Richard, J. F. (2002) *High Noon.* Oxford: Perseus Press.

Rifkin, Jeremy (1998) *The Biotech Century.* London: Gollancz.

Ritter, Ernst-Hasso (1987) Umweltpolitik und Rechtsentwicklung. *Neue Zeitschrift für Verwaltungsrecht* 11: 929–38.

Ritter, Hennig (2004) *Nahes und fernes Unglück: Versuch über das Mitleid.* Munich: Beck.

Roberts, J. Timmons, and Hite, Amy (2000) *From Modernization to Globalization: Perspectives on Development and Social Change.* Oxford: Blackwell.

Robertson, Roland (1992) *Globalization, Social Theory and Global Culture.* London: Sage.

Robin, Kiòrey (2004) *Fear.* Oxford: Oxford University Press.

Robins, Kevin (1996) *Into the Image: Culture and Politics in the Field of Vision.* New York: Routledge.

Rose, Hilary (2000) Risk, trust and scepticism in the age of new genetics. In Barbara Adam, Ulrich Beck and Joost van Loon (eds), *The Risk Society and Beyond: Critical Issues for Social Theory.* London: Sage.

Rose, Nikolas (2003) Neurochemical selfs. *Society* (November/December): 46–59.

Rostow, Walt W. (1960) *The Stages of Economic Growth: A Non-Communist Manifesto.* Cambridge: Cambridge University Press.

Rustin, Michael (1994) Incomplete modernity: Ulrich Beck's risk society. *Radical Philosophy* 76: 3–12.

Sachs, Wolfgang (1993) *Global Ecology and the Shadow of 'Development' – Global Ecology: A New Arena of Political Conflict.* London: ZED Books.

Scharping, Michael, and Görg, Christoph (1994) Natur in der Soziologie. In Christoph Görg and Michael Scharping (eds), *Gesellschaft im Übergang.* Darmstadt: Wissenschaftliche Buchgesellschaft.

Schelsky, Helmut (1965) Der Mensch in der wissenschaftlichen Zivilisation. In Helmut Schelsky, *Auf der Suche nach Wirklichkeit.* Cologne: Westdeutscher Verlag.

Schillmeier, Michael, and Pohler, Wiebke (2006) Kosmo-politische Ereignisse: Zur sozialen Topologie von SARS. *Soziale Welt* 57: 331–49.

Schirrmacher, Frank (2000) Zehntausend Jahre Einsamkeit: Wie wir unser Nachkommen von uns selber schützen wollen. *Frankfurter Allgemeine Zeitung,* 8 September: 49.

Schmitt, Carl (2005) *Political Theology: Four Chapters on the Concept of Sovereignty.* Chicago: University of Chicago Press.

Schumann, Michael (1987) Industrielle Produzenten in der ökologischen Herausforderung. Research proposal, Göttingen.

Schütz, Alfred, Luckmann, Thomas, and Zaner, Richard (1979) *The Structures of the Life-World,* vol. 1. Evanston, IL: Northwestern University Press.

Schwarz, Michiel, and Thompson, Michael (1990) *Divided We Stand: Redefining Politics, Technology and Social Choice.* New York: Harvester Wheatsheaf.

Schwimm, Thomas (1995) Funktionale Differenzierung – wohin? Eine aktualisierte Bestandsaufnahme. *Berliner Journal für Soziologie* 5/1: 25–39.

Scott, Alan (2000) Risk society or Angst society: two views of risk, consciousness and community. In Barbara Adam, Ulrich Beck and Joost van Loon (eds), *The Risk Society and Beyond: Critical Issues for Social Theory.* London: Sage.

Scott, John (2006) *Social Theory: Central Issues in Sociology.* London: Sage.

Senghaas-Knobloch, Eva (1992) Industriezivilisatorische Risiken als Herausforderung für die Friedens- und Konfliktforschung. In Berthold Meyer and Christoph Wellmann (eds), *Umweltzerstörung: Kriegsfolge und Kriegsursache.* Frankfurt am Main: Suhrkamp, pp. 53–71.

Shaw, Martin (1996) *Civil Society and Media in Global Crises: Representing Distant Violence.* London: Pinter.

Shaw, Martin (2005) *The New Western Way of War: Risk Transfer and its Crisis in Iraq.* Cambridge: Polity.

Shields, Rob (2006) Boundary-thinking in theories of the present: the virtuality of reflexive modernization. *European Journal of Social Theory* 9/2: 223–37.

Short, James F., and Clarke, Lee (eds) (1992) *Organizations, Uncertainties and Risk.* Boulder, CO: Westview Press.

Silverstone, Roger (2006) *Media and Morality: On the Rise of Mediapolis.* Cambridge: Polity.

Sloterdijk, Peter (1999) *Sphären*, vol. 2. Frankfurt am Main: Suhrkamp.

Soros, George (1998) *The Crisis of Global Capitalism.* Boston and London: Little, Brown.

Sossebach, Henning (2006) Schulz zieht in den Krieg. *Die Zeit*, 2 November: 17–20.

Spretnak, Charlene (1989) Towards an ecofeminist spirituality. In Judith Plant (ed.), *Healing the Wounds: The Promise of Ecofeminism.* Philadelphia: Green Print.

Steenbergen, Bart van (ed.) (1994) *The Conditions of Citizenship.* London: Sage.

Stern, Nicholas (2007) *The Economics of Climate Change: The Stern Review.* Cambridge: Cambridge University Press.

Stichweh, Rudolf (2000) *Die Weltgesellschaft.* Frankfurt am Main: Suhrkamp.

Strulik, Torsten (2000) *Risikomanagement globaler Finanzmärkte.* Frankfurt am Main: Campus.

Strydom, Piet (1999a) The challenge of responsibility for sociology. *Current Sociology* 47/3: 65–82.

Strydom, Piet (1999b) The civilisation of the gene. In Patrick O'Mahony (ed.), *Nature, Risk, and Responsibility.* Basingstoke: Macmillan.

Strydom, Piet (2000) *Discourse and Knowledge.* Liverpool: Liverpool University Press.

Strydom, Piet (2002) *Risk, Environment and Society: Ongoing Debates, Current Issues and Future Prospects.* Buckingham: Open University Press.

Szerszynski, Bronislaw, Lash, Scott, and Wynne, Brian (1996) Ecologies, realism and the social sciences. In Scott Lash, Bronislaw Szerszynski and Brian Wynne (eds), *Risk, Environment and Modernity: Towards a New Ecology.* London: Sage.

Sznaider, Natan (2006) Terrorism and the Social Contract: The Difficulties of Understanding Evil. *Irish Journal of Sociology* 15/1: 7–23.

Taleb, Nassim N. (2004) *Fooled by Randomness: The Hidden Role of Chance in Life and in the Markets.* 2nd edn, New York and London: Texere.

Taleb, Nassim N. (2007) *The Black Swan: The Impact of the Highly Improbable.* New York: Random House.

Therborn, Göran (1995a) *European Modernity and Beyond: The Trajectory of European Societies, 1945–2000.* London: Sage.

Therborn, Göran (1995b) Routes to/through Modernity. In Mike Featherstone, Scott Lash and Roland Robertson (eds), *Global Modernities.* London: Sage, pp. 124–39.

Thompson, John (1995) *The Media and Modernity: A Social Theory of the Media.* Cambridge: Polity.

Thompson, John (2000) *Political Scandal: Power and Visibility in the Media Age.* Cambridge: Polity.

Tucker, Alphonse (1996) The fallout from the fallout. *Guardian Weekend*, 17 February: 12–16.

Tulloch, John, and Lupton, Deborah (2003) *Risk and Everyday Life.* London: Sage.

UNFPA (2006) *State of World Population 2006.* http://www.unfpa.org/swp/2006/english/introduction.html.

Vogler, John (1992) Regimes and the global commons: space, atmosphere and oceans. In Anthony McGrew, Paul G. Lewis et al. (eds), *Global Politics: Globalization and the Nation-State*, Cambridge: Polity, pp. 118–37.

Volkmann, Ute (2000) Das schwierige Leben in der Zweiten Moderne: Ulrich Becks 'Risikogesellschaft'. In Uwe Schimank and Ute Volkmann (eds), *Soziologische Gegenwartsdiagnosen I.* Opladen: UTB, pp. 23–40.

Voss, Jan-Peter, Bauknecht, Dierk, and Kemp, René (eds) (2006) *Reflexive Governance for Sustainable Development.* Cheltenham: Edward Elgar.

Wallerstein, Immanuel (1974) *The Modern World System*, Vol. 1. Cambridge: Cambridge University Press.

Wallerstein, Immanuel (1990) Societal development, or development of the world-system? In Martin Albrow and Elizabeth King (eds), *Globalization, Knowledge and Society.* London: Sage, pp. 157–72.

Watson, Sean, and Moran, Anthony (eds) (2005) *Trust, Risk and Uncertainty.* Basingstoke: Palgrave Macmillan.

Weber, Max (1968) *Wirtschaft und Gesellschaft.* Tübingen: Mohr.

Weber, Max (1991) Objektive Möglichkeit und adäquate Verursachung in der historischen Kausalbetrachtung. In Max Weber, *Schriften zur Wissenschaftslehre.* Stuttgart: Reclam.

Wehling, Peter (2006) *Im Schatten des Wissens? Perspektiven der Soziologie des Nichtwissens.* Konstanz: Verlagsgesellschaft.

Weizsäcker, Ulrich von (1995) Hätte ein Dritter Weltkrieg ökologische Ursachen? *Der Bürger im Staat* 45/1: 57–8.

Wildavsky, Aaron (1994) *But is it True? The Relationship between Knowledge and Action in the Great Environmental and Safety Issues of our Time.* Chicago: University of Chicago Press.

Winner, Langdon (1992) *Autonomous Technology.* London: Sage.

Wittrock, Björn (2000) Modernity: one, none, or many? European origins and modernity as a global condition. *Daedalus* 129/1: 31–60.

Wolf, Rainer (1987) Die Antiquiertheit des Rechts in der Risikogesellschaft. *Leviathan* 15: 357–91.

Wolf, Rainer (1988) 'Herrschaft kraft Wissen' in der Risikogesellschaft. *Soziale Welt* 39/2: 164–87.

World Commission on Environment and Development (1987) *Our Common Future.* Oxford: Oxford University Press.

Wuthnow, Robert (1991) *Acts of Compassion.* Princeton, NJ: Princeton University Press.

Wynne, Brian (1989) Frameworks of rationality in risk management. In Jennifer Brown (ed.), *Environmental Threats.* London: Belhaven.

Wynne, Brian (1991) Knowledges in context. *Science, Technology & Human Values* 16/1: 111–21.

Wynne, Brian (1996a) May the sheep safely graze? A reflexive view of the expert–lay knowledge divide. In Scott Lash, Bronislaw Szerszynski and Brian Wynne (eds), *Risk, Environment and Modernity*. London: Sage.

Wynne, Brian (1996b) The identity parades of SSK: reflexivity, engagement and politics. *Social Studies of Science* 26: 73–91.

Yearly, Steven (1994) Social movements and environmental change. In Michael Redclift and Ted Benton (eds), *Social Theory and the Global Environment*. London: Routledge, pp. 150–68.

Yearly, Steven (1996) *Sociology, Environmentalism, Globalization*. London: Sage.

Young, Oran R., Demko, George J., and Ramakrishna, Kilaparti (eds) (1996) *Global Environmental Change and International Governance*. Hanover, NH, and London: University Press of New England.

Zapf, Wolfgang (1992) Entwicklung und Zukunft moderner Gesellschaften seit den 70er Jahren. In Hermann Korte and Bernhard Schäfers (eds), *Einführung in Hauptbegriffe der Soziologie*. Opladen: Leske & Budrich, pp. 195–210.

Zapf, Wolfgang (1996) Die Modernisierungstheorie and unterschiedliche Pfade der gesellschaftlichen Entwicklung. *Merkur* 1: 63–77.

Zimmermann, Andrew D. (1995) Towards a more democratic ethic of technological governance. *Science, Technology and Human Values* 20/1: 86–107.

Zürn, Michael (1995) Globale Gefährdungen und internationale Kooperation. *Der Bürger im Staat* 45/1: 49–56.

Zürn, Michael (1997) 'Positives Regieren' jenseits des Nationalstaates: Zur Implementation internationaler Umweltregime. *Zeitschrift für Internationale Beziehungen* 4/1: 41–63.

Zürn, Michael (1998) *Regieren jenseits des Nationalstaats: Globalisierung und Denationalisierung als Chance*. Frankfurt am Main: Suhrkamp.

Zürn, Michael (2001) Politische Fragmentierung als Folge der gesellschaftlichen Denationalisierung? In Dietmar Loch and Wilhelm Heitmeyer (eds), *Schattenseiten der Globalisierung*. Frankfurt am Main: Suhrkamp, pp. 111–39.

Index

accountability 26
see also responsibility
actual and known threats 127–8
actual vs anticipation of catastrophe 10,
11–13, 67–71
African aid 202
Agamben, Giorgio 78–9
ageing population 215, 216
al-Qaeda 68–9, 73, 95, 149
Albrow, Martin 174, 181, 183, 204
ambivalences
of anti-modernity 232–4
of individualization 219–23
and irony of risk 5, 6, 47–50, 55,
187–91
of more-modernity 231–2
Anders, Günther 28, 224, 225
antagonism of risk 140–2, 145, 195–7
anti-modernity
ambivalences of 232–4
dialectics of 223–31
anticipation of catastrophe 1–2, 9–11,
14–16, 70, 188
vs actual catastrophe 10, 11–13,
67–71
Apocalypse 73, 148, 213
Apocalypse-blindness [Apokalypse-
Blindheit] 192
apocalyptic rhetoric 219
Arendt, Hannah 38, 48–9, 58–9, 214,
226–7
Asian financial crisis 200
Asian tsunami 45, 58, 69–70
atomic bomb 224–5
authoritarian 'failed states' 79–80

Balzac, Honoré de 6
banks, reputation of 1–2

Baudelaire, Charles 98, 212
Bauman, Zygmunt 61, 113–14, 174, 226
Beck, Ulrich 19, 27, 32, 56, 65, 78–9,
83, 103, 147, 166, 176, 184, 203–
4, 205, 219, 223
and Giddens, Anthony, and Lash,
Scott 119–20
and Grande, Edgar 56
and Holzer, Boris 87
and Lau, Christopher 136, 194, 214
and Sznaider, Natan 166, 176
bell curve model 50–1
Benn, Gottfried 82, 222
blame and responsibility 7, 91
Böschen, Stephan et al. 47, 117, 119–20
boundless inclusion 58–9
Bourdieu, Pierre 120, 207
Britain
environmental issues 34, 81–2, 96, 103
prevention of terrorism 105, 106–7
Bush, George W. 10, 39, 63–4, 123, 151,
157, 196

capitalism 7, 8, 16
global 65–6
'green capitalism' 34, 60, 81–2, 102–3
neoliberalism 65–6, 200, 201
see also economic(s)
catastrophe
intended and unintended 76–7
see also anticipation of catastrophe
category of risk and ambivalences
187–91
Cervantes, Miguel de 5
chance
linear vs non-linear 51
vs purpose, typology of global risks
13–14

Chernobyl nuclear reactor 36, 116, 117, 171–3
and Asian financial crisis 200
China
    African aid 202
    environmental issues 31, 62, 104
    SARS outbreak 175
    US trade 75
chlorofluorocarbons (CFCs) 47, 117–18, 184
circle of evil 228–9
civilizational self-endangerment and global governance 183–6
'clash of risk cultures' 12, 71–6, 146–7
climate change 2–3, 8
    abstractedness of threat 71–2
    in British public consciousness 34
    chlorofluorocarbons (CFCs), ozone layer destruction by 47, 117–18, 184
    predicted impacts of 37, 84–5
    quasi-religious conversion response 205
    and state responsibility 62–4
    see also environmental issues
'coalitions of opposites' 95, 96–7
Cold War 147, 196, 222, 224–5
collective responsibility 197
communication across divides, enforced 59–60, 198
communicative logic 59–60, 191–2, 194–5, 198, 199
comparative regional studies 167, 173–4
compassion, globalization of 58, 59, 69–70
compensation
    non-compensatability of global risks 52, 53
    vs precautionary principle 118–19
    welfare state 116, 117
    see also insurance
conscious inability-to-know [Nicht-Wissen-Können] 126
'contextual universalism(s)' 205–6
conversion effect, in risk perception 196–7
conversion response, quasi-religious 205
'cosmopolitan harm conventions' 163
cosmopolitan hermeneutics 189, 206
cosmopolitan inequalities 176–8

cosmopolitan moment 15–16, 55–66, 233
    components 55–6
    definitions 48–9, 56–7
    of ecological crisis 91
    9/11 as 67–71, 153–5
cosmopolitan pathologies 181
cosmopolitan political realism 192, 198, 208–9
cosmopolitan realpolitik 66, 131
cosmopolitan state 66, 100–4, 103–4
'cosmopolitan vision' 19
cosmopolitanism
    enforced 61–2
    from above and from below 180
    methodological 177, 181, 205
    normative 177
        and descriptive 187–204
    political 177, 192, 207–11
    of risks 197–9
'crisis phenomena' 231
critical theory
    normative horizon 187–204
    political perspectives 207–11
    scientific basis of 204–7
cultural criticism 218, 219–20
    critique of 229–32
cultural perception of risk see anticipation of catastrophe

danger vs risk 112–13
decision paradox (threat–knowledge gap) 117–18
decision-makers and those affected 112–13, 140–1, 142, 143
    decoupling 161–2, 163, 168, 169
    see also global risk inequality
delocalization of global risks 52
denial, non-knowing [Nichtwissen] as 123–5
Dewey, John 59, 182–3
dialectics
    of anti-modernity 223–31
    of modernity 214–23, 231–4
dichotomization
    of smokers and non-smokers 144–6
    of 'West and the rest' 154
Diderot, Denis 5
Douglas, Mary 7, 79
    and Wildavsky, Aaron 84, 196
drama and sociology, commonalities and differences 129–31

Durkheim, Émile 191, 221
Dürrenmatt, Friedrich (*The Physicists*)
    129–31, 132, 134, 136

ecological neo-imperialism 87
economic(s)
    consequences of environmental
        destruction 37–9, 85, 92–3
    global risks 199–203
    model vs reality 18
    rationality 110, 113
    realism 209
    state vs market 62–3, 201
    see also capitalism
'end of the world' 217–19
enforced communication across divides
    59–60, 198
enforced cosmopolitanism 61–2
enforced enlightenment 57–9
environmental issues 36–9, 65
    affluence-induced vs poverty-induced
        destruction 199
    global subpolitics 93–5
        from above 100–4
        from below 96–100
    non-knowing 123–5
    as social problems
        [*Innenweltprobleme*] 161–6
    theoretical approach 82–93
    US policy 63–4
    see also climate change; global risk
        inequality; nuclear energy
environmental NGOs 94, 185
    Greenpeace 95, 96–7, 99, 180–1
epistemic communities 184, 185–6
Eppler, Erhard 147–8, 153
Ericson, Richard V., and Doyle, Aaron
    133, 134–8
error probabilities in risk calculations
    123–4
ethics
    of responsibility 15–16, 195
    of technological age 26
Eurocentric cosmopolitanism 180
Europe/European Union (EU) 28, 162,
    209, 213
    US relations 74–6, 197, 204, 208, 209
European novels 4–6
evil, circle of 228–9
Ewald, François 7, 52, 53, 91, 109, 138
expert(s)
    rationality and knowledge 124, 126–7

vs lay knowledge 11–12, 33, 86, 87,
    89–90
    see also science
export of risk 141, 150, 167, 169,
    170–1

Falk, Richard 93
    and van Steenbergen, Bart 93
fear 8–9, 139
felt war
    felt peace 151, 153
    staging (terrorism) 155–9
Fichte, Johann Gottlieb 232–3
financial crises 200, 201
financial markets 121, 136, 199–200
financial risks 202–3
for-us, anticipated catastrophe 70
Foucault, Michel 6, 79–80, 172
Frank, Manfred, and Haverkamp,
    Anselm 221
Frankenfeld, Philip 98
French nuclear tests 96–7
Friedman, Thomas L. 63–4
future generations 217
future shaping 230–1

Gauss model 50–1
gender relations 215
genetically modified (GMO) foodstuffs
    74–6
genetics and reproductive medicine 2
Germany 1–2, 43, 65, 232–3
    see also Holocaust
Giddens, Anthony 25, 121, 124, 201
    Beck, Ulrich, Lash, Scott, and 119–20
    and Pierson, Christopher 120, 121–2
global capitalism 65–6
'global community of threats' 8
global governance 185–6
global risk inequality
    models 163–6
    typology 165, 166–81
global risks
    hallmark of 52–4
    typology of 13–14
global space of responsibility 188
global subpolitics 93–5
    indicators, conditions of emergence
        and forms of expression 93–108
    of terror 104–8
    see also under environmental issues
global warming see climate change

God
  absence of 4, 6, 72–4
  as science 230
  and terrorist violence 148–9
Goldblatt, David 131–2
governance
  alternative forms of 64–6
  civilizational self-endangerment and
    global 183–6
government
  and politics, decoupling of 95
  as reinsurer of last resort 137
'green capitalism' 34, 60, 81–2, 102–3
greenhouse effect *see* climate change
Greenpeace 95, 96–7, 99, 180–1
Gulf War 152, 190

Habermas, Jürgen 33–4, 58–9, 120, 198
Häfele, Wolf 36
Halfmann, Jost 111
hallmark of global risks 52–4
Herbert, Ulrich 221
hierarchy
  of global risk inequality 164, 170–3
  of knowledge (expert vs lay) 33, 86,
    87, 89–90
Hiroshima 224
'historical falsification criteria' 206–7
historical perspective
  alternatives of cosmopolitan action
    64–6
  'end of the world' 218–19
  individualization 220–3
  metamorphosis of risk 5–6
  new character of world risk society
    192–3
  security and novel threats 28
Hobbes, Thomas 94
Hofmannsthal, Hugo von 227
Holocaust 225–7
homosexuality 221–2
Horkheimer, Max, and Adorno,
    Theodor W. 198, 226
hospitality 190–1
Hurricane Katrina 57–8
Husband, Charles 189
Husserl, Edmund 205
hyper-modernity 55, 65

Ignatieff, Michael 148, 153
inability-to-know [*Nicht-Wissen-
    Können*] 5, 17, 53, 115, 126

conscious 126
  political action and 124–5
  unintended 118–19
incalculability of global risks 52, 53
incidental war [*Nebenbei-Krieg*]
    151–2
India 75, 202, 225
individual liberty, restrictions on 1, 10,
    61–2, 105
individual responsibility 188, 195
individualizability principle of insurance
    139
individualization 54–5, 97
  ambivalences of 219–23
  and anonymization, smokers and
    non-smokers 144–5
  of global risks 169–70
  of war 107
industrial societies
  decisions and side effects 91
  norms and institutions 91
  phases 86
  and reflexive modernization 213
  as risk societies 109, 110
  see also modernity
industrialization 25–7, 29–30
industrializing countries 37
inequality *see* global risk inequality;
    West–Third World/rest relations
institutional constructivism 90–3
institutional contradictions, theory of
    193–5
institutionalization 7
'institutionalized reflexivity' 121
institutions
  international economic 100–1, 201–2
  national, cosmopolitan state and
    transnational networks 103–4
  from trustees to suspects 54
  vs basic principles of modernity
    214–23
  see also global subpolitics
insurance 109, 211
  criticism and counter-criticism 131–9
  'maximum credible accident' (MCA)
    27–8, 29
  uninsurability 110, 113, 133–4
  see also compensation
intended catastrophes 76–7
intentional non-knowing [*Nichtwissen*]
    118–19
interdependence 208

international economic institutions
100–1, 201–2
International Monetary Fund (IMF)
201–2
international organizations 208–9
international politics
environmental hazards 184–5
terrorist risk 39–41
inversion of values, smokers and non-
smokers 146
Iraq War 53, 65, 123, 151, 158–9, 196
irony and ambivalences of risk 5, 6, 47–
50, 55, 187–91
Islam/Muslims 105–6, 148–9

Jasanoff, Sheila 33

Kahn, Paul W. 153
Kant, Immanuel 61, 122, 190, 191, 233
Kasperson, Jeanne X., and Kasperson,
Roger E. 173–4, 179
Kellow, Ansley 180
Keynes, John Maynard 18–19
Knight, Frank 17
knowledge 115–19
hierarchy (expert vs lay) 33, 86, 87,
89–90
perspectives on 'reflexive
modernization' 119–28
see also non-knowing [*Nichtwissen*];
science
known and unknown knowledge
(insurance principle) 135
known non-knowledge 126
Kuhn, Thomas 206
Kundera, Milan 4

labour, 'environmental politicization' of
38
laissez-faire distributions of burdens of
proof 102
Lash, Scott 121, 122
Beck, Ulrich, and Giddens, Anthony,
and 119–20
Latour, Bruno 27, 90, 130, 174, 198
Lau, Christopher 111–12
Beck, Ulrich, and 136, 194, 214
law/legal norms 29–30, 31, 35, 191,
229–30
legitimation of 'risk war' 150–2
Levy, Primo, and Sznaider, Natan 150,
176, 225

lifeworld phenomenology 204–5, 206–7
linear models of technocracy,
invalidation of 110–13
linear vs non-linear chance 51
linear vs non-linear theories of
knowledge 125–6
Linklater, Andrew 163
Loon, Joost van 197, 198
Luhmann, Niklas 112–13, 120, 143–4,
145, 156, 183, 193, 194, 229–30

Mandelbrot, Benoit, and Taleb, Nassim
51
Marcuse, Herbert 218, 230
marginalized, voice of 57–9
Marx, Karl 31–2, 233
mass media 10–11, 12, 50, 194
Asian tsunami 45, 58, 69–70
enforced enlightenment 57–9
globalization and auto-stigmatization
of Muslims 106
moral import of global threat 189–90
staging 72, 98–100
and terrorism 104, 107, 158–9
war 148, 152, 153–4
mass tourism 70
'maximum credible accident' (MCA)
27–8, 29
medical knowledge 116
methodological cosmopolitanism 177,
181, 205
methodological nationalism 166–70, 210
methodological problems 163
Middle East 147–8, 156–7, 208, 225
migration 169
military imperative of terrorism 157–8
modernity
basic principles vs basic institutions
214–23
dialectics of 214–23, 231–4
dilemmas 231–4
first 73, 80, 92
hyper-modernity 55, 65
second 74
as workshop of certainty 217–18
see also anti-modernity; industrial
societies; industrialization
modernization 6
of knowledge 122
more-modernity
ambivalences of 231–2
dialectics of 214–17

Müller-Jung, Joachim 1
Muslims/Islam 105–6, 148–9

'naïve' relativism 132
'national interests' 65
national public spheres and global
    public opinion 154
national security and international
    terrorism 39–41
nationalism, methodological 166–70,
    210
nations *see* state(s)
natural disasters 50
    Asian tsunami 45, 58, 69–70
    Hurricane Katrina 57–8
'nature'
    and 'destruction of nature' 89–91
    and 'ecology', indeterminacy of
        concepts 82–5
neoliberalism 65–6, 200, 201
network analysis, SARS risk 174–6
new historical character of world risk
    society 192–3
'new' wars 147–9
Nietzsche, Friedrich 48, 72, 233
9/11 terrorist attacks 67–71, 133–5, 137,
    153, 159, 196–7, 203, 227
non-compensatability of global risks
    52, 53
non-governmental organizations
    (NGOs) 185–6
    environmental 94, 185
    Greenpeace 95, 96–7, 99, 180–1
    terrorist 40
non-knowing [*Nichtwissen*] 47, 53, 54,
    115
    as denial 123–5
    downplaying central role of
        16–19
    drama and sociology 129–31
    intentional 118–19
    manufactured, as existential condition
        116–17
    typology of forms 126–8
non-knowing, wilful ignorance [*Nicht-
    Wissen-Wollen*] 115, 126
normalcy–exception overlap 76–9
normative cosmopolitanism *see under*
    cosmopolitanism
norms
    formation of 183
    legal 31, 229–30

novels, European 4–6
nuclear energy 1–2, 43, 96–7, 217
    see also Chernobyl nuclear reactor

Obama, Barack 63
'objectivity' 127–8
'old' terrorism 149
'old' wars 147, 149
Ong, Aihwa 174–5
ontological insecurity 45–6, 195,
    199
organized irresponsibility 27–9, 31, 139,
    193–4
other(s)
    'end of the other' 37
    recognition of 56–7
ozone layer, destruction by CFCs 47,
    117–18, 184

Palestinian–Israeli conflict 147–8,
    208
peaceful war 151–2
Petryna, Adriana 171–3
The Physicists (Dürrenmatt) 129–31,
    132, 134, 136
plurality of voices 189
pluralization 143–4, 145, 147–50
political action and inability-to-know
    [*Nicht-Wissen-Können*]
    124–5
political catharsis 60–1
political cosmopolitanism 177, 192,
    207–11
political individualism 222–3
political reflexivity 42–8
politics *see* governance; government
postcolonial social movements 211
Potemkin insurance protection 138,
    139
power differences 125–6, 142
    see also decision-makers and those
        affected; global risk inequality;
        relations of definition; West–
        Third World/rest relations
precautionary aftercare [*vorsorgende
    Nachsorge*] 28
precautionary principle 53
    and errors in risk calculation
        124
    vs compensation principle 118–19
    vs *laissez-faire* distributions of
        burdens of proof 102

private actors *see* epistemic
    communities; non-governmental
    organizations (NGOs)
private insurance *see* insurance
provident state [*Vorsorgestaat*] and
    providing state
    [*Versorgungsstaat*] 109
public co-insurance (subsidies) 134
public sphere 44–5, 58–9, 154
purpose vs chance, typology of global
    risks 13–14

'racial profiling' of suspected terrorists
    105–6
rationality/rationalization 16–17, 18–19
    expert 124, 126–7
    vs emotions 198–9
    vs 'subjectivity' 11–12
realism–constructivism, environmental
    debate 85–90
reciprocity, global risk inequality model
    166
reflection, concept of 120–1
reflective non-knowing 126
'reflexive communities' 122
reflexive globality 181–3
reflexive modernization 55, 94, 109,
    114, 142, 213
    two perspectives on 119–28
reflexive realism 89
'reflexivity of uncertainty' 15–16
reflexivity theory 197–9
relations of definition 194–5
    as relations of domination 29–36
    and relations of production 31–2,
        33–4
    smokers and non-smokers 145–6
religion
    conversion response to climate
        change 205
    of individualism 221
    Islam/Muslims 105–6, 148–9
    see also God
responsibility
    and blame 7, 91
    collective 197
    cosmopolitan 163
    ethics of 15–16, 195
    global space of 188
    individual 188, 195
    and organized irresponsibility 27–9,
        31, 139, 193–4

    social 188
    state 62–4
retirement benefits 215, 216
risk 4–6
risk calculus 7, 11, 25–7, 28, 29
    error probabilities 123–4
    incalculability of global risks 52, 53
'risk communities' 188, 197
'risk contract' 7
risk cosmopolitan law 191
risk definitions 111–13
    see also relations of definition
'risk donor countries' and 'risk recipient
    countries' 30–1, 164
risk management 130, 135–6
    models 50–2
risk perception *see* anticipation of
    catastrophe
risk society 6–9, 15, 24–5, 30, 50
    industrial society as 109, 110
    as revolutionary 76–9
    as self-critical 110
    see also world risk society
'risk war' 149–50
    cosmopolitan publics 153–5
    legitimation question 150–2
'risk-transfer war' 150
Robins, Kevin 190

SARS risk 174–6
Schelsky, Helmut 110–11
Schmitt, Carl 78
science 5, 6
    basis of critical theory 204–7
    God as 230
    industrialization and law 29–30
    The Physicists (Dürrenmatt) 129–31,
        132, 134, 136
    and technology 6–7, 8, 34–6,
        212
        invalidation of linear models
            110–13
        and nature 83–4
        security strategy 14
    see also climate change; environmental
        issues; global risk inequality;
        knowledge; nuclear energy; risk
        calculus
selective assumptions 126
selective exclusion of terrorist risks
    136–7
self-confrontation 109

self-criticism, critical theory as 194,
    209–11
self-endangerment
    civilizational 183–6
    and endangerment of others 87
self-entrepreneur terrorists 107
Shaw, Martin 147, 150, 153, 158, 183
Shell oil company 96, 99
Short, James F., and Clarke, Lee 124
side effects 18–19, 29–31, 37–8, 41
    catastrophes 77
    concept of 127
    latent 141, 161, 162, 167–8
    living 141, 142, 143
    reflexive modernization 119–20
    unintended 109
Silverstone, Roger 228
Sloterdijk, Peter 182
smokers and non-smokers,
    dichotomization of 144–6
social constructionist perspective 29–30,
    31–2, 127–8, 194–5
    institutional constructivism 90–3
    realism–constructivism,
        environmental debate 85–90
social delocalization of risks 52, 77–8
social movements 15–16, 43–6, 77
    emergence of 222–3
    postcolonial 211
social problems [Innenweltprobleme],
    environmental problems
    [Umweltproblemen] as 161–6
social responsibility 188
social vulnerability 178–81
society, transformation of concept of
    14–16
Soviet Union, Ukraine, impact of
    Chernobyl reactor catastrophe
    171–2
spatial delocalization of risks 52, 77–8
staged non-staging [inszenierten Nicht-
    Inszenierung] 141
staging
    felt war (terrorism) 155–9
    mass media 72, 98–100
    organized violence 146–55
    of the reality [Realitätsinszeninerung]
        of global risk 10–11, 12–13, 16
    see also global subpolitics
state(s)
    authoritarian 'failed states' 79–80
    cosmopolitan 66, 100–4, 103–4

environmental movement–industry
    relations 3, 60, 86–7
provident [Vorsorgestaat] and
    providing [Versorgungsstaat]
    109
responsibility 62–4
    and social movements' power 77
    sovereignty 78–9, 103, 233
    and terrorist power 78
    vs market 62–3, 201
    see also welfare state
Steinmeier, Frank-Walter 65
Stern, Nicholas (Stern Review) 84–5,
    101–2
Strydom, Piet 163, 193, 197
'subjectivity' vs 'rationalist
    understandings' of risks 11–12
subpolitics see global subpolitics
suicide attacks see terrorism

technological age 26
technological citizenship 97–8
technology see under science
temporal delocalization of risks 52,
    77–8
terrorism 10–11, 39–41, 65
    al-Qaeda 68–9, 73, 95, 149
    anticipation of 1, 10–11, 67–9, 134–5,
        234
    as global staging of felt war
        155–9
    globalization of 157
    9/11 attacks 67–71, 133–5, 137, 153,
        159, 196–7, 203, 227
    as privatization of violence 148–9
    as social, spatial and temporal
        unlimited state of exception
        77–8
    subpolitics of 104–8
Third World see West–Third World/
    rest relations
'totalitarianism of defence against
    threats' 8–9
transformation
    of concept of society 14–16
    and pluralization of war 147–50
transnational actor-networks 173–6
transnational cooperation 41
transnational regimes 185
trust 121–2
    loss of, in institutions 54
tsunami, Asian 45, 58, 69–70

typologies
  of global risk inequality 165, 166–81
  of global risks 13–14

uncertainty
  modelling 50–2
  vs risk 17–19
unconscious non-knowing 126–7
uncontrollability, theoretical vs factual
  41
unintended catastrophes 76–7
unintended inability-to-know [*Nicht-
  Wissen-Können*] 118–19
unintended side effects 109
United Nations (UN)
  Economic Security Council 201
  Security Council 150, 153, 154,
  209
United States (US) 2, 3, 10–11
  airport security 14, 107
  George W. Bush (administration) 10,
  39, 63–4, 123, 151, 157, 196
  Centre for Disease Control, Atlanta
  175
  Congress scientific commission
  217
  environmental issues 60, 63–4, 104
  Europe relations 74–6, 197, 204, 208,
  209
  government as reinsurer of last resort
  137
  and international organizations 209
  military unilateralism 209
  passive smokers 145–6
  terrorist attacks (9/11) 67–71, 133–5,
  137, 153, 159, 196–7, 203, 227
  terrorist risk 39, 41, 47–8
  WTO Dispute Settlement Body 74–6
universalization of risk conflicts 143–4,
  145
'unknown unknowns' 40, 127

virtual war 148, 149, 152–3
voice(s)
  plurality of 189
  of underprivileged and marginalized
  57–9
vulnerability
  social 178–81
  to terrorism 156–7

war(s)
  Gulf 152, 190
  Iraq 53, 65, 123, 151, 158–9, 196
  staging organized violence 146–55
  on terror 10, 11
  transformation and pluralization of
  147–50
Weber, Max 6, 16–17, 18, 33, 91–2, 120,
  198, 204, 206, 217–18
welfare state
  compensation 116, 117
  and globalization 215
  retirement benefits 215, 216
West–Third World/rest relations 87,
  154
  global financial system 201–2
  migration 169
  modernity and alternative modernity
  182–3, 186
  terrorism 107–8, 156–7
Wildavsky, Aaron 123–4
  Douglas, Mary, and 84, 196
work scarcity 214–17
World Bank 201–2
World Health Organization (WHO)
  175
world risk society 9–11
  theory of 191–2
World Trade Organization (WTO) 162,
  185
  Dispute Settlement Body 74–6
world ugliness contest 3–4